THIS
SIDE
OF
GLORY

Other books by Lewis Cole

A Loose Game
Dream Team
Never Too Young to Die

THIS SIDE OF GLORY

The Autobiography
of David Hilliard
and the Story
of the Black
Panther Party

David Hilliard
and
Lewis Cole

Little, Brown and Company

Boston   Toronto   London

First Edition

Library of Congress Cataloging-in-Publication Data

Hilliard, David.
      This side of glory : the autobiography of David Hilliard and the story of the Black Panther Party / by David Hilliard and Lewis Cole. — 1st ed.
          p.   cm.
      1. Hilliard, David.   2. Black Panther Party — Biography.   3. Afro-Americans — Biography.   4. Black power — United States — History — 20th century.   5. Black militant organizations — United States — History — 20th century.   I. Cole, Lewis.   II. Title.
      E185.97.H55A3   1993
      973' .0496073 — dc20
      [B]   92-29388

10   9   8   7   6   5   4   3   2   1

MV-NY

Published simultaneously in Canada by Little, Brown & Company (Canada) Limited

Printed in the United States of America

Acknowledgments

THE funeral in 1989 of Huey Newton, my friend and founder of the Black Panther Party, provided the catalyst for this book. I had begun writing about the Black Panther Party and my involvement in it twenty years ago; however, that effort was put aside and not completed. The reader of this book will understand why. The occasion of Huey's funeral brought together friends and comrades, many of whom I had not seen for ten or twenty years. It deepened our determination to tell our story in our own words. Shortly after Huey's funeral Marty Kenner invited me to his house in New York, where he had invited many of my Panther comrades as well as others who had worked with him in support of the Panthers. That event gave birth to this book.

In acting as my agent and adviser Marty Kenner brought to this project the same intelligence and steadfastness that he displayed in the days of the Party. Marty and my brother June contributed with their knowledge of Panther history. We knew that the key to making this the most authentic story of the Panther Party was to include the voices of a wide range of Party members; sadly, our efforts were limited by time, money, and geography. Most sad of all, so many of our comrades were killed along the way; no acknowledgment would be complete without honoring the selfless contributions of Bobby Hutton, the first to fall, murdered in Oakland; Bunchy Carter and John Huggins, murdered in Los Angeles; Fred Hampton and Mark Clark, murdered in Chicago; Sam Napier, murdered in New York; and Peggy

Carter, Masai Hewitt, and my son Darryl Hilliard, all killed by the stresses of the struggle.

D.H.

"I would not have the anniversaries of our victories celebrated, nor those of our defeats made fast days and spent in humiliation and prayer," writes Grant about the Civil War, "but I would like to see truthful history written."

The story of the Black Panther Party has been distorted, forgotten, and repressed over the last twenty years. One purpose of this book is to show and reaffirm the true concerns and practice of the organization and the experience of the men and women who made up the Black Panther rank and file, to tell, through the story of one person, a collective tale of daunting personal sacrifice and still to be recognized historic accomplishment.

To achieve this, we interviewed numerous members. Without their wholehearted participation we would never have accomplished our goal; their generous donations of time, patience, and memories embodied the selflessness and comradeship that was the core of the Black Panther Party's spirit. At the same time, we must note that our book is a far from comprehensive account of Black Panther Party history—a complete, objective record remains to be written. We particularly regret not including the experiences of the Winston-Salem chapter and its Deputy Minister, Larry Little.

People throughout the country helped us as guides, hosts, and analysts. They include: in Mobile, Etna and Paul McCovery, Allen, Ted, and Joseph Hilliard, Isum Clemons, Floyd King, and Ollie Kiel; in New York, Martin, Max, and Camilla Kenner and June Hilliard and Frances Carter; in Chicago, Bobby Rush, Gwen Swaghammer, and Steve Tappis; in Los Angeles, Donald Freed, Sam Hurst, Mark Rosenberg, Esther Soriano, and Paula Weinstein, Van, Rose, and Van, Senior, Hilliard, and Dorion and Valery Rene Hilliard; and, finally, in Oakland, Linda Fullerton, Frederica Slaughter Newton, Melvin Newton, Mickey and Carla Phillips, and Carol Rucker.

Both authors received enthusiastic support from the leadership and members of their professional affiliations: Larry Gerber and the staff of Local 790, SIEU, and Annette Insdorf and the faculty and students of the Film Division of Columbia University.

Alex Hoffmann, Stew Albert, and Dale Walker gave helpful and thoughtful readings of the manuscript, Alex and Stew supplying uniquely detailed tours through the labyrinth of Berkeley and national radical activity in the late sixties. Paul Chevigny performed a signal service by lending us his highly prized copy of that treasure trove of government criminality, Book 111 of the "Final Report of the Select Committee to Study Governmental Operations with Respect to Intelligence Activities," otherwise known simply as the final report of the Church Committee. All quoted material about the FBI comes from the section of this source titled "The FBI's Covert Action Program to Destroy the Black Panther Party."

For the record of government attack against the Party, we also relied on three other books: *Agents of Repression,* by Ward Churchill and Jim Vander Wall, South End Press, Boston, 1988; *Racial Matters,* by Kenneth O'Reilly, Free Press, New York, 1989; and Sara Blackburn's *White Justice,* Harper and Row, New York, 1972.

Quotes from Huey Newton, Eldridge Cleaver, and George Jackson come from, respectively, *Revolutionary Suicide,* Ballantine Books, New York, 1974; *To Die for the People,* Random House, New York, 1972; *Eldridge Cleaver,* Random House, New York, 1967; and *Soledad Brother,* Coward McCann, New York, 1970. All these important literary and political documents are currently out of print; it's to be hoped that they will once again become available to a wide audience.

Ron Griele, director of the Oral History Research Office at Columbia University, bravely backed the endeavor at its inception with financial support for the interviews; the transcripts are to become part of the permanent collection at Columbia, which is open to the public.

With her flawless ear, fastidious judgment, and unfailing sense of responsibility, Andrea Miller once again proved herself to be the world's most reliable, intelligent, and sensitive transcriber.

Jennifer Hengen, Peter Matson's assistant, and Geoffrey Kloske, Roger Donald's assistant, performed numerous, invaluable, thankless tasks, all of them doubly trying because they had to be done twice. David Coen copyedited the manuscript with a sympathetic and patient pencil in a demanding and difficult situation. John Williams conducted the legal reading of the book with an eye to keeping as much in, rather than taking as much out, as possible; and Mi-Ho Cha and Beth Davey early on adopted the book as a special project, enthusiastically promoting a story they had not known before.

Jerry Rubin encouraged this project at its inception; Martin Kenner worked tirelessly to realize it.

Peter Matson, our agent, staunchly insisted on the work's commercial value and historic importance; and Roger Donald, our editor, agreed with him not only in theory but in practice, offering us a contract ample enough to let us write it. Their worries for the project coupled with their keenly felt and consistent celebration of the work provided the necessary encouragement and demand to keep us going.

The members of the Cole and Yglesias families all offered wise advice and loving concern; Cathy Wein proved a sympathetic and loyal friend; Aaron Cole demonstrated an heroic tolerance of a frequently distracted father.

Frederica Slaughter Newton and Matty Oden helped prepare the manuscript at a crucial time, and Frederica provided emotional and material support without which the work couldn't have gotten done.

Finally, a personal note. Writing this book accorded me several privileges. One was to meet the Hilliard family, all of whom — whatever their personal doubts — welcomed me into their homes and shared their pasts, the children especially speaking with a breathtaking honesty. I was similarly accepted by ex–Party members. Neither of these honors could have happened without the intervention and personal example of David Hilliard: these people extended themselves because of their trust in David. "You do me wrong to take me out o' th' grave," Lear says toward the end of Act IV. "Thou art a soul in bliss, but I am bound/Upon a wheel of fire, that mine own tears/Do scald like molten lead." David Hilliard took himself from the grave and resolved to tell his story. Having set upon his course, he never flinched from meeting an impossibly high standard of personal honesty. Our collaboration was not easy and, under the pressure of deadlines and publication, was almost rent by issues of trust and appreciation. Readers can agree or not with our judgment that the final result made all our wrangling worthwhile. But even without the book finally in hand, there was for me never any question about the value of our enterprise: to be entrusted with the Promethean tale of David's life and the stories of the modern heroes who were his comrades in arms was, and will always be, one of the transfiguring events of my life.

L.C.

Cast of Characters

The Hilliard Family

Lela, *mother*
Lee, *father*

Theodore, "Bud"
Allen, "Pig Iron"
Nathaniel
Van   *their sons*
Roosevelt, "June"
Arthur
David

Rose Lee
Sweetie
Dorothy Mae   *their daughters*
Vera Lee, "Black Gal,"
    or "B.B."
Eleanora

Bojack and Maisie, *Rose Lee's children*
Michael and Gail, *Bud's children*
Ted, *Allen's son*

David Hilliard's Family

Pat, *wife of David*
Dennis, *Pat's son*

Patrice, "Trice," *daughter*
Darryl, *son*   *David and Pat's children*
Dorion, "Doe", *son*

Dassine, *David's daughter*
Brenda Presley, *Dassine's mother*

John and DeMario, *Patrice's sons*

Gene McKinney
James Phillips, "J.J."
James Crawford
Ernest   *friends*
Ray-Bell
Chico Higgins
Cleon Harris
Irving Kindler

Minnie, *a girlfriend*

The Party

Huey Newton, *a childhood friend, founder and Minister of Defense*

Melvin Newton, *Huey's brother*

Bobby Seale, *Chairman*

John Seale, *Bobby's brother*

Donald Cox, "D.C.," *Field Marshall*

Emory Douglas, *Minister of Culture*

Eldridge Cleaver, *Minister of Information*

Kathleen Cleaver, *Communications Secretary, wife of Eldridge*

Fred Hewitt, "Masai," *Minister of Education*

Elbert Howard, "Big Man," *an original member of the Party*

Sam Napier, *head of distribution,* The Black Panther

Li'l Bobby Hutton, *the youngest member of the party*

Charles Bursey, *member*

ILLINOIS

Fred Hampton, *Deputy Chairman, Illinois branch*

Bobby Rush, "Rush," *Deputy Minister of Defense*

Mark Clark, *Defense Captain, Peoria branch*

William O'Neal, *Head of Security, a police agent*

LOS ANGELES

Alprentice "Bunchy" Carter, *Deputy Minister of Defense*

Elmer Pratt, "Geronimo" or "G.," *Deputy Minister of Defense*

John Huggins, *Deputy Minister of Information*

Elaine Brown, *Deputy Minister of Communications*

NEW HAVEN

Ericka Huggins, *Deputy Minister of Education (widow of John Huggins)*

Frances Carter, *founding member, New Haven branch (later married to June Hilliard)*

Peggy Carter, *founding member, New Haven branch*

Lonnie McLucas, *founding member, New Haven branch*

George Sams, *a member*

Alex Rackley, *a member*

NEW YORK

Michael Tabor, *a member of the New York Panther Twenty-one*

Richard Moore, "Dharuba," *a member of the New York Panther Twenty-one*

Zayd Shakur, *founding member of the New York branch*

PRISON

James Carr, "Jackal Dog"

George Jackson, *Field Marshall*

Jonathan Jackson, *brother of George Jackson*

Comrades in Arms

Stew Albert, *member of the Red Mountain Tribe*

Beverly Axelrod, *legal defense counsel*

H. Rap Brown, *member of the Student Nonviolent Coordinating Committee (SNCC)*

Stokely Carmichael, *member of the Student Nonviolent Coordinating Committee (SNCC)*

Judith Clavier, "Gumbo," *member of the Red Mountain Tribe*

Mark Comfort, *an Oakland community organizer*

Ron Dellums, *a supporter and member of US House of Representatives*

James Forman, *member of the Student Nonviolent Coordinating Committee (SNCC)*

Donald Freed, *founding member of Friends of the Panthers*

Charles Garry, *legal defense counsel*

Tony Gibson, *a prison inmate*

Emmett Groggan, *founder of the Diggers*

Tom Hayden, *radical activist and defendant in the Chicago conspiracy trial*

Alex Hoffman, *legal defense counsel*

James "Doc" Holliday, *a prison inmate*

Marty Kenner, *founder, Panther Defense Committee*

"Kumasi," *a prison inmate*

Father Earl Neil, *minister, St. Augustine's Episcopal Church, cofounder of the Breakfast for Children program*

Mickey Phillips, *Arlene Slaughter's son, a supporter*

Jerry Rubin, *founder of the Yippies and a defendant in the Chicago conspiracy trial*

Raymond Scott, *a prison inmate*

Betty Shertzer, *cofounder, Panther Defense Committee*

Dan Siegel, *president of the Berkeley student body*

Arlene Slaughter, *a supporter*

Frederica "Fredi" Slaughter Newton, *Arlene Slaughter's daughter, later married to Huey Newton*

Dr. Tolbert Small, *cofounder, Panther Free Health Clinics*

Faye Stender, *legal defense counsel*

Steve Tappis, *a founder of Rising Up Angry in Chicago*

Elsa Knight Thompson, *head of Public Affairs, radio station KPFA*

Sandy Turner, *David's spiritual adviser in prison*

Hannah Weinstein, *political activist and fund-raiser for Panther Defense Committee*

THIS
SIDE
OF
GLORY

Prologue

ALL those years waiting for the news and when Melvin calls I'm sleeping.

"David," he says, "wake up." His voice is even, controlled. "Huey's dead."

"What do you mean?" I stutter the question. I'm half asleep, half awake, and all alone: Pat's taking care of Mom in Alabama.

Melvin repeats himself. Huey's been killed. Shot in the street. In West Oakland.

"What are you saying?" I ask again. I shut my eyes hard, concentrating on his words. "What are you saying?"

"David, wake up." Melvin tries to talk sense through my surprise and distress. Maybe he thinks I'm still using. "Listen to me. We're going to the hospital. Meet us there or at the house. We always knew this was gonna happen. We just didn't know when."

I tell Melvin I'll see him at his house and turn on the TV. The two faces of Huey cover the screen. Then: the famous beret and shotgun, Huey baby-faced and clear-eyed. Now: a recent mug shot, Huey wearing a wrinkled shirt, head cocked in his inimitable manner, both asking and confronting, chin stubbly, eyes clouded.

The reporter's voice-over states the facts:

Place of death — outside a house on Center Street, around the corner from a dope house.

Time — five in the morning.

1

Circumstances—a verbal altercation followed by gunshots. Assailant unknown.

I listen, organizing my ideas. Yes, Melvin's right. I can't pretend to be surprised. I've expected something like this for ten years, since Huey came back from Cuba. He has so many enemies in Oakland—police from Party days, gangsters and dealers from the days after. And then there's Huey himself, never giving up the drugs, his grandiosity assuring him he's a special case, always able to outsmart everyone. The man was living on the edge. And recently he had gotten real bad. Hey, David, the brothers would tell me, your boy's got to cool it. People ain't gonna be hearing all that stuff. He ain't got them Panthers with him no more. He can't be around here thinking he can keep doing people the way he used to.

So, no, I am *not* surprised Huey's dead.

But I am in a state of disbelief.

Not the fact, but the *idea* of Huey's death fills me with awe. No matter that he abased himself—"incomprehensible demoralization," as the AA program calls it. For me he remained an apotheosis, my leader; with him, I felt I was near greatness, that something really spectacular would happen any moment. And most times, it did.

After calling Pat and my brother June, I shave and dress, trying to figure out what's happened. Did Huey strong-arm somebody? Did someone try to rip him off? This is Huey after all; anything is possible. I don't want to get caught up in madness I had nothing to do with. I've been sober for a year and a half now. Huey's assassin could be anybody. The killer might even be waiting to murder me—thinking I'm organizing people to avenge Huey's death.

I start my investigation, phoning people from the streets, reliable sources who have known me and Huey, users, dealers, the brothers and sisters off the block whom we used to organize into the Party.

"Hey, you know, Huey just got shot."

"Hell, I just heard it."

"Well, you know, see what you can find out and let me know. I don't want to walk into something I don't understand."

Checking it out, like I used to in the Party, taking charge, taking care—that was my job.

I drive by the bay shore. New, shiny San Francisco skyscrapers loom opposite; on my side huge white raised cranes guard the Oakland shipyards like Robocops or *Star Wars* creatures.

I remember twenty-two years ago.

Late October.

Four or five in the morning.

Huey's stopped by a police officer named Frey. There are some words. Then gunfire. Frey is shot dead, Huey badly wounded.

At the time the Party is almost dead. Twelve members, no survival programs—there isn't even the *idea* for the survival programs—the paper appearing erratically, Huey not yet a national figure. In less than a week we're in action, borrowing a psychedelically painted double-deck bus from one of the local white political communes, cruising the streets blaring, "Free Huey! Free Huey! Can a black man get a fair trial in America—even if he was defending his life against a white policeman?" Meanwhile Melvin and I start looking for witnesses to the shooting, using my street smarts to track down people we've heard saw what happened.

Been searching...

Melvin sings as I drive, doing his best version of the Coasters, and within a week, we find witnesses who can blow the case wide open. By then we're in gear: we've created the Huey Newton Defense Committee and held the first rallies at the courthouse, brothers marching, sisters chanting. In February we host the grand birthday party attended by H. Rap Brown and Stokely Carmichael. Huey and the Black Panther Party are becoming known nationwide. Every day people call headquarters wanting to give money, start chapters. The second life of the Party has begun. When Huey leaves prison four years later, the Party has thirty-three chapters, over four thousand members, an international section, a weekly newspaper with a hundred thousand–plus readership, and free Breakfast for Children, shoes, medical and legal programs in operation from Winston-Salem to Seattle. J. Edgar Hoover calls us Public Enemy Number One, "the most active and dangerous black extremist group in the United States." Huey himself has been changed. He's no longer Huey, but Huey P. Newton, founder, main theoretician, and Supreme Servant of the Black Panther Party, the creator of the Ten Point Program, the revolutionary who calls police "pigs" to their faces, stands them down in the street and courts, son of Malcolm, an internationally recognized political figure, a warrior of ideas and actions, my leader—no matter how much he drives me crazy.

Twenty-two years ago.

And now I'm doing the same. Driving to Melvin's. The two of us seeing about Huey. Putting together the conclusion to that thing that began so long ago.

*　　*　　*

I reach Melvin's, a large split-level up in the hills above the city "flats" where we grew up and first knew each other. Cars line the driveway. The family is arriving—the Newton clan and supporters. Ministers and community leaders, people from UC-Santa Cruz, where Huey got his doctorate, old Party members, and the press, already an enormous amount of press, press from everywhere: I mean, Huey's been killed.

Melvin and I hug and he asks me to stay with him until the funeral. We're used to working collectively; in the next few days there will be many political decisions, and he wants my counsel. Besides, Huey's gone: Melvin and I both need the comfort of our brotherhood.

Right now there are two priorities. There's no money for the funeral and we've got to find out what really happened.

I tell Melvin the information I've gathered from my calls. Huey was hit three times. The weapon was a nine-millimeter. Melvin and I say the murder looks like a professional job. If the killer had been a young gangbanger, the shooting would have been a drive-by. This killer came close to Huey when Huey was unarmed. So Huey must have known his murderer and either trusted or despised him: Huey never would have left himself at a tactical disadvantage with a respected opponent. Finally, there's the third bullet. The coup de grace to the back of the head. A sign of a professional making sure Huey was dead. The one that sickens me.

We go through possibilities from the past. People burnt by the Party or who split from it. I don't think any are responsible. But the killing *looks* professional; and Huey is so important to me I secretly want his death to have significance—even if only the drama of a big-time drug hit. Still, something tells me that's not what happened.

"No," I tell Melvin. "I don't think this has *anything* to do with the Party. There's something else going on here."

We decide to drive around West Oakland, see what we can discover.

For me the ride is like being home. Huey became my friend when I was eleven. We've stayed by each other's side more or less ever since: same parties, women, and of course the Party and later drugs. But though I loved Huey, I was never fully comfortable with him; he was so extreme—talking at you, checking you out—that I was often on edge. Whereas I can spend hours hanging out with Melvin.

"We're doing it again," Melvin says as we head downtown, remembering our investigations after Huey's shoot-out with Officer Frey.

"Yeah," I say. "Huey seems to keep us going—in life and in death too."

We recall other war stories. Flying to Los Angeles for the first meeting with Bunchy Carter. The New York visit to the United Nations. My expulsion. Everything feels far away and ever present. The walking wounded, Masai Hewitt used to call us, the ones who survived, veterans from our war with the police and government, as hurt as any who had served in Vietnam.

We cruise the streets near the death site, stopping people I know: Hey, have you heard the news? Oakland might be a big city with two professional sports teams and its own airport, but to me it's a small town with friends on every block.

We drift by the murder spot.

The scene is quiet—only a few television crews and a couple of police, maybe fifty or sixty people standing around. In the next week the numbers will grow, people paying homage, strewing flowers, leaving personal mementos and messages of grief. The street looks genteel and quaint, a weird setting for carnage, tree-lined with cracked redbrick sidewalks and pastel-painted gingerbread one-family houses with carved lintels and widow's walks. Outsiders would never guess the place was a major drug market.

The house Huey left this morning stands on the corner, a large white and bluish gray two-story wood building; the back of the second floor served as the crack house. A black-and-white stuffed toy dog with large round eyes stares out the window of the Victorian cottage next door. In the yard lies an abandoned, dilapidated kid's car seat, a small dumpster, and a used milk carton.

"That's where they found him," an old woman who says she lives opposite tells me. "His head was right in my mother's rosebushes. His body was in the street. He came by here every morning right at eleven. He used a little red car. That day he parked at the top of the block. Stayed all day and night. There was a dark gray car parked in front. I want to know how they knew he was coming out. It was set up, I tell you. They told him to get in the car and he said no and that was when they blew him away—mad-dog killers. This used to be a nice neighborhood. Now it's Dopeville."

Driving back, I think about what she's said. I remember the time I missed death. I was on San Pablo Avenue, selling some syringes to get crack money. Waiting for the guy to return with the cash I become paranoid—I'm high as a kite. So I try the hotel lobby door. It's locked. Now I'm really going crazy. I pound on the door. I don't know what's going on. The night manager comes out. But he's not letting me in. Who does he think he is? I tell him. I rev myself up. You know, I'm David Hilliard, Chief of Staff of the Black Panther Party! Let me in here! But the night manager won't back down.

Furious, I go back outside to a friend. I'm screaming about this night manager when my friend shouts: "David! Watch out!"

And he hits somebody.

I turn around.

The night manager stands there holding a gun. "Motherfucker! I'll blow your brains out!"

I'm saying, "Who? What's up?" I don't know what's going on.

My friend pushes me away. "David, go! You're out of your mind! The guy is trying to kill you. You don't even know what's happening."

So I walk home, no longer high but clear as a bell, saying: "God! Did I almost *die?*" convinced life was just about to end for me.

I don't want to believe—I *hate* to believe—Huey died in some similar madness. But more and more I'm convinced that's what happened.

Outside Melvin's, the media have set up camp.

We wade through the crowd. The reporters shoot questions, stick mikes in our faces, trying to get some statement. We say the same thing: "We'll let you know when we're prepared for a press conference. Nobody can come inside now. We'll let you know."

The easy half is the funeral: we'll tell people to send donations to a foundation we'll establish.

The hard part is deciding what to say about Huey's death, framing the event. The left is already spinning out theories. One group is spray-painting images of the young Huey, shotgun in hand, with the slogan

Who killed Huey Newton?
It wasn't you or I.
No, it was the FBI.

Other people compare his murder to George Jackson's and Malcolm X's, implying the police conspired to kill Huey.

None of us want to go along with that. But we do have a problem figuring out what to say about Huey and drugs. Realistically, we can't deny Huey's addiction. Huey has been busted for possession every day, up and down the street. But the press will focus on any admission we make about his habit. Ever since the Party fell apart they've wanted to prove he was a monster.

"Most of Huey's life was not about drugs and alcohol," Melvin says. "It was about *ideals*. It was about a social *movement*. It was about social *change*. That's what we have to be determined to talk about. We can't allow the press or anyone else to reduce his life to its worst element."

We gather on the living-room couch—Melvin, Frederica (Huey's wife), my-self—and for a half hour spar with the reporters. What was Huey doing down there?

Was he dealing drugs?

Is it possible the guy who killed him acted in self-defense?

We skirt the issue. Well, Huey had *business* down there. He had *friends*. He was born and raised in West Oakland. It wasn't like he was visiting some foreign country.

The more we duck, the more they attack.

But what about the time?

What's somebody doing down there so early in the morning?

Cool, collected, Melvin keeps coming back to the central issue.

"Well," he says, "if you forgive Huey for the sins he's committed against himself and other people, then we'll forgive America's sin for committing the murder against the red men and slaughter of the Japanese people in Nagasaki, and what they've done to blacks."

I chime in on the same note. The FBI put a lot of pressure on the Cubans not to import their cigars, I say, and you can't find Cuban cigars. So maybe if the FBI put the same effort into seizing Colombian cocaine you wouldn't have a growing crack population and incidents like Huey P. Newton's.

That kind of stuff. Rhetorical. Not making the point. Not making the point at all. Inside I'm uncomfortable. I've been going to AA and have been in recovery for almost two years now, and I keep hearing the fourth and fifth steps of the program: "Make a fearless moral inventory of yourself." That's not what's going on. I'm shirking the truth, not admitting it.

Afterward, I drive Frederica home.

"Look Fredi," I say as soon as we're in the car, "I need to know what's going on here. What's Huey been into?"

Fredi tells me he had been down to LA, trying for a movie deal. But this project had fallen through like the others and he was very, very depressed. And also Huey had lost a lot of money on a drug deal. Maybe as much as seventy thousand dollars.

I press her. Could some dealers have been out to kill him?

"No," she says, "I don't think that's it."

What about Muslims? I've heard Muslims in the Acorn—a project where we used to hang out—had problems with him. Maybe they decided Huey was too negative an influence on our youth and wanted to eliminate him.

Again she says no. Farrakhan had tried contacting Huey, and she had heard some Muslims talked to him, but nothing happened.

"Fredi," I say, "you *got* to tell me what's happening! What am I into here? What's going on?"

"I don't know," she says. "I swear to you I don't know. He's been doing really *super* in the last six months."

She describes their last afternoon together. They were at her house, Huey helping her with the crack babies she's been boarding for the last year. Then he has to leave: a state investigator is visiting and the law forbids caretakers contact with felons. Fredi gives him twenty-six dollars and he splits.

My own experience and the program tells me what happens next.

Huey is beat, depressed. Here's Huey Newton, who defined power as the ability to define a phenomenon and make it act in a desired manner. Now he can't define even his own life.

So he relies on his own willpower; he tries to do things on his own, use his own devices. He goes to his usual haunt for dealing with problems—the crack house. He plans to forget. Because that's what you do when you smoke cocaine. You involve yourself in the excess of where the drug takes you. And you forget.

He smokes, runs by his girlfriend's house, smokes, comes back to the crack house, goes by his girlfriend's again, smokes some more.

Then it's five in the morning. He returns to the crack house. Two guys stand on the street in front of a car. Huey asks one guy for dope.

The guy's a street hustler, strong, young, a weight lifter—his neck muscles bulge like a bull's; the only thing he knows about Huey is that once he ran the Panthers and now he's sprung on crack.

He tells Huey there ain't no more dope.

Huey gets belligerent—like me on San Pablo, crazed on crack.

"Go away," the guy says to Huey. "We ain't gonna give you no more drugs."

But Huey isn't going anywhere because he wants his dope, even if he doesn't have any more money. He argues with the guy. Details don't matter; what they say is all the same; it's all drug talk.

Until Huey says one thing too many and something happens: the guy hits Huey on the head with his gun.

Now Huey never backs off from a fight. Huey's whole thing is to elevate the fight, raise the struggle to a higher level, challenge force with new force, threat with new threat, never to show fear because the other person is bigger or stronger or holds a knife or gun but to equalize the difference. His instinct—his response to danger—*is* Huey; when he was a kid and a gang beat him up, he came back with a hammer, daring them to a new fight, and many times, as a Panther, he faced down police with his shotgun. He perseveres; he is unwilling ever to give up. Defiance is Huey's essence.

So now imagine him. He's staggered by the hit, cracked out. The street's empty. He's alone. No wife, girlfriend, running partners. There's only this black-and-white round-eyed toy dog staring at him from the window and this over-muscled, under-brained, apolitical, scared punk who has just pistol-whipped him in public.

He pauses for a moment, trying to absorb what's happening.

"Man, why do you do that?" he says.

And then the old Huey comes up—the intrepid rebel, bold, angry, intractable.

"You might as well kill me," he taunts the guy. "Go on, nigger, make history."

Maybe the guy backs off a moment, scared even then of old Huey's power. Or maybe he taunts Huey more. Either way Huey has taken over, forcing the situation to its logical conclusion.

"Go on," Huey says. He's turning things around, just as he did with the cops, using his powerlessness to humiliate the guy. "Kill me, motherfucker! I'm not afraid of death!"

He stands there, hands out, feet spread wide. "You can kill the body, but not the spirit, motherfucker! Go on!"

The guy raises the gun.

But Huey doesn't care. He's Huey. He's faced down death. He's beaten fear.

"You ain't doing nothing here."

Knowing he's stung the boy, Huey becomes merciless.

"You ain't doing nothing here! Whatcha gonna do?"

He throws his arms even farther apart, putting himself completely at the fool's mercy. "Whatcha gonna do? Make history?"

And then it happens.

History.

"Motherfucker!" the guy says.

And he pulls the trigger.

Bam!

And Huey Newton—whomever that was—who walked upright and was born of woman, comes to the end of his road.

Which is what the program tells you: you always have another high but you might not have another recovery. Sooner or later you'll self-destruct—

homicide or suicide. You'll do what you're programmed to do, because that's the way addicts operate. You'll go where you find some relief. The disease tells you one hit of cocaine isn't going to matter because all you've got is twenty-six dollars anyway. So that's where Huey went, only this time he didn't come back. The name of his murderer doesn't matter; he was killed by the insanity of the drug culture. As it almost killed me. Huey *just* didn't make it this time. Period! He died messing around with drugs. And that's how his death happened.

I leave Frederica off and come back to the house.

After telling me about the funeral plans and when I'm scheduled to speak, Melvin asks me whether I'll appear with him on a local television show later that night. I agree and go downstairs, where some people watch a tape of Huey in his last television interview.

"The movement is wiped out and people are having a field day telling stories," he's saying. He did the show a few months ago during a brief time when he was off drugs. It's a vintage performance. Eyes alert and flashing, head cocked upward, he gives forth ideas and contradictions almost too fast to follow.

"I will accept being an outlaw," he says, "because to change the laws you must step outside the laws. If you do that and the people are with you, then you will become a hero, but if they are not, then you will become a criminal. I will accept being a deviant. I deviate from being docile. This government destroyed the movement, destroyed the revolutionary community fervor, destroyed the role models, and of the role models that were left they destroyed the character, and so now what you have is drugs in the community and police surveillance of the community—which is despicable because they use drugs as an excuse to abuse everyone in the community. The same things we fought against are still present today. This is sometimes depressing to me. But what's more depressing is that I'm not active anymore. But I'm looking for movements to rise up. Revolutionary movements come in waves, and as I look around I see movements in the community growing. They are in their infant stage, but I believe in time binding all wounds."

Hearing his words makes me miss him. Huey's jabber drove me crazy when he was manic; but the same voice—twangy, agitated, tripping over itself with all its ideas—came out with the clearest, most original analyses about the world or people I've ever heard.

"I don't know you anymore," he told me when he got out of jail. "You act like Eldridge. When I sit here and listen to you, I might as well just tune in

Eldridge. You're starting to look like him, walk like him, act like him. You don't know who you are. Which is very insulting to me."

And he was absolutely right.

Or he would talk about intercommunalism, his global vision negating nationalism, seeing the world as communities, some under siege, some besieging.

Standing there, looking at his image on the screen, I realize I'm never going to hear that voice say something new again. What am I going to say about you, Huey? I think. What am I going to say?

I go upstairs to rest. Huey's voice keeps going through my mind. His talk drove me craziest when we smoked. Because when we'd get high Huey would chatter endlessly about the drug, its effects on people, then about Panthers: You and me, David, he'd say, we're fallen stars! On and on he'd ramble, from six in the evening to six the next morning, nonstop, all the time expecting me to sit there like a sounding board, never letting me get a word in edgewise. Almost a kind of torture. Until suddenly he'd ask, "You following me?" Just to see if I was really listening. And he'd stare at me, pinning me. So I couldn't lie to him then. I had to tell the truth. And if the truth was that I had been pretending to listen, he'd call me. "Don't ever do that, because I'll read you. Don't ever play like you're understanding me." So I could never relax around him.

Finally we stopped smoking together. I went into the program; he kept getting worse. Which was ironic since I had started him smoking crack in the first place.

It was around 1985. At the time he was saying he thought nobody could get high off crack, that the one time he'd tried basing, the dope didn't do anything to him.

But I told him no, he wasn't getting high because he wasn't smoking right.

"Oh no," he says. "That stuff just doesn't work. I don't understand why anybody wastes their money, just burning it up. Just going up in smoke like that."

I reintroduce him to an ex–Party member who runs a dope house. After a while he sends back a message: "Tell David he's right. I finally got a good hit off this stuff. I didn't know what I was doing."

So Huey and I start smoking together. And immediately Huey is making plans off the crack, figuring to organize these dealers; the government has impoverished him through embezzlement cases and he doesn't have a house or a car, and crack seems a way to make money.

But dealing isn't what I have in mind at all. At the time I'm living in one room, down in the Acorn, sleeping literally on the floor. I've been on crack for five years, an alcoholic for as long as I can remember. I've shuttled from place to place — doing "geographics," as they say in the program, trying to fix your life by changing your address — but my dependency has only grown more powerful and I have suffered every possible humiliation: banned from my brother's and sister's houses, locked up for fighting with my wife, threatened by my own kids. So I don't harbor any grandiose schemes of getting rich. I just want to be high. To do what I can to keep a supply for my own addiction.

"No," I tell him.

My refusal frustrates him.

"You don't want anything," Huey says. "You know, you don't want any money. You're just a dope fiend."

"Well, that may be," I answer. "I'm okay with that. I don't want to be a drug dealer. I don't want to be walking around with guns. It's bad enough trying to wade through these motherfuckers to *buy* with all these guns, let alone trying to have shoot-outs with them."

Which Huey himself has told me about. Because when I first live in the Acorn I have no sense whatsoever of fearing the dealers. They're the sons of old friends and running partners, and in my mind I'm still the Chief, David Hilliard, Chief of Staff of the Black Panther Party, who has taught these kids about guns. So if on occasion I get *burned* and they take my money without giving me drugs and talk crazy to me, I talk madness right back at them, acting like I own them, speaking with authority, never even imagining they might hurt me. That's how insane the dope has me. And I never get hurt: sometimes the dope acts like a blessing and keeps you out of harm's way.

But when I go with Huey he backs off.

"David," he says, "these motherfuckers don't know who we are, man!" He's laughing. "These guys were only ten years old when we were Panthers. Besides, they're dangerous. They have no values. They're not like us. They don't have any respect for life or anything. You can't talk to them."

But I still don't believe him.

Then one day I'm leaving the dope house and see some sellers lifting weights. I go over to them. I say, "Wait, hold this. Let me lift weights."

They just laugh. "Old nigger, the heaviest thing you gonna pick up is a base pipe."

Their attitude shocks me. Contempt. For *us!* Me and Huey Newton!

"You motherfuckers ain't doing nothing but buying dope is all. You niggers ain't what you all used to be. You all are history."

*   *   *

Soon after, Huey and I stop smoking together. He starts becoming paranoid—
the way he had acted in the Party when he accused members unjustly, including, finally, Pat, June, and myself. One night he smokes with Pat and my son
Darryl all *night* in my house, without me ever touching the dope.

The next day Frederica comes looking for Huey because Huey has their
car. I say I'll see if I can find him. I go around back and tell him Frederica is
there.

Huey very coldly dismisses me.

"Whatcha do with my dope?"

"What're you talking about?" I say.

"I know you're smoking over there in the apartment," he says. "You stole
my dope."

"Huey," I say, "Huey, what is wrong with you? Dope? I don't have any of
your dope. You took your dope with you."

I leave feeling really, really bad and angered that I even let him come to
my house, because I know what's about to happen: he's going to accuse me
of stealing his dope, a replay of his old distrust. So I decide never to be
around him—not as long as he uses drugs.

Finally one night we quit dodging each other.

"Well," he tells me, "Melvin said that we're family and you probably
didn't take the dope from me. So I forgive you and I'm asking you to forgive
me for it. But I'm *not* gonna beg you."

"Well, that's all right," I answer. "I didn't ask you to beg me. Besides,
I'm the guy, remember, that you could trust over everybody! You know, why
would I steal dope from you? I gave you your organization back, you know?
I mean how could you *possibly* think I would steal drugs from you?"

He says, "Because everybody steals drugs from each other when they use
that stuff."

It's two years later before I see him again. I run into him at Melvin's.
Huey's shuttling back and forth between Melvin's and Frederica's. Shielding
an addict from hitting bottom contradicts every rule of the program. But
Melvin's Huey's brother; I have the same weakness with my son Darryl. Besides, this addict's not just Melvin's brother; he's Huey.

I walk into the kitchen. Huey's on his way out, going to West Oakland,
doing his thing in the Acorn with his drug friends.

"How you doing?" he asks me. He looks based out. "You still sober?"

He doesn't ask the question resentfully. Huey is a master of psychology.
He's suspecting I'll be back out there with him in a very short time. And he

probably would be right, except by now I've been in recovery a year and a half and I know one thing: I can't control my use of dope or liquor and can't be around him or anybody else who messes with them.

Then he declares himself, warning me not to give him any program talk. "I don't want to be friends with nobody that don't have drugs." He smiles.

"Well, I certainly don't have any," I answer.

It's our standoff, magnets keeping each other away, bound by our energy, but not touching: You know, Huey often tells me, you're the only friend I've never fought with.

"Oh, you doing all right?" he says.

"Yeah," I tell him, "I'm still sober. I'm doing okay."

"Well, I'm not," he says. "I'm not doing well at all."

"Well, you'll do all right when you get ready, Huey," I say. "Just as I have."

No answer, but a smile. I can picture his smile now. Then he pulls away. "I'll see you later." And he goes on about his business.

A few weeks later, I call him. A newspaper article in the *Tribune* says the city should erect a monument to the Panthers. Even against so much adversity, the Party scored significant victories. The federal government itself took over programs we initiated like the free Breakfast for Children program and our free tests for sickle-cell anemia. More than twenty years after Huey first wrote it, the Ten Point Program remains a complete, concise statement of what minorities need and want. And in Oakland, we changed local politics, electing the city's first black mayor, bringing blacks onto all the city's governing bodies, taming the police.

I've been doing community work and think maybe the memorial would be a good focus for my energies. But I don't want to do anything about the Party without Huey's approval.

I call Huey at home.

"How you doing?" he says. He sounds good, obviously sober.

I tell him about the memorial. Should I work on the project?

He thinks for a moment. Then: "No, let them handle it. The community should start a fight to build something like that. And let's just see what they do."

He promises to call me again in a week, but I don't hear from him, and not starting contact between us is part of my discipline. But I do talk to Melvin, asking him how Huey's faring. "Well," says Melvin, "you know, he *sounded* straight on the phone." He pauses, a little remorseful. "I owe him a phone call. But I don't know. I'm tired of him being in my life. All he does is bring problems. Ever since he's a kid. And I don't know why I still bother with him. I'm sick and tired of him, and I don't want to see him again this side of Glory."

"Oh, Melvin," I say. "Come on. You know. That's Huey."

Two weeks later Huey's gone. This guy who causes havoc in my life and the life of anybody with whom he's been personally involved—he's gone. I realize what I'm feeling: relief. Relief for myself and also for Huey. Because I think Huey was just a bit tired himself—exhausted of being here, weary of himself.

The interviewers on the local show adopt a tough cop–nice cop team approach, trying to pry a revelation out of us.

What was Huey doing?

Was he a dope addict?

Melvin stays cool, answering the questions with a calm, self-assured voice. I hate being there. As far as I'm concerned the interviewers are eating us up. As the show goes on I see things more and more clearly: I want to take the sting out of the press's bite and deal with the truth. Our statements will be more viable, more powerful if we admit Huey's addiction instead of denying it. If there's anything people will understand it's Huey being a crackhead in West Oakland in the 1980s. My God, Elvis Presley named his home Graceland—and he was nothing but a common dope fiend. So people will certainly understand about Huey; they just need to be told.

Halfway through the program a guy phones in.

"I know Huey Newton," he says. "I was in a nightclub with him, in a speakeasy, after hours, and they were getting ready to close the club, and Huey Newton had his bodyguards pull guns on the bartender, demanding drinks."

Melvin takes the call.

"Well," he starts. "What do you expect? Somebody in an after-hours, full of alcohol. What's so unusual about that? Anybody who drinks acts more abnormally than when they're not drinking. What are you trying to say? How do you act when you are messed up off of alcohol, and, besides, what are you doing in a speakeasy anyway?"

His answer is his first public admission that Huey had a problem. I think: Good. Now I've got the go-ahead, we can talk. After the show I start.

"Melvin," I say, "we got to stop this. The press is tearing us up, using this stuff about Huey's addiction. We got to put it to rest. And the way we do that in the old Party methodology is to *give* it to them. Let's knock the wind out of it by *admitting* it. Then they can't beat us with that. They can't hurt us with that anymore."

We're driving out of the lot and the yellow and white street fog lights stripe Melvin's face.

"Okay," he says.

As soon as I enter the house an old Party comrade calls.

"What are you doing?" she demands. "All you guys are in denial around Huey and his addiction."

I defend myself. "What do you mean?"

She says, "Huey's a dope addict, and you ought to know better! How can you go on television and attempt to cover him up?"

"I'm not in denial," I say. "If you saw the television show, you heard Melvin admit right there that Huey. . ."

She interrupts me. "It's not just that incident they're talking about. Melvin's covering up. How could you accept that kind of defense of him? That's not it."

Now my mind's divided; the Party comrade doesn't share my respect for Huey, but she's speaking the truth.

"You're in recovery yourself," she goes on. "So how can you be denying it? Just being on television like that and letting them get away with all these apologies for him."

"I'm not doing that," I repeat. "What are you talking about? What do you want me to do?"

I don't know the answer.

I don't wish to hurt Huey's family. But I love Huey. I feel I must say something *decent* about him, to *free* him, talk about him with clarity, conviction, speak as Huey would have spoken. I don't want him to pass out of life with lies surrounding him, a strange, dark, negative figure.

So I'm caught, stymied, having to choose my words, instead of simply speaking freely and saying what I know and believe. Nothing's coming out right.

Outside I meet Father Neil, the Episcopalian minister who helped found our first Breakfast for Children program.

I tell Father Neil I need some spiritual peace, ask him to pray with me. We kneel together while Father Neil talks to God.

"Give David the strength to do what he thinks is right."

I follow. Years ago I needed strength to join the Party and face the risks that came with membership. Now I ask for a similar fortitude.

"I need courage to do what's right again," I say, addressing God.

"I need courage not to be a victim to dishonesty and denial. I need courage to confront things and face them head-on, and I am making a decision now to do that."

As soon as I finish, my path becomes clear. I can hear the family inside getting ready for the next day of mourning. But the clarity of my understanding makes me feel alone. In the Party, we used to call certain moments "colossal events," situations that defined new realities—Sacramento, Huey's shoot-out, Li'l Bobby Hutton's death. Huey's death has been a colossal event for me. It's not Huey I must confront with the truth, not Huey I must face. It's myself.

Part
ONE

Chapter

1

THERE are few people in my life I know less about than my father. I was his twelfth, last child, and we were pretty much strangers to each other—he was already in his fifties when I was coming up. On his background, schooling, family, even the names of his mother and father, I draw a blank. "Marengo County," he used to answer when we asked where he came from, nothing more specific. Maybe a town called Sinai. Before that maybe British Honduras— British Hondu, he called it. Even my mother doesn't know. "I just know he came from another county," she says. "It was up north. I never knew his family except for his siblings."

Because of this, my memory of him tends to be fragmented. My father gives me a quarter, places a cigar band on my finger, plays checkers and the harmonica, votes for Republicans (even when we tell him Democrats favor poor people) because Republicans freed the slaves, curses the Cajuns, his word for all white people: "Them kissified people. You can't trust them Cajuns." He's dark, with *tight* black skin, short—"low and lively," my cousin Boy Collier calls him—and so strong that I disregard his physical height and consider him a giant: I grow up hearing stories of him dominating bigger guys.

Most of all, he's sweet smelling. Scents, sachets, perfumes, colognes; he wears them all. I recall vividly the whiff of freshness that fills the room as he leaves his nightly bath.

"You're smelling like a Harlem sissy," my mother teases.

"That's my kissified perfume," he answers.

* * *

Smelling good meant a lot to him, I think, because he worked so hard. No one worked harder than my father. Idleness was anathema to him; ask any of my brothers and sisters and they'll tell you he was the hardest-working man they have ever known—a *strenuous* worker, in the words of my brother Van.

Work was his whole life. He started in the second grade when he left school to help his sharecropper parents in the fields. Later he became a lumberman, bunching logs and chipping boxes—tapping turpentine—in the Alabama pine forests. When he moved to Mobile, he served as a hand on boats and as a dishwasher in the Sheraton Battle House—"Daddy," I used to ask, "what's a battle house?"—and Morrison's Cafeteria. Once he couldn't find a job; he left and we didn't hear from him. I believe my mother thought he had abandoned us. After several months, we received a letter. He was working in a northern Alabama lumber mill; illiterate, he had to find someone who could write to tell us he'd be home soon. Even when he was over sixty-five and too old for anyone to hire him, he still looked for work, too determined, proud, and energetic to accept staying at home "to draw my pennies." Throughout all his difficulties and struggles, he maintained his appearance: shined shoes, fresh clothes, brushed hair, soaped, scented skin, taking pride in his labor, but not wanting the smell of work on him.

"Kissified" was one of his words. "Datblasted" another. Also "conflummicks" and "bumfuddled and shot-to-pieces." Get away from me, he'd say, waking up in the morning, I'm all bumfuddled and shot-to-pieces.

No one knew the origin of the weird-sounding concoctions. Some, like "conflummicks," may have been mispronunciations—my father tried arduously to read, poring over the Bible at home, or newspapers, sounding out words whose first letters he recognized. "Bumfuddled" and others seem to have been expressions from the area where he grew up—home words, as my brother Allen calls them. Whatever their origin, they were a constant part of his vocabulary, a way of expressing himself.

"Stop your conflummicks," he would say when my brother Arthur sneaked up behind him as he played checkers.

Arthur was one of my favorite brothers. He was a devil. Once he went into my grandfather's field and offered a cow a corncob. When the animal refused the gift, Arthur hit it on the head with a hammer. So, naturally, when my father told him to stop, he didn't listen. He tickled my father under his arm instead.

Except you didn't touch my father. You didn't goose him. (And you didn't call him "P. Whittler" or "Sapsucker." P. Whittler or Sapsucker and you were already gone: he'd beaten and cut you.) So when Arthur touched him, my father exploded, flailing in the air, arms and legs upsetting the board and throwing the checkers over the living room.

"You kissified bastard!" he yelled.

Kissified was his worst curse. He was hot then. He used it if you touched him with a broom. "Kissified bastard!" he'd curse and snatch the broom and spit on it, breaking the magic—being touched with a broom meant he was headed for jail. He'd be really furious at what he considered a basic violation of his self-respect.

He had other superstitions—"My daddy was an old-country man," says my oldest sister, Rose Lee. If a black cat crossed his path, he'd turn around and walk away fast: nothing could induce him to head into the trouble waiting for him down the road. He refused to let himself be photographed; photos captured your soul. And whenever we had bad thunderstorms, he covered the mirrors with sheets. Lightning and thunder were the work of "Old Master" and no one was ever to fool with Master. Many times he told us the story of his cousin, Hoseah, who carried an ax to church planning to avenge a wrong done him by a congregation member; as Hoseah mounted the stairs, a bolt of lightning struck the ax head, knocking Hoseah to the ground. "Old Master wanted to teach Hoseah respect for the House of the Lord!" my father told us. "Hoseah should have known better than to tempt Old Master!"

Like Old Master, my father also had a temper. Not that he had a short fuse. But when he got mad, you had to watch out because my father was lightning-quick and always made sure to get the first punch. Once, my brothers tell me, a two-hundred-pound guy in a lumber camp started bothering him, making obscene gestures. "Don't jaw-jack me!" my father told the man. But the man didn't listen. Instead, he put hands on my father. My father grabbed the guy by the pants, flipped him, and busted open his head. Then he went for his knife. That's the kind of guy my father was. He didn't care who his antagonist was: if you got hit, you'd better hit back. That was the rule we grew up with. *Who* hit you—white or black, big or little—didn't matter; we couldn't come home unless we'd stood up for our self-respect.

My father figures in my life as an influence; looking back, I can trace his qualities in me—his anger, style, desire for knowledge. My mother is there as a constant presence, sacred, secure, a figure of strength dispensing equal portions of love to each and every child, the center of her kids' lives. To this day, I don't know what I and my brothers and sisters would do if my mother died; and throughout the four years I was in prison, I prayed that nothing would happen to her.

When she meets my father—in 1916—she is only sixteen, just a little over half Daddy's age and his opposite in almost every way: taller than him, with big bones and a lighter, tawnier skin. Also unlike him, she comes from a well-established family. The Williamses are important people in Rockville, her hometown; shortly after the Civil War, they use six cows and twenty bags of grain to buy 140 acres and become the first black landowners in Clarke County. (My mother still owns twenty acres of the original property.) The family homestead stretches over a rise of hills—my grandmother's house, then her sister's, and finally the church, a one-room, hard-benched, white-shingled chapel. Dick Williams, my grandfather, serves as sexton, ringing the bell that announces deaths, services, and the "Big Meeting," a communal feast my sister Rose Lee remembers to this day. "It started on Sunday and lasted for the week," she says. "Everybody would come together and bring food—pigs and calves roasted on spits over coal and pies and cakes for the kids. There'd be food for hours and hours."

Although a wide gap separates my mother and father socially, there seems to be no opposition to their union. (My sister Rose Lee says my father's work habits endeared him to the clan.) I've heard my mother's brother, David—I'm his namesake—disapproves, but the family certainly doesn't: the Williamses give my parents land on which to build a cabin, a plot between my grandmother's house and the church, a clearing in a thickly treed hollow surrounded by a steep-banked, clear-running creek.

"You'd walk down behind the church and there was a baptizing pool, and it was cold water too, fresh," recalls Boy Collier. "A little farther and you'd get to the Hilliard house. That was in the woods. *Deep* in the woods. *Down* in the woods. I didn't go by myself there. I was scared. Because along in that time there would be animals that would bother kids and things—wildcat, foxes, and panthers, all across them woods in there. And they would jump on kids."

As Boy indicates, Rockville—my mother's town, where she and Father live—is *country*. Sixty miles north of Mobile, the town is a settlement of hand-built, mostly off-the-road cabins threaded together by red-dirt roads that wind through the pine, chinaberry, and oak woods of the Alabama hills, a link in the chain that makes up the black belt, the African-American community that stretches through the five states of the deep South.

"I started working on a farm when I was twelve," Boy Collier says, describing life back then.

Plowing and farming. We raised cotton, sweet potatoes, corn, okra, greens, tomatoes, peas, beans. At lunchtime I would haul lunch from the house out there to the hands. Got fifty cents a day. Three dollars a week. All of that. We'd grow the food and market it. Some families — like your mother's family — of course also owned their own land. But even they had to mortgage it because otherwise they wouldn't have the money to get a mule or horse that they needed to till the crops.

We did all the work for Mr. Allen. Charlie Allen. He was a white man. Owned a lot of land around there. He had a lot of cows too. He lived out in the piney woods. That's where the white folk kept themselves. "I've got to go out to the piney woods," you'd say, and cook or cut for such and such or pull corn or pick beans, chop cotton.

Back then, I was scared of white people. Back then, black man had to mostly do what the white man wanted. If he didn't do it, the white man would do something to him. First they would talk to you. Tell you what they wanted you to do. Then, if you won't do that, you'd get in trouble.

One time they whipped my mama's first cousin about shooting a cow. The cow had broken into his field, ate up all his crop. He had worked all year for it, and then Charlie Allen's cow comes and eats it all up. Now he didn't have nothing! So he shot the cow! Well, Charlie Allen didn't know who shot his cow, but the boss man for Charlie was my mama's first cousin's cousin. He was a limber-legged man. Had a boy who would come and set him up on his horse and he'd stay on that horse all day. Well, he told Charlie Allen. So one night Charlie Allen and the whites come out of the piney woods down there into Rockville. They took my mama's first cousin and put him in the back of a pickup truck and carried him to Jackson where there's a creek. And they dropped him in the creek. Tied his hands behind him and hog tied him. And they — all of them — had their pump guns and shotguns. They didn't whip him, but they made him tell that he had killed that cow. And then he had to *quit* his job and go to work for Charlie Allen to pay for that cow he had shot.

Boy's world was changing a lot by the time I was born. New social conditions — the Depression and the mechanization of agriculture — produced a mass migration to the north, of which my family was a part. The exodus stripped the town of population and turned fields of cotton, corn, beans, and greens into untended forests. Fewer people now live in Rockville than when my father first courted my mother.

Yet Rockville remains a profound influence on my life. Through all the journeys taken by my family, Rockville and its way of life endures as a standard. Not that I am happiest in Rockville, or even more comfortable. There are things I can't stand about that life—I still dislike snakes, and many of my memories of growing up involve hunger and fear—and I keep my visits to my siblings in Alabama short. But spending time with them is to me the equivalent of an Italian-American returning to Sicily: Alabama remains home, the place where life is lived as it should be. "We're going back to the old country," my cousin Bojack used to say when we were growing up and preparing for a trip south. Rockville remains the closest I can get to my origins, to *being African.*

It amazes me how much the past has remained alive down there. (Not always a good thing. In true Jim Crow fashion, the roads to Jackson—the county seat, where whites live—are paved; the ones to Rockville are still dirt: a stranger wouldn't know he was passing through a town until someone told him.) For all the VCRs and portable telephones—and crack too—you'll now find in Rockville, the old culture, life as it was in my father's time, still endures. To this day, I can show up at the home of relatives with whom I've been out of touch for twenty years and be greeted with fresh-fried river catfish, corn bread, and iced water. As when I was a kid, families casually drop in on one another. Everyone works and shares the tomatoes or corn they grow. Even though the television is always on—color sets, usually out of focus and showing weird oranges and purples—you sit and trade talk: jokes, news, recipes, gossip, stories, everything important, that is, being passed on verbally. Is yellow catfish better than channel catfish? My brother-in-law Paul always has some tale of outside life: a guy who was bitten by rattlesnakes so often that the snakes would die after puncturing him. Everybody goes by a nickname: Pig Iron, June Bug, Bud, Molasses, Hot Shot, and Shipyard Fats. They're called after the food they like, their neighborhood, or just their physical stature: Big Poppa or Big Church, a guy so large they had to make his name *Big* Church to accent his size. People are accepted with all their foibles.

This sense of the South—the black South—as home is not peculiar to me.

"I left the South when I was about eleven years old, and I was thirty-one years old before I came back," says Melvin Newton, Huey's brother, who comes from Louisiana.

I had a strange kind of spiritual experience. My father had died the previous year. And as I drove on Highway 10, starting to get into Louisiana, I felt the presence of my father. I felt his presence in some very clear kind of way. It was almost like I could hear the mule wagon with wooden wheels that he used to drive in the Louisiana lowlands. I wished my father were there, but I also had a feeling of being close to some people I had never known, could never know, because they were gone. But they were there. And what I found further was that families were there, because that's where we began in the United States. You had families, people who developed their own institutions, churches and schools and businesses. You had cemeteries! Out here, in the West, the graveyards are set aside from the community. But there, the graveyards are *in the community,* in the churchyards! So even in death, people aren't separated. Here's Uncle so-and-so, here's Grandpa, here's my father, and so on. They're there, even though they're gone.

When I think about the influences that inspired the spirit and work of the Black Panther Party—many of which are still not understood—this culture figures large among them. Many of the most important members of the Party—people like John and Bobby Seale and Geronimo Pratt, Bobby Rush and Fred Hampton—were imbued with the moral and spiritual values of their parents; and the work that went into the Party, our dignity as an independent people, the communal ideal and practice that informed our programs, all stem in part from the civilization of which my mother and father were so representative a part.

Down in the hollow by the creek, my mother and father make their life.

Mother constructs the cabin—a bungalow with a front room, two bedrooms, and a kitchen, rather than the simpler shotgun style. My brother Allen hands her the scrap lumber boards my father has gathered from the mill; she nails them together, hanging them vertically, rather than horizontally. There's a front and back porch; the heat is a family story.

"Daddy built a chimney to try to make heat," says my sister Sweetie.

He built it out of some old, brown bricks—we call them sand bricks— and red-dirt clay. You'd stick them together with the clay and make a chimney. And it comes a big rainstorm. All that clay and stuff got wet and it *fell* down to the ground. Just washed down. And just left a big hole. And we didn't have nowhere to make heat. So Daddy made a heater, out of a piece of tin drum. Cut a hole in the top, put a pipe in it, cut a hole in the side, and made a door to it. You could open or close it. Stoke it with wood. You'd go into the woods and get the wood. At evening time.

Out back my mother grows her garden.

"Greens, peas, okra, watermelon, cucumbers," remembers Sweetie. "All that kind of stuff."

In front one of the kids dusts the dirt yard every day.

"You'd cut long *bushes*, a big ball of them, and tie 'em together and *sweep* the yard!" says Sweetie. "In those days, your yard was just as clean as a carpet in a house."

There's no plumbing, of course, so a little ways back—in "the jungle," as Mother calls it—Father builds a spring.

"The water came out of the ground onto a big, tall bank—clear, clear, pretty water," says Sweetie. "We'd use that water for everything. Washing, bathing, cooking."

Clothes are washed every Friday—a long, hard job.

"The boys would go in the woods, cut down these big oak trees, stack them up, and make a big fire," says Sweetie. "Then we'd take the iron—a big, old heavy iron—and set it to that fire and it'd get hot. You'd have your ironing board up there, and every time you get ready for ironing, you'd get your iron and iron your clothes."

Bathing is daily, the kids soaking in large tin tubs.

"You had to wash your feet if you didn't take a bath," says Sweetie, "because they'd be *dirty*. Couldn't get into Mama's bed unless you wash your feet. You fell asleep early, she'd wake you up. 'Get up! Got to wash them feet before you go to bed!'"

School is Christian Valley, a one-room building behind the church that kids stop attending regularly once they're old enough to work.

"We used to hoe in the fields and pick cotton and stuff like that," remembers my brother Allen. "You know, for a buck or fifty cents a day. With dinner. We wasn't compelled to do it. But if you wasn't lazy, you'd get up and go and do something. I started because my mother sent me to school one morning and she looked like she was sick when I left. I went and tears were running down my little cheeks. Because I figured I'd be more help with her at home than I could be at school. So I turned around and came *back*. She told me: 'I ain't gonna whip you today! You come back for a reason!' I say, 'Yeah, Mama, you was sick.' And I didn't attend no more school after that."

Mother and Father work all the time. Mother is in the fields, earning money from Charlie Allen—when she isn't bedridden with one of her twelve pregnancies. Father is mainly away.

"He would be gone from the house for a week or two at a time," recalls my brother June, "because he worked in logging camps and there was no way for him to get back home." Sweetie says he never missed a day of work. "He just worked *all* the time. Believed in his work. Hard-working man. Cutting logs. Sawing logs. All that stuff."

First he bunches logs with his brother Oscar cutting pine and gum trees with a crosscut saw for three cents for every eight- to twelve-foot log. After cutting the trees, he and Oscar stack the logs and the company mules drag them to the sawmill. Later, he taps turpentine, "chipping boxes." He skins the bark with a draw knife—a two-handled straight-edged blade—and nails a tin scoop with a box into the trunk. The resin runs down the tin groove into the box. Each week, he removes the boxes, scraping out the resin to fill large fifty-five-gallon barrels later gathered by the turpentine company.

On weekends, when Mother and Father are home together, they share the domestic responsibilities.

My father leads the expedition to the general store in the piney woods.

"We had to walk a *long* ways," says Sweetie. "I guess it was about eight or nine miles through the woods to that grocery store. So we had to leave early in the morning, walking *fast*. Daddy would have a big sack across his back. He'd have two or three of the children with him. And that's the way we brought our groceries home from the store—on your back in a sack."

Liking to cook, he makes his specialties: salmon croquettes and tomato gravy.

"He'd put some shortening in the pan," remembers Sweetie. "Then put the flour in there and let it brown. Just stir and keep it from burning. And open a can of tomatoes and dump it over in there. Put some water in, season it up, and make gravy out of it. Good gravy! Eat that on rice, biscuits, everything."

He's also a native pharmacist.

"One of us got a stomach ache or cold or something, he did all the working on it," says Sweetie, who still collects the roots of special plants for cures when she visits Rockville, "making teas, and home remedies and stuff like that." (The main ingredient in these concoctions seems to have been turpentine. When we had a cold, his antidote was tea brewed from whiskey, lemons, Vicks, turpentine, honey, and water. After we drank this we were sent to bed to sweat out "the cold bug." I always perspired so profusely my sheets became wringing wet, and I would have to dry my underwear by the living-room wood stove. But years later, when we had a flu epidemic in the Party, I brewed some of my father's medicine. The comrades refused to drink the foul-tasting mixture, but I ordered them, drank some myself, and none of us got sick.)

Meanwhile my mother fishes.

"She used to fish a lot," says Rose Lee. "She had another sister. They'd get up before the daybreak in the morning. They'd pack them sacks and those earthworms and whatnot and go fishing. They'd fish till *late* over in the evening before they'd come back. She *loved* to fish. She *stayed* on that water."

My father's relaxation is closer to home.

"For him, a good time was setting down and laughing and talking," recalls Boy Collier. "He never did drink that I know of really. He could play checkers. He could *throw* those checkers. He'd play his brother, Uncle Ben. He'd say, 'Uncle Ben, you're nothing but a chump!' He'd go to win and be so fast on them checkers, he'd be skipping them and Uncle Ben wouldn't even miss them."

Mother and Father also share the discipline. We're most afraid of my father.

"He could look at you and you knew that what he wanted you to do, you'd best do it," says my brother June. "You knew that he never *would* hit you, but he would always let you know: If I *have* to hit you, I'm gonna *hurt* you, and I don't *want* to hurt you. So we never did provoke him to that extent."

But most of the time Daddy passes the task off to Mother.

"If we did something that had to get a whipping," Sweetie remembers, "Daddy would say, 'Uh-huh, I'm gonna tell your mama. Make your mama whip you.' "

My mother's blows stung.

"She was very strict with us," says Sweetie. "She didn't care nothing about how old you were. When you did something you didn't have no business doing, she'd get on you. She would get that belt or a switch off the beech tree and she'd tear you up. Yes, she'd get on you."

Even when Mother puts the job back to Daddy, he tries to get out of it.

"Sometimes, if we were real bad," says June, "he'd go to this tree peach and get two branches, give each one a branch—we call them 'switches'— and say, 'Now you discipline each other.' We would hit each other on the legs and on the behind and stuff like that. First one start crying, we'd stop it. It was his way of showing us that if we were gonna fight and create a problem, then we had to mete out the discipline for doing that. To each other. I guess it helped kind of build a bond to each other. We'd say, 'Well, if we got to do this, maybe we shouldn't fight.' "

Sometimes even Daddy's resistance breaks down; he whips us with a leather belt or thin, little branches, stinging our bare behinds. But these times are rare. He seems to have a genuine reluctance to use force on us.

"Daddy didn't believe in giving us a whipping," says Sweetie. "Daddy would stick up for his own. If people would ask us to go into the field and help them to hoe their corn or chop cotton and we would drag around like we didn't want to go, he'd tell Mama: 'Don't make them go. If they want to go, they can go on their own. But don't *make* them go. Because I don't want my children to come up like I did. Working hard in the fields and things.'"

Chapter

2

IN the thirties, the turpentine company relocates my father and the family moves around: Chunchula, then Chickasaw, finally back to Rockville. There I'm born.

"Mother was sickly," Rose Lee says about Mother's delivery. "Headaches and fever. A lot of fever. The night you were born my grandfather rode to Jackson on an old mule to get the doctor. Grandpa had to ride real hard to get there in time."

Soon after, my oldest brother, Bud, changes our lives. Bud is close with Daddy—they've worked together in the woods—and my father listens to him. He tells my father and my brother Allen there's work for them in Mobile.

"Bud had gone down there," says Sweetie, "and he kept worrying until he got all of them to come down."

We move to Maple Street, a sun-drenched block of two-story brick buildings and wooden shotgun houses. Davis Avenue—renamed Martin Luther King Boulevard after riots in 1968—is the neighborhood's main thoroughfare. Like everything in Mobile, Davis Avenue is provincial. For all its impressive history—founded in 1520, Mobile was supposed to be the capital of French America—Mobile is nothing more than a secondary port surrounded by pockets of communities, including a French quarter and business district with antebellum mansions, a black neighborhood, and an industrial sector called Prichard whose one massive paper mill belches gases all night long. But even though Davis Avenue is only a few brightly lit blocks, the street seems big-time to my young mind: a boulevard as grand as 125th

Street with night spots on every corner, especially the Harlem Dukes Social Club, where my brothers see the great blues performers.

Our home is a shotgun shack, four rooms straight through, kitchen in the back. Mother lines the wood floors with linoleum. Curtains serve for doors. We use the four-eyed, potbellied kitchen stove for both cooking and heating. In other rooms we have wood heaters: you open the grate, throw the log in, and get the pipes to glow.

The kitchen is the true center of the house, the only room supplied with running water; we bathe as well as eat there. A small cupboard holds the watermelon rinds, pear and plum preserves my mother puts to store every summer. An icebox with a daily delivered fifty-pound cake of ice acts as our refrigerator. For cool water, we chip pieces off the block and let them melt in a glass. Water is important. We scramble to keep food on the table, different family members working jobs that supply us with food. Arthur brings fish, even frog legs ("We don't want them frog legs jumping all over here," we say. "That stuff's alive"). And from the local store down the street—for which my mother kills and dresses chickens—we get chicken, beans, and pork neck bones—"naked bones" we call them. But with twelve kids there's never enough food, and Mother always insists I drink a glass of water before meals to make sure my stomach's filled.

Outside lies the yard. The area near the back steps—where mother dumps the dishwater—is foul smelling and covered with flies. Sometimes I stand for hours swatting the flies with a slat from an old apple box; I kill so many their blood stains the wood. But somehow there are always more. I hate the flies. On summer afternoons when I try to nap, they crawl on my face and drone past my ears. I nuzzle into my mother's lap while she fans them away, letting me close my eyes in peace.

The bathroom is an outhouse by the banana tree. It has scary cobwebs, bugs, and vermin; its nauseating smell and splintery board seat terrify and disgust me, and I look forward to visiting my older sisters and aunts with their new flush toilets. When I use the outhouse, I hold my breath so I won't smell the funky odor, and leave gasping for air.

I'm especially afraid of going at night. Not only the snakes and bugs fill me with fear. I'm frightened because of the eerie voices and spooky stories I hear on the radio: "The Fat Man," "The Shadow," Sidney Greenstreet in something called "Inner Sanctum." Plus, I've heard family members talk about ghosts outside the Rockville church, petrifying, compelling tales about things on horses that appear and vanish in the night. When I go to bed with only an oil lamp for light I'm scared stiff I'll meet one of the shadows in my room.

In order to stay indoors we keep "slop buckets" by the bed. We call them "pee cans" (we only urinate in them).

"My mama say she want a *pee* can," I tell the man behind the Broad Street store counter proudly one day when my mother gives me seventy-five cents to buy one.

He says: "Tell your mama I don't have no pee cans, but I got some mighty fine slop *jars*."

So I run back home:

"Mama, mama! The man say he don't have no pee cans, but he got some mighty fine slop jars!" It's a family joke until I'm twelve years old.

But even in bed I'm afraid of the slithery things I've seen in the outhouse. I lie under the quilt, unable to sleep, a vision of snakes and insects crawling into my room paralyzing me with a shameful, undeniable fear.

"I can't sleep!" I complain. "I'm afraid."

"Go to bed! Nothing's gonna come in here. And if it does, you call."

But my imagination won't stop. I cry until finally I get my wish: sleeping next to my mother, safe in her warmth.

Davis Avenue is only a short walk from the port and commercial district, a semicircle of narrow streets with a few imposing hotels and one fancy movie theater. But although we're near downtown, we still have minimal relations with whites.

Our main contact is with the Smiths; the owners of the local grocery store, they're the Charlie Allens of our block. Old man Smith is a hellion, a drunkard and racist; his only interest in blacks is to make money off them, call them dirty names, and sleep with the ladies. His wife is a decent person. She hands June an extra ten or fifteen dollars when he works for them, and when her husband isn't around she gives my mother or sister extra food at the store's back door.

June isn't the only one they employ. My whole family—except for me—gets paid by them. One brother, Nathaniel, becomes so close to the Smiths that they often leave the store in his charge, certain he won't take even a piece of candy without telling them. Our dependent relationship with them—common in the South—is a kind of continuation of slavery: the black family reliant on the white one.

My mother's job for the Smiths is to kill and pluck chickens; instead of money, she gets to keep the feet, gizzards, and head. She makes soup from the chicken feet—an old custom. (My father once told me he had seen so many chicken feet and so few chickens that he was thirty-two before he knew the birds came with only two feet.)

She kills the birds on the back stoop, right where she dumps the water. She brings them home in a cage and wrings their neck. Afterward she and my sister dip the still-bleeding bird into hot water to free the quills, then singe the bodies over an open fire to remove the pin feathers. Sometimes they pluck as many as a hundred birds on a single day.

I watch, disgusted by the feel of the warm blood on my hands. But soon I get cold to the kill. She uses one quick, powerful snap; the chicken flutters once and dies. I try to imitate her. I hold the wrestling, scrawny chicken and twist. The head flops and starts to bleed, but my victim—unlike hers—doesn't die. Instead the fowl squawks around the yard, flapping and bleeding. I take a stick and pursue him, beating the chicken in the head, smashing him like I do the flies until he's a bloody lump.

Our other main contact with whites is during Mardi Gras.

The holiday captures Mobile's schizophrenia toward race: the city is a Jim Crow, mulatto society.

The port is a big influence on Mobile culture. The city has one of the great bays of the world—a characteristic it shares with Oakland—a broad opening that fills the swamps created by the Tombigbee River. When I'm growing up, the bay connects remote inland Alabama towns with the Caribbean basin. Skip boats and rafts carry vegetables and timber from Monroe County, while tankers loaded with bauxite steam up from Cuba and Jamaica. The commerce democratizes everything: black and white, the unionized stevedores work together while the colored Cuban and West Indian sailors from the bauxite boats walk the streets of downtown, their trade solicited by the white store owners eager for their money.

The Creole influence of the town also leavens the strict, southern segregationist bias. The people don't just eat gumbo—our own kind, with a tomato base, rather than the New Orleans roux—they are a sort of gumbo. "In 1702, your countryman Chestang entered our (the BLACK PEOPLE's) home at 21 mile bluff," reads a pamphlet published by one of the city's local African-American historians. "He fell in love with one of our BLACK women. . . . With good-looking women, the smell of magnolias in the air, free, tasty, beautiful food, good river travel to the Mississippi sound, Chestang knew that he had entered the second heaven." Besides this, the area is ruled by many different nations—Mobile is cosmopolitan for its time, another similarity it shares with Oakland—each with a separate legal code; the result is a greater flexibility in race relations. When Spain controls the Gulf—then called Old West Florida—in the late eighteenth century, slaves buy their freedom by paying their owner a price set by arbitration. "Negroes attained more prominence than before," says one history of the town. "Free black men and free mulatto women are often named in official papers. Free blacks even own slaves of their own. There was a military company of free blacks and mulattoes."

Even Africa influences the town. There are stories throughout the area of Africans who escaped from slavery and lived with Indians—Geechies, we call them, referring especially to blacks from the Carolinas with straight black hair and chiseled facial features. An entire section of town is called Africa-town. It's existence is one of the lesser known anecdotes of our country's history. Shortly before the Civil War, a white southerner named Timothy Meaher bet a hundred thousand dollars he could successfully evade the national embargo against the importation of slaves. Meaher hired the schooner *Clotilde* to bring 116 Africans. The ship entered Mobile Bay and the slaves were spirited off the *Clotilde* onto another boat and hidden in a canebrake to avoid discovery. Meaher, still an important name in the town, took thirty for himself. "Between 1859 and 1865 the thirty Africans from the *Clotilde* established themselves as part of the free Negro class," writes a local historian.

> According to African folk tales of Mobile, the Africans from the *Clotilde* survived in the swamps, bayous and river systems of the area. . . . Because of a strong spiritual belief provided by the church, the Africans endured. They bought property, worked in the mills, fished, hunted, planted gardens and fruit trees, and hoped for the day they would return home to Africa. Each Sunday after church they would gather at the home of Potee Allen, Cudjoe Lewis or Zuma Levinson to discuss the welfare of the group and to settle differences which might come about in the town. By 1890, the Africatown settlement was known to be the only community of its kind with a distinct ethnic and tribal code of government for its people, a retention of the traditional African language and Tarkat customs, and the largest and probably the only community of pure-blooded Africans in the United States.

On Mardi Gras, the blacks hold their ceremony first. The men don headdresses with feathers like chiefs; the women wear colorful serapes and scarves. I don't understand what they're doing—now I realize their costumes celebrate the great African kings and warriors—because I am more concerned with the *real* Mardi Gras: the white one where you get the best booty.

The exciting day starts early. During the year my mother has managed to save enough money to buy us five or six pounds of peanuts. Now, while it's still dark outside, my nephew Bojack and I roast peanuts in the kitchen stove, burying the nuts in the ashes. When they're done, we parcel them in little brown paper bags we will sell for ten cents apiece, hustling to get rid of our goods before the floats and parade turn the corner at the north end of town and start the procession down Government Street.

Just being on Government Street is thrilling; it's the town's main drag, an oak-lined boulevard of antebellum mansions with balconies and white pillars, some of which date back to the first European governance. (One of them houses the city museum. The large, dark, wooden-floored rooms pay full tribute to the white South—including a triptych that shows Robert E. Lee, Stonewall Jackson, and Jefferson Davis, depending on where you stand—while giving little reference to the city's important African-American culture. The museum exhibits some pre-Columbian pottery—which as far as I can tell has next to nothing to do with the town—but ignores the Mobile black community and the slave auction block that existed only a few streets away.)

On Government Street, we stand in special sections. Riding by on their powerful motorcycles, the police make sure we don't come out and touch the floats. Their concern only whets our appetite for the forbidden thing. An unacknowledged game of dare and double dare ensues. The police drive as close as possible, seeing if they can run over our feet. Meanwhile we stick out our toes, pulling back at the last moment. I love the challenge of the moment, waiting for the last possible second before jumping clear. The cops, though, have more firepower than us: when the motorcycles don't work, they employ their flares, dropping the torches on us, one of them burning a big plug of Bojack's hair.

As the floats pass by, the people on them throw sweets to the kids: the reward for coming. My favorites are the Paydays   salty outside, sweet inside. The afternoon reaches its climax. All the kids dive for the candy lying on the street. In the excitement, you can't keep black and white apart. We go after the same bars. For once we have no restrictions on us; we're all the same. We scramble with the white kids for the chocolate. The street is a free-for-all. Taking advantage of the melee and high spirits, I get my revenge: in the presumably playful struggle for candy, I quite purposefully land a shot or two.

Bojack, my nephew, is my closest companion. Or at least my most constant one: all my brothers and sisters are considerably older than I, and Bud, Allen, Sweetie, and Rose Lee have already left home and have families of their own.

Bojack is the son of my oldest sister, Rose Lee. He suffers me. The youngest child, I feel I must prove myself by physically dominating my peers; poor Bojack gets the brunt of my determination. I bully him, slapping him on the head, and employ my own fears to terrify him: knowing Bojack likes sitting in the outhouse with the door closed even less than I do, I kick the door shut whenever I get the chance.

"You used to do a lot of strange things," says Rose Lee. "Keep the other children crying. Pick on them. Pass by then and tap Bojack on the head. You were just devilish."

But because of my position in the family I get away with my behavior.

"You were a little, weaselly, skinny child," says Sweetie, "and Grandma always thought Mama shouldn't whip you. Thought you was too little for Mama to whip. 'Oh don't whip him. He's too *little*. He don't know no better.' She didn't want nobody to whip you."

I also have life easier than any of my brothers. June, for instance, already works a man's job when I'm still a kid, pulling a rickshaw-like cart loaded with wood through the Davis Avenue area. In the winter cold, June hauls the stacked cart earning a dollar a day. "Wood man!" he calls. "Get your wood! Wood man! Wood man!" I run after, pushing the wagon, but he doesn't need the help of my spindly arms and tells me to go home. He doesn't even get to keep the money, throwing it into the household's communal pot to help feed the family.

I'm also an entertainer. My older sister Dorothy Mae is a drum majorette at Central High. Every day she practices twirling her baton, stepping high and "bending back"—arching her body over the floor—which she sometimes does with one hand, her other spinning and catching the baton. During football season she performs each week, marching at the front of the band behind the drum major, Bo Diddley. I love the flash and style of Bo Diddley's walk, a rhythmic, intricate step; whenever the band passes, I run into the street, mimicking him, using a broomstick for my baton, parading five or six blocks with him until poor Dorothy Mae can't tolerate my antics and breaks rank and chases me home. (Dorothy Mae also wants to sing. But she marries at eighteen and moves to Prichard. She's one of the sisters I love visiting: her house has an indoor toilet.)

Although my father is loving and attentive, his age and constant working keep us apart. I know he's Daddy and that he takes care of things, but we don't have a father-son relationship. I disdain the fact of his illiteracy and that he must work at menial jobs. Instead my brothers and sisters become my teachers and exemplars, providing me with knowledge and experience.

Van—originally my parents name him February after his birth month; he finds the name funny and changes it—marries Rosemary. Soon after, Rosemary's stomach grows. I've seen women with goiters on their necks and assume Rosemary has a stomach goiter. When she comes back from the hospital, I ask her where her baby came from. She answers the child has grown inside her stomach and Van has put it there.

Her explanation is my first understanding of sex. I have been precocious from the first. I've come upon some of my brothers making love and once surprised my parents; when we make our yearly summer visit to Rockville I see the animals. So at nights when my mother bathes us in the kitchen, I have experimented. As my nieces—Rose Lee's daughters—lean over, drying off, I buck up against them from behind.

"What are you doing?" my mother asks.

"I'm doing like the dogs do it," I say.

The whipping I receive doesn't stop me. That night when we go to bed I slide to where my niece lies—we sleep sometimes four and five to a pallet—and try to have sex while she's asleep. But not until Rosemary explains to me about the growth in her stomach do I understand even vaguely what sex is about.

Other brothers provide me with models to follow.

Arthur is fearless. Days he drives a truck for the Starfish and Oyster Company; nights, he hangs out at the clubs. Every Friday night, we know when Arthur is coming home because he jacks off six rounds of his .22: pow! pow! pow! Arthur's a little nuts. When the family still lives in Rockville, he and my sister Vera Lee—B.B.—get into a fight. Vera Lee dares him to cut off her toe. When Arthur double-dares her back, B.B. removes her shoes, puts her foot on the chopping block. Well, Arthur's like B.B.: he refuses to back down from a dare. He brings the ax down, nearly severing her toe.

"Arthur was a typical young fellow," remembers June.

He liked to party and have fun, to gamble and to drink heavy. But he wouldn't bring his money into the house and put it in the pot with the rest of us to help make ends meet. We would talk about that a lot, getting around and criticizing him for that. After a while he started bringing food from the fish market—where he was working—and he would drop fish off to try to help make the ends meet. We'd never just sit around and have any roundtable discussions about politics. But there were discussions about how we were surviving, and what it took for us to survive, and what we had to *do* to try and make it easier on the family as a whole. That type of political discussion. Because that is politics in a sense.

Allen—Pig Iron—is the next oldest after Bud and Arthur. To my mind, he is a master, tall, thin—now that he's aged, Allen looks like a *griot,* one of the African tribal storytellers—a smooth talker who can verbally outmaneuver any challengers when the guys are sitting on the porch trading small talk and friendly insults. Allen also drives a truck, and I consider him an expert mechanic. He mixes an extreme gentleness—women like his courtly manner and solicitous ear—with a sharp temper. One night he and Arthur are in a bar when Big Church slaps a smaller guy. Allen kneels before Big Church. "Slap me, too, so that I can kill you," he says. He's crying—Allen cries easily. Big Church refuses. Allen becomes so incensed he picks up a chair and beats Big Church out of the club.

The fighting I hear about is constant. Quick, powerful hands are something to respect; and there is nothing strange about people being beaten, cut, even killed. Violence is an accepted condition of life. If you go to the store or clubs you run the risk of a fight. On Friday nights, and whenever there's a family argument, and especially when people start pouring their alcohol, you can be fairly certain that somebody's going to do something before too long. There's going to be some shit, as the saying goes. Violence is the norm; because of this, violence is part of my personality, part of my value system. I grow up expecting it, always on the alert, never relaxed, never lowering my vigilance.

Partly this proclivity to violence is, I think, a southern trait. Down south, everybody is armed, whites and blacks. (When I arrive in California, the locals are amazed I carry a knife.) But what's true for my family and for many blacks is that we turn this violence inward. We fight among ourselves, taking out on our own people the frustrations we're forbidden to level against society. (In fact, not until my twenties, when I listen to Malcolm X for the first time, do I hear about respecting the race; only then do I start to have a new value system, liking brothers rather than being afraid something will happen if I look at another black guy when I walk into a room.)

Mobile culture encourages this bloodshed. The town has the aura of southwestern Cajun cowboy macho. My brother Nathaniel doesn't sing blues but Hank Snow and Hank Williams:

> *Jambalaya, crawfish pie, file gumbo!*
> *'Cause tonight I'm gonna see my chere mio!*

Old downtown Mobile even looks like a western town. The buildings lie low to the ground under a high, wide sky, and at noon the place has an eerie, sleepy emptiness I associate with the stillness before a shoot-out.

But my favorite sibling is Vera Lee, "Black Gal," or B.B., as we call her. B.B. is beautiful. She has pitch-black, *tight* skin; she straightens her hair with a hot comb and sports a gold cap on one of her front teeth.

B.B. is a hell-raiser. At night she runs around with Arthur's girlfriend. Both are armed. Arthur's woman holds a razor soaked in garlic and lemon juice, and she can really handle a blade; once she cuts a woman from head to toe, slicing her clothes clean off. B.B. carries a Coke bottle, ready to cold-cock any guy if a fight breaks out.

I love B.B. She personifies adventure and good times. Some Fridays she sends me to the store to buy beer. I run down to the Smiths and put the money on the counter:

"B.B. wants some beer."

Mrs. Smith wraps the bottle in a paper bag. Proudly I deliver the package and get a sip as my reward. At seven, I already know about liquor. When Allen and the family sit around, they drink "shinny"—clandestinely manufactured alcohol that my father sometimes helps to distribute. My mother puts some in a cup and stirs in some sugar; occasionally she lets me take a sip. Sometimes some shinny is left standing out and I taste the drink raw, my gut filling with the alcohol's burning heat.

One day B.B. takes me to a stranger's house. It's an airless Sunday morning and I'm still dressed for church, wearing my one suit, an all-white outfit I hate. Boy, you're too black to wear that all white, people tease me. You look crazy with that white on.

Inside the woman wears an apron over her bare skin. She's sweating and distracted. A teenage boy stands by the door; a couple of men sit in the living room, one of them sipping shinny, one sound asleep, his head resting on the wall as though he were dead. There's a jukebox in the kitchen; the rooms are bare of furniture except one or two couches with the pillows piled high on top of one another. B.B. gives the woman two dollars and the woman pours some whiskey into a half-pint bottle. The place is a "hit-house," a clandestine dispenser of shinny, the neighborhood unlicensed bar.

B.B. and Arthur's girlfriend adopt me. At night I lie awake in my room listening to them recount their adventures in the clubs. During the afternoon, I crank the Victrola while they dance to Louis Jordan and Cab Calloway records. For laughs they teach me "Rag Mop" and "Caldonia." I manage to memorize "Rag Mop" but can't remember "Caldonia." Instead, I run around the living room shouting, "Caldonia, what make your big head so hard!" B.B. and Arthur's girlfriend go off into gales of laughter. Later I snuggle up to them when they sit on the couch. "Oooh, look at his eyelashes," they exclaim over me: "He's beautiful!" I know I'm B.B.'s special baby brother and pretend to sleep, laying my head close to her breast and listening to them talk about me.

But my biggest influence of course is Mother. I love her. For me she's synonymous with life. I can't imagine living without her. I pray I die before her. When I am in her presence, I feel the world is all right, everything is well. Her unconditional love for me — she never undercuts, betrays, or second-guesses me — confirms my sense of self.

I sleep in the bed with her and my father. One night I wake up. She has moved away from me; my father touches her. She puts his hands away. He whispers something, caresses her again. The feeling between them is gentle, as though they are playing together. At that moment I hate my father. I feel completely left out, abandoned. I want to push myself between them, hug my mother, keep her to myself. I close my eyes so they won't know I'm awake.

"Shhh!" my mother says. "Not now!" She tucks his hand away. "He's right here!"

"Boy's sleeping," my father says, giving one more try.

She turns toward me, figuring the odds. Then she thinks better. "Tomorrow," she says. I'm still furious with him.

Another morning I wake up and the bed is empty. She's gone fishing with Sweetie. I miss her so much — I'm so frustrated and afraid — that I become hysterical and throw a tantrum. When she is gone all day I resolve to make it impossible for her ever to slip away. From then on, I get up every night and climb into my parents' bed, sleeping between them with my arm around her, holding her tight, making sure that if she moves and tries to escape, I'll wake up, clutching her.

She also takes me fishing after that. We ignore the old downtown wooden pier. We fish off the banks, up the Tombigbee where its waters run into the bay. The brackish water is a fisherman's paradise; we catch mullet, pompano, red snapper. Sometimes we take nets and seine for shrimp. Mother uses a long cane pole with earthworms for bait; when a fish hits, the cork sinks instantly. I wait for that moment — the thrill of seeing her pull the fish in, release it from the hook. Then we go home, take whatever we've got — oysters, crabs, shrimp, fish, fish heads — and throw the mess in one pot, make our gumbo.

You never get far from the sea in Mobile. Twice a day, you smell the ocean, the raw, salty funk of the tidal flats mixing with the man-made foulness from the Prichard paper plant.

"The Gulf's letting her drawers down," my brother Bud says. "She needs to pull her drawers on."

Chapter

3

WHEN I'm six or seven we move to Congress Street, opposite the county hospital, a three-story, antebellum structure topped and surrounded by painted white brick chimneys and walls. It's an imposing, scary building; in one classroom window, the student doctors hang a skeleton. Our house has a flush toilet so I don't have to brave the outhouse anymore, but remembering the country stories about ghosts, I always walk in the opposite direction from the hospital.

The hospital figures in our life in another way, too. On Fridays the carcasses of the fish served for lunch are left outside in big, ice-filled wooden barrels. We wait in our house, looking out the window, wanting to make sure we get first pick. My mother has sheets of newspaper all ready for us; as soon as the super lugs the barrels we dash out into the street, wrapping the best leftovers in the newspaper and bringing them back to the house. The wastefulness of the hospital shocks us: there's still lots of good meat, which Mama cooks for us, on the bones. Besides, we can always use the head for gumbo.

We always need more food at our house. I constantly crave more. We rarely eat at regular hours and sometimes must wait until one of my brothers or sisters brings home a paycheck so June or Nathaniel can go to the Smiths—they admit us even after the store is closed—and buy the beans and neck bones that make up our daily fare. I grow to hate beans so much that when I see them on the table I throw my plate on the floor. Finally my mother feeds me off a pie pan so I won't break any more dishes.

Supper itself is a struggle for survival. At table the firsts are meager, the seconds rare. Sometimes Bojack eats quickly so my mother will forget he's already been served. If she catches him, she whips him from the table, paddles his behind and shouts: "Bojack, you a lying bastard! That's what you is! Don't you ever do that again!" Another time, a friend of June's comes over. When June isn't looking, the friend tries to snatch something off June's plate. Quicker than lightning, June plants his fork in the guy's hand. He turns and teaches me: "Don't ever let someone take your food," he says.

We never eat out. We're taught to refuse if a neighbor asks us for dinner, saying we're not hungry even if our stomachs are growling. It's not polite to take food from others who might not have enough to eat themselves, my parents say.

There are other adventures on Congress Street — strange, enticing things.

Down the block from us lives Waterhead. He's a hydrocephalic whom I tease with this awful name. Waterhead sells reefer for his mother on Davis Avenue. Whenever he passes our house heading toward his post on the avenue, I call out the nickname, heckling him and defying my parents: Mother and Father think people who smoke reefer go mad, and they refuse to let me play with Waterhead or go near his house.

Even more mysterious is Mr. Sam. He's big, bigger than Big Church. Three hundred pounds and always dressed in overalls — no pants would close around his waist — and a cap we call "pieces of pie."

To me, Mr. Sam is fearless. Everybody is afraid of him. Not just on the block, but — big as he is — everybody in the whole world. He carries a .45 on him all the time. One day he gets into a fight and a man cuts him before running away. My sister Eleanora and I are by the Streamline Cleaners on Davis Avenue when the man who knifed Mr. Sam rides by on his bike. Out of the blue, Mister Sam appears with his .45 and shoots — pow! pow! pow! Eleanora and I run home to tell my mother.

"Mama! Mama! Mr. Sam shot at that man! And that man outran Mr. Sam's bullet on his bike!"

Mr. Sam is a poacher. Every now and then he comes home with livestock in his trunk: cow, pig, once a giant turtle. He always confuses me. He says he's "going fishing" and returns with meat, says he's going hunting and returns with fish. He butchers the meat in his backyard, giving the cuts to his neighbors on the block.

Because of him I get the worst whipping in my life. One afternoon Bojack and I are sitting on the porch enjoying one of my favorite occupations: counting out-of-state license plates. I fantasize as we add up the passing

Michigans, Illinoises, and New Yorks. Maybe later, I'm thinking, we'll shoot marbles. I have a new honky, one of my favorites because when you shoot it down the middle of the ring the big marble clears the whole circle.

A truck barrels down the street and a hundred-pound sack of beans falls off the back. Beans are scattered all over the street and the bag lies in the middle of the road. The driver doesn't notice; he goes on. But Mr. Sam sees and grabs the food.

I run inside to tell my mother what's happening. She goes out. Soon she and everybody else on the block is portioning out beans.

A little while later I'm still on the porch and see the driver walking down the street, knocking on everyone's door. He has come back to ask about the beans.

I go inside and tell my mother: "Mama, this man is coming to look for the sack of beans."

"Keep your mouth shut," she tells me. "If you tell anybody what you've seen, you're gonna get a whipping."

I wait for the driver to come up. I'm scared and excited. I've seen something forbidden; plus, Mother is afraid of what I can say—I have some power over her, a rare thing. Besides, she stays in the house, leaving me alone on the porch.

The man comes up. "A sack of beans—"

Even before he finishes the question, I start blurting out the truth. "A man took—"

Suddenly my mother's strong hand grabs me.

"The boy don't know nothing," she tells the driver, pushing me behind her. "He's just running his mouth."

As soon as the driver leaves the block, she locks my head between her thighs and paddles me good: "Don't you *ever* go and tell anybody when I tell you *not* to. You don't go around and tell people that we took beans or that we took anything. Don't you *ever* do that!"

Crazy Mary is another reason I'm paddled.

She lives opposite us, a very pretty, light-skinned woman in her thirties. Every morning she goes into her yard and yells, telling the world to kiss her ass, pulling up her dress, cursing on and on. Then she runs out of the yard, strips off her clothes, and parades naked in the middle of the street. Traffic stops while Mary stomps up and down, leveling her filthy-mouthed tirade at the cars, making quite a show until her mother and Eli—her son, a friend of June's—come and carry her back inside.

No one knows why Crazy Mary is crazy. My father tells me a scary story about her. While visiting in Louisiana, Mary drank a potion that induced her insanity. For a cure, her family sent her to a "mojo" woman. As Mary approached the woman's house, a snake wound itself around the knob and opened the door. Inside, the "mojo" woman gave Mary a strange tea brewed from Spanish moss and other herbs. But even all that power didn't help Mary.

Mary's skin entrances me. "Kiss my black ass!" she yells to no one in particular in the hot, early morning. Well, I've seen her ass and the imprecation makes no sense to me; her bottom isn't black, but a light pink I find beautiful and arousing. In the mornings, I hang out by the fence waiting for a glimpse of her pretty rump. One day I'm so bewitched by the sight that she catches me peeking. Before I can turn and run, she's up and out; she seizes me by the throat, choking me so hard I can't even yell. Bojack—he's always by my side—screams for Mother, who runs out hollering and brandishing a broom with which she beats Crazy Mary until the woman lets me go.

From then on, I spend every morning hurling obscenities at Mary. I don't want to get her mad, I want to encourage her to use new curse words: I learn new dirty words from Mary, and there's something charged in hearing her unloose her barrage of sexual language. "Show me your ass, Mary!" I shout, egging her on. "Come on, show me your ass!"

By lunchtime, I'm fired up. I come in the house loaded with new curse words. On the table there's nothing on my lunch plate that I like. Because the only thing I want is bacon or sausage and we rarely have either. Instead I'm looking at biscuits and "naked" bones. Mother has made them with red beans today, but the choice of beans makes no difference. I've eaten naked bones every which way—red beans, white beans, lima beans, rice, with gravy, without gravy—and there's no way that I've ever enjoyed them.

I drink my required glass of water and go into my act, throwing the tin plate on the floor:

"I don't want this stuff. I want bacon!" I sprinkle some of Mary's new curse words into my declaration.

"Stop saying those words," my mother orders. She returns the plate to my setting. "I don't have bacon. You'd better eat this."

But I'm out to test her. Grandmother will always tell her not to hit me too hard, that I shouldn't be whipped because I'm too little, too puny. So I continue.

"I don't want it!" I toss the plate off again. "I want bacon!"

That does it. "Go get a switch," she says.

My anger won't let me show that she scares me. I march into the yard. I'm not scared of my mother — not like I am of my father. Hard as she hits, I can take her blows. I yank a branch from the low-growing peach tree out front. I want to hurt the tree. Then I stalk back and taunt my mother with my defiance: "Here!" Over I go, head between her legs, while she strikes me. The stick stings, but she whips me long enough only to drive her message home. Then I'm free. Instantly I run outside and stick my head through the window.

"Dirty bitch!" I use the curse words I've heard from Mary all morning.

"Don't you call me that," she says, "I'm your mother!"

I say the worst thing I can think of: "No, you're not, you dirty bitch! No mother would ever treat her kid like that! You're a dirty bitch! You ain't my mother and I'm gonna tell Grandma you hit me!"

Mama takes my threat in stride. "Well, you got to come back in here before the night's over," she says and ignores me.

Mary's pale skin haunts me. I'm one of the darkest children in my family — all my nieces have lighter skin — and we are all acutely aware of color. "African" is a fighting word to us. So is "black." Our worst insult to each other is "black African." "Black African" is fighting words. "You black motherfucker. You nigger. You black, liver-lipped, nappy-haired black African." The curses are part of the internalization of hatred: our hatred of ourselves. My sister Eleanora is black like me, with tight charcoal skin, and she fights regularly whenever the kids call her a black African.

Then, when I'm about seven, I meet Raoul, a Cuban kid who lives down the street. To me he's a mystery — speaks another language, comes from another culture. Raoul carries himself with self-assurance. We share two things: bananas — our backyard banana tree reminds him of home — and our curly black hair. And Raoul is the cock of the Congress Street walk. All the girls go for him. He controls them, especially Geraldine, whose pretty light skin reminds me of Mary's. I want Geraldine as my girlfriend. But I'm thankful, not angry, at Raoul for winning her: when I see that Geraldine is fascinated by Raoul and loves to play with his curly hair my self-respect is strengthened.

Later that summer, in Rockville, I let my female cousins play with me like a doll: "Come on, David, put your head in the spring. We want to wash your hair." They love how the strands straighten when wet. (The memory shows the irony of prejudice. My cousins like my hair because they associate straightness with beauty, a European standard of beauty. But their approval fosters my sense of inner security and confidence.)

*   *   *

My self-esteem whets my resentment and envy at richer blacks and whites.

One target of my anger is Donald Baker. Donald lives up the hill from us in Toulminville. Donald always wears sharp clothes, corduroy knickers, argyle socks—argyle socks! I'd give anything for a pair of argyle socks!—and a matching cap, all one piece, and his father owns a mortuary besides being the principal of Central High School. I'm in a love-hate relationship with Donald. We hang out during school, but I always pick on him, try to take his hat, and at the same time social codes divide us almost as though we were white and black: we never visit each other's house.

My envy is even greater of whites. One day I notice a white boy riding by my house on a bicycle. I have almost no toys. Crazy Mary's brother has made us kites of willow sticks, colored tissue paper, and homemade paste. We attach long tails to them with razor blades at the end and float them high in the air, tugging them through dogfights, trying to cut each other down. I also have a red wagon from Grandmother, and I've amassed a lot of honkies, the large, agate marbles I covet. But the thing I want most is a bicycle. I'm always walking. Dragging after June as he carts his wood. Trudging after my mother. To have a bicycle is to fly, escape the ground.

So every day I watch the kid. I entertain a fantasy. We'll make friends. He'll let me share the bike. I even come to believe the kid wants a friendship too; after all, he's driving up and down my block every day.

Sure enough, one day he stops in front of our house. I run down the steps.

"That your bike?" I ask. I know my question's foolish, but I have to start the conversation somewhere.

"Yeah."

I can't tell if he's shy or unfriendly. Guided by my hope, I plunge on.

"Can I ride it?"

His bike is a beautiful machine, a silver-framed Raleigh with black rubber-tipped handlebars and a bright red leather seat. I've seen it advertised in the Archie and Jughead comic books my older brothers read. Sometimes June will buy me a Roy Rogers comic book as a special treat and there'll be a kid saying he got his Raleigh by selling packages of candy. Packages of candy! And he gets a bike! Meanwhile June pulls a whole wagonload of wood and we have just enough money to pay for the comic book. But I've also seen the bikes in true life—the white kids swooping down Government Street on them, fast as birds.

"I see you riding by here a lot," I answer.

I begin to suspect something's the matter. He's looking at me with a superior squint. My anger starts to build. I'm sure he lives in Spring Hill; the idea that he can drive through our community, drive down *my* street, while I can't venture into *his* neighborhood, makes me resentful.

"You live here?" he asks. His voice has the slight nasal twang of the Cajun accent. I look at my house, checking to see if any of my family is watching. I hear my father warn me: "Don't trust them. Those kissified people will hurt you."

I tell him yes.

He asks what my mother does.

"She goes to college," I say.

I don't even think about the lie. My mother in college. The idea is ridiculous. Right now she's on the banks of the Tombigbee, angling for any fish that will bite. But in my child's mind I'm hoping something else: he'll believe the lie and banish the awful inequality separating us. I even imagine he'll go along with me, even if he *knows* I'm lying, accept the lie for truth so we can be friends.

He retorts immediately. "You're lying! Niggers don't go to college. My mother's been to college and she told me niggers don't go to college!"

Caught, I fight back. "That's not true!" I yell. "Colored folk do too go to college. My mother does. You better take back what you said!"

"I'm not taking back anything," he answers. His accent is ugly with contempt.

I must hit him. Striking first is the smaller man's main advantage. But my blow glances off. He punches back — a hard sock right in my eye. In the moment that I'm blinded he seizes the opportunity, pummeling my face and body. When he's done, he rides off.

I lie in the dust. I'm crying, but more from anger and shame than hurt: I've let my mother be insulted and a white boy beat me.

In the next weeks, I plot my revenge. I tell nobody about the incident — not June, Nathaniel, not even my mother. I cringe at the possibility they'll hear a white boy bested me. Finally I work out my plan. I have a good arm, the result of our local broomsticks–and–bottle caps stickball game. I pile some ammunition of rocks and earth behind a fence down the street and wait. One afternoon I see the white boy bicycling. I run to my fort. As he rides by, I pelt him, furiously tossing stuff too fast for him to pedal away. One clod hits him square in the head and he falls. I unload my cache, pelting him as he lies there crying. It's a victory, but I almost feel like crying too, and I hate this boy for everything that has happened between us.

Exhausted and charged up, I turn and run to my house — directly into the arms of my mother.

"What's happening?" she asks.

"I had a fight with a white boy. He said you were stupid and niggers don't go to college." I still don't tell her that he beat me up.

My mother looks at me, then calms. "I don't care what color that boy was," she says. "If he hit you first you had a right to fight him. In fact, if you *hadn't* hit him, I would have hit you."

But not all fights with whites turn out so well. Soon after we move to Mobile, my brother Bud gets into an altercation with a white man. Bud works as a janitor at the bus station. One afternoon a passenger kicks him slightly on the leg, telling him to pick up a bag. Bud reacts: he pushes the man down, jumps on his chest, and pokes a pocketknife in the man's face, calling him a son of a bitch and telling him he might kick his dog, but Bud's a man and he can't kick him. That night he leaves for California.

Sometime later Van joins him there. His run-ins with the white establishment are more bizarre and dangerous. Van works in a Mobile cleaners. One day a white serviceman leaves his uniform. The soldier returns a few hours later with a policeman. He asks to see the uniform and after looking through the pockets claims to have left a hundred-dollar bill that Van has stolen. Van denies the charge. His bosses back him up. But the serviceman presses charges and Van spends sixty days in jail. When his case comes to court the serviceman doesn't show. (We assume he's a con man; he hoped the owners would take his word over Van's and reimburse him the money.)

Shortly after, Van leaves for California with his wife, Rosemary. I assume the reason for his departure is the soldier incident and don't find out the real cause until years later. Van was having an affair with a white woman in the dry-cleaning store. One day he was with my cousin Boy Collier and met the woman; she kissed Van in public and held his hand. Boy was terrified. He hurried Van down the street and told him the woman was crazy and that if any whites saw what was going on they would hang him. Then he went to my parents, described the incident; my mother and father insisted Van leave town.

As I grow older, I become obsessed with my frailness. Nathaniel, who is training to be a boxer, teaches me to fight, building me a set of weights from pipes and concrete-filled syrup buckets. He also brings me Wheaties from the Smiths—Wheaties, the breakfast of champions. I imagine myself a boxer, a contender. One day Nathaniel comes home with a patch over one eye—a stick with a nail in it has temporarily blinded him—and says he can no longer box; my ardor for the ring cools.

Still the world with its praise of violence and power taunts me. I stare at the Charles Atlas ads in the Dell comic books. Skinny sits on the beach with his girlfriend. A well-muscled bully kicks sand in Skinny's face, taking away Skinny's girlfriend. But Skinny's no chump. He takes Charles Atlas's body-building course, finds the bully, beats him up, and wins back the girl. I imagine myself standing, scared and alone, on the beach—what am I going to do? I search for models.

More and more I find my exemplars not on the street, or even in my family, but in the movies. I love the movies. Every Saturday I attend the Pike or Lincoln, second-run houses on Davis Avenue. Furnished with wooden seats, they cost only twelve cents. The ripped screen dangles only a few feet off the floor; sometimes guys or girls scream as a rat as big as a cat—this is the South we're talking about—darts under the screen, but I don't share this fear: crawly things frighten me, not a rat that I can see and stomp on.

My favorites are the chapter movies. I like Buck Rogers and a character called Atomic Man who runs into caves and exits with gravity-defying rockets on his back. The owners break full-length features into parts; a flood chases Green Arrow down a tunnel and the screen goes black. You've got to come back to see him escape.

The very best are westerns and war movies. The Black Hawk Commandos. All of the Marine Corps stuff. Bataan. Bombing the hell out of the Japanese. Lash La Rue. Johnny Mack Brown. Allen Rocky Lane. Allen Rocky Lane is a tough cowboy. He has a horse named Black Jack—all these guys have horses smarter than themselves—who can jump over the Grand Canyon. In the stuffy, close darkness of the movie theater—"air-cooled," they say, in reference to the fan responsible for spreading the smell of popcorn throughout the theater—I watch these adventures, imagining myself as swell-looking and heroic in California.

Of all the war heroes, I like Don Winslow and his Commandos, the Fighting Devil Dogs, the most. They're super-tough, a gang of white Americans who almost single-handedly win back the entire Pacific. I am glued to the screen as Don and his buddies mow down Japanese. I identify with them completely. "Kill the Japs!" I shout in the almost empty theater. "Kill the Japs!" My eyes are glued to the screen. Every time the camera shows a close-up of a slant-eyed, nefarious-looking devil, I warn Don, cheering him on: "Dirty Jap!" When the matinee is over and I must go outside I continue the combat. I'm no longer in Mobile but on Bataan, and I'm not David but Don; dirty Japs hide in the branches of the banana and oak trees, lurk behind the corner at Robinson's Cafeteria, lie in ambush at the alley behind the Harlem Dukes Social Club. I explode my enemies with grenades, chase them from their bunkers using flamethrowers even hotter than the blasts of air coming out of the cleaners.

Sundays, we travel downtown to the Sanger, a movie palace near Morrison's Cafeteria, where my father now works. Outside, the Sanger has a splendid, curved marquee; the women on the fresh posters look more voluptuous, the men more handsome than the faded characters I see in the coming-attraction windows of the Pike and Lincoln. Inside, the red plush velvet seats match the color of the carpets; ornate carvings and flowing drapes frame the giant screen; the air-conditioned blackness feels as cool as water.

The Sanger is Jim Crow. We buy our tickets on line with everybody else; but inside we're shuttled upstairs into the balcony. We resent the discrimination. We don't care about being next to whites, but if a fire breaks out, the people in the orchestra will be able to run, while we'll burn to death. We revenge the abuse by sitting near the front row and, whenever the ushers aren't near, lobbing wads of gum, paper cups, and candy wrappers over the balcony. One Sunday we decide to turn the tables on the whites, start a fire, and escape, leaving them to burn. We've piled a bunch of combustibles onto a seat when a young black man comes over and warns me that if I strike the match he personally will kick my ass.

One Sunday my nephews—Bojack and Ted, Allen's son—can't come. I don't like going downtown by myself, but Daddy has handed me an extra quarter on payday and I don't want to spend the long, hot afternoon in the yard.

I catch the Davis Avenue bus and sit in the back. Less than a mile separates Congress Avenue and the Sanger, but the two places are worlds apart. When I get off, downtown is jumping, the shops along Joachim Street bustling with sailors and shoppers. The crowd and their carefree weekend mood excite me. I want to be part of their high living, one of these men I see buying something expensive for his woman. Even with all my envy and resentment, I am charged up by their energy. In my innocence, I still think that sharing this exhilaration is all right to do with white people. I am aware of all the obstacles, hatred, and viciousness that limit my life, but I reject the restrictions. Beyond all that the South represents, I still find another world, a world I am going to live in, where *their* life will be *my* life.

I wait on the line and give the rouged, henna-haired woman in the box office my twenty-four cents and climb the stairs. I sit in the front row of the balcony, safe and excited in the darkness.

The curtains open. The movie starts. I settle in. I don't know what the story's about, but it takes place in my magic place, California, the Golden State, land of Lash La Rue and Allen Rocky Lane. It has songs, which I like, and it's funny, guys climbing up and down furniture. Plus, it stars Debbie Reynolds, and I love Debbie Reynolds. When Gene Kelly finally kisses her, he starts to dance, blissed out because he's in love, tapping on his toes, drenched in happiness on Hollywood Boulevard, splashing and spinning. I imagine myself him, in love, cool and exuberant, sharp and smooth. I'm sitting there, alone, hands gripping the balcony rail, and what I want is to *be* him, *be* where he is up on that screen. Not as a star, but enjoying his life, surrounded by smiling people, friendly cops, and pretty women:

> *I'm singin' in the rain,*
> *Singin' in the rain,*
> *What a glorious feeling*
> *I'm hap-hap-happy again!*

I watch, entranced. California! Singin' in the rain! That's where I want to be when I grow up!

Chapter

4

BUD'S another reason I fantasize about California. Bud serves as my ideal of manhood. He's big—weighing about 170 pounds—with tight, dark skin, broad shoulders, and impressive African features. He is what he likes to call a "Mandingo type." He's the first to do everything—work with my father, leave home, get married, have children—and also a notorious ladies' man: when I spend summers at Rockville, I hear stories about Bud's teenage conquest of seemingly every woman in the town.

Bud has prospered in Oakland, where he has settled, and his return home makes him my hero. He drives up in a new Hudson or Nash and emerges like a conqueror: salt-and-pepper mustache, smelling as fresh as my father, but dressed like a dude, his beaver Stetson set at a striking angle. I always climb into the front seat as soon as he arrives. Bud buys special macaroon cookies in California; on the long cross-country trip the sweet smell permeates the interior. I sniff the sugary aroma, relishing the flavor almost as much as I do the cookies. Then I enact my fantasy; I sit on the edge of the softly cushioned seat and turn the large, flute-edged, ivory steering wheel, pretending I'm leaving the flies and Crazy Mary and driving across the country to golden California.

"You gonna come to California with me?" Bud asks.

The Golden State, we call it, and I take golden literally. Streets paved with gold, even the Golden Gate Bridge made of gold. A state where every town—Oakland, Sacramento, Los Angeles—is Hollywood and you can meet Gene Autry and Roy Rogers and Allen Rocky Lane on every street.

"Can I?" I ask. "Can I?"

"My baby," Bud says—he always calls me his baby—"whenever you want to come with me, just let me know."

"I'm going to California," I yell, running through the house.

Even long after he leaves and I'm back on the porch counting license plates or yelling at Crazy Mary, I treasure his promise, believe one day his invitation will come true.

There's no joy when Bud finally makes the proposal. He arrives with his two kids. They've come to bury his wife. She has died mysteriously. No one talks about her death in a normal voice. Only later do I piece together the facts: she hemorrhaged while trying to abort herself.

At the time I have just experienced a terrible fear. We've been warned that if an old person points a finger at us, we'll be cursed for life. One day several friends and myself are playing marbles when Miss Lizzie walks by. She's a wizened old lady with wispy white hair. She always acts unfriendly, never giving us any candy. When she accidentally kicks our marbles, scattering them over the dirt street, I get angry and throw a rock at her. With my pinpoint aim I hit her square in the back. She wheels around. Her lips hang loosely and her pulpy gums are empty except for a few golden teeth. Pinched-faced, evil-eyed, she points her scrawny finger at me and issues her curse: "You won't live to see your eleventh birthday!"

Pretending to be brave I yell something back. But inside I'm trembling. First I'm afraid Miss Lizzie will tell my mother; when time passes and Miss Lizzie doesn't say anything, I start to worry about her threat. I think Miss Lizzie will kill me. Maybe not herself, but perhaps some snake like the one in the Louisiana "mojo" cabin Crazy Mary walked into. I try to forget the fears, but when I lie in bed my terror overwhelms me. What's that sound? Is there something crawling toward me? I can't fall asleep because I'm checking the floor, feeling the walls to make sure nothing is approaching. I worry about every shadow. Even when I fall asleep I wake instantly, afraid that at the moment of losing consciousness Miss Lizzie will attack and destroy me. Never before has the thought of death—of the end of my life, my consciousness—been so sharp, so vivid. Each night becomes a torment as the time to sleep approaches. But I don't tell anyone of my fear. The night of my eleventh birthday I stay awake, afraid to close my eyes for an instant, terrified of dying in my sleep, waiting for midnight. Finally it's twelve. Nothing. I breathe, blink my eyes. I'm alive. I lie back to sleep and startle myself awake: maybe this is her trick and she'll strike now when my vigilance is relaxed. But no, there's nothing. I'm still alive, myself, a man.

*　　*　　*

One night soon after this I find Mother and Father talking at the kitchen table. Their voices are low, calm, my mother saying what she thinks, my father listening.

I'm excited and happy because it's early spring and we're preparing for the yearly school Maypole dance, one of my favorite events.

Enjoyment is a rare thing at the Broad Street Elementary School down the block. Other than the Maypole dance—and reading, I love reading and excel at deciphering words and incorporating them into my vocabulary—I have only one pleasant memory of the place. One day our reading instructor teaches us "Alouette, gentil Alouette." The song sounds crazy to me—she doesn't explain the words are French. (And even if she did, I wouldn't have understood the concept.) But I love the pretty melody, the strange sounds; plus, we perform the tune as a round, my first experience singing harmony.

Besides that, the place is hateful. The classes are boring. The students are all mixed up. In our class sits a tall, fat thirteen-year-old who has recently moved to Mobile; every day he brings his lunch—rice, beans, and greens mixed together and topped with biscuits—in a syrup bucket and eats with a spoon he carries in his overalls pocket. I look at him, trapped like Gulliver among the Lilliputians; his enforced presence in our class, I imagine, must be painfully embarrassing to him.

And the place is ruled by a tyrant, Mrs. "Kushfoot"; tall, dark-skinned, with sparse gray hair and a deep, masculine voice, Mrs. Howard, the principal, walks with a limp because she has a clubfoot. If you're referred to her office, she whips your palms with electrical cord.

But the Maypole is pure pleasure. Each class has its own Maypole. Each child holds one strand of the different-colored ribbons attached to the top. With music in the background, we weave past each other, plaiting the ribbons around the pole, covering the wood with a rainbow as we twist and thread our paths around one another. I love the stepping and skipping, and the special clothes—red ties and *white* suits: for once, I don't stand out in my only fancy clothes. And the Maypole is a competition—whoever finishes first wins the prize; the mothers sit on the sidelines, clapping and encouraging us. (I was shocked, but not surprised, when I later heard that the Mobile School Board, deciding the Maypole was a Communist celebration, banned the festivity.)

In the kitchen I hang by the table. Mother speaks with a lot of purpose, telling my father that Bud doesn't want the kids to be brought up by a stranger. B.B. and Sweetie will still be in Alabama, she says, and they can take care of my sister Eleanora; Mother will just take Bud's children, Michael and Gail.

My father listens. He looks old to me. He's in competition with lots of younger men for the menial positions he works, and the years are catching up with him. He sits hunched over, his face tilted downward toward the red-and-white-checked oilcloth, absorbing what she is saying. Eyes squinted in concentration, hands folded before him, legs crossed, his foot jiggling, he keeps nodding. He never disagrees with my mother about domestic matters anyway, and certainly not about helping Bud.

But my mother's plans upset me. The point is very clear. She's going to Oakland with Michael and Gail. And if she's going, I am too. No possibility of compromise on this one. I don't care that I'm eleven and consider myself a man or that my father's present. In my mind my plan is set: I'm going to stop any decisions either one of them might make about leaving without me. I'll make a scene.

"You're not gonna leave me," I say.

"No, you're gonna go," my mother says.

But something about her manner doesn't convince me. The plans for the trip, anyway, are unclear. She'll go for a short time, during the summer, and maybe my father will come out later. Maybe she means I'll come out with my father. Which is not what I want at all. And besides, even if that's not in her mind, I want to impress her with the fact that there is absolutely no way in the world she's leaving without me.

"You got to take me!" I scream.

My mother pats her lap. My tantrums don't impress her, but they work.

"What's the matter with the boy?" my father asks.

My mother ignores him. "You're going with me," she says, gathering me in her arms, trying to soothe and smother my rebellion.

"You're not gonna leave me!" I shout. "I have to go! Or you can't go! You got to take me!"

"Come on, here," she says, bringing me to her. "Don't worry. You're coming with me. You're my baby."

Bud stands at the door. "Sure you're coming. You're my baby too."

"I need you to come with me," she's saying.

Slowly I calm down, believing her.

"I need you," she says. "You got to read the signs so I'll know when I get there."

The Daylight Unlimited from Chicago leaves at twelve. The whole family sees us off at the station. We drive down in Allen's truck, the Starfish and Oyster Company name on the side. I sit by the window, next to my mother. Only one thing interferes with my intense excitement: Mother has insisted I wear the white suit. She wants me to look starched and fresh, but I sweat immediately in the hot day and the white cloth shows every stain; I already feel more soiled than I would in regular clothes. As we pass Davis Avenue I see one of my buddies wearing jeans, a Buster Brown shirt with vertical stripes, and penny loafers, dressed the way I want to be.

As soon as we enter the station, I start reading the signs, leading us to Platform One. The train waits like a huge monster, huffing and puffing, car after car stretching the entire length of the track. Redcaps bustle up and down the platform, stuffing away luggage and collecting tips. Families lean out the windows, waving to friends, shouting out last instructions. The departure fills me with an exciting sadness. I butt my head into the chests of my sisters when they hug me, trying to keep them from humiliating me by marking my cheeks with their lipstick. I mount the steps, every inch of me conscious of my new role: the oldest now, I have the solemn responsibility of making sure Mama gets to Oakland.

The heavy door whooshes closed and the cool of the compartment captures me. The conductor escorts us to our seats, heaving the bags onto the rack. From outside, B.B. calls: "Hey, David!" Tall and lithe, she stands on the platform in a polka-dot sundress, her gold tooth glinting, her hair black and shiny. "You take care of Mama now!"

Mother settles us, creating a little home out of the two facing seats. She arranges our food basket overhead and fixes pillows for Michael and Gail; I have some comic books at my post by the window. She checks our luggage again; besides clothing, the trunk contains her Bible, in which she has written down all her children and grandchildren's birthdays, and stores her important letters and documents. I want to run and explore the train, but Mother has her hands full with Michael and Gail and doesn't want trouble. Instead, I fix myself at the window, watching the landscape. I must know where we are and not depend on the conductors. I hear my father: "You just be careful dealing with these people. Them kissified people will do something to you."

The train travels due west to New Orleans through flat pine forests. I sit at the window, pushing off Michael, who wants to play, my face glued to the glass, watching for signs. I have a knife in my pocket for protection, and reassure myself by clutching the handle.

The first sign starts with a "C."

"We in California yet?" my mother asks.

"I don't think so," I say.

I sound out the "ch" sound as the teacher has taught us. "Ch—ch—oc—

taw," I pronounce, then state my conclusion, fulfilling my duty: "No, we're not in California yet."

Instead we're on a bridge, a vast span rising into the sky like a giant arm, stretching across a bay bigger than Mobile's. Slowly, we climb higher and higher. The roller coaster fascinates and scares me. What's going to happen when we get to the top? The dull oily brown bay spreads out below. Seabirds scatter from their nests as we move by. I press my head closer to the glass and look behind me: the train extends all the way down the bridge, an incomprehensible length.

"Mama," I say, "this bridge is as long as the state."

"That's right," she says, but Gail needs some tending to.

I return to my post. We're up so high the trawlers and shrimp boats look like toys below. I turn the other way and see we're approaching the top. I don't want to scare my mother, but I steel myself for the ride down; I imagine the locomotive's weight pulling us to earth. We reach the peak. I push against the glass, staring at the steep downhill ahead. We're going to fly! I think, but our descent is just as stately as our climb up.

We can't move much around the train. A few cars up is a fancy dining car, every table covered with starched linen and glittering and polished glasses and silverware. Next is the parlor car, with its long windows and comfortable seats. I envy the businessmen tipping the liveried porters who serve them glasses of ice-cold ginger ale. I yearn to wander around, but Mother doesn't let me go out of her sight. When we come to stations, men hawk candies, sandwiches, and sodas from the platforms and Mother lets me buy Paydays through the window. In Houston, we stay in the station and I ignore Michael, who's holding my hand—I'm beginning to understand how June must feel as I tag along behind him—and stand on the top of the steps looking at the busyness around me.

For the rest of the time I keep watch by the window. I stare at the vast, hot landscape, eyelids itchy from the sun's glare, the train's motion lulling me. I doze for moments, then wake. My mother puts her arms around me; I curl on the seat, drifting into sleep as I rest my head on her lap, then wake because the conductor shouts something and I must be sure to read the black-and-white-painted signs to know where we are. I don't care what the conductors say; words, the words I read, are the only truth to me. I and I alone—no brothers or sisters—am responsible for my mother, and nothing is going to fool me.

One night I stay up, peering at the featureless desert, waiting to see the sun rise. We pass through small towns, the names lit by single spotlights. I thrill that I'm finally seeing the homes of my license plates: Texas, New Mexico, Arizona. As morning comes, billboards welcome us: "Lucky Lager! You're Lucky to Live in California!"

"Mama!" I say, nudging her out of sleep. "Mama! We made it! We're here! We're in California!"

Getting to Oakland takes almost as long as it does to reach California. I keep my post, waiting for my dream California to appear.

"There's gold in them thar hills," I say to Mother, repeating the line from the chapter movies, the wooden seats and stale air of the Davis Avenue movie theaters a million miles away.

We travel inland, up the San Joaquin Valley; I'll get to know the way intimately in the next ten years. But the hills are brown, not gold, the towns plain farming communities, baking in the hot sun; the men walking the station platforms wear normal clothes, not the Gene Autry or Roy Rogers chaps, boots, and spurs I have expected.

Finally we arrive. We carry our luggage down the steps and look for Bud. He's not there. We wait, expecting him to show up as the conductor announces the train's departure. The Daylight Unlimited leaves and we're still standing on the platform. A redcap comes over and asks if he can help. We tell him we're waiting for Bud who lives in Oakland.

"This is Richmond," he explains.

Mother has Bud's number; he's working at Elder Buick, delivering cars: he attaches a motorcycle to a car the garage has fixed, drives the auto to the customer, and rides the motorcycle back to work. He talks to the redcap and the man explains what we must do: "You're gonna have to take a bus to San Jose. There you can catch the train to Oakland. Your family will meet you at the Sixteenth Street Station. Now you know where you're going to go? San Jose?"

I repeat the name.

"That's right," he says. Dutifully I write down the name of the town, spelling out the words the way they sound: "San A Zay."

Holding tight onto the piece of paper, I board the bus with Mother and the kids. After a short ride the bus driver tells us to get off. I look at the sign: San Jose.

"This isn't it," I tell the man.

"Of course it's San Jose," the man tells me. "It's the end of the line. You get off here and take the train to Oakland." He's a large, florid man with red hair and a pockmarked nose.

I point to the sign. "That says San Josie," I say. I take out my piece of paper. "We're going to San A Zay."

"Where?" He laughs.

I show him the piece of paper.

"You spelt it wrong," he tells me, chuckling. He smells of sweat and ciga-rette smoke. I don't believe a word he says.

"What are you talking about?" I shout.

I'm frustrated and furious. The man is telling me one thing; my sign says another. I'm supposed to be taking care of my mother, but I really don't know where we are and I'm without the usual protection of brothers and sis-ters. Plus, I am self-conscious because people are looking at me and I'm still in my white suit.

"We're not getting off the bus until we get to San A Zay," I shout. "I know! I can read! I can write! We're going to San A Zay and this isn't San A Zay!"

The bus driver appeals to my mother. He points out the train across the street and offers to help her with the bags.

Mother's torn. "My son says it's not San Jose," she says.

The bus driver gets an idea. "Lemme see that paper," he says.

He studies the scrap I thrust at him.

"You see," he says, "what you wrote was San Jose in English." He points to the sign. "But you're in California now. We spell these names in Spanish!"

I realize his explanation will allow me to escape from the situation. Grudg-ingly I pick up the bags and we trudge across the square to the waiting train.

Bud is worried to death by the time we finally arrive. He wears his Elder Buick uniform: white overalls, a leather bomber jacket with a fur collar, and a chauffeur's cap. He looks sharp. Plus the motorcycle he uses for his job is attached to a blue-bottomed, gray-topped, big-fendered, sharp-looking car.

He hugs his children and tells me I did a good job. "What do you want? I'll get you anything you want. You're in California now!"

He doesn't have to ask me twice: I want clothes. I'm in a new city and a new state and all I've got to wear is this white suit. I need new clothes.

We pile into Bud's car and he drives us home, a two-bedroom apartment, the second story of a one-family house. There's no yard except for a single tree in front surrounded by a skirt of lawn. Inside, the modern place is cleaner than the Congress Street house and I like the new stove, refrigerator, and bathroom; but the idea of my aunt dying in these bare, windowless rooms mortifies me. The only good thing about the place is that Mother and I will sleep in the same room.

Almost as soon as Mama starts unpacking, Bud says he'll get me some new clothes and gives me two dollars. His gift is more money than I've ever had before. Feeling rich, I walk down the block. The cool, moist air has none of Mobile's airless funky stench. I head toward a store at the end of the block. The outside stands are stacked with fruit. I gawk at the nectarines and pears (I've never seen either before); the aroma from oranges and plums as big as softballs sweetens the air. A Chinese man comes out. Another first. He stares at me, wondering if I'm going to rip him off; I look back, awed by his color, eyes, and straight black hair. He gestures and speaks:

"You want? What do you want?"

I clutch my knife, then move toward the dark, shiny purple plums.

"Plums?" he asks.

"I got two dollars. I want some plums," I tell him. I take out my bucks. He nods and stuffs what must be twenty plums into a brown paper bag. When I go into the store to pay I'm met by the familiar sweet smell of Bud's macaroon cookies. Tomorrow I promise myself I'll buy the cookies and try some of the strange-looking fruits on the stand.

Back at Bud's I sit on the steps, getting ready for serious eating. Almost as soon as I take my first bite a kid comes by.

"Give me a plum," he says.

He's bigger than me and wears jeans.

I move the bag closer to myself and keep eating.

"Give me a plum," he says again.

I'm remembering what June Bug has taught me: Somebody takes your food, you wipe them out.

"No," I say again. I'm not being selfish; I would give him a plum if he asked politely, but he's trying to intimidate me. If he tries again, I've already decided I'll go off on him; I'll have to teach him, establish myself in the neighborhood.

When he reaches for the bag, I punch him in the face and whip out my knife.

"Get out of here!" I yell. "Don't try to take no plums!"

The kid is shocked. "You're crazy, man!" he shouts. But he backs off as Bud comes up.

"What's happening?" asks Bud. He's carrying a bag.

"He hit me," says the kid. "I tried to take one of his plums and he hit me. He went to pull his knife on me."

Bud laughs and introduces us. The boy is Dennis McDaniels; his family owns the house and lives on the ground floor. We shake hands; we'll soon become good friends.

Inside my mother asks what happened.

"My little brother is making himself at home," Bud says proudly.

He shows me what he's got: three pairs of jeans and three Buster Brown T-shirts with vertical stripes. I go into the bedroom where Mama has put everything away and strip off the hated suit, savoring my new clothes. I save the shoes for last, slipping into the tan penny loafers and filling the neat slots with shiny pennies. I've got new clothes, money in my pocket, my knife, and my bag of fruit—something to barter with. I feel pretty much in control. I walk out, new kid on the block, ready now for my new summer home.

Chapter

5

CALIFORNIA is nothing like I imagined. There's no gold in the hills, much less the streets, no cowboys, no horses. The real blessings of the lucky state are complete surprises: huge oranges, nectarines, and peaches, strange-speaking Asians with light yellow and brown skins, the even coolness of the days.

And television. Bud has his own set. The privilege is new: in Mobile the only TV we see is on Fridays when we camp in front of my cousin's snowy black-and-white small-screen Emerson to view the latest episode of "The Cisco Kid." But now I lie on the floor from morning to night watching "Little Rascals," "Laurel and Hardy," and "Howdy Doody" on Bud's nineteen-inch sharp and clear RCA. "Who's that knocking on this barrel? Who's been knocking on this barrel?" Phineas T. Bluster demands as the Howdy Doody peanut gallery howls in delight. (How do those kids get on the show? I want to be there.) Another show named "Captain Midnight" features a contraption called the Kazziggafikal Machine. Kazziggafikal rhymes with Michael. I pop my little nephew Michael on the head. "Who's that knocking on this barrel?" I ask as I nuggie him. No one interferes with my torture. Mother is shopping while Bud's at work. I answer myself, tattooing Michael's helpless curly head: "Kazziggafikal-Michael! Michael-Kazziggafikal!" As he starts to cry, I repeat the routine, tapping his skull. "Who's that knocking on my barrel? Kazziggafikal-Michael!"

Michael replaces Bojack. An orphan at two, he has been adopted by the en-

tire family, usurping my position as favored son and family entertainer, and I
resent the attention he receives.

One Sunday we take our weekly outing, driving over the Bay Bridge to
the zoo. We cross the long span from the port to Yerba Buena Island, and
Michael asks where we're going.

"San Francisco," my mother answers patiently.

Michael repeats the name in baby talk and the adults laugh, telling him
he's cute, encouraging him to say the word again. How can I compete with
his adorably thick Hilliard eyebrows, soft brown eyes, and nonsense syllables? I slap him on the head, pronouncing the word right and taking away
the adults' attention.

Michael starts to cry.

I flick his head again. "San Francisco," I say.

Michael's in tears.

"David!" my mother shouts, grabbing my hands. "Stop that! You're the
baddest little bastard I've ever seen!"

She comforts Michael as we near the outcrop of buildings marking downtown.

"I was playing!" I protest.

My mother shoots me an angry stare; her disapproval only increases my
annoyance at Michael. When she's distracted by the skyscrapers—the city is
bigger than a hundred Mobiles—I whack him quickly again: "Kazziggafikal-Michael!"

Michael wails. My mother admonishes me; I protest and sulk, but I also
enjoy my triumph: at least they're no longer cooing over him.

On weekends we pile into Bud's Mercury and take a long ride down the Valley.
I sit in the back, near the window, enclosed in my own world: too young to
be an adult, too old to be a kid.

We pass the warehouses and railroad tracks that ring Oakland. Everything
here is new, fast, large, electrical. When I go downtown, around tree-lined
Lake Merritt and the white courthouse, I spend hours watching the trolley
cars, awed by the sparks flying from the overhead wires. The excitement ex-
ceeds the thrill of seeing the sailors in downtown Mobile with their money
and girls. Oakland is no lazy southern capital but a city that generates power,
a magnetic energy.

We drive into the Valley. Instantly the heat shoots up ten degrees. The car
becomes a hot box. I roll my window down and stick my head out. I squint
in the blistering, blast-furnace air and look at the dirt roads that trail off the
main two-lane highway toward isolated farmhouses. The West. I forget

about Michael and stare at the stark, brown, distant hills; they look nothing like Rockville's rolling mix of farms and forest. This is cowboy country. Gullies and gulches. Flash floods. Steep-walled canyons where John Wayne and Randolph Scott shoot it out with Indians. I peer at the broken horizon, almost expecting Allen Rocky Lane or some other hero to lead a wagon train over the mountains.

After an hour we arrive at the pick-your-own farms in Modesto. My mother and the rest collect greens, peaches and nectarines, paying for the produce by weight. Then for a dollar or two we fish the stocked lakes for catfish and bass. The mountains cast their shadows over the farmland; the aroma of the orchards sweetens the air. I stop at a wooden table, lured by chunks of cured meat.

"Hey, Bud!" I shout. "Can we get bacon?"

The farmers sell meat by the pound.

"Sure, my baby," Bud answers. "Whatever you want." Bud's generosity is legendary; he loans friends twenty and thirty dollars whenever he can. With him we never seem to be without money; I always have cash for fruits or macaroons at the Chinese store.

"I want some bacon!" I tell the farmer.

"How much?" he asks, moving the sharp knife up and down the slab.

"This much," I say, and slap two dollars Bud has given me on the table.

I walk off, the prize clutched to my chest. Bacon!

"I'm trying to convince Mama to stay here," Bud confides to me. "Get Papa to come here. I can afford it. What do you think?"

"That's all right," I say, hugging the bacon. I'm not sure yet what I think about not returning to Mobile.

"Mama!" I shout. "I got bacon! I'm never gonna throw my plate on the floor again! I got bacon!"

As Bud and Mother decide the future, I explore my surroundings. "There is no there there," Gertrude Stein has said about Oakland. But she's not speaking for natives. Oakland has a distinct, important history; and you certainly can't understand the Panthers without having a sense of the city's unique blend of southern black, militant trade union, and western American cultures.

Originally Oakland served as the railhead for the transcontinental railroad, a ferrying point for goods shipped to and from San Francisco. Populated mainly by Italians and Portuguese, the Victorian houses that line the streets also housed Pullman porters, members of the first organized black trade union—Congressman Ron Dellums's uncle was a secretary of the radical union—who, as they crisscrossed the country, passed the word about the liberal, thriving town. By the twenties Oakland was attracting blacks from the Gulf states. Because a nucleus of local industrialists increased their power in the state, the port won important contracts; when World War n began all Pacific Theater forces left from the Oakland docks, promoting a surge in the city's growth that attracted more blacks, a migration that continued into the fifties. (Blacks weren't the only southerners to get jobs in the ports; whites from the Gulf states came too, many of them joining the Oakland Police Department, thereby giving that organization an especial notoriety.)

The newcomers — like my family — settle in the "flats," the tableland that stretches from the port to the hills inhabited by the city's traditional power brokers. No one in the flats has money, but there are still distinctions within this working-class community. From the piers up to Lake Merritt you're in West Oakland, a tract of largely treeless streets filled with broken glass, boarded up houses, and decrepit schools — a ghetto whose squalor seems even worse to me than Mobile's, larger, grayer, more inescapable. From Lake Merritt to the hills, you're in East Oakland, away from the industrial sector, traveling through streets of single-family houses and well-tended parks: a promised land outside the ghetto, its avenues lined with the beauty shops and barbecue joints that make up the low-cost, fast-profit start-up businesses of black entrepreneurs.

But we don't only change Oakland. The newly emerging western city also affects us. First, the place is a raw settlement, a boomtown, violent and full of adventure. Vigilantes play as distinguished and important a role in the area's life as, say, Irish politicians do in Boston. Plus, the area has a rich union tradition. The area's local hero is not a college football coach but Harry Bridges, head of the radical longshoreman's union. When I'm growing up, Communist Party members openly recruit at the docks and in union halls, and there's no stigma attached to their ideas or practice. The political environment encourages the idea of internationalism; solidarity is the watchword, and we are surrounded by examples of people collectively asserting their power.

The internationalism is emphasized by the fact that Oakland, like Mobile, is an integrated community. You don't simply find whites and blacks, but yellows, browns, Native Americans too. These groups coexist in a particular way. New York is famous for its many ethnic communities. But whenever I visit there, I'm surprised at how groups don't mix: the city is multiracial, not intraracial. But on July 4, when the young people of Oakland crowd the park by the bay to watch the fireworks, the array of skin shades is beautiful and impressive; couples claim five and six strains in their blood, setting the basis, perhaps, for the first truly color-blind society in America.

Finally, there's a rawness to the Oakland character. This is Oak Town, the city of the A's and Raiders. Its two most important cultural figures are Bill Russell and Jack London—rebels both.

We—the Party—are another expression of this defiant energy. Our audacity and persistence in claiming power and expressing ourselves is particularly American. Huey himself is a sort of real-life Martin Eden. (And there's something of Huey in Jack London too.)

But there is one significant difference between us and our Oakland forebears. In creating and developing the Party we refused to glorify our rootlessness. Instead we shaped and focused the anger and energy of our members, creating a revolutionary organization of workers and the poor that combined the internationalism of the radical trade union movement with the communalism of my sister Rose Lee's Big Meeting and, for a while, captured the imagination of an entire generation—black, white, and everything between.

When I'm not watching television, I hang out with my new friends—Dennis, who lives downstairs, Toby Jackson, Thomas Ingram, guys from the block. We play ball in the school gym across the street or loaf in De Fremery Park, a square of large green shaded lawns that includes a municipal swimming pool and a Victorian mansion in which the city holds arts and crafts classes and weekend dances.

But mainly we fight. At least at first. Even after my scuffle with Dennis, I still must establish myself in the neighborhood. Short and frail looking, called "skinny bones," I tie on with the local guys every day. (Without June—and I miss June a lot—I have no choice.) For us, fighting's like words: a way to work things out. We fight to make friends, get rid of our frustration or boredom, assert our identities. Fighting is a creative outlet.

One day, Toby Jackson tries to jump me on the lawn in De Fremery Park. I pull my knife from my pocket, flicking the blade open as I swing the shaft forward, mimicking Allen: he's taught me to keep a wooden match under the blade, allowing you to spring it open with your thumb.

Toby backs up, looking at Dennis and Thomas, trying to explain his retreat. "He's got a knife!"

"Well, don't you guys carry knives?" I'm saying.

"No, man," says Dennis. "It's a fair fight."

"Sure it's fair," I say. "I got a knife."

"But he doesn't," says Thomas.

"That's his problem," I say.

"No, man," says Dennis. "Fair fight means no weapons. Put your weapon down. You got to. It's a fair fight."

*   *   *

The only friend I don't mix it up with is Huey. I don't fight with Huey. Not then, not later. In his book *Revolutionary Suicide* Huey says my reputation as a battler drew him to me. "If the neighborhood boasted a good fighter, word got around. That was how I first heard of David Hilliard. . . . David was no bully; he never looked for trouble, but when attacked, he had great courage. He won renown in our neighborhood as a brave adversary who never backed down. That is one of the qualities I have always admired most in him, and the bond that was formed then, eighteen years ago, has held." He wrote those words in 1973; even during the worst of the next sixteen years we never laid hands on one another.

I meet him when we move at the end of summer. Living around the block at Forty-seventh and Market, Huey's a neighborhood curiosity already a fighter and talker, known for his toughness and his high-pitched, rapid-fire voice. (In fact, Melvin thinks the voice provoked a lot of Huey's fights. Kids made fun of him and he defended himself.) Always immaculate, clean, sparkling, he reminds me of Donald Baker, the principal's son back in Toulminville. He uses Dixie Peach—the best grease you can find, he tells me—slicking down his hair into handsome, soft waves. He washes his face so well his cheeks look polished. His teeth sparkle: some mornings he brushes them fifteen times. Instinctively I want to be around this sharp-looking, smiling guy who's always walking, going someplace, as though he's on a quick march, head straight ahead, full of purpose.

Almost immediately I'm accepted into the Newton family and feel completely at home there. Mother—we call Mrs. Newton "Mother"—adopts me as another son, feeding me and including me in any advice she gives Huey.

Mr. Newton is a minister who earns his living working for the city. A staunch disciplinarian, he speaks sternly, expressing himself with firm conviction. But he's also a very funny man, making sure to include some levity even in his most serious pronouncements. The child of a rape—his mother was fourteen when he was born—he is famous for defying whites in Louisiana: "He never yielded," Huey writes about him in his autobiography, ". . . he never hesitated to speak up to the white man."

"In our family," Melvin Newton says,

> my father was a legend even while he was still alive. My mother and brothers and sisters recited his heroics down south in protecting his family. We sat at his feet and he taught us self-respect and discipline. He told us stories of the heroes—Moses and Samson, David, Daniel in the lion's den. He always valued loyalty to your family and friends and yourself

above material things. Once you had loyalty, then nothing could happen to you. Once your spirit was secure, it didn't matter what happened to your body. You had no fear of living, nor of death. You were already beyond that. He used words like "drink muddy water"—meaning if you had to give up fresh water, than you drank muddy water rather than violate your own spirit. He said, "You can take a killing, but you can't take a beating." His belief in people went beyond the material person. He felt there was a constant number of spirits and souls out there that occupied bodies, and that the continuum of that spirit depended on how you lived; and in addition, this continuation of people in death from life meant that you didn't have to be afraid of living or dying. He had a strong belief in the ideals of Judeo-Christian religion. Huey once shared a conversation with me that he had with my father.

"What do you do if your brother offends you?" he asked my father.

"You don't strike your brother," my father answered. "You try to reason."

"What if he continues to offend you?" Huey insisted.

"Well, he's not going to continue to offend you," my father answered.

Huey pressed the issue. "Yeah, but what if he does?"

"Then he's not your brother," answered my father. "You strike him down."

The reason we move is my father. Bud has convinced Mama to stay, and in the fall my father leaves Mobile with June.

"Bud took Mother first," remembers June,

because he needed Mother right away. And you were of course her baby, so she wasn't gonna leave you. Me and Dad would come later. It wasn't something that he readily related to wanting to do wholeheartedly. You knew that something was bothering him, something wasn't right, the way he would answer you, or phrase certain words, or even his refusal to say anything. But he did it because of his love for his wife and his kids.

On the drive we never stopped to sleep, only to fill up with gas and get something to eat. Every time we stopped, he was reminding me: "You be careful out there. Them kissified people will do something to you out there, boy, so you just be careful dealing with these people." You didn't go through the front. They would always have us go around to the back to pick up sandwiches. He'd always be afraid that they was gonna shoot us back there, hang us, whatever his fears was. I'd always have that in the back of my mind; I'd look around and make sure that everything looked normal. I kept that up. To this day, I do that. Some people say I'm paranoid. But to me it's just a heightened sense of awareness.

Papa doesn't get happier when he arrives. Oakland is too big for him and he can't find a job. Every day he goes out, dapper and dignified, looking for work, returning home frustrated and silent; when we say he can relax and collect his Social Security, he rebukes us, telling us he doesn't want to draw his pennies.

I share none of my father's feelings. I'm excited about the start of school. I will attend Santa Fe, the elementary school. The first day I'm amazed. I'm used to integrated streets by now, but I never expect the classes to mix white and black kids together.

The first week I get into a fight. In the schoolyard we're tossing a ball around, playing "Four Square" with Charles Petrie, a tall, strong white kid. Charles and I get into an altercation and Charles throws the ball, hitting me in the chest. Everyone around us witnesses the moment of intimidation. I hold the ball. Petrie waits for me to do something. I must answer him: if I don't, kids in school will think they can take advantage of me.

I go over to him. "Why'd you throw the ball at me?" I ask

The outlines of the situation are clear. I've got to hit Charles back. If not I'm going to get hit again. That's the way things go.

I let my mind go blank I don't want to think about what's going to happen, don't want to analyze the situation. Any sort of thinking will only weaken me. What matters now is intuition, my sense of when I should tee off and throw the first punch, because if I don't strike first I'll probably lose the fight and get busted in the eye or something like that.

"You don't know how to—"

Before he even finishes I drop the ball, fire on him, hitting him hard, right in the mouth.

Stunned for a moment, Petrie then slams me back.

The kids close around. Because of Petrie's height and weight, there seems to be no contest between us. But my mind is concentrated only on the fight now, not thinking about comparisons, only figuring how to damage him as quickly and thoroughly as possible. I know I'm quicker than him and that my first punch has surprised him, so I hit again. Fast. Straight on the lip. And hit him again.

"You're bleeding," one guy says.

Backing off, Petrie dabs at his lip. He isn't crying but doesn't want to continue. I'm waiting, poised, ready to spring again. His buddies surround him; slowly he backs away, ending our bout. Now all the boys throng around me. I feel courageous for having stood up to the bigger kid and beaten him. And all the kids around me are absolutely awed — because Charles Petrie is a big guy.

"You got fast hands, man," one says.

I start to hang out with the "slow learners," the kids who fill the back of the classroom. I shuttle from the rear seats right in front of the closet with its wood sliding door to those up front, facing the teacher, Mr. Bentz. During the mystery of math I stay in the back; during reading and history I move to the front, sitting next to people like Petrie, eager to display what I know, anxious to learn more words and discuss ideas.

Mr. Bentz is white, but he takes an interest in me, believing I show academic potential, impressed by my love for words and reading ability. He urges me to join the Boy Scouts, buying me a twenty-four-dollar uniform and taking me on all-night camping trips with the troop. He also suggests I become a "sign slinger": hold the sign up and kids march across the street at the crosswalk, lower it and the black-and-yellow-licensed cars speed by.

Being a traffic boy is the "in" thing at Santa Fe; every student wants to wear the rust orange jacket and yellow, peaked soldier's cap. I'm so proud of my new station and responsibility that I bring my costume home and practice in my room, raising the sign and blowing the whistle. When I make the shrill, commanding sound I feel like I'm Ken Maynard in the Beech-Nut Spearmint gum commercial. "Beech-Nut Spearmint gum!" Ken says, his breath so fresh that it stops a charging locomotive. My power and competence in some weird way sums up the difference between Mobile and Oakland. Down in Mobile you get run over walking across the street. But Oakland is so civilized that even I — eleven years old! — can control the traffic!

Huey lives around the corner. Now every morning we go to school together. I wait on the small porch; like clockwork he approaches, quick stepping, well-washed, telling me something even before he reaches me. I jump off the porch because Huey doesn't stop. He's going to school, jabbering, one idea after another. Huey's not a good reader, believing that adulthood will bestow on him the instant ability to read, he doesn't try to improve his literacy, and his IQ score is somewhere down below dull-normal. But he does possess a

powerful memory, reciting "The Bells" and "The Raven," and "Easements."
This morning he's repeating the Rubáiyát of Omar Khayyám, telling me the
quatrains he's heard recited over the radio by "Cool Mon-i-que."

A loaf of bread
A jug of wine
And thou

I rush to keep up; I like the image of the lines, their romantic listlessness.
There's no one like Huey. He always has something to say, something interesting. He won't let anything go. When he and our friend James Crawford
get together they spend half a night trading dozens because James invents
rhymes much better and faster than Huey.

"I fucked your mama on Twelfth and Vine; the baby came out drinking
cold white wine," says Huey.

"I fucked your mama from city to city," answers James, "and the baby
was sucking from titty to titty!"

But Huey always refuses to surrender. I watch them, laughing and mar-
veling until finally, as always, the dozens disintegrate into a fight and James
and Huey tie one on.

The older I get the more confusing school becomes. Every day you must
choose. What are you going to be? A guy from the streets or a *saditi* like
Melvin, a bookworm? I love dictionaries, for instance; looking up words —
reading all the different definitions, discovering their histories — fascinates
me. Sometimes I think I could spend days turning the fragile pages of the
thick book. Yet though I admire learned people and am fiercely proud of and
awed by, say, the ability of my brother Allen to tell a story or of Huey to explain an idea, the world and my own instincts guide me to revere someone
like Clyde, the hippest kid in my junior high, who comes from New York,
smokes reefer, and wears the coolest pair of pants I've ever seen, shoestrings
lacing up the ripped-open seams along the side. Plus, at the same time, I cut
myself off. I don't know why, but once I learn how to read, for some reason I
think there's no more reason to go to school.

And for all the talk in school about studying hard, a lot of the teachers indicate something else.

The worst is music. I love music. I've always been told my voice is
sweet; music is like smell to me — a natural sense for me, a kind of knowledge. In junior high, myself and my friends Irving Kindler, Ray-Bell, and
Gene McKinney organize a group, singing a cappella imitations of the
Moonglows and Satins.

"Oh, we had harmony!" remembers Gene.

You guys could sing. You didn't need no music ! No bands, no guitar, no nothing. You could just fill up the whole room with your voices. I was the only one who couldn't hold a note. I remember I once went into music class. Did it to meet girls because I didn't think I had to sing, thought it was just a little old, simple, easy class. Then the teacher says, "Are you a tenor? You solo this here." That kind of gives me butterflies and stuff. But I start to sing and someone says, "Gene, you're off-key, man!" So I get to be something like the manager because I don't want to mess you guys up. Only thing I can never manage is what to call the group. Every other week it gets a different name.

The kids think my group is pretty good and I'm proud of our effort. At the time we have a chorus class taught by a guy with thin black hair, thin lips, and fat cheeks. He loves classical music and European culture. He lectures us endlessly about Mozart and Vienna. We don't mind his lessons, but we would also like to sing some of our songs. When we ask him whether we can perform, he tells us no and hands wt a new sheet of music.

Immediately the kids start laughing.

"What's this? What's this?"

The joke travels through the class. No one can read the title. It's not English. Our teacher has gone nuts. He loves Europe so much he's not even teaching English now!

" '*Stille Nacht*' !" he replies, distributing the sheets.

" '*Stille Nacht*'?" asks my buddy Irving Kindler. "What's that?"

The music teacher goes to the front, squinting at Irving with his hard, thin-lipped sneer. "German. '*Stille Nacht*' is German."

"German! Man, we hardly know English!"

We laugh to ourselves. "*Stille Nacht*." Big joke. We repeat the phrase, Irving singing the strange words in his bass.

"It means 'Silent Night,'" the teacher says, waiting for us to simmer down. "You do know 'Silent Night,' don't you?"

His contempt makes me angry. Who is this man, anyway, teaching me how to sing? I know singers—*great* singers! Sam Cooke sang with my sister Dorothy Mae in the church choir in Mobile.

"Course I know 'Silent Night,'" I say. "What do you think?"

"I think you're a dumb black bastard," he says. He tosses the curse aside, coolly, as though the insult is a private joke between us.

"You shouldn't say that," a girl reproves him.

"I heard one of you say that the other day," he answers.

"That's different," the girl continues.

"You mean you can say something and I can't?"

He loves to torment us. His hatred makes me hard and cold, as though I'm a stone, wanting to smash something. Not only because I hate his hate, but because he shuts me out: I want to know that weird-sounding "*Stille Nacht*," his beautiful Vienna, and his glorious Mozart, to understand the majestic, moving foreign sounds I've heard in his class.

Chapter

6

HOOVER Junior High marks the start of my adulthood. There I begin the two activities that soon occupy me full-time: drinking and sex.

Originally the alcohol is no big thing. We start with Vino di Tavolo, boosting "short-necks," or "puppies"—half-pints—from Mr. Costello's corner grocery store.

"What're you doing?" he yells as Huey and I study the candy rack.

We take offense. "Deciding what I'm going to buy," I say.

"Decide outside," he says. He comes out from behind the counter, waving us away with his hand. "You want to browse, go to the library. This is a store."

"Hey, Mr. Costello—"

"Out! Out!"

But as he ushers us out, Gene McKinney and some other kids enter. Guessing instantly what's happening, Gene grabs some candy bars.

"Hey! Come on!" shouts Mr. Costello.

"I'm paying, Mr. Costello," Gene protests.

Accidentally on purpose I lean against the candy rack; the sweets come down and one kid grabs a Mounds.

"Gimme that candy!" shouts Mr. Costello.

Mardi Gras! Kids scramble for bags of potato chips, candy, and soda. Mr. Costello runs after the nearest offender while scooping up chocolate bars. Meanwhile, Huey and I edge our way to our goal. Vino di Tavolo. We grab two bottles and run for the front. Mr. Costello sees us coming.

"Stop!" he yells, dodging toward us.

Huey and I split up. Huey makes the door, but Mr. Costello grabs my shirt.

"Huey!" I shout and toss him my bottle. The glass shatters on the concrete.

"Goddammit!" Mr. Costello cries. As he lunges for Huey, I twist free and seize a last bottle off the shelf.

"I just wanted a candy bar!" I shout, holding the bottle before him.

Around the corner we meet up with Gene.

"Gimme that bottle!" he says, laughing.

We hand him one, then Huey takes a second from under his shirt. Gene looks on in amazement.

"Man," he says, "how'd you get *that* one too?"

Later, we graduate to Bitter Motherfucker. (Bitter Dog we call the mixture in the Party.) The brew is immortalized in a popular song:

> *White port and lemon juice*
> *What it do to you*
> *Tastes so good*
> *It makes you feel so fine*

We open the bottle, drink the top part of the almost sickeningly sweet, cheap stuff—the "poison," we call it—pour in half a can of lemon juice, shake it up, and enjoy ourselves. Less than a dollar for the whole thing and we're wired for the afternoon. Later, we experiment buying Rainer's Ale—Gene calls the stuff Green Death—and even Thunderbird, combining ice-cold bottles of the wine with lime Kool-Aid. Looking like embalming fluid, the stuff makes your brain itch; compared to Thunderbird, the Bitter Motherfucker is a fine Burgundy. (Years later, I'm in Washington representing the Party and taken to a fancy restaurant. Condescendingly my host suggests I pick the wine. Château White Port, I coolly reply.)

Drinking makes my days in Hoover even more frustrating and boring than before. On graduation day, I'm drunk when I stand on the stage dressed in a black robe with a stupid tassel dangling over my cap. By the next year, I practically never attend class.

"Now you were a boy who *hated* to go to school," remembers Gene.

Unless we were having fun, or something was happening, you would always cut school. "I'm not going to school today!" I remember thinking, Man, how does his mama let him get out of going to school every day? Because my mama, she'd be: "Hey! You *got* to get your ass out of here!

You're going! And you'd better learn something!" But you didn't go.
That's one of the things I dug about you. Because you'd be almost like
teaching yourself, because you'd read and write a lot—dictionaries,
every kind of book. And I understood where you were coming from. Because a lot of the teachers weren't that good. Some of them didn't care,
didn't give a damn. You seemed like you were more advanced than the
other people in the class. Sometimes I thought that was why you wouldn't
go, because the class was boring to you. And that was what made me
feel so good about you. Because you did like you liked.

High school only increases my dislike of education. I attend McClymonds, a
West Oakland high school famous for its athletic tradition: it counts sports
stars Bill Russell, Frank Robinson, and Paul Silas among its graduates.
McClymonds looks like the massive Prichard paper plant and smells only
fractionally better. Its linoleum floors and cinder-block walls stink of stale
sweat and too many cooked lunches. I think school should be a clean, fresh-
looking place, with orderly, welcoming classrooms. Dingy McClymonds has
the stench of a warehouse, a human depository, and most teachers treat us
like unused stock, extra inventory.

"You can go," my math teacher tells me and my running partners, Chico
Higgins and Cleon Harris, when he enters the room.

He opens the door with a flourish. "You never have to return," he says,
ushering us out to the laughter of our classmates. "Don't worry about your
mark. I give you an A in ignorance."

We stalk out. I never surrender my pride, but inside I'm mad: he should
be encouraging us to stay, not aiding our escape. We gather on the third-floor
landing and decide to cut next period too; we're scheduled for gym, which I
dislike because if one of the other guys makes a comment about my thin
build I'll have to fight, and I don't want to.

We light our first joint and Cleon takes a drag.

"Don't hot-box it, man," Chico reprimands him.

"What are you gentlemen doing?" a voice suddenly demands.

"Tasting the goods," says Cleon.

The monitor doesn't think the joke funny. He tells us to put out the offending joint and march down to Mr. Ellsworth, the principal.

"The three H's," announces Mr. Ellsworth as we enter his office. He's
proud of the nickname he's invented—the three H's stand for Higgins,
Harris, and Hilliard—the three bad musketeers who are conveniently blamed
for everything bad that happens.

Mr. Ellsworth warns us for several minutes. Then he dismisses Chico and

Cleon. I sit nervously in a straight, wood-backed chair as he tries to encourage me.

"David," he says, "you could be a really good student. All you have to do is put out a little more effort."

I shift away from him, intensely uncomfortable. I don't like being singled out from my friends, and at the same time Mr. Ellsworth's attention pleases me. But I don't believe I'll succeed with my studies. Anyway, who's he to tell me I can be a good student? *I* know I'm intelligent and can work hard. It's his teachers, school, and textbooks that fail me; it's he who humiliates me by separating me from my friends and making me feel disloyal—disloyal to the bone.

"Look, you don't care about my being a good student," I explode. I burst out with words as though we're fighting and I'm teeing off, getting in the first shots to silence my adversary.

"David, that's not true."

"This is a gladiator school," I say. We've seen *Ben-Hur* at the fancy Lake Shore Theater, where we buy tickets for the balcony, then sneak into the loges, smoking Pall-Malls and downing a Vino di Tavolo. Charlton Heston didn't thrill me like Don Winslow used to, but the scenes of the gladiators training remind me of the McClymonds gym. "You don't care about good students. You want everybody to be a warrior. You care about good football players. And I'm not one." When I first speak I am scared, uncertain of what I'm saying. But as I continue I gain confidence in my ideas. The more I explain why I can't be a good student, the more persuasive and articulate I sound. "I'll never be a good student here. I don't belong here. So just leave me alone and I'll leave you alone and I can go about my life later on."

"You don't have to feel like that, David," Mr. Ellsworth says.

But I don't want to agree with him. I want to get out of the office, be on the third-floor landing or outside in the schoolyard with my running buddies.

"Well, that's the way I feel, and it doesn't matter to me that I don't have to because I do."

I get up, staring down at the floor, needing to leave.

Mr. Ellsworth stares at me, trying to shame me into remorse with his anger and disappointment. Does he think an occasional pep talk can change me? A hard core of resentment tightens in my stomach, pulling my head down: I'm afraid that if I look at him I will feel forced to say something, tell him some of the other reasons for my not applying myself.

"All right, David." Mr. Ellsworth gives up. "We'll have to tell your mother about this latest incident."

I don't care. I leave and stroll down the wide, ugly hall past the glass show-case displaying the bronze plaques and statuettes celebrating the school's past heroics. A drink would be good, I think, and go find Chico and Cleon.

We cut out the back way toward our new hangout, a grocery store around the corner from De Fremery Park, up the block from my family's new house. In the last year we've moved to a large Victorian house with room enough for everyone. Mother has finally put her foot down, insisting I sleep alone. Without her the nights are terrifying. My back room faces a funeral home. The first night there I lie in bed staring at the mortuary, remembering the skeleton hanging from the window of the Mobile hospital and worrying about ghosts. Unaware of falling asleep, I dream I am in the dark, trying to open the door as things I can't see crawl over my skin. I wake gasping; my sweat soaks the sheet.

We buy our pints—the store is famous for selling the coldest wine in Oakland—then stand on the corner, downing the wine, making small talk to passing girls. As is often the case recently, I miss June deeply. A few months ago he decided to join the Air Force, and I feel vulnerable without him.

"Remember when June messed up Billy McDaniels?" I say. It's a famous incident that happened soon after June arrived in Oakland. Playing basketball in the school gym, some of us start debating who's stronger, June or Billy McDaniels—no relation to my downstairs neighbor Dennis—a local famous for his tough, street-fighting reputation. I'm saying June because no one can whip June; June's as strong as a mule; June's carted a whole wagonload of wood around Mobile; no Billy McDaniels can take him. My bragging causes trouble. McDaniels overhears me. Deciding to take things into his own hands, he goes over and pushes June in the middle of the game. June doesn't say a word. He picks up McDaniels and body-slams him to the floor, lays him out, then walks away and keeps on playing ball. Everybody looks amazed at his feat, but I'm nonplussed because June is my hero and I'm never surprised at his strength. "I said you can't mess with June," I tell the guys.

We laugh about the exploit. But the story only makes me feel lonelier. Now June's gone to some far-out place like Idaho or Wyoming much too distant to visit. And Papa is saying he wants to leave too. Every night he is-sues the same complaint: *I don't want to draw my pennies and I can't get no work here. I want to go back where I can work, where I can get me a job. These kissified jobs here. I know I can get me a job in Mobile.*

Let him go, I think, downing some wine, let him go. He doesn't want to be here; he doesn't want to be with us; let him go.

Already buzzed, we finish the first bottle and mix up a second batch.

"What's that?" Cleon asks, pointing to a woman coming toward us who's wrapped in sheets and wearing a veil.

"Be cool, man," I say, "that's the Moolah."

"The what?"

"The Moolah, man."

"Why's she dressed like that?"

"That's the way they dress. With those head rags on. Even the kids walk around in white—with dresses on. They're weird."

I tell Cleon about the kids' uncle; he rides a bike, selling a bleaching cream called Skin Succession and a record called "A White Man's Heaven Is a Black Man's Hell." Skin Succession, my sister Eleanora and I call him, deciding these people are truly strange.

We get into Cleon's car and pick up Gene after school. As we drive around, we see some good-looking girls.

"We're giving a party," one says. "In Richmond. Come on over."

"Okay, baby," Cleon says. He fancies one of the girls already and thinks he's going to make her. "I'll be there."

"Tonight. Come on over."

Two hours later we're driving out to Richmond. I'm not looking forward to the evening, but everyone else is up for fun, and we're dressed to kill in our double-breasted suits, pleated, cuffed pants, and "stingy-brimmed" Stetsons—a style we've fashioned by taking old hats, trimming and re-hemming the brims—trying to be as dapper as our idol, Cab Calloway.

"Cleon, man," Gene says, "don't you see? That pretty little girl is using you. She just wants you to get her old man jealous."

"No, man," says Cleon. "She loves me."

"Oh my God." I laugh. "Cleon, you're asking for trouble. We shouldn't be going here."

"I'm getting some pussy tonight," says Cleon. "I got to have that."

"Maybe she love me/Maybe she don't/It don't matter/If I gets what I want!" I say, repeating one of Allen's favorite chants.

"That's good, David," says Gene. "It rhymes out!"

We get to the party and within a few minutes Cleon is sweet-talking the troublemaker, while Gene hasn't had any trouble in finding a friendly female. With his large build and gentle ways, Gene's a born lover, a fighter whom I can always rely on, with all of Huey's heart but none of his craziness.

I stand and watch the scene unfold. I know I'll be fighting in a moment, but the shenanigans amuse me.

Finally, someone interrupts Cleon's patter. Cleon objects. I go over, intervening.

"Hey, man," I say to one of the guys, "you don't need this. We're going."

I can see the girl enjoys the tension. I make eye contact with Gene; he's ready. I'm aware these strangers don't know my reputation and that my size will help convince them to fight: they won't want people to hear a skinny kid bested them. By now we're on the lawn; the group grows in size behind us. I look at Gene and we don't have to say a word. Suddenly he dashes for the car. Instantly, the guys tumble on us, taking us down. But Cleon and I are ready, mixing it up for a moment until Gene races by with the car and I grab Cleon, pulling him with me as we pile through the car windows.

"You're strong, David," Gene says. We're breathing hard.

"I'll mingle with them," I say.

"Hey," says Gene as we relax, enjoying our escape, "you got to bring some ass to get some ass."

Later we pick up some local girls and go to the pipes, a large lot down the block from my house filled with disassembled machinery. We hide behind the stacks of rusted equipment and toke up, getting high off the sweet pot, then split up, finding some secluded, hidden spot where we can have sex.

Sex is something I'm good at. I know a lot about it and I'm not shy. Girls appreciate my confidence. Inarticulate, unable to verbalize my feelings, I act out my feelings: I walk up to a girl, grab her, and, without warning, kiss her, then tell her that I want her to be "my woman." My precocity helps me. I may mispronounce *"Stille Nacht,"* but I know you taste better if you open your mouth and use your tongue when you kiss.

We experiment everywhere—hallways, cars, parks. In our basement we gather for hours with two girls from down the street, fine, shapely, very desirable young women who are the neighborhood heartthrobs. Our music is a record by Hank Ballard and the Midnighters:

> *Work with me, Annie*
> *All night long*
> *You got to roll with me, Annie*
> *You got to get it while the getting's good*

Then we flip it:

> *Annie had a baby*
> *Can't work no more*
> *She has to stop working*
> *And start sweeping up the floor*

Whites consider the lyrics obscene and (as they do with 2 Live Crew thirty-plus years later) ban the record from the radio; the notoriety only increases our delight in the song. We turn the lights down and line up to "scrunch" with the girls, performing a grind like the Lambada, the girls gyrating closer and closer with each new guy, a contest to see who can make the other hotter. The couples clutch each other tight by the cheeks, rub their chests and hips together. The room is sweaty, passionate. Dancing with one of them at the end of the session is a torturous delight. Both know how to throw it, and all inhibitions are forgotten; I stick my hand under their skirts and through their blouses, and I'm stiff as a board pushing up against their frenzied softness and completely frustrated: a rule of scrunching is that we never unzip our flies and it's uncool to come in your pants.

So when I meet Minnie in tenth grade I am ready for some serious loving; a few years older than I, Minnie is ready to teach me. We spend afternoons together in her mother's house, making love. I don't use birth control—I've experimented with rubbers, and I hate the feel and the discipline of disengaging at exactly the moment of passion; besides, Minnie never complains—and after a couple of months Minnie tells me she's pregnant. Minnie says she wants the child, and her mother—a warm, generous person—tells me she'll buy us a house.

"Do you want to marry her?" Bud asks me.

I've gone to him for advice; Papa has long since traveled back to Mobile, where he shuttles in and out of the hospital fighting a pneumonia that won't be altogether cured. Besides, Bud is experienced in these matters.

"I don't love her." I say what's on my mind.

"Well you got to tell her mother that," he says. "But you got to help with the child."

Help is no problem. Gene has gotten me a job working the popcorn machine at Hale's Department Store downtown. I earn about thirty dollars a week, contributing some money to the household and using the rest to buy clothes, a suit and "stingy-brim."

But telling Minnie and her family the truth is difficult.

To my surprise, Minnie believes in me, imagines I can become someone of importance.

"You ought to be a lawyer," she says when we talk about things. "You can really, really convince people."

No one has ever said that to me before, and I've certainly never imagined myself as a lawyer. In her words, I recognize love.

But I don't love Minnie. The longer I'm with her, the more I realize the limits of my feeling. And although many of my friends act as though I shouldn't even consider her feelings, I feel guilty about my lack of passion, feel that I have misled her. In my confusion, I compound the problem, double-dealing with her family, finding excuses, ducking the question. Because of her feelings, Minnie is afraid to find out the truth, and her mother—to protect Minnie, I guess—also doesn't press me for an answer. The predicament completely puzzles me. I feel I should marry her, but guys I talk to say you don't marry a woman simply because you get her pregnant; I feel that there is something shameful in my fatherhood itself since I'm not her husband, but I'm surrounded by people who praise me when they hear the news. When my son is born I take him home, showing him to my mother and the neighbors. Proud of my paternity, I parade him on the block, basking in the compliments and approval of my peers. I'm a father and only seventeen years old! I'm not a kid anymore. I'm a man! The whole world changes around. Suddenly I don't have to go after these young girls anymore; they look at me with interest. I savor my masculinity. The situation is so fulfilling and exciting that soon Minnie and I start having sex again.

One day Allen calls from Mobile: Papa has died.

"I think he just didn't like California," remembers Ted, my nephew, Allen's son.

> Papa wanted to be around people like us. You know, he was an old country man. He came out of a different era and the races didn't mix and he didn't like the mixing of races in California.
>
> I slept in the room with him and my mother's father. They were two old men and liked smoking tobacco and talking to me, telling jokes and talking about old things that happened to them, the railroad where my mother's father used to work, and the two mules they had to pull the logs out of the woods.
>
> He kept himself neat and clean all the time. Kept his shoes shined. He had about five or six pairs. He had a small foot—something like a seven and a half. I was a young boy then, and when he found out I could wear them he gave me a pair. They were so clean and shiny. And he gave me a nice-looking vest, a sweater vest he had. Yeah. Papa was a nice, clean, well-dressed gentleman.

We pile into my uncle's car for the drive, an old black-and-white, flathead-six Pontiac station wagon that Bud likes to say can outrun a spotted ape. Whatever that means.

We drive straight, heading south, stopping only for gas. In Texas a gas-station owner won't let Van use the john and tells him to go out back. Looking very disappointed, Van laughs and shakes his head.

"Things are still the same down here," he says bitterly.

Worried that I'll make a scene if I'm bothered, Mother insists we pull off the road when we're in Mississippi and I need to go.

"You're not gonna get out there and start messing with people," she says. The injunction is unusual for her, though common in the South. ("Southern Black women have always had to be careful about how they bring up their sons," Huey writes in *Revolutionary Suicide*. "Through generations, Black mothers have tried to curb the natural masculine aggressiveness in their young male children, lest this quality bring swift reprisal, or even death, from the white community.")

We cross the state line and soon pass through the flat streets of Prichard and enter Happy Hills Projects, where Allen lives.

A small group gathers by Allen's porch, watching us; the returning family is a big event here.

"Goddamn!" I hear one of the kids say disparagingly, "your cousins came here in a ambulance!"

I'm mortified by their mockery. But I try not to show anything; I want to act very adult, very cool throughout the whole trip, prove to everyone that I'm no longer the young kid who left here, but a man. I've even had my mother buy me a gray blazer with a red, white, and yellow crest sewn on the breast pocket.

My opportunity comes the next day in Rockville. I walk very stiffly, showing my maturity with every ramrod-straight inch of my body.

Mac, one of my mother's cousins, comes and gives me a hug. "What's that?" he asks, pointing to the crest.

For all my sophistication, I can't think of anything to say. "I don't know," I confess. "Just some sort of sign."

We go inside. Everybody's crying, sitting on wooden slatted chairs. I need to distinguish myself from all these relatives, from this entire state. I'm not going to cry, I tell myself, I'll show strength. Papa lies in the casket, neat as a pin. While people break down and lament his death, I stand in my blazer, directly by the coffin, remaining very stoical and detached, staring at him with a smile, determined to show everyone how to accept death.

Because of my father's death, I feel that I have taken on some of the family leadership. The next day my niece Maisie, who's eight months pregnant, says she wants to come with us back to California; everybody tells her no, she shouldn't take the chance. I hate their scared, cautious thinking. What

I've realized is that everything small and scared comes from here; if you want to live a real life, where you're not always fearful of the outhouse, you must leave.

"Come on, Maisie," I say. "You can make it. It's okay. You'll be fine."

And, to my amazement, I'm listened to. Maisie takes my word over everyone else's and joins us for the long ride.

Six months later, I'm drinking with Chico on the corner and suddenly start to cry. Maybe the liquor causes my tears or the fact that I'm in love and feeling soft and tender. Whatever the reason, I realize I haven't cried for my father and now, having swallowed my half-gallon of Bitter Motherfucker, I start to bawl.

Chico is appalled. We're on the street, after all. "What are you crying about, man?"

"My father," I say.

"Your father's dead," he answers.

"I know," I say, "but you know I didn't cry at his funeral. I want to cry now."

Chico won't hear it. "Oh, man, you're a punk. You don't cry."

"Yes you do," I insist. "What's the matter with me? Why didn't I cry for him. I owe him tears."

"Punks cry, David."

"No, men cry too, Chico. My father deserves my tears."

We get into a sloppy, halfhearted fight, tossing punches, not really wanting to hurt each other. By the next afternoon when the strange man passes us we've made up.

He's a strong, powerful-looking guy, older than us, with rusted red hair cropped close to his head and piercing, challenging eyes. He's always dressed in a gray business suit with black shoes —no sense of style at all, very plain and very direct—carries an attaché case and wears a knowing smile that somehow isn't supercilious or condescending. He wears a strange ring with a design that reminds me of a Masonic symbol.

"It's the Moolah," Chico says. We've seen him before and know he's visiting the strange family down the block, though what he does exactly I still haven't figured out.

"*As-Salaam-Alaikum*, brothers," he says to us as always in his steely, confident voice.

We come back with our standard reply, goofing. "Yeah, I slung Lincoln too," says Chico, laughing already.

"And I slung Washington," I say.

The stranger answers with his enigmatic smile.

"Yeah, I got him a full nelson," says Chico.

I go over to the man. "That Masonic?" I ask.

"No, brother," he answers, "this is a Muslim ring." And he invites me down to the temple.

That afternoon I get a copy of the record, "A White Man's Heaven Is a Black Man's Hell." The words make sense, pointing out that what's good for whites is bad for blacks. By myself I attend the mosque. The guy's lecturing, talking powerfully, explaining that whites oppress blacks, and that we came here as slaves and will never be free until we have our economic destiny in our own hands. I leave completely sold on the new program. Now I say *As-Salaam-Alaikum* all the time and lecture my family, telling my mother whites are evil.

"David," she says, "where you getting all this stuff from?"

"From the people next door," I say.

"Skin Succession man? David, those people are crazy," she says.

"No they're not," I answer. "They're not Moolahs, they're Muslims, and that's why the women dress that way."

June walks in—he's returned from the Air Force—and I embark on my next crusade, informing him he must divorce his wife because even though she's part Cherokee, she looks white and white people are blue-eyed devils.

"Well, what are you going to do?" I demand.

"Nothing," he answers. "I think I like her very much and plan to stay with her."

I let him know my disapproval, denouncing him furiously, and, when I'm done, leave to meet Chico and the other guys on the corner for our nightly drunk.

Chapter

7

THE person I love is Pat. She's a little younger than me, tall, light-skinned, with large brown eyes and a sexy, sometimes husky, confident voice. I have dreamed of marrying a pretty woman, prayed to God to give me a beautiful mate. Pat's my dream come true: the most desirable woman I've ever seen. I want her to be mine instantly.

We meet at one of Melvin's college frat parties.

"Look at that girl," I tell Huey.

We're posing, as we say, or profiling, standing in a corner where the girls will see us and we can check out the action.

"I know her," says Huey. "She used to go to Wilson with me."

He introduces us.

Pat couldn't be less interested. "Pleased to meet you," she says and walks on.

But I am smitten. I wait until she comes back through the doorway, approaching us. As she passes, I stick out my foot, tripping and then catching her.

"Hey," I say, smiling, "you fell for me. I got you. Now you gotta be my woman." And I ask her for her telephone number.

This is my usual line, preempting any resistance. But Pat resists me, righting and freeing herself with a frosty, feisty "Excuse me" that leaves me empty-handed.

Then she transfers to McClymonds. Now I apply myself to the pursuit. Luckily, I've just acquired a new status symbol: June has given me my first car, a 1947 Plymouth. After my gang and I paint the rusted body white we go for a drive. Gas fumes drift up from the floor.

"You gotta give this car a name, Doc," says Darlene, a girl who runs with our gang. Doc's my nickname.

"Well, what do you think I should call it?" I say.

"The modulator."

"Why? What's that?"

"Because it's so gassy in here it modulates my breathing capacity."

I hang out in the Modulator every day, waiting for Pat by school.

"Hey," I tell her. "No way you're not gonna be my woman. You gotta be my woman."

She just keeps walking down the street, leaving me behind.

"Hey," Darlene says to her in the hall after class. "You know Doc really likes you. He wants you to be his woman."

"Well, who's Doc?" Pat says.

"You know, the guy in the white Plymouth."

"I don't know nothing," says Pat and walks away.

I find out things about Pat. Huey tells me she was a good student back in Wilson, a good reader, from a Catholic-school background. But she also has a wilder streak. She hangs out with older girls — they invite her to Melvin's frat party — and already has a one-year-old child.

The split — I don't know this then, but I find out — is the key to Pat's character. Her mother and great aunt moved to Oakland in the thirties to run a whorehouse for a white man from their Louisiana town. But early on Pat's mother abandons her, leaving Pat with her great aunt. Pat grows up with brothers and sisters who act as though they're her cousins and Minty, her adopted mother, who constantly denies the family past.

"He came here because there were sailors and other things," Pat says of the white man from Louisiana.

So he got my aunt out here and they had a red-light house and the rest of the family followed. She worked in the house. I'm quite sure that they worked as prostitutes first. Then, after they got other women to work there, they were more or less running it. They wouldn't ever talk about him, wouldn't say anything. We used to go up by the California Hotel to catch the trolley car to go downtown. My mommy, she'd see these prostitutes and stuff, and would say, "I'll sure be glad when they get 'em off the street."

By then she had married someone else, my father, who was a jazz musician, and bought a whole bunch of houses. She had a lot of money. She rented out one house and was a real Christian and had a room where you'd pray at, a room with candles and religious pictures and all that stuff.

Mommy always treated me different. She always told me, "You make good grades. You learn. Because I want you to be able to take care of yourself. You always say you want a lot of children. But you have to go to school. You have to learn to have discipline." She constantly compared me to my cousins—I mean my sisters and brothers—saying, "You're not going to be like that. You're gonna stay in school. You're gonna learn how to take care of yourself. You're not gonna be on welfare, you're not gonna have to depend on nobody but yourself."

And my father was the same way. "Frog," he'd say—because that was his nickname for me because of the way I'd get on my stomach when I was a baby after a bath—"Frog, I want you to go to school."

But I was very confused because so much was hidden from me. I didn't even know I had brothers and sisters. I kept bothering Mommy. I'd say, "How come I'm always alone. I'm tired of being by myself and being alone." She would try to help me. She gave me dolls. I had *dolls* everywhere. I said, "They don't talk to me." Then she tried to adopt a child. Finally my older sister called my mother and told her because she knew how much I didn't like to be by myself, "You have to tell Patricia that she has brothers and sisters." I was eleven by then. It's something I've always felt I needed to find the answer for in my life. Because my mother—my biological mother—had four kids in front of me and two behind me, and how did she manage to raise the four before and the two behind, but not me? I knew the truth. It was always in my head. But I didn't want it to be like that so I never talked about it.

So finally, in the fourth and fifth grade I got rebellious. We had this big house, and I'd go in what she called the "guest room" and hide under the bed, and she would leave. One day she came in and I was looking at television with my other cousins.

She said, "You haven't been going to school. But it's okay. I'm gonna take you downtown tomorrow and get you a couple of pair of shoes, and then maybe I'll take you to the city and find you a coat."

So she took me straight down to the Juvenile Center, which was on Eighteenth and Union.

I said, "Well, I don't want to go up here. Where are you going?"

She says, "Oh, I'm going to talk to this woman. You just come on, Patricia."

I went in there and I waited and I waited. And Mommy never came back.

Instead a lady came back and she says, "Well, you're gonna stay here with us for a while, because we have your records where you haven't been going to school. And if you don't go to school you have to live here. With us."

Which was very frightening, because it was right there in the neighborhood—West Oakland. So from then on I was an A student until eighth grade. By then I wanted to go to school with boys. But Mommy wanted me to go to Catholic school. So I got this bright idea. I was going for testing up at Holy Names High School. I went there and marked all the wrong things: "Who is the President of the United States?" I put down Lincoln. I mean just really screwing up. Then I ended up going through to the ninth grade in public school, and then in tenth grade I got pregnant and I had Dennis. But my Mommy saw me through it. She always had an expression—"You got to pull your little red wagon now"— for when things didn't go the way you wanted them to. So then I had to pull my little red wagon.

After Pat has Dennis, Minty charges the boy's father with rape and puts him in jail. Minty adopts Dennis, bringing him up, and Pat continues in school. Pretty, eager, Pat has plenty of admirers. When I meet her my competition is John Aikens—the school's second-best basketball player after Paul Silas—and an Afro-Latin conga player. Aikens is tolerable—he's my age. But the musician enrages me. He's older than Pat, older than me, twenty-five, with a wife and two kids, and I can't abide the idea that he's poaching on younger men's territory. Plus, I idolize him. He plays the drums really well, dresses very flashily and elaborately; I want his new clothes, envy how the girls admire his musical prowess. In my mind I resolve to take her away from him because he's an older man.

For days I pursue her, waiting outside McClymonds in the Modulator, telling her every chance I get that she's going to be my woman. But Pat still resists. I've never known someone so strong-willed. I can't accept her rejection. When I hear she's seeing someone else, I declare war. I find out she's going to a party with him, and Gene, Chico, Cleon, and I pile into the Modulator, following them. When they get out for the party, we harass him, trying to provoke a fight. Pat acts like nothing's happening. We follow the two inside and keep up the fire, bothering the guy. Finally, when he comes outside we ratpack him, the five of us beating him up.

The next day the war continues. Part of the Oakland male ethos is that you should degrade a woman if she doesn't come around to you — "beat her down," as the youngsters say today. So I park in front of the school, waiting. When Pat comes out, she sees me but doesn't stop. I call her name, but Pat ignores me again.

"Pat!" I yell.

She keeps walking.

Now what am I supposed to do? I desperately want this woman and she's refusing me. Plus, she rejects me in front of all my friends. Her rebuff is impossible to accept. Deep down, I know she really wants me, is attracted to me.

"Pat!" I yell as she sashays away.

I must stop her. The desire to be wanted mixes with my shame and produces the same anger and frustration I experienced with the white boy back in Mobile. I find a rock. I still have good aim from my bottle-cap-throwing days, and though she's not riding a bike, I do want to knock her off her pedestal.

"Pat!" I shout and fling the rock, not hitting her but coming close enough to let her know the next one might nick her. I think she's going to say something, and I start walking toward her, asking her who she thinks she is and repeating that she's my woman. Before I'm halfway to her, she throws my rock at me.

"What the hell are you doing?" I demand.

"You're throwing rocks at me," she explains.

"Just give me your phone number," I insist. "I just want your phone number."

"Well, all you gotta do is ask," she says.

That Sunday, Bud, Mama, and the rest of the family go out. I'm alone in the house. I have Pat's number in my hand, but I have wanted her for so long, cared so deeply about possessing her, that now I'm apprehensive. With Minnie, I was very clear within myself: I had wanted her sexual confidence. But Pat stirs other feelings, deep, uncontrollable emotions. I don't know whether her resistance increases the power of these feelings or whether my attraction to her is simply growing stronger, but my heart pounds when I dial the number: if she's there and refuses my invitation, then the game is over and I don't know what I'll do. And from the way she behaves I am sure she will reject me.

Instead she agrees to see me.

I get myself together, wash up, splash on my cologne. Before she arrives at the door, I see her in my mind's eye, disbelieving my fortune. Could she really be coming here? Is all this effort and desire going to be rewarded? I am well aware that because I'm the youngest in my family everyone thinks I'm spoiled. But my life has never appeared that way to me. My family protected me, but at the same time I believe I've had to fight to be heard and to claim what I need; the deepest sense I've experienced of the truly wonderful things that have happened in my life is amazement and doubt. Quite the contrary of expecting them, I have responded to them only with gratitude, never quite believing that I deserved them. There has been more than one occasion when I have all but wondered, What am I doing here? How did I get here? experiencing a thankfulness at my own fate, an awe that maybe accounts for the sometimes matter-of-fact way I will then act, a taking-things-for-granted that belies my anxiety and sense of disbelief. Joining the Party was one event like that, of course, and there were events afterward that were unimaginable to me, moments when the door of life opened and dreams walked through— the days I began to believe in the possibility of my own recovery. They are the magic moments of life, when your dreams and reality mix. Pat ringing the doorbell, standing there waiting for me to answer, is one of them.

First Pat and I are together after school and in the evenings; then I start picking her up at lunch and keeping her out of school, going over to a friend's house and drinking wine and making love.

Yet Pat still resists me, wanting her independence, flirting with the notion of seeing other guys.

Things come to a head on the Fourth of July. I'm on the corner of Eighteenth and Chestnut with my friends. By now we've graduated from shortnecks to half-gallons. Proud of our alcoholic professionalism, we get a large barrel—the size my father used to collect the resin from the trees—and start filling it with drained bottles; when people come by and ask if we've drunk all that, we proudly answer yes, as though the empty bottles testify to our adulthood. We plan to go over to Tillman Park for barbecue; Pat's told me she wants to stay home and that I should meet her afterward, but this isn't good enough: Pat's my woman and my woman does what I tell her to do. So on the way to Tillman Park, we stop by Pat's. She's not there.

Now I become enraged, crazy with anger. Where the hell could she be? She must be with some other guy. The gang cools me out, saying they're sure we'll hook up with her later and that we should just forget about it and go to Tillman. Thwarted, and half stupefied already by the liquor, I get in the car. We drive up the long hill to the park and descend down the brown, brush-filled slope, heading toward Wildcat Canyon, barbecue smell mixing with sharp eucalyptus. I'm downing another bottle of wine when suddenly I see a car passing by us: Pat's inside with a guy named Aaron Pointer, a local baseball star.

I go crazy. "Stop the car!" I yell. "There goes Pat!"

They're already past us, so we can't follow them. But I figure they're coming back and we park at the bottom of the road, blocking access, forcing them to stop. The liquor fires me up more and I prepare what I'll do when the car reappears, talking madness with the gang.

"Can't let no bitch two-time you."

"You goddamn right. Bitch says she's staying home, she'd better be home."

"Don't let no bitch treat you like that."

By the time Pat and Aaron drive back there's a crowd waiting for the showdown.

They halt and sit in the car, Pat staring at me. Aaron's cool; at any rate he's not going to mix in the middle of this lover's quarrel, especially with my buddies standing around.

Holding a wine bottle, I go over to the car. As I approach her I'm out of my mind. Not simply crazy, but not myself, someone else, taken over by the wine and my anger. I don't know what I'm going to do next. I'm walking toward this woman because I love her; but my heart beats with fury and I can't find the words to express the hurt and meanness I feel.

"Why the fuck are you   you know, you lied to me!"

"I didn't lie to you," Pat shoots back.

"You said you didn't know —"

"I said I'd probably stay home. Which was none of your business anyway." Amazingly Pat's as mad as I am, sticking her head out of the car, attacking me hard as the people gather around us, enjoying the confrontation. "I don't got to tell you everything I—"

I can't listen, can't hear her words. Humiliation builds up inside me along with my anger and frustration.

"Shut up!" I tell her.

"You don't tell me—"

Over at the Modulator, someone laughs. I lift the bottle.

"You told me—"

Her voice is high now, pitched at a defiant whine. "Whatever I told you, what I'm doing is not your business and—"

I have so much rage inside me that I'm afraid I'll kill her.

"If you're my woman—"

"I didn't say I was your woman, what I said was—"

I smash the glass against her head. Flat against her skull. Before I even know what I'm doing.

The glass explodes around us.

"David!" Gene jumps forward.

A switch turns off. A moment ago all I wanted was for her to stop. Now I'm mortified—more humiliated then before. Pat sits dazed. But there is no blood: a miracle has happened, the bottle breaking cleanly, the glass shattering without cutting her. In the stunned silence, Aaron revs the car, taking off. My guys surround me. I want to cry from gratefulness, shame, and fear—I have scared the hell out of myself—go down on my knees and beg her forgiveness, cry: I've never been this mad before, never cared for a woman (except Mother) as much, never tried to hurt someone whom I've cared for as much. But there's no possibility of this. Gene's in front of me.

"You all right, Doc? I didn't know you were going to go off on her. She's just a little doll, man."

I feel trapped, as I did with Minnie. I hate myself for my behavior. And I can see in the eyes of some of the guys deep disapproval of my violence. But that's the trick. Because the way they look at me also indicates that I'm special, capable of a kind of ferocity they could never manage, a violence and wrath they can't equal. My viciousness makes me a big shot, someone to deal with, the thing in me I despise adding to my reputation, which I enjoy.

So when I see Pat later that night I don't apologize. Instead I stifle my disgrace and fear at my own behavior and berate her, telling her she was responsible for my craziness by two-timing me and embarrassing me in front of my friends, making me look like a punk.

And another miracle happens. For some reason, in my tirade, Pat listens past my self-justification and hears another note: the note of love.

"Then that's when we started dating," she says. "After that we became a twosome. What do you call it? Puppy love. Yeah, it's puppy love."

Partly, of course, the liquor makes me crazy. But the wine isn't the only source of my violence. Everything that surrounds me encourages me to believe in the rule of force. The society at large glorifies violence, from Don Winslow Devil Dog chapter movies to the thuggish Oakland police who torture guys with impunity in the Alameda County Courthouse's twelfth-floor "hole." And in my immediate life, my family and friends confirm this brutal view of the world, victimizing themselves and their loved ones with physical force. In his drunkenness one New Year's Eve, Hershey, my sister Eleanora's husband, decides to test his mettle against the Hilliards.

"Be cool, Hershey," I say.

I'm not warning him about myself but Bojack and June and Arthur and Bud, all guys who will destroy Hershey. Especially Bojack. My little nephew has grown into a man who stands only five feet two but believes he can whip anyone, and I have come to understand that most of fighting is mental; you surrender your rationality to every instinct of hate and survival and you win.

"I'll bet you, Horse," says Bojack. (He calls everyone Horse.) "Horse, I can throw you if I get my hands on you! I don't care how big you are! I'll bet you!"

Bojack starts for him. I grab Bojack before he seizes Hershey and body-slams him to death.

But no good deed goes rewarded.

Hershey takes advantage of my intervention. "Come on," he threatens. "You punk-asses! I'll whip you—"

Bud walks up and smashes Hershey with a beer bottle.

Hershey staggers. "I'm gonna get you, David!" Hershey yells.

"Me! What did I do?" I yell. "I tried to *save* your life. Why are you talking to me?"

But Hershey's made up his mind. "I'm gonna get you!" he repeats, running out.

For weeks after I live in fear: Hershey's considerably bigger and older than me. Finally my mother asks what's the matter. I tell her my worries.

"Get the car," she tells June.

"Where we going?" I ask.

She doesn't answer; we drive down San Pablo to Burt's Pawn Shop, where she tells the man to give her a .22 pistol and a box of bullets.

"Here," she says and hands me the gun. "You put six bullets in it and when Hershey comes to do something to you, you shoot him with every one of them bullets in this gun!"

I hold the gun; the metal rests in my hand with a certain conviction. And I'm not going to argue with my mother. So I go with a buddy looking for Hershey. When Hershey sees me, he comes up. My buddy warns Hershey, telling him to go away. But Hershey won't listen. He's still bad. He walks to the car door. As he reaches for the handle, I put the gun in his face.

"My mother said that I got to shoot you with every one of these bullets," I say. "So if you want to die, you touch this door. Because I ain't gonna give this gun back because she bought it and told me to shoot you with it."

Hershey waits, measuring me. I hold the .22 with both hands, steadying the gun against the bottom of the window, my feet pressing hard on the floor.

I'm praying he goes and daring him in my mind to make a move: I will kill him dead.

He goes.

A little while later Pat tells me she's pregnant. This isn't like Minnie. I need Pat and love her; my experiences over the last year and my desire to be with her convince me I can take care of her, want to take care of her. I'm eager for the responsibility and about to tell Bud and the family what's happening, when we receive a call from the Juvenile Detention Center.

"I was waiting for you," remembers Pat.

The doorbell rang. I didn't even ask who it was and it was the police. They asked to see my mother and asked her was I the one that she wanted to take to Juvenile because I was pregnant again. She told them yes. So they picked me up and took me into Juvenile. They kept me there for three days. My father was mad. He always disagreed with Mommy and I used to manipulate the two of them. Tell him something Mommy had said and he'd answer, "Oh, don't listen to her." So now he raised a lot of hell with Mommy. "Don't worry about her," he said. "I make enough money." Meanwhile you were calling to speak with me and everything, and my mom didn't give you any information. She says she's giving me a choice: "Either you leave my house or you go back to jail," she says, "but I'm keeping Dennis."

Finally, I got a chance to call on the phone. I told you where I was. You and Bud came down and you said you wanted to marry me. I didn't expect that. Like my older sisters would have babies, but the men would never be around. And I just thought that's what happened, that's what it was all about: you get married or you raise your kid yourself. All I had wanted was somebody, a baby to be with me — and she had told me she was gonna take Dennis. But then along came you with a whole family of twelve. Now I didn't ever have to worry about being alone or without anyone to talk to. You filled up all the spots in my life.

"Look," I tell Bud. "You got to help me out. I want to get married but we've got to get her out of Juvenile."

Bud accompanies me to the Juvenile Detention Center, where we pick up Pat. Then I'm over to her mother's.

"Sweets," I say, "how could you do this to Pat? That you love so much? How could you lock her up?"

"Oh," she says, "Patricia's hardheaded."

"I love your daughter," I tell her.

"You do?" she asks.

"I want to marry her," I say.

"Well," she says, and I can see her easing up, "maybe she'll do what you say."

The next day I go to school for the last time and have my final confrontation with Mr. Ellsworth. "I know you're a bright young man," he says, lecturing me as I sit in the hard-backed chair. "Even the substitute teacher in Mr. Clark's English class could tell that after one period. If you attend classes you'll do better. You'll make something of yourself. So why don't you get it together?"

I get up. No need to listen to this anymore. I'm going to be a married man. I'm going to be a father. We're equals now. "I have other plans," I tell him. "I'm gonna get married and raise a family. Good-bye!"

And I stalk off.

A few days later we wait until the clerk calls our name in the Berkeley City Hall. The ceremony takes place inside a small room; when the perfunctory judge hears we don't have money for a honeymoon, he gives us two dollars and we go and have the largest hamburgers and milk shakes we can find. Pat stays with me at my family's house because her mother is still so angry with her. But our place is very crowded and Pat's father works on her mother, convincing her that things will work out for the better while fixing up an apartment for us downstairs. A few weeks after the marriage, we move into Pat's mother's house. Mr. Ellsworth could not have been more wrong, I think, bursting with pride. A kind of sweetness mellows me as I lie in bed in my new house. I feel I'm a man. My other partners are still on the corner. But I've got a house and a wife. My whole life is getting meaning. My dream is coming true.

Chapter

8

I go for jobs. I have no true skills—I have no idea where I fit in the work world—but I'm smart and personable and have a taste for style. I can convince people to take a chance on me. Besides my dream's a simple one: to wear a suit and tie to work.

Sug—Walter Grimes, a buddy I've grown up with in West Oakland—gives me my first break. He says Youth For Jobs—a CP (Communist Party) organization—is looking for a counselor. The job sounds promising. From school and the street corner I know I can influence people; plus, I'll be working in an office, wearing a suit, fulfilling a responsible position that has some power. I like the idea.

Sug invites me to a Friday-night recruiting meeting in Berkeley. That afternoon, when I tell my street-corner buddies I've got to go, Quack—a neighborhood legend, an older member of the infamous Earring Gang, who can kick his leg up six feet high—says he'll come along.

"It's not a party, Quack," I explain. "It's being given by the Party."

"I don't give a goddamn who's giving it as long as it's a party," says Quack.

"No, man," I try again. "Not like that. Not a party, but *the* Party. The Communist Party. The Party's an organization."

"I don't give a goddamn," says Quack. "Whatever kind of party they want to be is all right as long as there's dancing."

There's more politics than dancing at the gathering. Lots of whites fill the room, discussing the Freedom Rides. I don't share everyone's admiration for the demonstration — me and my buddies think these people are crazy to let themselves be brutalized. But I keep my opinions to myself: I enjoy the talk, and, besides, I'm here for a job, not a debate. And when Sug introduces me to a young white guy named Bill Proctor I get what I want: Proctor tells me the counselor position is filled but that he can help me secure a training position at the shipyard.

The next day I'm at the union hall. I sell myself hard, telling the guys I need a break and that I don't care if I start at the very bottom — I'll do anything, just give me a job.

I mean this sincerely; yet from the first day I abhor the work. My job description is "laborer" and I'm responsible for the plainest, meanest tasks: cleaning up after the skilled electricians, plumbers, and welders renovating the ship's hold. The work pays six dollars an hour and comes with medical benefits, but I hate the demanding, dirty drudgery. I push the wheelbarrow filled with plasterboard, nails, and tiles, thinking, I'm better than this, I don't deserve to be here. I've been up since six, throwing garbage around for the last two hours, and want a drink badly. I don't feel proud about earning money for Pat and myself; I resent the fact that this tiring, spiritless slaving is the only way I can make an income. I dump my load from the wheelbarrow into the vat and dust and noise surround me. I feel trapped, that time is passing me by; as I haul the wheelbarrow back to collect more junk, I see myself as an old man before my time, already all used up.

"Man, this is hard," I complain.

"That's all right," a welder tells me. "Hard work is good for you."

No it isn't, I think.

Besides, his answer misses the point. The work *isn't* hard. The work is *dumb*, demanding neither skill nor intelligence and earning not an iota of respect.

The frustration — a bitter, blind anger   builds in me.

I think of Ernest, an older buddy from the street corner. He lives in Acorn Village, old Army housing sites recycled by the city as a low-income project. Ernest doesn't work steadily. Instead he shuffles unemployment, welfare, and temporary work to make a living. But he has a roof over his head — he pays low rent — all the creature comforts you can want, including a stereo, color television, and car, and his freedom. Why shouldn't I live like him, rather than minding the clock?

Besides, work is supposed to let people know who you are. Is this what I am? Laborer? Picking up trash? Not in my mind. The thought that being a laborer is the best I can achieve infuriates me. But what else can I do? All around me I see people pursuing their lives, purposeful, respected, satisfied.

I want to be one of them. The idea that perhaps this vision of myself will remain only a dream, that I'll never find my connection as they've found theirs — that maybe there is no connection for me or that the only connection is clocking hours and getting drunk — terrifies me.

"Who wants to work anyway?" I declare later on the street corner where I go every afternoon, drinking with my buddies. Standing in front of the store, surrounded by my friends, downing the Bitter Motherfucker, checking out the street action, is the one time and place where I feel relaxed.

"That's right," Ernest says, like one of the deacons in the old Rockville church encouraging the minister to keep talking.

"Hard work is *not* good for you," I continue. Trashing work is a favorite pastime here. We confirm our mutual misery about making a living.

"That's true," agrees Ernest.

"I mean life has got to be simpler than getting up every morning and going to somebody's *job!*"

"Well, that's right," Ernest agrees.

"I don't care what anybody says. Hard work'll kill your ass just like it killed my grandfather." Which is a total lie.

"Why are we here?" asks Ernest, meaning the United States. "To work. That's why we were brought here. To work. We were brought here for slaves. Damn work. You know we're supposed to be free and all that."

I'm transferred to another job. Now I'm a chipper, working on the deck, attacking the floor with a tool whose blades break the tiles, cleaning off the paint. The job carries more status than laborer: it demands a degree of skill and comes with a tool. Yet I feel more trapped than ever before. My father had been a chipper once in Mobile, and every time I sink to my knees and face the endless tiles — more tiles than you can chip in a day, more tiles than you can clean in a week — a despair settles over me: I'm repeating my father's life. Besides, I hate kneeling down; when I kneel down my back goes sore and my joints stiffen. I look at the older men performing the positions I should be aspiring to — welders, electricians, painters. What do they have to show after twenty years of service? A watch?

Besides, all these hard workers are hypocrites. When the boss is there they work arduously; then the boss leaves and they stop. I just want to keep doing what I'm doing.

"Hurry up," they say, "the boss!"

"I don't care whether the boss is here or not," I answer. "I'm not gonna speed up because the boss is coming around. I'm working at my own pace. I refuse to work myself to death."

"Well that's the way we work here."

"Well maybe you should change the way you work," I say.

"Man, I've been working here for five years. I'm not gonna change now."

The idea is inconceivable. "Five years! How can you stay on the same job for five years? What kind of crazy stuff is that?"

The longshore work is temporary and the job periods are too short to permit me unemployment benefits. So I fill the rest of the time working at the huge canneries that hire during the harvest — Del Monte, Hunt's, the packing plants for the Valley of the Jolly Green Giant. We stand in front of the gates, waiting to be called, the straw bosses selecting the workers every morning, pulling the people they see regularly.

One day Huey comes with us, a rare treat. Since I've gotten married he and I spend less time together, our paths separated not by choice but necessity. I'm trying to work and hanging on the corner; Huey's in school and running around doing petty criminal activity. But he hasn't changed his brand of ironic humor.

"Name," they demand, as they let you through the gates.

"Manual Labor," Huey says, pronouncing the words as though they're Spanish, our little inside joke.

At the canneries I hear there are full-time positions at the Gerber baby food plant. I go and demand one, making a big stink until the dispatcher gives in.

"Okay, okay," he says, trying to shut me up. "We'll give you a job."

Next day I'm stacking baby-food boxes on ten- to twelve-foot-high pallets, arranging the cartons in a pattern that balances the weight and keeps the construction steady: ten across one way, tie the box, ten the other. The job's simple — I know it's simple. But I have a problem with patterns. I can't visualize shapes. (I fail those parts in tests, even now.) Plus, I become anxious, anticipating that I'll mess up the configuration. So I stack the boxes, keeping everything perfect until the last two or three rows. Then I make a mistake. When the forklift comes and scoops up the load, the boxes tumble off. I'm working with J.J., James Phillips, and he laughs at my error, joining the foreman. I don't find my failure humorous at all.

"Shut up, J.J.," I say.

"Hey, Doc, it isn't anything. I'm just laughing because you do it so well and then the last couple of rows you screw up."

"I know I screw up," I say.

"Well you can do it, Doc. You do it to the last couple of rows, so of course you can do it."

"Of course I can do it," I say.

After J.J.'s vote of confidence I swear I'll get the pattern right. I concentrate on arraying the boxes correctly. Pressure builds inside me as I near the top and success. Okay, I think, now this is where you screw up, so think hard. In my mind I plan out exactly what I must do, then I proceed.

I start to crown the stack with the last box; I even feel a little cocky — I've beaten the monster once and for all. Then I realize I've done it again! Somewhere I've screwed up. The boxes are still wrong.

I stand there, contemplating my flawed masterpiece, wanting to punch myself. I've got to fix the pattern. But getting the boxes right isn't easy; I have to rearrange lots of rows, an enormous amount of work. And the forklift driver is already coming up. I'm always under the gun to go faster because my problem with the patterns makes me slower.

Frustrated, confused, angry, I lie to myself. Don't say anything, I think. Maybe the boxes will work anyway.

The driver starts to lift and —

— the whole thing crumbles with a crash.

J.J. and the foreman stand there, laughing and shaking their heads.

"Goddamn!" I shout.

"What's the matter with you, Doc?" J.J. says.

"Put me at the end of the line," I say to the foreman. "I can't do this work."

Nice enough, the foreman obliges me. But my failure stays with me. I return to the boxes, trying them again, frustrating myself until I quit, just walk off the job. I go by the corner, drink some wine, and come home, telling Pat about the fiasco.

Bud doesn't understand my problems. He bothers me all the time. June has more sympathy.

"I came up during a time when I was indoctrinated by my father into the work ethic," June says.

But when you came along, that wasn't so. You were allowed to realize yourself, just go around and enjoy the leisure life, or do whatever you thought you wanted to get into and become a part of. You didn't have to go out and hold down a job to eat every day and have a place to stay; it wasn't necessary for you to have a job for the family to realize food on the table and a roof over their head and clothes on their back, because by the time you had a family we were all working.

So when you had this trouble with jobs you responded differently to it than I would. I would have just kept on working. But you — you would leave. The jobs were never interesting enough to make you stay. They were just jobs, nothing challenging there. You was always looking, searching for something bigger and better, something that you liked to do, something that allowed you to use your mind and skills and talent. Because just going and using your hands — manual stuff like that — you were never capable of for very long periods of time.

And there was one other thing. You were *given* to me, in a sense, and I was always looking after you. Now I had gone through a lot of hardship when I was young. I didn't have a bicycle. Everything I got of what you might call "luxury items," I had to buy and get for myself. And I wanted to make sure that *you* didn't have to go through that, make sure that if I was able to do that for you, that you would *have* those things. I didn't want you to *want* for the same things that I wanted for.

Pat is also very understanding.

"I don't think you really knew that most of the burden — the brunt — of a marriage was on the man, for the man to provide for the family," Pat says.

Plus it was very bad times for black men to work. I could see how hard it was — your father, a man fifty-six years old, making a dollar twenty-five an hour washing dishes. I looked at that and I knew the system wasn't very just as far as black men were concerned. I looked at my brothers and all my nephews and I could see they couldn't keep their jobs — if they got a good job, they might work three or four months and then be laid off. It's just like in history: black men had to get up and move from place to place to work and the woman was always the head of the family. My mother had made sure that I knew enough to be able to take care of myself. To be independent. She always said, "I don't want you to fall in love. You just have different boyfriends you go out with. Because black men always leave — for whatever reason it is."

By now we've already had two kids, Patrice and Darryl.

Patrice is perfect, made to order, a daughter, which is what we both want, with my color and Pat's fine, expressive features. Above all, she has all this hair — "the wild lady from Borneo," I call her with intense pride.

People think I name her after Patrice Lumumba, who's constantly in the news. But at the time I don't even know Lumumba. Then I see a photo of him. I'm impressed by his handsome, unusual appearance. He parts his hair stylishly and wears pince-nez glasses; even in the black-and-white dots of the tabloid his eyes shine with a deep intelligence and conviction and a rock-hard dignity that reminds me of the guy who stays with the Moolahs and strides down the street. To have your photo day after day in the newspaper and be so concentrated and sure of yourself: that's also something to aspire to. But Lumumba's not the inspiration for my daughter's name; I name her after Patrice Munsel, the singer, whose sweet voice I admire.

Trice goes with me everywhere. Everybody loves her because she's so pretty and petite. I take her in the stroller to the corner, where Ernest and the other guys buy her things; her bright eyes looking around, she stays with us as we drink and carouse until my sister comes and picks her up.

Darryl's born a little less than a year later. From the first he's in trouble: he has a hole in his heart. Without warning he turns blue, losing oxygen, and I must rush him to the hospital. So I keep an eye on him constantly.

The first time he gets an attack I run with him to the car.

"Goddamn, Darryl, breathe!" I sob as he gasps for air, his little body shaking spasmodically. I don't know what to do. A part of my mind thinks this nightmare will end and he will suddenly be all right. Another part sees him dying in my arms. I hug him to my body; then I become afraid I'll smother him and pull him away abruptly.

"Help my baby!" I yell, running into the hospital.

When they bring him back, Darryl's breathing regularly, his eyes staring at me under his fierce, thick, black Hilliard eyebrows; I thank God for the miracle and go back to the corner drinking.

A year later comes Dorion.

"He's never going to look older than this," Pat says, holding the baby, looking at his furrowed brow and shriveled skin.

"That's like the picture in the book. Let's call him Dorion, after Dorian Gray," I say.

And perhaps there is another reason. Dorion is an accident; some contraceptive foam Pat's got from Planned Parenthood didn't work. On top of my troubles with the jobs, the addition of a third child — with the eight dollars a week I'm now supposed to send Minnie for child support — seems overwhelming: I am becoming old before my time.

Meanwhile I try.

Try anything.

One day I'm a car salesman on San Pablo ready for big commissions and wearing a suit and tie. Except that you don't get paid until you make your sales. By the middle of the first afternoon I've had only two customers and not even a hint of promise for future money; I leave.

Another day I decide I'm as good-looking as these guys in *Jet* magazine; I'll become a model. I borrow a large cardboard Seagram's VO display from the liquor store where Pat works—a good job that helps keep our liquor costs down—and Bojack photographs me next to the poster, all duded up in a very classy suit I've bought especially for the occasion. We send the picture to a San Francisco modeling agency. They never answer.

Then there's ABCO Weatherproofing, located around the corner from our Magnolia Street house. I'm intrigued by the sign and the large truck always parked outside. Maybe there's something here?

One afternoon I present myself to the barrel-chested boss named Al.

"You work fast?" he demands, looking skeptical.

"I work tirelessly," I say because I'm sure I will devote myself if given a skill.

He asks me my name and thinks the matter over. His clothes smell from dried sweat.

"This is what I'll do, Hilliard," he announces. "You take care of the truck and clean up the tools and everything, and I'll train you as a weatherproofer."

I quickly agree. I'll have a skill. Delighted with pride, I go home to tell Pat, who's very excited by the news. You're going to stay with this job, she tells me, proud and encouraging.

The next morning I start. The present contract is at UC-Davis. I drive in the truck with Russ, an older guy who's Finnish; he has a half-moon of soft, mink-like hair that surrounds a shining, smooth skull and makes him look like a monk. He calmly tells me my responsibilities: after helping him erect the scaffold, I'll refill and bring him the caulking gun.

"You ever do this sort of work before?" he asks.

He reassures me when I tell him no. "You're a smart young man," he says. "You'll do fine."

It's fun working with Russ. He speaks in a soft, firm voice, explaining things very clearly, always letting me know whether I'm doing right or wrong, performing his own work with a tranquil competence.

Al, though, is another story. He always yells:

"Hilliard, goddammit, pick up the gun!"

"Hilliard, what the hell are you doing!"

"Hilliard, get the hell over here! I'm paying you to work!"

He hollers at me to mix the caulking compound faster, collect the tools faster, do everything faster, while calling me names and muttering under his breath. He's enraged at something and has made me his target, and I appreciate his attitude about as much as I do the stale smell of his unwashed shirts.

"He screams too much," I tell Russ while we drive home.

"He's an Italian," he says. "They're a very excitable people."

I enjoy talking to Russ. As we drive back and forth, we exchange stories. An ex-seaman, Russ listens to my frustrations.

"You seem to be a smart kid," he says, and suggests books for me to read, *The Varieties of Religious Experience* and a book called *The Mind Reaches Forth.*

The title catches my imagination. The mind reaches forth. I imagine a darkness into which I extend myself, my hand, arm, whole body, not fearfully as I might fumble in the darkness of the outhouse, but with purpose, calmly looking for the connection, the connection that will make me whole. I borrow the book from the library and try to follow the author's explanation of the principle of fight or flight in humans. Fight or flight, I think: that's my history with jobs.

That weekend Al tells me to take the truck home and clean it. I feel pretty proud: like my older brothers Allen and Jake, I have a truck of my own now.

June says he'll give me a hand, and Sunday morning I pick him up.

As we pull into my driveway I see Pat's back-talking to Al, who's already in a state. I get out of the truck and Al yells at me:

"Hilliard, what the hell are you doing driving the truck?" He pronounces my last name as though the syllables are dirt, spitting out the sounds and making them sound ugly.

"Hilliard, I didn't tell you to drive it," he says sticking his face directly into mine. "You're not supposed to drive, Hilliard. I told you to clean it."

"I was about to clean it," I start.

I see Pat with her arms around the kids. Trice looks worriedly at Al, her gorgeous hair flailing out from her head like an electrified halo.

"It's Sunday," he shouts. "What did you do yesterday, Hilliard?"

"I'm supposed to have the truck clean by—"

"You haven't done a goddamn thing. You're not supposed to be going to parties, Hilliard, you're supposed to do what I tell you to—"

He shouts at the top of his voice, crazy with rage, humiliating me.

"Daddy!" Trice cries.

I flip. I've never been scared physically of Al—I've whipped men twice his size; the only reason I've laid off him is that he pays my salary. Now I no longer care.

"You crazy son of a bitch!" I yell.

Al is surprised. He's never seen me angry.

"Get the hell out of here!" He's mistaken if he thinks he can make more noise than a Hilliard.

"David," Pat warns from the porch.

"Don't talk to me."

I'm past arguing with the guy. I charge into his truck. He wanted his truck, he'll get his truck.

"Hilliard," he screams, running after me. "What the hell are you doing?"

Jamming the key into the ignition, I blast the motor.

"You trying to threaten me?"

The fool stands his ground. I back up and start coming right at him, screaming through the window. "Who the fuck you think you are, insulting me in front of my family! I'll run you over!"

"David!" Pat screams.

Al beelines for his car. I drive after him, following him down Magnolia Street, yelling out the window:

"I'll kill your Italian ass! Nobody insults me in front of my wife and kids! Nobody!"

After that I give up on jobs altogether. I no longer need real reasons to quit; I make them up. I adopt and abandon jobs like I change clothes, shuffling things, like Ernest, working schemes on welfare and unemployment. One year Pat wins seven thousand dollars from a negligence suit. Later, when we have no money, Huey schools me in suing, and we set up false lawsuits, faking accidents, convincing the defendants to settle out of court for a couple of grand.

Each new scheme costs me another part of my self-respect. For several weeks I work a night job cleaning out meat barrels in a San Francisco packing plant. I start the job with the same false hopes as before: in time I will become a boning man and later perhaps a butcher. Meanwhile I rinse out and oil the large steel drums, line them with cellophane bags, and roll them outside so that the meat inspector will find a perfectly clean shop in the morning. My boss is another Italian, a Mr. Figoni, an affable, enthusiastic man who encourages and praises me. I promise myself not to drink on the job, but even so one night I lapse. Before I know it, I'm fantasizing that blacks from Hunter's Point will come and burglarize the place. All I really want is to get away and drink, but instead I use my fear as an excuse and drive away without having done my work. The next morning, Mr. Figoni calls, furious because his plant hasn't passed inspection for the day.

"You're fired," he tells me.

"You can't fire me," I tell him, trying to salvage my own dignity. "I quit!"

"You quit another job," Pat says. She's already come home from her work as a salesgirl at Irene Sergeant in downtown Oakland.

I just want to shut her up. I'm mad at myself, the job, her; the liquor swims through me. Suddenly hunger overwhelms me. I grab some chicken she's made, rip at the meat, eating it over the sink.

"Fuck that," I say. "I don't want to hear that shit, and I'm drunk anyway. Leave me alone and don't mess around if you don't want to get into a fight."

There's another reason for my anger: I'm cheating on Pat. I can't claim a specific cause to explain my wandering. I love Pat and have always loved her — she's the one thing that makes me feel complete, and I'm proud my street-corner buddies envy me my wife. But somewhere during the pregnancies I start to want more. I'm disappointed with my jobs, discouraged by my life. I want more and that includes more women, more experience. I'm twenty-one. Why can't I have what's available out there? If one's good, a hundred must be better. Besides, every guy I know has several women. I don't want Pat less, I tell myself, but something else more, some variety, some change.

Some change appears, a woman who I can tell is interested. Plus, I've heard guys saying she plays around. When the next occasion presents itself, I don't waver, but move with a kind of blind purposefulness, quelling my fear by jumping off the cliff. When I come home, back to Pat, I want her desperately, feeling an urgency in my desire that has been absent for a long time.

Everything becomes a justification for getting drunk. That fall of 1962, the world goes crazy with the Cuban missile crisis. We all watch Khrushchev on television lift a glass of water. "I toast you — I send you a boom!" we say. We certainly know what the gesture means: you toast fools with water. We like President Kennedy, identify with him, agree that America shouldn't be bullied by the Russians, and take a great pride in our nationalism. But at the same time we think nuclear war is imminent and our reaction is simple: we just might as well go and stock up and party because there's nothing we can do to stop the end of the world.

Drinking is no longer simply something I do, drinking is me, the only time when I feel right about the universe, free of frustration, free of torment. Sober, I'm confused about everything; drunk, I see things clearly. Sobriety, not alcohol, is the reason for things going wrong in my life. People's speeches about alcohol abuse are meaningless. They talk about drinking as though it's a sickness. Quite the contrary. The Moolahs and the *saditis,* who save their alcohol for one weekend a month, are the sick ones, the ones with something wrong, not us. I like being drunk. Being drunk is when I'm in control, better than the rest; being drunk is when *I* excel. I can drink more, faster, and hold my liquor better than a dozen other guys. Whatever original reasons I might have had for drinking are bypassed by now. I drink as someone else would work: because on the street corner with the bottle in my hand is where I make my connection to the world, where I fit in. This is my skill.

The final humiliation is with the best job of all. I become an inspector of bottles at the Fanta plant. Nothing to it. Just sit on a stool looking at bottles going by, make sure they don't contain any foreign particles. If you see something through the special illumination light, you toss the bottle into a big fifty-pound drum—just like we do on the corner. The job pays seven dollars an hour, and Pat's ecstatic when she hears about it. One lunchtime I go to the car to get the sandwich Pat has packed me, and instead of eating I drive to the liquor store. It's as though I haven't made the decision; the decision has taken control of me. I know I'm doing wrong, hurting myself, but drive anyway, cursing myself and the plant the whole way to Ernest's, where he meets me with a look of incredulity. Man, you've quit that job too! And I spend the night drinking with him, too ashamed to tell Pat.

The next afternoon I go to meet my girlfriend at a hamburger stand. As I'm picking her up Pat comes by. Later Pat and I have it out.

"Sex isn't love, Patricia," I tell her. At the moment, my heart swells with love for Pat. She herself is love; in her selflessness, honesty, and commitment, she personifies true love.

"That's not the way I see it," she says. "I love you one way and you love me another. I love you unconditionally. Anything you do is okay. That's what I have to do as long as I'm with you. But that's not true for you."

In my despair and anger I seek solutions. Between the alcohol and my blues I can't sleep at night. One day I tell an old high school friend who says she suffered from the same thing until a Japanese doctor gave her some pills.

"That's what I need," I tell her. "I need something so very bad. Because my life is just going to pieces. I don't know what's happening to me. I never had this much pressure in my life. I just feel completely overwhelmed."

I go to the doctor, who prescribes the pills. I take them happily, and they work well: now I sleep all the time.

"This is crazy," I tell Pat. "Now I can't do anything. At least when I'm on the booze I can do things."

Everything seems a lie. The only time I can relax from the scheming and the terrible anxiety that drives my lies is when I'm drunk. On weekends, sometimes we load up with nine or ten bottles of wine and get into the car to visit the family in Los Angeles, driving the long straight miles down the Valley, drinking, then partying for the weekend, sometimes buying weed or bottles of "red devils"—fender benders we call them, because they're downers and you'll nod out on them if you don't watch out—from the Chicanos in East Los Angeles and selling them up in Oakland.

Shortly after one trip, I come home to find Pat watching the television. Kennedy's been shot a week ago and a black man is speaking to Mike Wallace, pointing his finger at Wallace; he talks with such clarity, energy, and purpose that his finger seems a sword, cutting through Wallace's purposeful obfuscation. He wears thin glasses and speaks in a familiar steely voice, staring at the camera with piercing eyes. He's talking truth. Truth I've never heard before: in this society the victim is called the criminal and the criminal is turned into the victim. The man *uses* language, explaining his reality, taking words away from Wallace, and cool, unflappable Mike is fumbling, trying to meet the challenge.

I freeze.

"Pat," I say, "I know that guy. That's the Moolah. The guy who would come down Eighteenth Street."

"Shhh," she says. "Listen to him."

I lock on his face. He's saying what I'm thinking, but even before I frame the words in my mind, expressing his ideas with a tense, controlled authority.

Do it to him, Malcolm, I root him on silently, like I'm cheering a great hitter at the plate. You're making sense out of my years of frustration. You're giving me words. You're speaking the truth; you're matriculating me; you're connecting me; now I know where I'm going.

Chapter
9

OR do I?

I agree with Malcolm and the Muslims about America: a white man's heaven is a black man's hell. And Malcolm—with his razor sharp mind and wit—speaks my language. He's no *saditi;* he could easily hang on the corner with us. But I don't return to the mosque after my one visit, and stay away even after Malcolm's television appearance. For one thing, my street buddies won't go, and I like running with my partners. Plus, the Nation of Islam is a living contradiction for me. I respect their personal discipline, but like to drink, dress up, and party; I champion their militancy, but relish American culture. I don't want to opt out of America. I like America. I think and feel American. I don't have a problem if I want out of the society. My problem comes from wanting in.

I have equally divided feelings about the people who are fighting to be included.

I'm impressed by the oratorical ability of Martin Luther King—Martin Luther Cool, Chico calls him—and his precise, clever imagery: "We have come to cash a check and the system has returned it to us saying insufficient funds." I admire that. I envy his power to move and influence people. Listening to him, I recall the minister in the Mobile True Vine Baptist Church and experience the same excitement that overwhelmed me as a boy, loving the give-and-take of the sermon, answering him back, swept up in the crowd and the euphoria he manages to create.

But I completely disagree with him. First of all, he *is* a preacher and I've never overcome my contempt for our local ministers who would accept tithes from their poor, hard-working, spellbound congregations: they preached false glory, and King's no better. In fact, he's worse. There's not false glory, there's *no* glory in getting your brains beat out.

"Why don't these people fight back?" I ask Pat angrily as the Alabama police pursue the crowd stumbling off the Selma bridge. The passivity of the civil rights demonstrators contradicts my family's most fundamental belief: you don't stand idly by and be kicked, you fight for yourself.

"What is wrong with them to allow this to happen?" I ask. I am so incensed I want to cry.

At the same time, the idea of taking political action into my own hands is completely foreign to me. Local organizations made up of people working out of the unions and community organizers like Mark Comfort, who's been trying to mobilize West Oakland for some time, are trying to meld the militancy of the Muslims with the broader vision of the civil rights movement. But I have no experience with organizations, no faith in my own power.

Then the family member one would least expect to be political gets involved in a protest. Since settling in Los Angeles, Bojack hasn't had too good a time; he drinks a lot and suffers blackouts, often losing the two- or three-hundred-dollar southern California wreck that is his jalopy for the month.

"Bo," we say, "where's your car?"

"Well, I don't know," he answers, dazed. "I lost it."

The dialogue becomes a family joke.

Then, one afternoon—we're in the summer of 1965—we hear there's a riot in Watts, the center of the black community in Los Angeles. For the next few days I stay glued to the television, recognizing the street corners, liquor stores, beauty shops, and bars that have become a war zone. The images of troops marching down the avenues remind me of Don Winslow; but now it's guys like Bo, my little nephew, who are Devil Dogs tossing Molotov cocktails. I cheer them on, envying Bojack, a wild thrill rising in me. Burn! I think, glued to the chaos on the screen. Burn! This is what should happen! We should never accept our situation! Hate and fury flow through me. Before, such powerful feelings have always pulled me inward, making me clenched inside. Now my rage and contempt pour out, as though they're a song or a kind of exuberant, defiant love.

On the corner we talk about the riots, everybody saying the brothers are right to defend themselves. Fired by the example, I apply the lesson to an immediate problem, intimidating a store owner who threatens to repossess some furniture Pat and I have stopped making payments on.

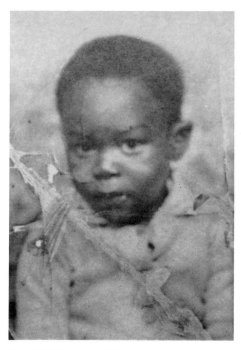

David's father, Lee Hilliard, in California

David Hilliard as a child

Bud Hilliard (*right*) and friend

David, age twenty

Pat Hilliard as a young woman

David and Pat

Stephen Shames

Dorion Hilliard

Darryl Hilliard

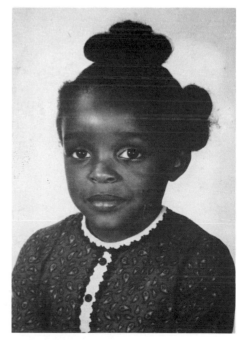

Patrice Hilliard

Brenda Presley and daughter Dassine

Left to right: June Hilliard, Lela Hilliard, Nathaniel Hilliard, and Betty Scott Hilliard at Vera Lee ("B.B.") Hilliard's funeral

"Listen," I say to him, liquored up and furious, "and you'd better listen carefully because I'm only gonna say this once: You bother me again about this furniture and we're gonna burn your store. So stay away from me."

Then the excitement of Watts fades. I realize my life still hasn't changed. And that's what I want, a different existence, a calling, something that removes me from my aimlessness, gives my days reason and purpose. Even working a good, new job on the docks that earns me weekly expenses in two or three days and provides me with the finest whiskeys and brandies money can buy, I remain deeply discontent. The next summer the Cleveland black community goes to war, guys my age seizing the Hough for two days. I stare in awe at pictures of them on television and in *Life* magazine. Their courage and defiance is monumental. What do you want? the radio interviewer asks them. More ammunition, they say. I start to read again, first the books Russ, the Finn, suggested, then others. Malcolm's *Autobiography* has recently come out. I buy the book and, for the next days, don't leave the house, don't drink, just lie on the bed, putting the words together, feeling I am not reading Malcolm's life but my own.

In the midst of this period, Huey starts coming over—he's recently served a short term in the Alameda County Jail, including a month in solitary, the notorious "hole"—drifting by at night, partying with me, June, and old high school friends, talking and drinking the cognac that the Japanese sailors sell cheap for American dollars.

One afternoon he announces he's putting together a new political organization and mentions Malcolm's name. I'm instantly excited.

"I got to be part of this stuff," I say. "You don't understand, Huey. I mean this is what I'm reading. What are you gonna do?"

"We're gonna defend ourselves," he answers. He refers to Malcolm again. "Malcolm talked about the right to defend ourselves by any means necessary—"

I interrupt him because the night before I read Malcolm on self-defense.

"Huey," I say, "this is amazing. I was just reading the man."

Huey smiles. "We're gonna be the personification of Malcolm X's dreams."

"I gotta be part of this," I say.

Huey tells me he's creating the organization with a brother named Bobby Seale, an aspiring stand-up comic whom Huey has done political organizing with at Merritt College. We drive over to Seale's mother's house, a rambling ranch house with a spotless living room, the couch and chairs sheltered inside clear plastic slipcovers.

In the back Huey introduces me to his new friends. He tells them about the old days, says I was one of the bravest fighters he's ever known. Then he shows me the guns: shotgun, revolver, a .45, one or two smaller pistols, an M1.

"But what are you going to do?" I ask. My head swims. I feel proud to be connected to Huey and his plan—things will definitely happen in Oakland now. But the guns scare as much as thrill me, and the whys, hows, and whats of the organization baffle me. I only know he's talking about an organization that will right some wrongs against black people.

"We're gonna organize the brothers," Huey says. "All these other organizations deal with students or the churches. We're gonna get the brothers and sisters off the block like you and me. Like Malcolm would have done."

I nod my head—what Huey says makes sense—and ask, "To do what?"

"Get power," Huey says. "True power is the ability to define a phenomenon and make it act in a desired manner. That's what none of the brothers have. None of us have it. And we have to band together to create it."

Bobby shows me the Ten Point Program. The document has two parts: What We Want and What We Believe.

What We Want: We want freedom. We want power to determine the destiny of our black community.

What We Believe: We believe that black people will not be free until we are able to determine our destiny.

What We Want: jobs, housing, education, an end to white businessmen ripping off the black community, an end to police brutality, trials by juries of our peers, freedom for all the brothers and sisters in jail, and finally a UN–sponsored plebiscite to determine whether we want to be part of America. (The final section in the What We Believe part is a quote from the opening of the American Declaration of Independence.)

"We call ourselves the Black Panther Party for Self-Defense," Huey says. He explains that the name originates from Lowndes County, Alabama, where Student Nonviolent Coordinating Committee (SNCC) organizers formed the first all-black party. "The nature of the panther is that he never attacks," explains Huey. "But if anyone attacks him or backs him into a corner, the panther comes up to wipe that aggressor or that attacker out, absolutely, resolutely, wholly, thoroughly, and completely." He tells me about the police patrols. Under California law a citizen can carry a loaded gun as long as the weapon is not concealed. Taking advantage of the law, the Panthers have been driving around armed with their guns and a law book. When they see an incident occurring between a cop and a brother they stop and make sure the officer follows the law. The cops have been totally furious and scared at the sight of blacks with guns, but so far the police have always backed down and there have been no shots fired.

Bobby straps on his over-the-shoulder holster, sets his beret at a perfect angle; Huey slings the bandolier over his chest and picks up his shotgun. Until this moment I've imagined Huey was talking abstractly — as though all this would happen someday in the future. Not now. Certainly not today.

"Where you going?" I ask them.

"On patrol," Huey says, getting into the car.

"To patrol the police?" I ask. Bobby lives on a quiet block lined with the usual stucco homes. I ask myself, Is this really happening? Here? Now?

"That's right," he says and closes the car door. And it becomes clear to me why he's not asking me to join them: Huey wants me to make up my own mind. He's giving me the choice.

"Power to the people, David," he says, and raises his clenched fist.

"Power to the people, Huey," I answer.

The next few days I am totally preoccupied. What am I going to do? Go with Huey or not?

Aware of what I'm thinking, Pat worries about my next move.

"Huey came by," she remembers.

I wouldn't even open the door for him. I knew he was into the civil rights movement and I knew what the problems were here in Oakland. But I had known Huey from before, in high school, and he was crazy. He was always very pretty, neat as a pin, and from his appearance you wouldn't think he would do what he did. But he was crazy. One time he got into a fight with some boys about his light skin. They got the better of him because they jumped him. But then he came back two weeks later with a hatchet and he got his revenge and had them jumping out of windows and stuff. So when he came around now I still had in the back of my head how he had protected himself then, and I was afraid he'd take you away — that you wouldn't be around me and the kids and would get involved in the movement.

June is also ambivalent about my working with the Party. "Man, you don't need to get into that," he says. "Just stick with your job."

I do, but I also make up my mind, telling Huey I want to go on patrol.

The next night we drive over to Bobby's. There, inside the car, Huey gives me the handgun. I'm really wired, not knowing what to expect. I've never backed down from a fight, but I don't relish confronting armed police at night in West Oakland.

"Let me carry the shotgun," I say. I want to overcome my fear and embarrassment that these other guys are more courageous than I.

"Actually," Huey answers, "I think I should carry the shotgun."

"You can trust me," I argue. "Like when we were young."

Enjoying the situation, his eyes shine, but he speaks with great authority. "I carry the shotgun. You carry this. Now let's go."

As I drive the car down the street I ask my next question—I have questions all the time now. "Now what should we do if the police stop us."

"If they stop us we have to defend ourselves," he explains.

"Oh," I say, looking down at the gun in my lap. In the back of my mind I still think that somehow Huey doesn't really mean his statement, that he's fronting—a lot of guys threaten to shoot cops and then let themselves be arrested. I don't blame them. I'm a realist. I don't expect them—and I don't expect Huey—actually to shoot it out with the police. He'll still command my respect. So I imagine his actual plan is for some talk, some compromises, a tit for tat in which they lower their guns and we lower ours.

The evening is an anticlimax, no confrontation with the police. But when I come home finally, the M1 in hand—Huey has given me the rifle to keep—I am utterly exhausted, completely wound up. I store the gun in the closet and Pat asks what I'm doing. I haven't even thought about asking her permission. Not out of disrespect; her opinion simply doesn't matter. My mind and heart have been captured. The Party—not another woman—has taken me away from her. For the first time since I can remember I no longer feel adrift.

During the next several weeks Huey and Bobby become local heroes from their standoffs with police. After the tense scenes, Huey comes by, sipping cognac and telling me incredible tales, talking a mile a minute, no different from the twelve-year-old kid with whom I used to walk to school, his head full of brilliant, mischievous, fascinating ideas.

But he's also a different Huey. I've been wrong. The Panther confrontations the last weeks have proved these guys are *not* like everybody else. They're not fronting. They're for real. They put on guns, load their ammunition, and don't back down when they find trouble.

And I ask myself, How do they do it?

Because I've never known anybody like that before.

But Huey I have known.

And yet, Huey is one of them.

And not just one of them—but their *leader*, the one they look up to.

And I know Huey and I've always been equal to Huey. In fact, when we were growing up Huey would come down to run with *us*.

So the past tells me I can join him. Huey's no superman; Huey's only Huey, the same person as ever, my friend, running partner, brother. And it's not Huey testing me, but a part of Huey inside myself, urging me, You can do this, David, meaning not just shoot at police, but—what scares me much more—take the intellectual and moral leap from the street corner into this world of action, ideas, and revolution.

"Why should I read it?" I challenge Huey. We're riding in the Volkswagen that belongs to LaVerne, his girlfriend. Huey's been going on about Castro, China, Aleister Crowley's *The Greatest Beast* all in the same breath, and now tells me I must study a book by an Algerian psychiatrist. "What's an Algerian psychiatrist gonna know about America?"

"Because he's talking about us. The wretched of the earth. That's what we are, David. The lumpen, the field niggers, the oppressed, the implacables. In Algeria the wretched of the earth threw out the French and created a revolutionary socialist society. Which is what we have to do here. So he has a lot to say to us. Revolutionary nationalists like us are not narrowly parochial, David."

We're driving down San Pablo, going to the Bos'un Locker, the bar where we hang out. The same sense of unreality and disbelief I've experienced before overcomes me, a kind of light-headed wooziness as I look at the familiar streets and people and see them in a new light: battlegrounds and revolutionaries.

"Huey," I say. "How do you know all these things? How'd you get so smart?"

"Reading," he says. "You can do it. I'll teach you. I'll tell you what to read. You can do it."

Maybe I can. One night Betty Shabazz, the widow of Malcolm X, comes to speak in San Francisco and the Party joins with another Bay Area group who also call themselves Panthers to serve as her bodyguard. I'm at work when the groups meet Betty Shabazz's plane, but when I attend her speech I hear there was a showdown at *Ramparts* magazine: Huey stood down the police, but the other group was fronting, with no ammunition in their guns, and would have been useless if a real shoot-out had occurred.

"They're not Panthers," I say and remember a phrase I've come across in Mao's Little Red Book. "They're paper panthers."

"That's right," Huey says. "That's good, David. Paper panthers."

I enjoy the moment. I've applied an idea to a situation—analyzed something. Maybe I have a gift for revolution after all.

*   *   *

I get Huey's book, *The Wretched of the Earth* by Frantz Fanon. I lie down, unconscious of my family's presence, my mind totally absorbed with the Party and politics, eager to absorb the lessons of what Huey calls "the black bible."

I open the yellow and black cover, struggle through the preface written by a Frenchman named Jean-Paul Sartre, and start reading the first chapter, "Concerning Violence."

"National liberation, national renaissance, the restoration of nationhood to the people, commonwealth: whatever may be the headings used or the new formula introduced, decolonization is always a violent phenomenon."

What?

I reread the paragraph.

I'm lost. I have the dictionary in one hand, the book in the other, and I can't get past the first page, can't get past the first paragraph, barely the first sentence. I might as well be reading a foreign language. Practically every word is unknown to me. I shuttle from the book to the dictionary, looking up these abstract, abstruse concepts—colonialism, decolonization, spontaneity, self-consciousness, tabula rasa, mutatis mutandis—figuring out the dictionary definition, then trying to apply the meaning to the sentence. By the time I've put one together, I've forgotten the previous two.

I close the book.

I feel as frustrated as when I'm on the job. Only this time ideas are falling down, not boxes of baby food, and I can't give up because Huey has told me this book will help enlighten me, and I trust Huey's opinions.

I skip ahead:

"You do not turn any society, however primitive it may be, upside down with such a program if you are not decided from the very beginning, that is to say from the actual formulation of that program, to overcome all the obstacles that you will come across in so doing."

Try another page:

"The natives' challenge to the colonial world is not a rational confrontation of points of view."

And one more:

"At times, this Manichaeism goes to its logical conclusion and dehumanizes the native, or to speak plainly it turns him into an animal."

That's it.

I drive over to Huey's house, furious at him for recommending this bedeviling book and at myself for not understanding it.

"Look, man," I say to Huey as he lies in bed—Huey always does a lot of his most important thinking in bed. "How the hell are we ever gonna educate people? *I* don't even know what's going on. I mean I read Malcolm X and I understood him, but I don't understand this at all! So how can I get other black people to understand it. They don't even understand *me* when I'm talking about Malcolm!"

"Let me tell you a story," Huey answers. He doesn't speak like a guru but in a fast, light voice, his words practically tripping over one another, his eyes darting, Geiger counters measuring his articulation and my comprehension; he's a brilliant, spellbinding chatterbox.

"Imagine people living in a cave. They've been there all their lives. At the end of the cave shines a light. Now one person among them knows the light is the sun. The rest are afraid of the light. They've lived in darkness and think the light is some kind of evil. Now let's say the person who knows about the light tells them it's not evil and tries to lead them out of the cave. They'll fight and probably overpower and maybe even kill him. Because all they know is darkness, and so quite logically they would be fearful of the light. So instead he has to gradually lead them toward the light. Well, it's the same with knowledge. Gradually you have to lead people toward an understanding of what's happening. So don't take this stuff all together. Just bit by bit understand it, and as you understand it you can give it to other people. Remember: One never drops a flowerpot on the head of the masses."

His words don't help me to understand Fanon, not one bit.

But the story does give me hope. Huey's right. I myself have been in the dark. But if I read and study the book, apply myself, struggle to understand the concepts, rather than just become frustrated by them, I will begin to understand what Fanon is saying. *The wretched of the earth*—that's not only the peasants Fanon talks about, but us, myself, J.J., Ernest, Chico.

Soon after, I attend one of the Party's political education classes. Bobby leads the session. He's talking about national culture, discussing dashikis, using the terms of colonizer and mother country, but speaking plainly so we can understand.

"We're nationalists," Bobby says, "because we see ourselves as a nation within a nation. But we're revolutionary nationalists. We don't see ourselves as a national unit for racist reasons but as a necessity for us to progress as human beings and live on the face of this earth. We don't fight racism with racism. We fight racism with solidarity. We don't fight exploitative capitalism with black capitalism. We fight capitalism with revolutionary socialism. All of us are laboring people—employed or unemployed, and our unity has got to be based on the practical necessities of life, liberty, and the pursuit of happiness. It's got to be based on the practical things like the survival of people and people's right to self-determination, to iron out their problems by themselves without the interference of the police or CIA or armed forces of the USA. We don't care about changing what we wear; we want power—later for what we wear. Dashikis don't free nobody and pork chops don't oppress nobody."

With their guns, the Panthers demonstrate in North Richmond against the police killing of a young brother named Denzil Dowell. Shortly afterward, I drive with Huey and Bobby to San Francisco; there we meet Eldridge Cleaver and other Panthers and put out a four-page mimeographed sheet with the headline "Why Was Denzil Dowell Killed?" That April a bill is introduced in the California legislature to ban people from carrying guns in public. Huey sees the possibility of a "colossal event." He decides to send Bobby and a delegation of thirty Panthers—twenty-four men and six women—right to the statehouse in Sacramento, loaded with guns and with a message to the people:

> America has historically reserved its most barbaric treatment for non-white people. . . . The enslavement of Black people at the very founding of this country, the genocide practiced on the America Indians and the confinement of the survivors on reservations, the savage lynching of thousands of Black men and women, the dropping of atomic bombs on Hiroshima and Nagasaki, and now the cowardly massacre of Vietnam all testify to the fact that toward people of color the racist power structure of America has but one policy: repression, genocide, terror, and the big stick.
>
> Black people have begged, prayed, petitioned and demonstrated, among other things, to get the racist power structure of America to right the wrongs which have historically been perpetrated against Black people. All of these efforts have been answered by more repression, deceit, and hypocrisy. As the aggression of the racist American government escalates in Vietnam, the police agencies of America escalate the repression of Black people through the ghettos of America. . . .
>
> The Black Panther Party for Self-Defense believes that the time has come for Black people to arm themselves against this terror before it is too late. . . . A people who have suffered so much for so long at the hands of a racist society must draw the line somewhere. We believe that the Black communities of America must rise up as one man to halt the progression of a trend that leads inevitably to their total destruction.

After carrying their guns into the State Assembly and reading Huey's message to reporters, the Panthers are arrested on a variety of trumped-up charges and put up on bail. To free them, Huey and I invest part of five hundred dollars he gets for speaking at San Francisco State—his first paid speaking engagement—in a pound of marijuana, breaking it down into "nickels" that we'll sell on the street.

As we're transporting the dope in the Volkswagen, a cop car drives by. I understand this could be a very, very bad situation because not only do we have the dope but we also have the guns in the car as usual.

"Hey, Huey," I say, "what are we supposed to do if the police stop us?"

Huey laughs. "We *shoot* them. You know, we fight."

Even with the preparation of the last several weeks, I am unprepared for the answer.

He goes on. "We don't give up our guns. We don't give up our dope. I mean, that's what I don't understand about these brothers. They get busted and they have guns with them, which is all the police have, but they give up their guns *and* their property. No. If the police come and mess around here, they've stopped the wrong car."

I look at him. Huey's completely serene, not scared or macho, just real clearheaded about the situation, certain of one thing: if the cops stop us, they are going to be the ones in trouble, not us.

The silence grows. I have to answer him. In my mind history has always happened differently, almost as though the events I read about were according to plan. What Huey and the rest of us are doing all seems much less organized, erratic. And I still doubt myself: Can we really be something of value? And yet Huey's knowledge and supreme self-confidence and my own excitement make the idea of turning back absolutely unacceptable.

"Okay," I say, watching the police car draw away in the rearview mirror. "Okay."

That fall of 1967, the students in the Bay Area organize a demonstration called Stop the Draft Week. For five days they try to shut down the Oakland recruiting station using nonviolent tactics. Neither Oakland nor the rest of the country has seen anything like these white kids—-mother country radicals, Huey calls them, adopting one of Fanon's terms—defying the laws and police, "shutting the mother down," as they say, making chaos be the cost of the war.

Throughout the week, Huey and I sell papers at the demonstration. I listen to people's speeches over loudspeakers and mikes and then refer to the subject I've just heard as I hawk the paper: "Buy *The Black Panther*! Our paper speaks to this issue and our program—"

And people respond. "Yeah? What's this?"

"We're the Panthers! Want to see? Buy the paper!"

I sell a hundred papers in thirty minutes. Huey—who has first sold Red Books with Bobby on the Berkeley campus to get money for the Party— says, "God, you can really sell papers!"

My days become fractured. Some mornings I work longshore. I wake at five, Bobby driving me to the San Francisco dispatch hall and back to Oakland once my number is assigned a job. Then he takes the car, going off on Party business while I work in the hold. We load rawhides onto pallets, crisscrossing the leathers to secure them on the platforms. I hate the work; flies teem around the still-bloody, rancid-smelling skins. Overhead the walking boss looks down into the hold, shouting orders at me. The smell, dark, and insects nauseate me; I'm back in the outhouse in my mother's backyard at Mobile, and I curse the man every time his shadow passes.

Some mornings I don't report at all. I let a member of my crew sign for me and meet them at the dock or have someone else altogether use my number. They show up for work and I collect the paycheck, splitting the money.

"You gotta get to work," June tells me, getting on my case one morning after I say I'm too tired for the shape-up. "You're gonna lose your job. You got a family to support."

I get angry with him, curse him out, saying he has a slave mentality and that he should free himself from the white man's world. But Huey has the same attitude.

"Keep the job, man," he says. "Besides, it's a good job. I gotta get me a job myself. My girlfriend is getting on me."

"I hate the job," I tell Huey.

We talk at his girlfriend's house. It's the afternoon. Huey's hung over from our drunk at the Bos'un Locker the night before. He's lying in bed, reading Fanon.

"We gotta figure out what to do, David," he says, planted on the bed. "Things are really not going well. What are we gonna do?"

Together we review the past and formulate plans for the future. We've got a tubful of weed we can sell to raise some money, plus June's buddies like to play poker and we can hold a poker party at my house, serving and charging for spaghetti and fried chicken and taking a percentage of the pot.

By now it's four or five and we're ready to roll; there's a Congress of Racial Equality (CORE) rally this afternoon that Huey thinks we should attend.

"We need to revive the spirit of the Party," Huey says as we cruise through West Oakland. "We need a colossal event."

"Well what are we gonna do?" I ask.

He doesn't know. We stop on Seventh Street and Huey notices a good-looking hooker holding a clipboard.

"What are you doing," Huey asks her.

"Studying sociology," she says.

Huey cracks up. "Well interview me," he jokes.

At the CORE rally Huey stands by the door debating with people. When it's over we drift down to the Bos'un Locker.

"This is how you organize," Huey tells me in the car. "This is what Castro did. You talk to people. You organize the peasants. And the people here are in the bars."

Gene McKinney and some other guys from the old days are already there. Huey asks for three zombies, stiff drinks, and bets he can down all three, one after the other. Now June and his buddies join us. June is skeptical and standoffish toward Huey, but he buys him a drink too because — even as critical as he is — he loves to loosen Huey's tongue and make him talk on revolution.

"Go on, Huey!" they encourage him. "Talk!"

By now Huey is well into it, discussing Marxism and the Russian Revolution. I listen to his fervid oratory, fascinated by his knowledge and brilliance. Huey raps on Soviets and communes, the Bolsheviks and Mensheviks. The foreign names and distant countries no longer intimidate me. Instead I'm excited by them. Once all these people and organizations were the same as Huey and Bobby and me.

"Huey," I say that night as we drive home, "I gotta learn about the Russian Revolution and Marxism."

"Go see *Doctor Zhivago*," he says.

"What?"

"It's a movie. Go see it. Then we can talk about it."

I have other questions, but it's late; besides, there are always others questions; every answer raises another question. I want to continue — I feel an urgent need to know everything because I also believe I have never learned anything before this; the entire world is opening up to my understanding; things always dark and impossible to fathom are now perfectly clear, perfectly comprehensible — but I've got to get to work the next morning.

The next morning I'm tired and the stench from the cowhides is nauseating. From the first moment, the walking boss is on me:

"Get a move on, Hilliard! Move your ass!"

I explode at his irritating barks. "I'm moving as fast as I want!" I shout back. The other workers check me out.

"Don't you be yelling at me! You got something to say you come down here and say it to my face! I'm sick and tired of you standing up there yelling down at me! What the hell do you think this is? A slave ship? I'm gonna move as fast as I please. I'm not a slave anymore. And if you think differently you'd best not be up there when I come up!"

That night June gets after me. Pat remembers the scene.

"We were in the car," Pat says.

June was saying, "Man, you don't need to get into that. Just stick with your job."

But with me it was like, whatever you did was all right. I didn't want you to join because I was scared of death. But you wanted to join. You felt a need for yourself. That this was your chance to do something.

I said, "You do whatever you want. I'll work and take care of the kids. Just make sure the kids are okay."

Chapter

10

OUR other Party business is going to Eldridge's house. Eldridge is a writer, a master of words, and Huey has appointed him editor of the paper and Minister of Information. "Huey identified with Eldridge because he had these abilities to be so captivating in his writings," says Emory Douglas, an artist who studies at City College and who designs and lays out *The Black Panther*. "Most of the time we worked on the paper, we'd sit in the kitchen while Eldridge and Huey would discuss what should be in the issue and how it should be organized."

Eldridge is unique in the Party. He's older—his coterie call him "Papa" affectionately. (Also, sometimes, "El Rage," or simply "Rage.") Plus, he's starting to be a celebrity in his own right. Imprisoned on rape charges for nine years, Eldridge wrote a letter about his case to Beverly Axelrod, a Bay Area lawyer. Beverly—who gets lots of such requests—was impressed by Eldridge's command of language. She proposed they initiate a campaign to gain his release on parole and convinced *Ramparts* magazine to publish essays that Eldridge originally sent her as letters. The essays attracted national attention. Soon Eldridge was released and became a full-time staff writer for *Ramparts*. (The essays are to be published in book form, and *Soul on Ice* will become a best-seller.) Now his work has given him impressive contacts and authority in the Bay Area radical community and a growing notoriety: his speeches are so powerful, so incendiary that the parole board has had the audacity to order him to submit everything he will say in advance for its approval. (Eldridge beats the board on its attempted censorship.)

Tall, with a long, guarded face, Eldridge is always peering, looking through dark glasses, speaking from behind a haze of cigarette smoke. His hands are easier to read than his eyes. He talks with them, shaving off this point, hammering that one home, turning his fingers and wrists into tools of debate and emphasis as he coolly explains to some reporter that we must resist the pigs and seize control of our community.

Eldridge's verbal ability awes me. He's not scared of saying anything. I listen to him give interviews and think: I want to speak this clearly, make my points so forcefully.

Eldridge doesn't only explain things with words; he uses words to win people over. One day I drive him to the College of the Pacific. A Bay Area school, the place is a nunnery. The whole audience wears habits and rosaries — I've never before been in the midst of so much virginal holiness — and before them all stands Eldridge, black pants, turtleneck, leather coat, beret, commanding, a convicted, self-confessed rapist!

"I'm going to liberate you," he starts. "I'm going to lead you in a chant."

I'm standing there, listening, not knowing any more than the nuns what's going to come next.

"Okay," Eldridge starts, reminding me of Ras the Exhorter in *Invisible Man.* "Now here's the first stanza. I'll say it and you repeat it: Fuck Ronald Reagan."

I'm maybe even more shocked than the nuns. But one or two of them actually echo his words. I can hear them in the auditorium: "Fuck Ronald Reagan."

Now Eldridge gets into it, urging them on: "Fuck Ronald Reagan! Fuck Ronald Reagan!"

And the nuns are revving themselves up too: "Fuck Ronald Reagan! Fuck Ronald Reagan!"

The scene's an exorcism. Eldridge has proven himself true. The nuns are free; they are laughing and clapping and repeating the chant, all because of Eldridge.

"Now," he says after they burst into spontaneous applause, "you're liberated in speech. You've freed yourself from your fathers because you were imprisoned in the speech of your fathers because the sins of the father are visited on the children. And now you're free of that. You're free with your speech."

When I relate the scene to Huey, I can't help exclaim over Eldridge's genius.

"He's Ali Baba," I say.

"Eldridge is the master of the word," Huey agrees. "But I'm the master of the gun."

                                    *   *   *

Eldridge gets a lot of press. His fearless utterances make him a favorite with
the reporters, and, with Bobby in jail — he's serving time for Sacramento —
he takes on the role of Party spokesperson.

Plus, a group gravitates around him. Kathleen, his wife, is an ex–SNCC
organizer and college graduate; she's easy to talk to and tells me stories
about organizing down south that educate me and make me feel I'm part of a
much larger thing. Emory Douglas is another comrade. Emory has brilliant,
handsome eyes and long, delicate fingers; but his looks can be deceiving:
he's an artist but also a warrior; growing up in Hunter's Point he was a gangbanger for a long time, spending a couple of years in juvenile homes. A
brother off the block, he goes regularly on police patrols and was arrested in
Sacramento.

And finally there's D.C., Donald Cox. He's also older, a San Franciscan
who makes a living as a professional photographer. D.C. is well-liked by all
the Party members. He wears herringbone jackets, sports wire-rimmed
glasses, and slings a camera around his neck. But his sophisticated charm is
only part of his character. He can also don the field jacket and combat boots
of the urban guerrilla. He has organized a cadre in San Francisco, and it's
public knowledge that his group has recently ambushed and killed a cop in
Hunter's Point. (Eldridge later coerces and convinces D.C. to issue a public
admission.) Huey expresses nothing but respect for D.C. and names him
Field Marshall. "D.C. brought home the lion's head," he tells me often. El
dridge's reaction is more ambivalent. When I see him with D.C., I suspect he
feels he's in D.C.'s shadow. The openness and warmth that I feel between
Huey and D.C., or even myself and D.C., isn't there.

This isn't unusual with Eldridge. I never feel close to him. No matter how
often I hang out in the kitchen listening intently to him and Huey rap, I feel
shut out by him, as though in his judgment I'm merely Huey's friend, not a
true member of the Party. But I can never speak to Eldridge about this because I'm too intimidated by him. Whenever I try to make some kind of personal contact — talk to him directly, one on one — he gets away from me. I
can't ever seem to find the man; instead he's obscure, wrapping himself in
mystery. Huey and Bobby and I grow up on the street, standing on the corner, rapping. But Eldridge seems forged by his experience in prison, where
you want to control people because you don't know whom you can trust. For
all of Huey's madness, one thing is always true about him: he loves knowledge, loves knowledge for its own sake. That's why he can go on for so
long. He loses himself in exploring things, trying to understand them. Not
Eldridge. Not that he isn't smart. But for him knowledge always means con-

trol. For Huey knowledge is a tool of power. For Eldridge knowledge is a tool of manipulation.

That Friday we have the poker party, selling dollar-a-plate gumbo and chile and taking ten percent of the action.

At around two in the morning Huey and Gene show up. After a while Huey gets bored. Suddenly he jumps up.

"I think I'll go find my sociology professor!" he says.

"What sociology professor?" asks Gene.

I explain to Gene about the hooker.

"Come on, Gene," Huey says. "I'm going out on Seventh Street and go to school!"

They leave.

Gene remembers the rest:

We had been there awhile, but gambling's never been my thing. My old man used to run a gambling house, but it never did interest me that much because you never really have an upper hand unless you cheat.

So Huey and I leave. We have a little weed in the car. But we aren't driving crazy. Huey especially don't drive crazy. He abides by the rules and regulations.

We don't see the cops. Maybe they might have been looking or waiting for us. They act like they don't know the car, but they must know the car because that's the car we used to go put the paper out with, so I'm sure they had the car on the police blotter.

They come from the back, tell us to stop. We stop. The lights are shining on us. The cop gets out of his car. He walks over to us.

"Well," he says, "we got the great Huey P. Newton."

I'm sitting there. It dawns on me they're trying to kill us — trying to kill Huey.

Then the cop says, "Give me your license."

Huey hands him the license and I say to myself, "Oh, shit! There's gonna be some shit!"

The cop tells Huey to get out of the car. Huey opens the door.

"Gene," he says, "stay here. Stay right here."

I don't argue because Huey calls the shots. He's in the lead. What he was going to do was up to him. But whatever way it went, hey! we were together. I'm in the car, waiting. They start walking back. All of a sudden I hear this shot —

BOOM!

Oh man! Huey's out there! I jump out of the car. I don't worry about anything—I don't worry about the weed or stuff. Huey's out there!

I run back towards the police car, going by my instincts, seeing about Huey.

Huey and one cop are entangled; the other cop is shooting. I grab Huey and he's hit. I think, "Hey! I got to get Huey out of here!" I start running across the street and I see a buddy of mine coming in his car and I flag him down and get Huey into the car and, boom! we shoot over to your house.

Downstairs, Huey lies in the car. He's holding his stomach, bleeding, fading in and out of consciousness, talking about how much he's burning. Slowly we ease him out of the car. When he straightens to walk—he won't be carried—he shrieks with pain.

We bring him upstairs—we're holding the party on the second floor of Pat's mom's house, the "music room"—and lay him on the couch.

Pat gets some towels and Huey wraps them around his hands; he presses his gloved fists to his stomach, stanching the bleeding.

I start organizing things to take him to the hospital, and we help him strip off his bloody shirt and jacket. But Huey has other ideas. He isn't here for help; he's here to die.

"We got to take you to the hospital," I argue.

"If you take me to the hospital, all they're gonna do is *kill* me," he says. "And if I go to jail, I'll go to the gas chamber."

"But I *can't* let you stay here and *die*," I say.

But this is Huey. He's adamant. He wants to die! That's why he's here! To die!

I don't know what to do. June is frantic. Then Huey passes out. I tell everybody to clear out; the cops might be tracing him here at this very moment. Gene and Pat leave, and June and I pick Huey up, carry him to the car, and drive to Kaiser Hospital.

It's early morning. We cruise by, checking out the scene. Nobody's at Emergency. No cops, no attendants. We drive up the ramp. I open the door.

"Come on, June! Let's get him *out* of here!"

Together we pull him out, lay him in front of the entrance, rush back into the car, blow the horn, and take off. Afraid of the police, we drive the streets, staying off the main avenue until we get as close to the bridge as possible. There's still no roadblock. I tell June to go into the exact-change lane, where he dumps the coins and takes off immediately. In the darkness the bridge seems to span out into nothing. We pass Yerba Buena and San Francisco comes up in the darkness, the downtown buildings popping up like a cutout in a children's book.

"Keep looking," June tells me when I don't turn for the police.

We get off at one of the downtown exits and take a roundabout approach to Eldridge's. He's up, waiting for us.

"What happened?" he says. Kathleen is in the kitchen with him; he's smoking and listens to what I say with an intense glare.

"Brother Huey's holding court in the street," he says after I tell him about the shoot-out. "He's taken the struggle to a higher level."

He's scrutinizing me, as though checking to see whether or not I'm telling the truth. Then he asks me where the clothes are. "We gotta get rid of them," he says. He's already thinking about the trial.

I haven't thought about this.

"You gotta get rid of them," says Eldridge again. Is it my imagination or is he daring me? He squints through the haze of cigarette smoke, a hard, skeptical look.

Getting rid of them means going back into Oakland. There's some real risk here. By now cops might have staked out the house. We've already heard reports that cops busted into Mr. Newton's house, looking for Huey. If they think I'm involved in the shooting they'll go for their guns at the first chance.

But the problem is, I know Eldridge is right. Certainly *he* can't go. And I don't want to send other Party members to my house. Eldridge's proposition makes sense.

And there's another reason I can't refuse him. In Eldridge's mind I hang out with the Party. But I'm still not a member. I haven't passed my initiation, my test of courage like Bobby or Emory, who have served on the patrols and were involved in the Sacramento confrontation. I'm still Huey's man, his running buddy, undeserving to be included on my own merits into the Party leadership. If I reject this invitation, I'll be shunned forever.

I tell him I'll go.

Before I leave, I call up the comrades. I give everyone the same message; tell them what's happened and that they should get over to Oakland tomorrow so we'll be on home ground if the police attack.

I go back to the kitchen. Eldridge gets off the phone with Beverly Axelrod and gives me the rest of my orders. I'm to go back, gather the clothes, get rid of them. It's imperative that the Party be out in force the next day, in the office, on the streets, dealing with the press and the people, not taking a defensive posture, but letting our friends and enemies both know that we're not going anywhere.

His words inspire me. Eldridge has a powerful, strange quality. Even though I share none of the intimacy or brotherly feeling I have for Huey with him, he makes me feel worthy; I want to be respected in his eyes.

"Now I see why Huey values you," he tells me. "Now I understand why you're his best friend."

We backtrack over the bridge. The sun starts to glow over the bay. Usually I'm driving with my buddies to get to the docks at this time; now I don't know what to expect. June is completely quiet and concentrated at the wheel. He hasn't said a negative word since Gene and Huey came in, even though he mainly disagrees with Huey.

We approach the tollbooth. I'm wary of a roadblock, but we coast through. Then we take back streets into West Oakland, heading toward Magnolia. At the house there are no cops, nothing. Pat has already washed down the linoleum and couch, getting rid of the stains. The clothes—beret and jacket, shirt—are in a bundle. I pick up the bloody shreds and go outside. In the back we have a big metal barrel, the kind we use to toss our empties into when I'm on the corner drinking Bitter Dog. I throw the clothes in, douse them with gasoline. June's in front, keeping a lookout for the police. Then I drop the match. They burst into flame, the fire turning orange when it touches the metal lip of the can. In a moment, the evidence is ash.

Later that morning, a picture of Huey appears on the front page. He's naked to the waist, arms splayed back over his head, as though he's being crucified, handcuffed to a gurney while an Oakland cop strides away. Officer Frey— the cop Gene found holding Huey—is dead and Huey is going to be indicted for the murder; he faces the death penalty.

I pick up Pat at the liquor store.

"I was still working at a liquor store," Pat recalls. "You said, 'You have to go home. Too much stuff happening now. Come on.'

"I said, 'I can't go home. The owner's not here.' His name was Buddy.

"So you said, 'Well, you better call him and see how fast he can get here. Because you have to go.'

"I locked up that man's store ahead of time and never went back."

That afternoon I meet with Eldridge. He tells me I must keep contact with the family because the family and Party must be together on all legal and political matters. Then he praises me again.

"We gotta give David a title," he says. He thinks for a moment, then finishes the initiation. Eldridge is always good with words. "You're the Captain of the National Headquarters now."

Afterward I meet with Melvin. He's already been to the hospital, but no one has let him see Huey. The report is bad. There are stories that Huey is being tortured and that one doctor sliced his arm, using the needle as an excuse. But at least he's survived; what Melvin worries about now is the coming trial.

"I was concerned about the trial and his life being taken in the gas chamber," he remembers. "I could see down the road—what it would be like to be *alive* at the time your brother goes into the gas chamber. So the thing was, What can we do in order to keep him—not to get him out of prison—but just to keep him out of the gas chamber? That was my priority. And I felt we were alone."

I tell him he's not alone. We're going to beat this thing together. Until this moment, I have rushed through the last day. The clarity and logic of everything that has happened has impelled me forward with no time or desire to look back. But now I take a moment's pause. I am in a fight for life now, but strangely what I feel is freedom and relief. I've become a member of the Party; the problems of my life—my restlessness, my sense of purposelessness—are resolved. I'm working, but not on a job: my life and job have joined. I'm dedicated to a serious, deadly serious, goal. I think of my daily responsibilities, and one by one they drift away; they're unimportant now in the face of this new, greater duty. Now no more hides, no more walking boss. Even the things that once seemed so crucial to me—my clothes and car, and the material things I worked for—become trivial, burdens rather than satisfactions.

We go off to see Huey's family. I walk into the old house where Huey and I used to spend so many hours; everything is the same as always except for Huey's absence. For a moment I imagine him there, smiling, walking into and out of the kitchen, checking out the pots and what's being cooked for dinner.

In the center of the room stands Mrs. Newton. She's perfectly calm, soft-spoken as always. I want to say something to break the tension. On the wall behind the couch is a painting of cranes in a marsh. I've always thought the picture was very beautiful and was powerfully impressed when Huey told me, a few years ago, that he had painted it for his mother. I mention this and Melvin and Mrs. Newton laugh:

"David, how could you be so gullible?" Melvin asks. "Huey didn't paint that. We got that at a furniture store."

"My baby told you that?" Mrs. Newton says, chuckling with us.

"Well, you know Huey," I say. "He tells me these things without a hint of deception."

Our mutual enjoyment of Huey brings us together, breaking any stiffness. The warmth of our laughter and memory still present, I take Mrs. Newton's hands in mine and make my pledge: "Don't worry, Mother. No one's gonna hurt Huey. We won't let them. We're gonna free Huey."

Part
TWO

Chapter

11

MEETINGS.
Endless meetings.
Meetings all day.
Meetings all night.
Meetings in Berkeley.
Meetings in Oakland.
Meetings in San Francisco.
Meetings with the legal staff.
Meetings with the defense committee.
Meetings with the Party.
Meetings to plan the next meetings.

Serving as liaison between all three groups—legal staff, defense committee, and Party—I go to almost all the meetings. *Plus,* we're running the Party from my house and Bobby's, using our telephones as contact numbers on leaflets and my living room as a counting office, Pat and volunteers totaling up the money from each day's contributions, stuffing dimes and quarters into paper containers they take to the bank. The shoot-out has definitely been a colossal event. Before, we were twelve to fifteen guys with no office, money, media outlets, or program. Now we—we, my new way of thinking, no longer I but we, the Party—have to turn away new members, don't have time to fulfill all the media requests for interviews, and "Free Huey!" is becoming a national slogan.

"Eldridge," Bobby and I say, "we've gotta have an office. We need a place for the paper and where we can tell people to meet."

With some of Eldridge's book money we rent a storefront a few blocks from where Huey and I grew up. Grove Street is wide, gray, shadeless, but inside we've got plenty of space and the location provides us with a real base of operations. We cover the window with posters, including Eldridge's favorite: a photo Eldridge took one night at Beverly's of Huey sitting in a wicker African chair, spear in one hand, gun in the other. The pose makes him look like an African prince. Huey hates the photograph. But the image is indubitably striking. We put it smack in the middle to let the cops know Huey and the Party are here to stay and we're not backing down. We're revolutionaries, we announce, armed with a program and philosophy as well as guns. We stand for self-determination; we fight to let individuals and people decide their own fates. Our principles put us squarely opposed to the police. Not because they are individually racist pigs — which, in fact, Officer Frey is well reputed to have been — but because of their function in society. Unjust, abusive, they exist to maintain poverty and ignorance by force; without the threat of their billy clubs and guns, people would rise up, challenge the oppressive conditions of their lives. The police mission isn't to serve and protect but to deny power to the people. This is true for all police in any poor community, we say, but especially for police in a black community because black people are different. We're a colony, a people with a distinct culture who are used for cheap labor. The only difference between us and, say, Algeria, is that we are inside the mother country. And the police have the same relation to us that the American Army does to Vietnam: they are a force of occupation which will stop at nothing to keep us under control.

I don't talk much at the meetings. I'm intimidated. I'm used to speaking among family gathered around the table, everybody saying their mind, arriving at a joint decision, or rapping on the street corner, expounding to Ernest or Gene. But these meetings lack that easiness. They're tense with misunderstanding. Half the time is spent arguing over tiny details. When should the rally start? Who should speak? In what order will people appear? Nothing is simple. You don't speak to the point and have done, but give a speech listing five, six, seven reasons for your opinion, a stupefying oratory that overwhelms me. These people know what they think about everything and are never at a loss for words.

Eldridge impresses me the most. First of all he's extremely astute politically. From the night Huey's shot, he assumes increasing control of the Party. Second to Bobby in title—Bobby is titular leader, Chairman Bobby, as he's now called—Eldridge puts together the parts of the Free Huey movement. The coalition includes everyone from city councilman Ron Dellums to ex-inmates like Bunchy Carter and Baby Dee, new recruits to the Party. The center of the movement is a working coalition between the Party and the new left, white Bay Area community. Largely because of Eldridge, the Peace and Freedom Party—a recently formed radical organization dedicated to electoral politics—adopts the demand to free Huey. The issue gives Peace and Freedom a focus and urgency the organization would otherwise lack; and Peace and Freedom offers us a base of support in the white community. Together the two groups form the first functional black-white alliance since the civil rights mobilizations in the early sixties.

Plus Eldridge inspires me on a personal level. More and more I see him as the embodiment of Malcolm. Not only in his ideas—which, of course, are an extension of Malcolm's thought, translating his theories into practice—but in the way he conducts his life and what he has made of himself. Malcolm spoke of himself as an autodidact, and there's no one more self-taught than Eldridge. He was left to destroy himself in a prison cage. Instead he has mastered language and made the entire society listen to him.

At the same time there's an element in Eldridge that remains inaccessible, sometimes simply private, sometimes unsettling and suspicious. Even though he's increasingly involved with daily Party work he remains aloof, unsharing. My admiration for him, my complete respect for his powers and mastery, make me want to learn from him. Yet he rebuffs every attempt to reach him.

One night I accompany him to a fund-raiser; Honkies for Huey, they call themselves. I'm looking forward to the evening: I've come to really appreciate hearing the man. No matter how often I listen to him, he always invents something new and different, coining phrases at the drop of a hat—"Free Huey or the sky's the limit!" "You're either part of the problem or part of the solution!" Like a great jazz player, he spins off one idea after the next, coming out with a seemingly endless drift of talk, all of which makes perfect sense when you think about it.

That night his address is particularly brilliant. He's not a corruptor, as with the nuns, but more like Huey, breaking down ideas, not talking trash— murder-mouthing—but constructing an airtight, practical case for revolution. His words are straightforward, passionate, controlled; his organization of ideas is impeccable. I listen spellbound. The man may be addressing Berkeley lawyers and teachers, but he is explaining to me the change in my own life. I'm exhilarated to be his protégé, flushed with pride to belong to the Panthers. Throughout the question-and-answer period, I anticipate being alone with him so I can tell him the power of his performance.

Finally we finish shaking hands and passing out sign-up sheets—people are eager to come by the office, commit themselves to odd jobs.

"You fired me up, Eldridge," I say when we're outside.

Eldridge gets behind the wheel; he likes to drive, and we've spent a lot of time in the last few weeks cruising around the Bay Area, attending functions and speaking engagements.

"Teach me how to speak like that," I say. "I want to represent the Party like that."

I expect him to welcome my high praise with encouragement: "Yeah, okay, David. I'll teach you to speak like that. That's exactly what I'm gonna do."

Instead he says, "Uh-huh."

Just like that. "Uh-huh."

Acknowledging my remark but not reacting to it. Never breaking his cool.

I wait for a moment; maybe something more is coming. But Eldridge has spoken.

Frustrated, disappointed, I talk to Melvin about the incident. It's a few days later and we're hanging out around Seventh Street, right where Huey was shot, doing our nightly stakeout for two prostitutes who my street sources say witnessed the shooting and might be able to provide vital defense testimony. "The Bulldog Drummond Detective Agency," Melvin calls us, singing the words of a popular song by the Coasters, "Been Searching," as we drive out every night—

> *Gonna find her!*
> *Gonna find her!*
> *Been searching every which way*
> *And like Bulldog Drummond*
> *I'm gonna bring her home one day*

"He's distant," Melvin says after I explain my frustration with Eldridge.

Melvin looks off, as though he's receiving the ideas from some invisible source. (Although Huey speaks at a rapid-fire pace, and Melvin slowly, both love to talk, continuing conversations long after you want to leave; talking is their truest form of personal contact.) "He's a writer," he finishes. "Even when you're working with him you don't feel especially close to him."

Still my words bear some fruit. A week or so later, Eldridge says he thinks we should have a political education class. This way, he explains, he'll be able to disseminate his ideas to the cadre. He tells us to read *Beyond the Melting Pot,* a study of the struggles of different ethnic groups to achieve power. We start going through the history of the Molly McGuires and the Mafia; the sons of these rebels and gangsters are now politicians like California Governor Ronald Reagan and San Francisco Mayor Alioto, who call us thugs and racists. Suddenly Eldridge goes off on a tangent about *Moby-Dick.* He waxes poetical about Captain Ahab's obsession, explaining that it's not the size or strength of the whale but Moby-Dick's *whiteness* that lures Ahab to his doom: Moby-Dick symbolizes the power of racism, Eldridge says.

I'm mystified by the comment. Eldridge is speaking a language I don't understand, like my old music teacher back in Hoover Junior High talking about Mozart and Vienna and *"Stille Nacht."* His comment is the sort of thing Huey might say, psychological, philosophical, provoking me to know more. Forgetting whom I'm dealing with, I meet Eldridge after the class.

"Eldridge, what did you mean about the whiteness of the whale?"

Eldridge stares blankly, looking through, not at, me.

Uncomfortable with the silence, I go on, trying to explain myself. "How can you compare a book with a society? I need to understand these comparisons. To have your analytic ability."

I'm anticipating a Huey-like reaction, expecting Eldridge to welcome my interest.

"Read more," he says, ready to go. "Read more and keep coming to the PE class."

I try one more time. "That's not what I mean, Eldridge," I say. "I don't want to repeat what you're saying. I want to put my own ideas into words like yours. You got to teach me, man. You got to teach us. Teach us how to do this stuff!"

Eldridge goes back into his blank stare. "Okay. I'll give another PE class."

I keep a low profile in meetings because I'm unsure of my own opinions. There's a big debate about who should defend Huey, for example. Since the morning after the shooting, the phone rings nonstop with lawyers wanting the job. My pick is John George, a black Oakland attorney who has already represented Huey and other Party members in court and with whom Huey and I have often hung at the Bos'un Locker, drinking and talking. I assume he'll be the best person for the job.

But Eldridge argues Huey should be defended by a San Francisco attorney named Charles Garry. Garry has the influence and staff, Eldridge says, and the expertise: he has saved fourteen death-row prisoners from execution. ("I'm a better lawyer than Perry Mason," Garry is reputed to have said. "Mason's clients were always innocent.") Plus, Garry has the right politics; recently he defended a radical identified with the Communist Party.

Eldridge prevails upon Melvin to interview Garry. We go together. I'm immediately impressed. The son of Armenian immigrants, Garry grew up on the streets like us. He's a natty dresser — he sports a sharp, tailored look — and he's relentless, charming, tough, resourceful, a guy whom the judges have to listen to. And he's honest.

"Garry said the case would take at least three years, and cost a hundred thousand dollars," Melvin remembers.

"We said, 'We don't have any money. But we'll raise the money. Will you take the case, Mr. Garry?'

"He said, 'Of course.'

"And that was that."

The only thing left is for Garry to meet Huey. He goes to the jail the next day.

"Charlie just fell hook, line, and sinker," remembers Alex Hoffmann, a lawyer who is to work on the case. "I mean Charlie tends to fall for his clients, mind you. Even when they are Mafia types. And Charlie was left, but Charlie is anything but an intellectual. He's very much self-educated. Really working-class. Worked in a tailor shop and worked his way through night law school. And he was just totally enchanted by Huey."

And Garry isn't the only white we're working with. From the day after the shooting, two groups offer their support: Bay Area radicals — hippies, anarchists, the white new left — and the Communist Party. (Later, detractors of the Panthers criticize this support, claiming white allegiance, rather than our appeal to the black community, causes the Party's rapid growth. The charge is insulting and stupid: our four-thousand-strong black membership, not our white supporters, was responsible for the attention we received. It's ironic that commentators who desire a black-white alliance criticize the one black organization with the self-assurance to advocate that ideology.)

The Communist Party contacts Melvin through William Patterson, an historic figure who helped organize the Scottsboro Boys' defense and, in the Eisenhower fifties, charged the American government with genocide against black Americans. Patterson happens to be in Oakland when Huey's shot and meets Melvin through a mutual friend. Drawing on his experience, Patterson explains to Melvin the need to create a defense committee that can operate separately from the Party, raise legal defense funds, and propagandize about the trial. "He wanted my mother to go on a world tour, which would have been sponsored by the Communist Party, to carry Huey's story to the United States and Eastern and Western Europe," Melvin says. "He said he realized she wasn't young and that she could have a traveling companion—one of her daughters—and that she'd be well taken care of, particularly in Eastern Europe, where there were solariums. I wanted her to do it, but my mother didn't cooperate. She was a very provincial person."

Patterson is one thing. His dedication to political radicalism may be a little outside my immediate experience; still, I'm a southern boy and am sure he merits respect: no one can have put themselves on the line and lived as long as he has without knowing something. The other group—the white left—is another. Eldridge guides me through the maze of obscurely named and initialed parties, coalitions, communes, and affinity groups. Hippies, new- and old-left ideologues, intellectuals, they are a wonder. For one, they can't agree about any but the most basic things, applying and fighting over obscure doctrines. Plus, they're uptight—even when trying to be loose. They are always figuring out *how* to live their lives as revolutionaries, never doing it. Yet their commitment is unquestionably genuine. Complete strangers, they present themselves as comrades to the organization, helping at the office, turning up at rallies, pledging money.

Alex Hoffmann is one of them. Superficially, there's nothing similar between him and us. He's older, European—he's from Vienna itself, land of "*Stille Nacht,*" the son of left, Jewish refugees who escaped Hitler in 1938—and he's gay, though not actively at the time. Yet we become brothers.

"I had met Eldridge once at Beverly's," he remembers.

Then he invited me to a party to organize a support group called Honkies for Huey. It was this big house on Ashby Avenue and it was mainly white folks. Not only was the organization calling itself Honkies for Huey, with buttons saying "Honkies for Huey," but there was this presentation made, and there were questions from the audience, and someone started his saying, "How do you think we honkies can help?"

Well, one of you answered with a straight face, talking about what people could do, and I just thought, "My God, these are wonderful people that can sit here with a straight face!"

Alex serves as our liaison with Huey.

"Huey was totally isolated," he explains. "It was important that he be allowed to express himself and interact instead of going crazy in a jail with nobody to talk to. Plus, he had to be kept up-to-date in what was going on in the Party and being published in the Party paper, which proved to be very important, because [state prosecutor] Lowell Jensen in his cross-examination kept using stuff printed in *The Black Panther*."

Charlie can't visit Huey daily—he works in San Francisco and has constant court appearances—so Beverly Axelrod picks up the slack: she has proven herself a staunch friend and Huey trusts her. But a problem arises. Beverly and Eldridge have been lovers; when they break up, they fall out with each other.

"Eldridge had decided that for political reasons he shouldn't be involved with a white woman," remembers Alex,

even though Beverly was, with a tan, slightly darker than Kathleen. Beverly told Huey. Well, if that's the only problem, Huey decided, I'll issue a proclamation. And Proclamation Number One was: Beverly Axelrod is black. Then when Huey was in jail and there was a lot of communication it became very inconvenient for Beverly to serve as an intermediary to Eldridge.

One day Eldridge called me from Charlie's office and said, "Huey's been thrown in the hole and Charlie doesn't have time to go over there. Can you go down?"

I said, "Yeah sure." Shortly thereafter Eldridge told me Huey had requested I come and see him more often.

My other favorites are Stew Albert and Judy Gumbo—Eldridge has given her the last name (her real one is Clavier) because the two of them are a couple and make up Gumbo Stew. Stew and Judy belong to the Red Mountain Tribe, a collective that edits the *Berkeley Tribe* newspaper. (And not to be confused with the Red Family, another commune.) Stew is a mainstay of the Berkeley left, a lieutenant and adviser to many public leaders. Eldridge has met him through Beverly, and Stew has introduced Jerry Rubin and Abbie Hoffman, the organizers of the Yippies (Youth International Party), to the Party. Eldridge and I often hang out at Stew and Judy's house, drinking red wine and smoking weed. Simultaneously, Stew and Judy combine the best of the two sides of the white left, countercultural and ideological, and their temperaments are in synch with mine: not as intense and driven as Jerry Rubin and with a richer sense of humor than Tom Hayden of SDS (Students for a Democratic Society). They're a Mutt and Jeff team. Judy's short, wiry-haired, passionate, clever. Stew is huge, barrel-chested, crowned with long, curly golden hair, a hippie mountain man from Brooklyn. With Judy, everything is double time. With Stew everything is glacial. When he speaks, his New York drawl lingers so long over each word that I wonder whether he's going to lose track of his thought. But the torpor masks a smart, funny guy.

One evening Eldridge talks about the Party's problems with the "jackanapes," brothers who joined the Party early on and whose only interest is shooting police. Their uncontrollable, mad antics risk trouble for the Party. But Eldridge insists we protect them, saying they have a good value: they'll be the fighters on the first day of the revolution.

Stew listens to Eldridge talk about the latest problem caused by the jackanapes. He attends to Eldridge's rhetoric with a puzzled, thoughtful expression, occasionally pulling on his blond beard. Finally he interrupts with one of his painfully word-by-word-put-together sentences.

"Ummm, these brothers...ummm...seem to be...ummm...card-carrying members in the...ummm...stupid revolution," he says.

"I like that," I say. "That's good."

"Yeah," Stew says, delighted by my approval. "There's the black revolution and the student revolution and the stupid revolution."

Problems crop up between us and the hippies. For one thing, they look odd.

"Man, what is that?" Charles Bursey, a new member, asks when a hippie traipses into the Grove Street office. "Look at the dirty motherfucking hippie."

I know what's bothering Charles. Clothes and looks reflect who you are; with their stringy arms and pasty faces these long-haired, bell-bottomed, tie-dyed flakes stoned on acid or weed seem to have no self-respect.

"That's Mike Delacour," I say. "He's got the bus. We're gonna go out with him."

"What bus?"

I point out the window. A full-sized, psychedelically orange-, blue-, and green-painted bus waits outside the office, sides plastered with Free Huey! signs and posters.

I explain Eldridge's idea: Delacour will drive us around the East Bay while we propagandize about the trial through loudspeakers attached to the luggage rack.

"You're gonna go in that?" Charles asks. He's both joking and serious, pretending shock for comic effect.

"Yeah. It's colorful. It'll attract a lot of attention."

Charles looks like I just said we should shake hands with the police. "I ain't working with that motherfucker. Damn these crazy motherfuckers."

Li'l Bobby Hutton comes up. Bobby's sixteen years old and is an original member of the Party. "What're you talking about?" he tells Charles. "They're all right with me. They got good smoke. They got good weed."

I meet Kathleen and Emory at the bus, outlining our route to Kathleen, showing her the streets where we'll get a warm welcome. But I'm also apprehensive. I've never spoken through mikes before; the speakers are going to blare our message everywhere. I'm not even sure what to say.

"Say this," Kathleen tells me and hands me a piece of paper: "Free Huey! Can a black man get a fair trial in America—even if he was defending his life against a white policeman?"

I pick up the mike. Delacour waits in the driver's seat, ready to go, hair pouring over his ears. We'll cruise West Oakland first, our base of support. The importance of our task impresses me. We're about to embark on a lofty mission, and I concentrate on the paper, anxious to say the phrase right.

The door closes and I start.

"Free Huey!"

My voice booms down San Pablo.

I read the next words:

"Can a black man get a fair trial in America—even if he was defending his life against a white policeman?"

We cruise San Pablo, Market, and Grove, saturating Oakland and Berkeley with our cry. The bus is making everyone aware they'll have to deal with Huey. People gather to watch us, lots of them applauding and cheering: "Right on! That's about Huey! Right on!"

Kathleen suggests we stop at a busy corner. I hit the street with copies of the newspaper and a sheaf of flyers announcing the next rally. Instantly I'm swamped, people demanding details. I hand out the leaflets.

"Hey," I tell them, "you know what's happening with Huey. You heard it on the news. What do you think about it?" Not preaching, but talking like a friend. "We're having a class you guys ought to show up at. Talk about Huey. This guy, Eldridge Cleaver, is gonna be there. Why don't you just come down there and see what's happening?"

My worry vanishes. I am free and confident. I explain the trial and Panther philosophy. The phrases come more easily than when I'm standing up in a meeting. I may sometimes start slow, stumbling toward my subject, but I gain ground and speed and end up charging forward to make my point, sensing the change as I find the right words, my body straightening, my voice gaining energy and clarity. I love the give-and-take, feel like I'm back on the street corner talking to my buddies, hanging out. Huey's right. This is the stuff revolution is made of. Just like they did it in Cuba: speaking to people, hearing what they think, getting them to question their assumptions, telling them your ideas. When we return to the bus we have a new enthusiasm: we're reaching people. Plus, I realize something else. I'm good at this stuff.

"David," Kathleen says as we step back on board. "You're a natural. You remind me of the brothers down south. You can really teach."

The incident teaches me something else: the paper's importance. Huey has always stressed the significance of *The Black Panther.* From my experience on the docks and at Stop the Draft Week I'm well aware of the paper's function not only to inform but to organize: "Hey, brother," I say, flashing a copy in a stranger's face, "read *The Black Panther.* Find out what's really going on in this country. Open up your mind! Stop being one of the living dead. See what's really happening." If the brother takes the copy, I've made a potential convert; if he refuses, we get into a conversation that lures other people and ends in a general verbal free-for-all that's probably the most exciting event on the block in the last ten years.

But now the paper's existence becomes crucial to the daily work of the Party. Free Huey gives us a practical goal; putting out the paper — gathering the articles, laying out the pages, printing and distributing the final copies — gives us a practical task. In short time, the paper becomes the most visible, most constant symbol of the Party, its front page a familiar sight at every demonstration and in every storefront-window organizing project throughout the country.

Each week we follow the same formula. Front page — a thick color border anchored by a picture of Huey, beret cocked to the side, the shadows lining his face making him look handsome and defiant. Inside back pages — the Rules of the Party (Number One: "No member can have any narcotic or weed on his person while doing Party business") opposite the Ten Point Program, always printed underneath a photo of Huey with a bandolier slung over his chest and a pump shotgun cradled in his arms. Between the two — reports on the trial, news stories from community people, essays by Eldridge, poems and thoughts written by cadre, and messages of support for Huey.

And cartoons.

The cartoons are the favorites. Emory draws them. He uses three styles — lyrical woodcutting-like allegorical pictures of families and children, grittier etchings of brothers and sisters off the block, their dark gray and ebony faces in contrast to the vivid white of their guns and bullets, and, finally, real cartoons, funny, mean-spirited drawings depicting cops as pigs running away from the righteous, armed anger of the people.

"I was hanging around Eldridge at the time," Emory remembers of these early days.

They had already put out the first newspaper. It was just a mimeographed thing, stapled together. Now they were going to put out the second. Bobby had the stuff laid out on the table, and he was talking about how he was gonna do it. I had been doing flyers for cultural events and stuff. So I brought in my Instant-type and stuff and gave them suggestions and my materials. He was impressed and pleased that I would do that and *share* that information. They asked me, "Brother, why don't you come around and help us."

Now I had no basis for understanding what the Party would be about. I didn't know what they *meant* when they talked about cultural nationalism, which they were opposed to, or revolution. But I wanted to be part of it. I said I wanted to join. They said, "You're a Party member." Huey said I would be the Minister of Culture eventually in the Party, and that we would develop the whole area.

I started coming to meetings and what have you. It wasn't like they just gave you a gun and you went out into the streets and became part of these patrols. You had to understand what you were dealing with in these weapons. We had to be able to break them down, clean them; you had to have that basic, fundamental training before you even did anything.

Then we started going on patrols as observers. We went to Richmond and community rallies. It was impressive, because at the time you had all these killings that were going on of young blacks for so-called robberies, and they were shot down in the back and so-called preachers were standing up and not doing anything but getting out of the pulpit to come down and calm down the community. But the Party was confronting police with guns and constitutional law, and telling the brothers that they didn't have to answer any question but to give their name, address, and their phone number. So I was glad and proud to be a part of an organization that was standing up to that!

Anyway, one day Huey got an idea about the police. We had started calling the police swine because of the nature of their character — they had the most beastly character, dirty and filthy and abusing people and what have you. So Huey gets a picture of a pig and says he wants to put that in the paper — just on the front page — and put the badge of this policeman, who was in Oakland and who had been murdering and harassing people in the community.

But from my learning in art school I saw a way of carrying things a step further, improving on it.

I said, "My man, why don't we dress them up, like humans, and stand them up?"

And that's what I did. We put the cops on their feet and showed them running — bullets coming at them and them running. I think that captivated the attention. The black community was basically a nonreading community, and therefore we tried to make the headlines big and simple and make *big* captions — make them really big, so that senior citizens or anybody else who had bad eyesight could see them, and very simple so that the captions would be enough, if they weren't gonna read all the text.

The cartoons caught on like wildfire, people calling the cops "pigs" and saying "off the pigs," "death to the pigs," "fight with the pigs," the whole bit. The first thing they'd want to buy the paper for was the cartoons.

One night I join the madness. I decide I've got to do more than just talk about fighting the pigs. It's New Year's Eve, late, and I've been drinking with June and Bobby. We're standing on the porch of my sister B.B.'s house. I've been spending a lot of time with Eldridge, and now I'm saying we need to show some success in the struggle, that we've got to deliver a material blow against the pigs, not just give the brothers and sisters theoretical justifications for some future revolution that might never come. The talk and drink get heavier as the New Year approaches. As always during these discussions I feel an irresistible pull toward the violence, even though I don't yearn to shoot a gun or kill anyone.

Out of the blue a cop car rolls by the house. Well, I have a .380 Beretta in my possession. Why not now?

"This is a perfect opportunity to demonstrate how to carry out a guerrilla action," I tell Bobby.

Before he knows what I'm doing, I unleash the .380 and start firing at the cop car from the steps.

Bam!

Bam!

Bam!

Luckily I miss the car totally and the cops don't decide to fight. Who knows what they think? By now the papers are so full of stories about black revolutionaries and police ambushes that the cops probably believe they're about to be attacked by a platoon of crazies. They zoom off, tires screeching.

"David, you really shot at those guys," Bobby says.

"You're goddamn right," I say. But I don't feel proud. I have wanted to set an example, but I am humiliated by my action.

"We gotta talk about this," Bobby says. "That ain't right. That's jack-anape stuff. We believe in discipline. You gotta read and talk about Fanon, man, on spontaneity and its strengths and weaknesses. That's not what Huey would want at all."

"Well, explain it to me," I demand, his rebuke confirming my faith in the Party.

We drive to his house; until the dawn we drink and talk about violence, reading and discussing Fanon.

"This is what the man's saying," Bobby explains.

I listen, tracking the subtleties of Fanon's thoughts, not uncomprehending now. It's complicated, this stuff, I think—not simply what Fanon is saying, but being a revolutionary. Revolution is a science, not simply a matter of risking a lot or acting like a rebel. You've got to analyze and sort through things. This stuff is hard, I think; this revolution I've entered into takes time.

Chapter

12

MY Party responsibilities grow quickly.

Every morning either June or I—June's as solid as a rock; nobody's more reliable than June—open the Grove Street office. In the weeks since Huey's shooting, we've turned the deserted storefront into a revolutionary community center.

By ten the place is alive with people, a street corner inside four walls. Brothers and sisters off the block—the lumpen, guys and women like myself and Pat, street people, hustlers, pimps, prostitutes, whom we've come from and whom we want to organize—wander in and out, taking leaflets announcing Saturday's afternoon rally. Babies and kids run around underfoot, a Party member—man or woman, we're all used to taking care of kids—telling them to mind themselves, but getting distracted by some official business. Pensioners come by, offering advice, local gossip, complaints about landlords or local cops. Journalists hang out, eager to make friends and overhear Party gossip or get a glimpse of guns. Plus, there's a constant stream of left emissaries—Berkeley hippies, Peace and Freedom professionals, dashiki-draped nationalists, BSU (Black Student Union) kids wearing Army fatigues and shades like H. Rap Brown, union organizers, old-time CP'ers and members from every Bay Area radical sect. The Party serves as both a focus for the left and a source of energy. Huey is becoming an icon, "Free Huey!" the slogan of choice along with "Stop the War Now!" Supporting the Party is synonymous with revolutionary militancy and international solidarity. Each demonstration—we gather the troops if the state just whispers the name Huey Newton in court—has grown, Party members and supporters thronging the Alameda County Courthouse steps. Brothers in black leather, sisters standing to the side, naturals fluffed, fists in the air, the two groups chant slogans responsively like we used to in church:

> *Revolution has come!*
> *Off the pig!*
> *Time to pick up the gun!*
> *Off the pig!*

What's happening here? Bobby and I ask ourselves. Whatever the answer, it keeps happening, everything we do turning people on to the Party, bringing new members.

I go over to Sam Napier, the distribution chief for *The Black Panther.* Sam's tall, gangly; with plaits of hair sticking straight out like cactus shoots—Sam predates the Rastas—and a snaggletoothed smile, he can look like a wild man. The first time I meet him—at a CORE rally with Huey—he's so enthusiastic and energetic I think he must be a little crazy, but Huey tells me no, don't judge a book by its cover, Sam's a trustworthy comrade. Huey's right: actually Sam's an organizational genius.

Sam's handing out papers to some cadre. Cadre are required to sell copies every day. Most members love the work; as they hawk the paper, people gossip with them on the streets and even invite them for some food or drink—wine among the younger ones, bourbon among the old folks. Later, when Fred Hampton and Bobby Rush come from Chicago they make fun of us. "Where in the hell is your ghetto?" Fred will say. "All you gotta do is lay out in the sun under palm trees all day long. You gotta come out to the South Side and stand in the twenty-degree cold for a while."

But the newspaper has become more than an organizing tool. *The Black Panther* is the primary way we inform people about Huey's trial. The newspaper also helps us organize new chapters. "What do we do?" new members in San Diego or Sacramento want to know. "Sell the newspaper," we answer.

Plus the newspaper is our steadiest source of revenue. The quarters add up, providing a good deal of the Party's daily income. From the first we function collectively, pooling funds, living and eating together and sharing what we earn and own, including cars, clothes, and houses. Although we'll receive large contributions later on and also sign remunerative book deals, the paper, throughout my membership in the Party, remains the bedrock of the organization's finances, and all monies go only to paying the ongoing Party costs: cadre living expenses, legal defense, office rent, maintenance on cars and equipment—though a lot of this is donated—and, of course, the Party programs. Several times, later on, the government tries to mount income-tax and other financial charges against us for the years I'm a member, always unsuccessfully.

"Troops got to cover East Oakland today," I tell the cadre. "Remember, if the pigs harass you, take the arrest. Fight it in court."

I speak from personal experience. A couple of weeks ago, I'm standing in front of Tech High, handing out leaflets, when two cops hassle me.

"You got a permit?" asks the first. I know the cop from Eighteenth and Chestnut. He used to harass us on the corner, a beefy southern guy who always smokes cigars and looks like a big fat pig; foul nature, foul breath.

"I don't need a permit," I say, defending myself. "I have a constitutional right—"

"Let me see that," says the other. He grabs a sheet and the leaflets scatter over the sidewalk.

"You're littering," says Cigar.

"I am exercising my constitutional right—"

"Come on," says the other, and grabs my arm.

"You arresting me?" I demand. Kids stare at the commotion from inside the school; it seems a long time since I last went to school myself.

"You a wiseass?" Cigar answers.

"You arresting me?" I repeat. I want them to arrest me; I want to show them that they can't scare me off the streets, impress on them that I'll fight for my constitutional rights.

"What's your name?" Cigar says.

The other twists my arm behind my back and pushes me toward the patrol car. Cajuns, as Daddy would say—never trust them Cajuns. And these guys are worse; they think they're cowboys.

"Five," I say. Meaning the Fifth Amendment; it's what Huey has coached us to say.

Community people gather at the corner. Their presence inspires me. I'm apprehensive; the law's power is always scary, and Panthers and Oakland cops are sworn enemies. At the same time, I want to exemplify revolutionary behavior. And the Party rules help me keep my composure. The philosophy and practice endow me with discipline and purpose; without them, in a situation like this, I'd probably cuss furiously and get myself into more trouble.

"What do you mean, five?"

"Five," I repeat.

They open the patrol-car door, squeezing me inside.

"You'd better tell us your name," Cigar threatens.

"Five," I defy him and don't say another word until I call my lawyer.

The cadre leave.

"Damn," I say to Sam. "I forgot what I wanted to tell you." This happens all the time; I wake up at three or four in the morning, recalling something I should have taken care of that afternoon.

"The papers to New York," he says. Sam never misses a trick; he's right on time.

"That's it." A group in Brooklyn's Bed-Stuy have started their own chapter. Bobby and I plan to fly out there next week, but we want to make sure they understand the program and rules before we arrive.

"We still don't have the truck," he tells me.

"Well," I say, "figure out a way. The papers have gotta get there."

On my way back to my desk I see a brother standing idly.

"What are you doing, man?"

"They got enough people covering the street, Captain David."

It's no answer. We're in a war; there's no time for waste; there's always another task that can help you win the battle.

"How in the hell do you know? You'd better get out there and go sell some papers. All these papers standing around here. You'd better get out and educate the community or go get a Red Book and study and learn how to serve the people."

Eldridge drives up in his new Plymouth. The car's standard except for one feature: a phone. We welcome technology. Referring to Toussaint-Louverture, the Haitian revolutionary leader, Eldridge is fond of saying Toussaint had the good sense to know a revolutionary has two primary needs: a good shoemaker and a fast horse. We need a good car. We can't depend on some jalopy that might break down just when we need to get going.

We also need the phone. The cops, Huey says, have three powers: information, communication, and mobilization. Now we're under constant attack and the phone helps even the sides. Another weapon for us, it allows us to be constantly functional: with the phone we can't get caught isolated late at night and can keep in contact with the chapters starting to be established around the state. We talk to one another all day and night. Twenty-eight-hour days, George Jackson, a future member, later calls our schedules, the twenty-eight-hour day of the Black Panther Party.

Plus there's another reason for the phone. For us time is meaningless.

Days are endless; weeks and months disappear overnight. A meeting drags on forever; one colossal event begins before the last one has ended. We get used to a constant speediness. Ordinary time leaves us restless, fidgety; we need tension. Even when I come home exhausted, I pace around, craving contact and movement as powerfully as I yearn for cocaine later on. Phones and cars become our fixes. The phone puts you in touch with everybody. The car lets you know you're not standing still but going somewhere. I enter the new-smelling Fury and turn on the ignition, radio blasting; suddenly I'm there, free, an outlaw on a collision course with destiny.

Eldridge sweeps into the office, Kathleen behind him, black shades and knee-length boots.

"David," he says, "you come with me and Bobby to the one-o'clock press conference."

There's been another episode in the "stupid revolution"—the reason the truck's out of service and Sam can't deliver the papers.

Since the Party's become well-known, brothers masquerading as members have extorted payoffs from local businessmen. The rip-offs give us a bad community name, provide the cops an opportunity to blame us for criminal behavior, and completely controvert Party rules. We've sent a letter to store-keepers warning them to deal only with people showing proper Panther iden-tification and assuring them we condemn any gangster activity. But no sooner have we dealt with the problem than another pops up. We send some Panthers in our Panther truck—a contribution from a support group, it has a picture of a springing blank panther and the words "The Black Panther" painted on the side—to San Francisco on a distribution run. Couple of hours later we get a telephone call. Our Panther truck is in a shoot-out. The driver pulls up at a gas station. One guy—Bill Brent—goes to the john while the others gas up. Some time passes. The tank is full, still no Bill Brent. The members look around. Where's Bill? Oh, there's Bill: he's robbing the attendant. The guys in the truck are amazed. They don't know what to do, get him or leave? At that moment the third party arrives: some police drive by, see Bill with the gun, set off their sirens. Freaked, Bill forgets about the attendant and fires on the cops. The rest is pandemonium. Finally, a bullet grazes Brent and every-one's arrested; the Panther truck is seized. Next thing we know, the five o'clock news claims the Party has tried robbing a gas station in broad day-light for the grand sum of seventy-five dollars.

The incident is the last thing we need. Brent's behavior confirms every charge of the media, painting us as hypocrites and opportunists, members of an outlaw organization using politics to justify petty thievery. Plus, the sheer stupidity of the action makes us look asinine—a gang that can't shoot straight.

I say right on to Eldridge—we're spending more and more time together; Eldridge has even taken me to visit his family in Pasadena—and he goes off to his corner, a desk with telephone and old-fashioned typewriter, separating himself from the chaos. I hand a sister a press list we've put together. She's a college student; I like and respect the educated women we attract; they're incisive and independent, cut from Kathleen's mold.

"Make sure the reporters are coming," I say. "Tell them Eldridge is speaking. They can count on something outrageous to print."

Emmett Groggan sticks his head in the office. Emmett is the founder of the Diggers, a tribe—that's what some radicals call their groups—who organize the "street people" of the Haight into revolutionary activity. A few weeks ago, Emmett left off some bags of food his group distributes to the runaways, draft resisters, and freaks who have flocked to Berkeley, turning the town into the nation's counterculture capital. We told him to put the stuff outside the office: in a few minutes people were flocking by, stocking up on onions and potatoes. Now Emmett donates the food regularly. Like the newspaper, the food serves a double purpose, providing sustenance but also functioning as an organizing tool: people enter the office when they come by, take some leaflets, sit in on an elementary PE class, talk to cadre, and exchange ideas, all part of the revolutionary ferment I have imagined when listening to Huey describe Fidel and Che in Cuba.

"Potatoes and beans today?" Emmett asks. Nothing of the eager-to-please liberal about Groggan. He dresses out of *Rebel Without a Cause:* black motorcycle boots, jeans, white T-shirt, a pack of nonfilter Camels tucked into his rolled-up left sleeve. He thinks he can teach me about the streets. "You want it?"

"Yeah, sure," I say, "leave it by the door."

I feel more secure about my judgments. I'm not making policy—I lack the confidence and knowledge, I think, to map out strategies, and I'm still wary of public speaking. But I know now I can get things done, help people solve personal or organizational problems, figure out why something's not going right. I've heard Stew Albert say that if the Party is happening today, it's because of David. "You were the lifeline in relationship to making things function in the day-to-day," Emory says.

You were the guy sending out cadre, deciding what political work had to be done, listening and coming up with ways to deal with those problems democratically, dealing with the security of the Party, making sure that people in the Party were doing what they're supposed to be doing and not what they shouldn't be doing. The whole bit. You weren't awesome in the way that Huey was, and that was good too.

Bobby Seale enters as Groggan finishes unpacking the food.

"Chairman Bobby," Li'l Bobby Hutton—he's the officer of the day, overseeing the functioning of the office—calls, "it's for you."

Bobby picks up the phone and listens intently for a few minutes, then breaks in.

"Well, you got to come out here," he says. Someone's asking to start a chapter. We get calls all day long. Des Moines, Virginia Beach, Atlanta. Since we're three hours behind the East Coast, the requests often start as early as eight A.M. Our replies are always the same: people must come to Oakland, sell the paper, follow Party rules to the letter. We're not interested in growing for the sake of numbers. If we were a loosely knit organization— like, say, SDS, in which each group decides individually what it wants to do and believe—we could top the ten-thousand mark already. But for us the Party is a structure; the program and rules give us strength, a method of looking at things and understanding them. We want new members to increase this strength, not weaken it. We've successfully established an LA chapter, led by Eldridge's prison buddy Bunchy Carter; but chapters in far away areas pose different kinds of problems.

Right now our biggest problem in this regard is New York, the brothers and sisters in Brooklyn led by an Oakland native named Ron Penniwell. Penniwell's undisciplined, ostentatious style has stamped itself on the group. Their main activity has been trying to make citizen's arrests of police: completely contrary to Party program, they find cops asleep or drunk on the job and accost them, saying they're irresponsible and demanding they carry out their duties as guardians of the peace.

"This is not what the Party's for," Bobby and I say when we hear about these antics. "Let the police sleep. If they're drunk, good for them! Keep them asleep."

But at the same time, we don't want to write off Penniwell and New York. Even though his actions contradict our regulations—he shouldn't have started the chapter, called himself or anyone else Panthers, and he certainly has no power to name himself a captain—he has organized the chapter, is actually *arresting* police, which is admirable in its own way, and has earned the loyalty of his recruits.

"That's what you got to do if you want to start a chapter," Bobby repeats. "You got to come out here and we got to talk to you."

He hangs up.

"This stuff is getting crazy, David," Bobby says. "We got to go to Brooklyn next week. See what those brothers are doing and set them straight. Then we can use them as a model."

"All right," I say.

Bobby is a dreamer, but the best kind — a practical dreamer. Sometimes he props his feet up on the desk and talks about programs the Party should initiate. He makes everything sound simple. You listen to him ramble on and you feel like saying, "That's right, let's do that!"

I've started calling travel agents, trying to find the cheapest fares, when Li'l Bobby tells me Pat's on the phone. I pick up and Pat's talking about Li'l Bobby's mother. Li'l Bobby and I have become close friends. He likes my flair and style, and our discussions help me clarify my own ideas about violence and nationalism. He's been with the Party from the beginning — he lived near the first Panther office — and has a gut understanding of the Ten Point Program. Nights, we hang together, drinking wine and smoking dope while discussing politics and listening to jazz. But Bobby's political work creates trouble with his family, his brothers often looking for him because his mom, Dolly Mae, is worried and needs him home. Then Bobby gets mad, calls Dolly Mae to tell her he can take care of himself, Pat often intervening to assure Mrs. Hutton Bobby's all right. Last week there was a final blowup and Bobby said he'd had enough; if I'd drive him over to his house, he'd get his clothes and move in with us. I instantly agreed; Li'l Bobby's the younger brother I never had. Now Pat tells me Dolly Mae's worried again, and what should she say?

I understand Pat's in a difficult position. But between trying to get tickets, worrying about the press conference, remembering that we've got to come back for a newspaper meeting that Bunchy Carter is going to attend — which puts me a little uptight; I respect Bunchy and feel pressure in his presence to meet the high standard of a Party leader — I'm a little stressed out. Plus, I can't avail myself of my usual relief: drinking Bitter Dog on the corner with the guys would not only break Party rules but make me a sitting duck for the pigs who cruise by every ten minutes, shotguns at the ready.

So I blow.

"Don't bother me," I tell Pat. "I got too much going on, and you shouldn't be annoying me with that petty stuff anyway."

I slam down the phone and go to collect Eldridge, passing a brother who's acting nasty with a sister.

"I told you no," the sister insists. "I meant no."

"Hey, brother," I interrupt.

The sister slides away.

"We listen to what sisters say in the Party."

The brother starts defending himself, but I cut him off. I can predict what he's going to say. His justification is nothing new; many Party members are from the streets and their attitudes, like mine, are formed in an environment of exploitation and self-abuse.

"Listen to me," I break in. "We're not out on the street in here. We respect everybody's right to self-determination."

"I wasn't trying to get over. I just told her she was a fine-looking—"

"I know," I say, trying to put him at ease. "That's how a lot of brothers act. But that doesn't make it right. You want to belong to the Party?"

"Definitely," he says. The Party is the thing to join.

"Come to PE class," I say. If recruits attend classes and sell papers regularly, we admit them to the cadre, inviting them to sessions where we clean and assemble guns and discuss revolutionary activity and self-defense. "Bobby's going to be talking about this stuff from an article in the paper. You'll see what I mean."

"Right on," he says.

The Party's image of freedom and defiance attracts brothers and sisters— we have become the standard for black manhood, making guys feel like they're no longer less than men and telling sisters that if their men can't measure up to Brother Huey, than they had better get out of the bed. But people commit themselves because of our discipline, our insistence on respecting oneself and others.

At the last moment Bobby can't come, and, already late for the press conference, Eldridge and I hustle into the Plymouth.

We rush to the press conference while Eldridge talks about Huey's birthday party. Through Kathleen we've contacted Stokely Carmichael, James Forman, and H. Rap Brown; and now we're planning to celebrate Huey's birthday with a gathering at the Oakland Auditorium that all these heroes will attend. The idea of the SNCC leaders speaking at one of our functions blows my mind—I've come to revere these guys, especially Rap with his verbal dexterity: Detroit has become Destroy It, he says—but I'm aware that we are doing them the favor. SNCC is only historically important. To remain relevant to the black community, SNCC needs to join us, rather than us joining them. We, the Party, are the people taking the revolution's next step. We can easily survive without them; without us they're stuck in the past.

At the press conference Eldridge defuses the situation. The reporters think we'll shy away from our allegiance to self-defense. Aren't you violent? they ask, over and over again. No, we're not violent, we consistently answer. Violence is what is being done in Vietnam, where napalm burns the innocent to death. Violence is people going unemployed six months of the year, living with drugs and alcohol in their community. Violence is most assuredly a police force that harasses, terrorizes, and kills the people it is being paid to protect. But violence is not us standing with our guns saying simply, No, you can't come in here like you used to and shoot and maim and brutalize people at your will. So we're not violent. We're opposed to violence, opposed to war. But we are *for* self-defense.

But the distinction is lost on the press. Say the same thing over a hundred times and they come back with the predictable question once more: Are you violent?

Now Eldridge dismisses the whole problem; he confronts the accusation head-on.

"Look," he says, "Bill Brent has obviously flipped."

"Is the Party giving up the gun?" a reporter asks.

"It's not a matter of the Party using guns or not," Eldridge answers. "The point is, holding up a gas station in broad daylight for seventy-five dollars is not the Party's style. If we committed a robbery we certainly wouldn't do it in our truck, and we'd certainly get more than seventy-five dollars, and we certainly wouldn't get caught! So Bill Brent is obviously crazy as hell, and that's that!"

Going back to Oakland, we're stopped by cops demanding our IDs. Used to this harassment, Eldridge and I stay cool. Several nights ago cops have broken into his home, holding guns on him and Kathleen while searching for incriminating evidence they can use to revoke his parole. Getting Eldridge off the streets has become an obsession with the administration of Governor Ronald Reagan. We drive away and Eldridge mutters about unleashing the wolves and a day of retribution. It's jailhouse talk. The worse effect of the police on Eldridge is to bring him back into prison—not literally, but mentally, spiritually. He has struggled hard to free himself from the penned-in, brutal logic of jail, but when threatened by the authorities, he reverts back to the macho, sometimes self-destructive attitudes of his prison days. It's his great weakness, and he has no defense against it.

Because of the run-in with the cops we're late for the newspaper meeting. We've got to plan out the next issue. We've taken a lot of criticism for hiring

Garry instead of a black lawyer. Along with our insistence on self-defense, our attitude toward nationalism has made us notorious and unique. We're the only black revolutionary group to build a coalition with whites. We call our position "revolutionary nationalism," as opposed to "cultural nationalism," which limits the struggle for self-determination to appearances—dashikis, African names, talk about "new nationhood" and the black nation. For us, such emphasis is real problematical. Dress and language are definitely *not* what Fanon has talked about in *The Wretched of the Earth.* Instead he insists that the only worthwhile culture is a *revolutionary* culture. We say we won't free ourselves through steeping ourselves in an African past and folklore but by aligning ourselves with other liberation fighters, movements that have won their freedom through political and armed struggle. We are about gaining economic and political freedom; after that, worry about what you call yourself.

These conflicts have come to a head in Los Angeles. Bunchy Carter has organized and recruited impressive members, including an ex-Marine named Elmer Pratt who has served as a point man in the Vietnam bush and is called by the nickname Geronimo, or G. But Bunchy's success—like the success of the whole Party so far—has created tensions. The other influential black radical organization in Los Angeles is something called US (for United Slaves), run by Ron Karenga. US embodies cultural nationalism—the security guards are called "Simba Wachukas," and everyone sports African names and clothing. We could compete with them in a comradely fashion except that LA seems to be different than Oakland. Oakland is a community. In Los Angeles everything is territorial. Gangs control separate sections of the sprawling, flat miles that make up the ghetto. By mobilizing people we are invading US's turf. We don't care about this, of course; we want to organize the whole community and have been reaching the teenagers who live in the projects and congregate in the community centers, challenging Karenga's reactionary nationalism with our revolutionary vision and saying Karenga's taking black people nowhere. US's response hasn't been ideological but violent, its members threatening and attacking Party members. In the next several weeks things look to be really heading toward a resolution; we'll attend a Black Congress conference that US is sponsoring with SNCC, and even though Bunchy is a master at the intricate politics of LA gangs, we're tense at the prospect of the two-day meeting.

Inside the Magnolia Street house, Pat and volunteer younger sisters from San Francisco State count the latest financial contributions to the Party, rolling up quarters, dimes, nickels, and pennies, the loose change that Oakland's working people have given to our organizers on the street. Since I told her to leave her job, Pat has become the Party Treasurer, and even with the new office our home remains a center of Party activity.

"Suddenly there were a lot of meetings at the house," my daughter Patrice remembers.

> Bobby Seale, Bunchy Carter, Li'l Bobby Hutton. Bunchy was kind of laid back and very spiffy dressing. Li'l Bobby was wonderful. He related to us as if he were one of us. He was the one who, before a meeting, would come in there and play and talk and hug and kiss us. Me and my brothers used to love to go in his room because he always had change in his pocket. The change would fall out, and in the morning before we'd go across the street to school he'd let us get all the quarters, nickels, and dimes to put in our pockets and buy candies and bubble gum.

"You want something?" Pat asks. Our kitchen has become an all-night diner, everybody eating when they can. "I made some chicken for Bunchy."

I grab a thigh and breast. These days I'm never aware of my hunger. Sometimes I go for hours without food, just swallowing handfuls of vitamins until my stomach twists into painful knots; then I eat like a dog.

I go inside to greet Bunchy. Bunchy has become a key Party member. My age, handsome, with a high natural and burning eyes, Bunchy exudes charisma. He's a lover, revolutionary, and warrior, a genuine tough guy who never fronts. A gang leader from the Slauson — the area around South Central LA — he carries all the fascination, glamour, and repute of Los Angeles. His style is macho and lyrical. I am Bunchy, he says, like a bunch of greens, Reincarnation of Genghis Khan, the Mayor of the Ghetto! He distinguishes himself with a casual, flamboyant style. We're all into black leather sports jackets, straight cut, and wool berets. Bunchy wears double-breasted, down-below-the-knee leather trench coats and his beret has a leather strip. He dresses in green, drapes his coat, capelike, over his shoulder, and walks on the backs of his expensive shoes, treating them like slippers. He talks in extravagant metaphors — "letting loose the wolves" is his phrase — and writes fiery poetry about "automated slums" and "Charley," who's "in dread because he's in the red." We'll often ask Baby Dee, a prison mate of Bunchy's and Eldridge's, to recite "Black Mother," or my personal favorite, a takeoff Bunchy's written on a lyric by James Weldon Johnson, one of the poets of the Harlem Renaissance: "Any slave who dies a natural death does not weigh two dead flies on the scales of Eternity, and do something, niggers, if you only *spit!*"

                              *   *   *

We get down to business immediately, talking about the next issue, planning
the birthday party. During the long, intense discussion, I go into my usual
mode, sitting back and listening, trying to absorb as much as possible. My
silence makes me uncomfortable. In the last weeks, I've realized that when
people speak at meetings they're thinking on their feet, articulating their
ideas, applying basic principles to unfolding situations. The revelation helps
me: I understand I can do the same. But I still believe I must study more before I can approach the educational level of Bobby and Bunchy, guys who
can rap about Hannibal and African civilizations. Yet I can't continue in my
silence: we're Panthers and the other Panthers are all powerful speakers,
Bunchy and Eldridge, Kathleen, Huey and Bobby, and all with their own distinct style. If I want to be their equal, I've got to be able to talk.

   We keep going over the cultural nationalist stuff. Bunchy says the US
people talk militant but back off from any confrontations with the state. His
point reminds me of the "paper panthers," and I mention the San Francisco
situation.

   "That's why I called them 'paper panthers,'" I explain. "Because they
were fake. Some of those guys were out there to be on television. We're not.
Because once you have guns you can't decide what you're gonna do. Not
when the police have weapons pointed at you. Then it ain't no time for take
one, take two. You're not in Hollywood. No roll 'em. No do-overs. And
that's us. We're for real. We're serious business."

   I finish.

   Silence.

   Did I say something wrong?

   "I like that," Eldridge says, "take one, take two."

   Bunchy jumps in, staring at me.

   "How come you don't talk that much?" he demands. "You sit around all
the time, listening. You never say anything. What are you in the Party for?
You're the Captain of the National Headquarters. You got something to say.
Now I know you got something to say. You've got words. Good words. Use
them. I'm listening to what you're saying. You've got to talk more. In fact, I
demand you talk more."

At eleven, the meeting breaks up. People bed down, go home. I'm about to
take a shower when Li'l Bobby busts in.

   "Captain David," he says, abashed, "I gotta tell you something. I know
you're gonna get mad, but this brother I've been with is crazy. We go out
and walk into this liquor store and he just fires a shot up over the store

owner's head and everybody hits the floor and we go in and rob the place!"

"Is that how you've been getting all this money, Bobby?" I say. Bobby has returned home with satchels of cash every night; I thought the money was from legitimate contributions.

"Yeah."

"You gotta stop that," I tell him. "You guys are gonna get yourselves killed. You can't do that anymore. I won't tell anyone this time, but you can't ever do that stuff again."

I get into bed and Pat wakes up. I tell her that we're planning to go to New York.

"When?" she says.

"I don't know myself," I answer.

The discussion at the meeting is still going through my head and I'd like to talk out my ideas. But Pat's asleep again. Pat has a strange attitude. She thinks me capable of any kind of glory; but she takes no pride in me, none at least that I can see.

"You asleep?" I ask.

"I'm tired, David. I gotta get to sleep."

Suddenly I remember: the papers. I pick up the phone and get Sam.

"What?" he's frog-voiced.

"The papers," I say. "Did you get them to New York?"

"Yeah, yeah. June borrowed a van and ran them down. It's all right, Captain David. Go to sleep, man, go to sleep."

Ideas and images run through my mind. I've got to call someone, I think, a flash of anxiety buzzing me, and fall out, arms wrapped around Pat, dead until morning.

Chapter

13

BEFORE going to LA we take the long-awaited New York trip. I'm psyched. First of all, I've never gone farther east than Mobile. Plus, New York is a cultural capital; the Harlem Dukes Social Club was the main nightspot on Davis Avenue when I was growing up, and Manhattan's the home of Miles Davis and Coltrane. And finally, our visit marks a new level of organization for the Party.

The one thing I'm not looking forward to is the plane ride. Flying scares me. I strap myself in and immediately order some whiskey: liquor calms my growling stomach.

"David, relax," Bobby says, sensing my nervousness. "We're sitting over the wing; it's the safest place."

I trust what he says. In one of his many jobs before the Party he was a structural engineer for McDonnell Douglas. And there's another reason I feel safe. In this cabin in the sky there are no cops, no cars riding by, and there certainly won't be any shoot-outs or police kicking down doors. The unexpected peace makes me appreciate the anxiety and pressure I've lived under the last months; since the night of Huey's shooting I've constantly feared that I might be killed any moment and have often recalled the image of Huey after he was shot, clutching his stomach, bleeding to death. But now, up here, thirty-five-thousand feet above Ronald Reagan, Mayor Alioto, and the police, I'm secure.

"David, what are you doing?" Bobby asks. He's ready to talk all the way to New York.

"Going to sleep," I say, punching the pillow. I close my eyes for the best rest I've enjoyed in the last three months.

We drive to the Panther office, a storefront on Fulton Street in the heart of Brooklyn's Bed-Stuy ghetto. I'm impressed. Nothing I've read or seen has prepared me for the number of black faces we pass. Seven hundred thousand of them, one Panther tells us — and that's only in Bed-Stuy! Millions more live in the rest of the city. I have great faith in the Party — I've seen us grow to include many different kinds of members — but the idea of organizing all these people around the Ten Point Program blows my mind.

At the office we meet the cadre. Emory, Bobby, and I have already agreed on how to proceed: we'll find out the specific conditions of their community and their practice before coming to any conclusions about what they're doing — or should be doing.

Still we're surprised. These people are definitely cut from a non-Oakland mold. First there's a cultural difference. California blacks mix a western and Caribbean style — gumbo and red beans — whereas in New York they talk about peppered steak. And they certainly dress unlike us. The women wear weird side-slit boots and the wife of another self-proclaimed captain — Captain Ford — enters wrapped in a mink covered with political buttons, an ostentatious display totally out of line with Party discipline. Plus, the cadre are cultural nationalist. Some have adopted African names that none of us, even Bobby, who knows a lot about Africa, can pronounce. And they're also militaristic: they walk around with walrus or elephant teeth on rawhide loops and big, sleek, copper .45-caliber cartridges hung around their necks. Panther Bullets, they call them, though we certainly have never used anything like them.

"What is this stuff?" we say. "Panthers don't dress like that."

"They do in New York," they tell us, adding that they have their own style.

We've never heard this before. Bunchy may have his own style. But he's *Bunchy*. From the Slauson. LA gangbanger and leader. And besides Bunchy reveres the leadership of Huey P. Newton. "Huey is the baddest motherfucker that ever shit between two shoes," Bunchy says. But these guys treat us as equals, as though their opinions bear the same weight as ours. Which they most definitely do not.

"No," we say. "The Party doesn't have two styles. The Party doesn't work that way. Black Panthers have one way of doing things. And it's not how you guys think things should be done. It's how we say it goes."

*   *   *

For the next week we stay in New York, discussing the selections from "On Practice" in the Little Red Book and waiting for D.C.: D.C.'s ability to overcome differences will let him provide the chapter with confident, successful leadership.

We also start dealing with the city's political community. Everyone wants to talk to and at us, find out what we're doing. The rapidly changing radical movement contains a paradox. It's never been stronger—the antiwar movement holds huge rallies, students are shutting down campuses, even labor is starting to move left—while no one seems to know what to do. King talks about organizing a Poor People's Campaign to march on Washington, but the civil rights movement has stalled and maybe fallen apart in the North. The antiwar movement has no coherent ideology. Plus, there's no bridge between the two movements. The mainly middle-class or student antiwar leadership doesn't appeal to the brothers and sisters on the street; the white radicals are shunned by the cultural nationalists. Allying these two groups would clearly pose a real threat to the authorities. Under Huey's leadership and Eldridge's practical guidance, the Party is creating such a coaltion.

Our success makes everybody want to associate themselves with us; but they also all want us to follow their political vision.

The biggest problem is our position on cultural nationalism. Huey's statements have stirred up a storm. "Revolutionary nationalism is first dependent upon a people's revolution with the end goal being the people in power," he says in an interview with the *Movement,* a white-radical Bay Area newspaper.

> Therefore to be a revolutionary nationalist you would by necessity have to be a socialist. If you are a reactionary nationalist you are not a socialist and your end goal is the oppression of the people. Cultural nationalism, or pork chop nationalism, as I sometimes call it, is basically a problem of having the wrong political perspective. It seems to be a reaction instead of responding to political oppression. Many times cultural nationalists fall into line as reactionary nationalists. Papa Doc in Haiti is an excellent example of reactionary nationalism. He's against anything other than Black, which on the surface seems very good, but for him it is only to mislead the people. He merely kicked out the racists and replaced them with himself as the oppressor. Many of the nationalists in this country seem to desire the same ends.

We're especially intransigent about black cops. Are these guys part of the community or the police? The cultural nationalists defend them. We don't. Of course the colonizers—the white power structure—has its agents among the colonized; there's nothing new about that. Objectively black cops perform the same deeds and function as their white bosses: they are soldiers in the war against us and the community. Bobby Seale's house is broken into one night. We don't care if the guys busting down the door are black or white; either one is a pig, an armed oppressor trying to keep us and the community down. And the issue is ever more crucial because the cops have responded to the black community's revolutionary activity by sending in undercover cops, provocateurs who hide under the cover of black nationalist ideology.

We fly to the Black Congress in LA anticipating trouble.

When we arrive the place is a madhouse. A wave of people hand out leaflets, newspapers, copies of Malcolm's speeches, and buttons, posters, and incense. Organizers rush through the corridors; all wear the same serious, determined look, and each group—everyone's shown up; SNCC, CP, nationalists, the whole range of black radicalism—caucuses by itself, discussing a resolution it's determined to pass, what number its spokesperson appears in the order of speeches, a suspicion that a member is an undercover pig. The frantic preparations have an edge of paranoia too: every faction has its own bodyguards. The strangest are those for US. The Simba Wachukas wear all-black, two-piece, Vietnamese-like pajamas buttoned up to the neck and greet everyone in Swahili; they carry guns, as do we—we flew down from Oakland with our pieces tucked into our pants or under our leather jackets; metal detectors are still in the future—and we keep exchanging looks with them, each group daring the other to go first. (Though, personally, I trust Bunchy to keep everything calm: he knows many of these guys and can defuse situations, commanding their respect if not their agreement and able to negotiate them out of an aggressive, uncompromising stand.) Karenga is the strangest looking of all, a short guy wrapped in black Mao-jacket-like dashiki with a bald bullet-shaped head and a long Fu Manchu mustache. His weirdest quality is his voice—high, thin, piercing. I find it hard to believe he can attract followers. He seems almost comedic.

Right off, things go badly. Karenga, who hosts the conference and styles himself a revolutionary, has invited the Los Angeles police—white and black cops—to help with security. Their presence is of course unacceptable. We're more worried about the LAPD than we are about US. Aggressive, racist, LA cops use helicopters and massive amounts of force—they'll sometimes call in five or six patrol cars on one arrest—and the local Party chapter has already suffered several run-ins. Our opposition raises the nationalist issue right away.

"We can't support stuff where you got police who oppress and kill Panthers standing around and talking about being *security!*" we tell Karenga. "You know, we say a pig is a pig!"

After a fight, he agrees. But the handshake between us is just tactical. Karenga doesn't want to lose face; the confrontation has only increased the tension between his guys and ours, and we station ourselves strategically in the hall when the speeches begin, keeping an eye on the Simba Wachukas, ready for action.

Even more troubling are our dealings with SNCC. We expect a power struggle with US: important differences divide our two groups. But SNCC, presumably, is our ally. Huey plans to unite with them, not in a coalition—as with the white radical groups—but a mutually beneficial merger: SNCC will provide us with organizational and administrative expertise, their endorsement giving us legitimacy with the middle class and students, and we will supply them with our politics, energy, mass appeal, and charisma. Huey suggests we organize around a petition to the UN—originated by William Patterson—to investigate genocide against black Americans and conduct a plebiscite for their self-determination. His tapes and messages from prison direct us to name Stokely and Rap Prime Minister and Minister of Justice, putting them at the Party's helm. He has even raised the possibility of moving the Party to Atlanta, the first instance of his ambivalence toward our success: amazed at the massive support his case and the Panthers have received, Huey frequently indicates he's worried about the Party's future.

The LA conference is to be the first step in this amalgamation. From here we'll all return to Oakland for Huey's gala birthday party—both Rap and Stokely are scheduled to speak—and later meet in New York, where representatives of our two groups will hold a joint press conference.

But things don't go smoothly. We're of course impressed and honored by the presence and counsel of the SNCC leaders. In a private session James Forman explains SNCC's ten-ten-ten organizing strategy, each unit responsible for contacting another, creating a powerful, flexible network of cadre who can be mobilized overnight, an idea we quickly adopt (and that we employ throughout the Party's history).

At the same time, the presence of these heroes undermines us. They're more articulate and politically sophisticated than many of us, and it's harder to arrive at our own point of view with them around. Plus, we don't quite get along. Li'l Bobby and I like Rap Brown, with his beret, sunglasses, and combat boots; of them all, he has the most style, ironic and authoritative at the same time, someone we can connect with. But Stokely is a real problem. He's distant, arrogant, supercilious. His manner makes all of us—D.C. excepted—want to jump him. I have to hold Li'l Bobby back, and Bunchy threatens to give some SNCC people our special style of ghetto discipline if they don't listen to what we say. D.C. tells us to be more tolerant and treat Stokely in a comradely fashion; and, out of respect for our Field Marshall, we try to correct our attitudes. But Stokely continues to provoke us, acting as though he should be telling us what to do, rather than learning from us—which is what we think should happen since SNCC's only practice is organizing voter-registration campaigns, while we're about the business of armed struggle, involvement, and confrontation.

Our conflicts sharpen.

Our first fight comes before a press conference; to Stokely's annoyance, we demand he wear a Panther uniform if he's going to speak as a Party member. Then we go to Oakland and Stokely meets Huey in jail.

"[Stokely] had just returned from a trip...to Africa, Cuba, and Vietnam," Huey later writes in his autobiography, *Revolutionary Suicide,*

> and a lot of [his] ideas had changed in a short time. The only thing that would get me out of jail, he said, was armed rebellion, culminating in a race war. . . . He objected to the Black Panther alliance with the Peace and Freedom Party and said we should not associate ourselves with white radicals or let them come to our meetings or be involved in our rallies. Stokely warned that whites would destroy the movement, alienate Black people, and lessen our effectiveness in the community. . . . I did not believe him while he was running these things down to me. We were not into a racist bag, I told him. . . . I felt sure that Stokely was afraid of himself and his own weaknesses. I responded to his race analysis with a class analysis. We could have solidarity and friendship in a common struggle against a common oppressor without the whites taking over.

The next day we hold the birthday party. The Oakland Auditorium is jammed, the whole black community gathering in support of Huey—grandmothers and women like Li'l Bobby Hutton's mother, the housekeepers for the rich people who live in the hills, men of my father's generation, working guys like June, brothers and sisters off the block, students from the BSUs. And whites too, longshoremen and radicals, students and professionals from the Peace and Freedom Party. You can't find a seat in the place. Yet there's no sense of tension, only celebration. The outpouring vindicates everything

Huey and we have stood and worked for. When Eldridge welcomes everyone, the crowd stands as one to cheer him and us, the Party, and themselves: we haven't been frightened by the cops or any other authorities and have defied defeat, turning our trials into a cause of new life.

Eldridge introduces the speakers one by one. There's nothing of the showboat about Eldridge today. The gathering is the group he has assembled, the culmination of one part of his strategy to free Huey, and he is gracious and appreciative. In retrospect, I think the evening remains one of his finest hours.

Charlie Garry comes on early, leaning forward on the podium, talking to the crowd, encouraging them to attend court, telling them Huey will be free.

Rap follows, funny and sharp—even his voice has an edge to it, a little reminiscent of Malcolm's—raising his fists, leading the crowd in cheers. "It's their laws," he says. "They made them, we didn't, and we don't have to obey them. Because their laws are laws of white chauvinism. Their laws say everything about white is good and black bad. White cows give good milk and brown cows don't. White eggs are good and brown ones bad. Santa Claus is a white honkie who slides down a black chimney and still comes out white! You are either free or a slave. There is no such thing as second-class citizenship. Second-class citizenship is like being a little bit pregnant. The only politics relevant to black people today is the politics of revolution. They tell you your problem is unemployment. Well, I got a program that can employ all black people overnight!"

Next, Bobby matches Rap's anger with a calm, casual manner that the crowd also loves.

"Brother Bobby," he says, imitating Huey the short sixteen months ago when they created the Party, "we've got to create a platform for what our people need. We don't have time for complicated essays and debates. We just have to state the simple points of what we want and what we stand for." And he recites the Ten Point Program. Not as a political document, but as though the paragraphs are the lyrics of a poem, his voice caressing the words, making the demands seem so simple and undeniable: "We want land, bread, housing, education, clothing, peace, justice, and finally, as our major political objective, we want the United Nations to hold a plebiscite throughout the black colony in which only black colonial subjects will be allowed to participate for the purpose of determining the will of black people as to their national destiny. Peace."

Stokely strikes the only note of discord. He sits onstage all evening dressed in a regular jacket and black shades, smoking a cigarette, laughing and clapping. But when he takes the podium, he wears an African robe and carefully crafts his speech to further his program. He doesn't directly attack whites—the Peace and Freedom people are attending and he doesn't dare contradict Eldridge in the man's presence. Nor does he mention US. Instead, he says we should ally with all blacks—not only embracing Karenga and the cultural nationalists but even middle-of-the-road politicians.

"In talking about Huey P. Newton we must talk about black people in the world! In the world!" he says, his voice dropping with each repetition, each echo sounding sterner. "We must talk about genocide! In order for this country to come about, the honkie had to exterminate the Indian—and he did it! He did it! He did it! And if you don't believe he will do it check out what he's doing in Vietnam! The concept of a black man is one who recognizes his culture and historical roots—roots that lead back to the greatest warriors of all times, Africans! Africans! We have to recognize who the major enemy is! The major enemy! The major enemy is not your brother! The major enemy is the honkie and his institutions of racism! We're talking about survival and we will survive America! A black united front is what we're about!"

The crowd cheers Stokely, me with them. On this triumphant night we want to concentrate on points of unity, not difference. When we gather back at the Magnolia Street house I am overwhelmed by a sense of history: James Forman, Stokely, and Rap strolling through my living room!

We stay up drinking and talking. I spend time with Forman. He's my favorite among the SNCC people, an older man with a lot of organizing experience who has served as a behind-the-scenes theoretician, adviser, and teacher to Stokely, Rap, and the others. Now rumors say Stokely is angling to oust Forman completely from leadership. But though Forman sometimes seems frazzled, exhausted and confused, he's still eager to impart his knowledge. I sit next to him, imbibing his stories of the early southern civil rights crusades and tales of personal sacrifice and transformation. He repeats what Kathleen has said: I remind him of Sammy Younge, Jr. Once again I hear the story. A college student, Younge slowly devoted himself to organizing while attending Tuskegee Institute in Alabama. His SNCC work changed his life: transformed by his organizing experience, he became a political revolutionary. In 1966, he was killed by a white gas-station owner when he tried to use a "white" toilet. The accused man was later found innocent of all charges by an all-white jury, an acquittal that contributed a lot to SNCC's abandonment of nonviolence. The SNCC people consider him a martyr, an example of an ordinary person who became heroic through his commitment and honesty. To be included in his company is a true honor.

"How do you learn to be a good speaker?" I ask him.

My head still rings with the oratory of the previous evening. How do these people do it? Stokely, Rap, Eldridge, Bobby, each with their own tone, never at a loss for the right word. I'm still threatened and scared to speak in front of a crowd.

"Don't go out and stare at the audience," Forman answers. "Find some other focal point. And always speak about what you know. That's the starting point. The Party, the programs. That way you'll feel on solid ground. Don't talk about things you're not familiar with. Just concentrate on communicating what you have authority about. You'll do fine."

Talking to Forman, I feel more confident about the future. Our differences pale beside what brings us together. Besides, one thing Huey has taught me is not to fear conflict. Contradictions and change — flux, flux, flux — he says, are the ruling principles of the universe, and we embrace conflict because growth comes out of struggle. Other people can try to keep things as they are. We want to find out what's happening, look for the forces in contention, challenge things, take action; we want differences to break out, reveal themselves. So Stokely preaches a black united front; in time we'll find a true and powerful synthesis of our two positions.

A couple of nights later, someone pounds on the door at four in the morning.

"Let us in! Let us in! The pigs are after us!"

Soon as I open up, two members push inside; they're sweating and out of breath.

"Motherfucking pigs are after us!" One comrade sits at the table, looking out the window, paranoid.

"What's going on?" I'm exhausted; we've been working nonstop since Huey's birthday party.

They tell me the story: they've just had a shoot-out with police on Thirty-second Street. Nobody's been hurt, but they're afraid of getting caught.

"What happened?" I demand. I still don't know whether the police harassed them.

"We made a move on the pigs," one explains.

"Then what the hell are you coming here for?" I demand.

Sleepy, confused, Darryl wanders down the stairs. One of the comrades waves at him, making nice after putting my child in danger.

"Go on," I tell Darryl. "Go back to sleep."

Pat follows Darryl.

"It's all right," I say.

Now Patrice comes down.

"Go on! Get out of here!" I order and usher her out. When I turn back to the brothers I'm steaming.

"Where's your car?" I say. I want them gone.

"It's all shot up," one says.

"But don't worry," the other says. "We parked it around the corner."

I lose my control. "What are you doing?" I shout. "Nobody told you to do this stuff anyway."

"Eldridge says we're supposed to make moves on the pigs," one answers.

"Well, Huey didn't say it, and this isn't the way you do this stuff. The pigs know this is a Panther house. They're probably right behind you guys. This whole thing is brainless."

"Well Eldridge—"

I cut them off. Arguing with them is useless, and I can't throw them out. These comrades have been with Huey from the beginning, marching into the Assembly at Sacramento. I can't leave them to the cops and on their own. But I am definitely not placing my home in jeopardy because of their mad antics.

"You listen to Eldridge. Fine. Matter of fact, I'm taking you to Eldridge's house."

We drive to Eldridge's and I'm thinking, What have I gotten myself into? I'm furious at the brothers; their foolishness threatens themselves, the Party, my own well-being, my family's safety.

"What are you gonna do with them?" I ask Eldridge once we arrive. I believe in organization; you work with people, collectively, figure out the best plan, then do your utmost to fulfill the schedule. But these two have acted unilaterally while coming back to us for help, an unconscionable abuse of loyalty.

"We got to put them in a safe house," Eldridge answers.

Over the last few months, Eldridge has used his book royalties to purchase a small arsenal, stockpiling M1s with fourteen-round clips, shotguns, .45s— though later our ordnance becomes somewhat more spectacular. We've arranged to keep the guns at apartments throughout the East Bay Area.

"These guys are putting the whole Party in trouble," I say.

"These guys are the soul of the Party, David," he tells me. "We need to depend on them. They're the shock troops; they're the vanguard."

"They may be the vanguard," I say, "but they are definitely completely out of their minds."

"They're good for the first day of the revolution," he answers. "We can use the place in the Haight."

For a night or two, all's quiet. Then I get another call: they're taking potshots at hippies from the safe house.

"We gotta get them out of there," I say to Eldridge.

"All right," he agrees.

He sends them down to Los Angeles. But some damage has already been done. The police break into the apartment and find a bomb factory: beer cans filled with black powder, expended shells, the whole place a mess, an orgy of wishful adventuristic militarism.

"Eldridge, you gotta stop this," I say. "These guys are crazy."

"The brothers gotta let off steam," he says.

Chapter

14

THE incident with the two comrades isn't isolated. Everybody in the Party wrestles with the issue of armed struggle. We're not the only ones talking about revolutionary violence, of course; there's a general sense throughout the country of an impending explosion. But we're at the center of the pressure. The police have focused on us as their primary target, constantly driving by the office, harassing cadre selling papers, following our cars—the cops know every Panther vehicle by heart now.

One night we hold a PE meeting at Bobby's house, reading the Red Book and talking about H. Rap Brown. A next-door neighbor claims to the police that he has heard us conspiring to kill H. Rap Brown and Mao Tse-tung. Next thing we know the police arrest me, Bunchy, Bunchy's brother, and bust down the door to Bobby Seale's house, indicting us for conspiracy to murder.

"Who?" Charlie Garry demands of the Berkeley policeman during the preliminary hearing. "Who were they conspiring to kill?"

"A man named H. Rap Brown and Mao Tse-tung," the cop answers.

But the stupidity is gallows humor. The constant police persecution has a deadly serious goal: to intimidate and silence us. We take up the challenge. *Revolution has come!* we sing in front of the Alameda County Courthouse whenever Huey's to appear. *Time to pick up the gun!* Every issue of the paper features a new slogan. *Blood to the horse's brow,* goes one headline, *and death to those who can't swim!* The talk has its effect: we all feel the tension of having to set some examples, bring the lion's head home.

One night Melvin helps lay out the paper. Afterward he and Emory walk outside.

"There's gonna be blood," he says to Emory, expressing his worry about the future path of the Party. Emory's barely twenty; Melvin wants to impress him with the danger of our plans. And Melvin's not dissociating himself from the Party. He's gone down to Los Angeles with us to confront US and sleeps with a loaded shotgun in case of a police visit.

"Yeah," answers Emory, as though happy to confirm the prediction, "to the horse's brow."

Huey also worries about the Party's path. (We communicate every day, passing messages and tapes through Alex and movement journalists.)

Partly his problem is that the Party exists. He had never anticipated the organization's phenomenal growth or the appeal of the Free Huey movement.

"Huey was scared to death of being acquitted," says Alex Hoffmann. "He was scared of getting out. He never wanted the poster [of him in the chair] published. 'I'm not that poster,' he said. 'That's Eldridge's picture of who I am. That's not me. They're gonna expect me to come out of here and be that poster. I can't even speak in public.'"

His other problem is the form the Party's taking. He has never envisioned the Party as a military apparatus. First and foremost, it has always been the expression of a political agenda: the Ten Point Program and the idea of serving the people. "The original vision of the Party was to develop a lifeline to the people by serving their needs and defending them against their oppressors, who come to the community in many forms, from armed police to capitalist exploiters," he writes later in an essay about the Party's history. The police patrols attempted to educate the community and save some brothers and sisters from unnecessary brutality or jail. How can the Party operate and survive from day to day? How can the Party educate the people? These were the questions he was always asking before October 27, the night of his shoot-out. "The primary job of the party is to provide leadership for the people," he wrote six months before entering prison, in an essay called "The Correct Handling of a Revolution." "The main purpose of the vanguard group should be to raise the consciousness of the masses through educational programs and other activities. . . . The party must exist aboveground as long as the dog power structure will allow, and, hopefully, when the party is forced to go underground, the party's message will already have been put across to the people."

But since Sacramento the political message and actions of the Party have been confused. The press and public concentrate on the gun, turning the symbol into something different than what Huey intended. The gun is a tool of liberation for Huey. The Bullet or the Ballot? Malcolm asked. Huey has answered the question in practice, proving himself the heir of Malcolm, and the gun is the badge of his defiance, proof he's not fronting. But Huey never picks up the gun without provocation: he holds a gun in one hand and a law book in the other because we need to defend our lives, sends the Panthers to Sacramento to protest the "disarming" of the community and a fascist law that threatens to take away our right to bear arms. He never romanticizes violence. He follows Fanon, trying to analyze and employ violence, using violence as a tool of change, never a means in itself. "You know, it's not that I'm such a tough guy, David," he says one night when we're driving around in the early days of the Party. "It's that I'm a scared little fucker, and that's why I fight." Fear is what makes him fight so desperately, be so severe and extreme. He always *imagines* that what he does to you, you're going to do to him. So he beats you to it.

He also follows Fanon about the lumpen proletariat. He sees the brothers and sisters off the block as potential revolutionaries. "For the lumpen proletariat, that horde of starving men, uprooted from their tribe and from their clan, constitutes one of the most spontaneous and the most radically revolutionary forces of a colonized people," Fanon writes.

> This lumpen proletariat is like a horde of rats; you may kick them and throw stones at them, but despite your efforts they'll go on gnawing at the roots of the tree . . . the pimps, the hooligans, the unemployed and the petty criminals . . . these workless less-than-men . . . prostitutes and maids who are paid two pounds a month, all the hopeless dregs of humanity, all who turn in circles between suicide and madness will recover their balance . . . [and] once more go forward, march[ing] proudly in the great procession of the awakened nation.

But he also warns that "colonialism will also find in the lumpen-proletariat a considerable space for manoeuvering. . . . The oppressor, who never loses a chance of setting the niggers against each other, will be extremely skilful in using that ignorance and incomprehension which are the weaknesses of the lumpen proletariat."

So Huey always wants to make sure the brothers and sisters don't alienate the whole community, the older people and the church. He wants what happens at his birthday rally: everybody onstage, from his mother to Rap.

But Eldridge has a different style and vision. No one can express as powerfully and purely our contempt and rage at society. But Eldridge has no feel for the community. He's most comfortable among the brothers he's recruited from prison, speaking to political crowds and campus audiences. He quotes from the Russian anarchists Bakunin and Nechayez and the book *The Catechism of a Revolutionary,* saying the revolutionary is a doomed man. He curses furiously, denouncing the California prison and parole system. He always excuses the undisciplined actions of his disciples. These brothers are warriors, he says; they've proven themselves in prison, besting the racist wardens and guards, taking on the white-supremist Aryan Brotherhood. They'll make up the military wing of the Party, he argues. His imagination is fixed on war. We have to intensify the struggle, he says, up the level of struggle, take the struggle to the streets. Huey's held court on the streets and now that's the law: we've all got to hold court on the street. Everybody's fair game now. Stuff's got to get serious. He envisages the Party taking an action that will spark a revolutionary uprising of the people. He says we should seize Merritt College, a block-long building located near North Oakland, take on the pigs and hold out until the community rallies to our defense.

"No," I say to him.

I don't want to oppose Eldridge. We've been spending lots of time together. He has gotten to know and like Pat, and I've really come to enjoy listening to jazz with him while we put out the paper, talking to him about things and driving around the Bay Area. Still, I know his plan flatly contradicts Huey's, and Huey remains the Party's leader.

"That's not what Huey says. I think you should rethink your position."

The smoke curls around his face.

"What does Huey say," he answers.

So we call another meeting of the Central Committee and sit around the kitchen table, the Sony winding as we say hello and Power to the People.

"Huey," I say, "Eldridge is talking about carrying out an assault on the pigs. What's your opinion?"

The answer comes back on a tape the next day. "I've already *told* everybody how to handle that kind of stuff," Huey tells us, referring to "The Correct Handling of a Revolution." "You do not go in large groups like you would need to seize Merritt College, and you don't employ a whole *brigade* of Panthers and run around and talk about unleashing war against the system. This stuff is totally insane, and if you continue all we're going to have is a bunch of dead Panthers."

But Eldridge is stubborn. You don't survive nine years of the California penal system without a hard head.

"Well, Bobby's the Chairman," he answers.

This is true—but only in theory, not practice. Bobby's gifts for inspiration are invaluable to the Party. A practical visionary, he convinces crowds they can make a revolution, and has the same effect on the cadre. One day he enters the office after Emmett has left off bags of beans and rice.

"Damn, this is a good idea," he says. "We should do this."

"We are doing it," the officer of the day says.

"No, we should establish it. Every day. A Free Food Program. Get contributions from the local businessmen and put together packages. Help people survive."

And the Free Food Program starts.

But as a leader Bobby doesn't challenge Eldridge. He exercises his strengths — speaking publicly and doing day-to-day organizing, officiating at Party Central Committee meetings — and lets Eldridge advance Party policy, take the helm and move the Party forward theoretically. Eldridge writes all the major statements about Party ideology that appear in the centerfold of *The Black Panther*, forges the alliance with the Peace and Freedom Party, recruits the brothers like Bunchy who have furnished us with a major new source of energy. He's the real leader; his spirit has taken over the Party and everyone will follow his command, including me.

None of us can predict when the confrontation will happen. The possibility simply haunts us. When I was working I always knew that sooner or later I would hit the bottle; in the same way I now know that someday I'll be doing something almost unimaginable: in the streets, firing at the cops. Always, however, the event is linked with Huey's trial, now scheduled to begin this summer. *Free Huey,* we say, *or the sky's the limit!* So I imagine there's time — because of course we don't want to jeopardize the Party or Huey's legal standing before the trial begins.

Then on April 4, 1968, Martin Luther King is killed. I hear the news in the Grove Street office. Immediately people comment on the irony: we have criticized King for his nonviolent strategy, and now he's dead by an assassin's bullet.

I get on the phone to Eldridge. "What do you think?"

"Nonviolence has died with King's death," Eldridge says.

This is our general consensus: no more hoses, whippings, and dogs. People shouldn't be asked to bleed peacefully, Malcolm has said. People are too busy singing; they'd better start swinging. Now people will see we're right and support us.

The television certainly confirms Eldridge's claim. In the next twenty-four hours, black communities throughout the country take to the streets. We're organizing for a major fund-raising barbecue to take place this weekend in De Fremery Park, and every time we return to the office from distributing leaflets the television newscasters report a new addition to the list of riot-torn cities.

We don't want Oakland to be included. Three months of analyzing Fanon on spontaneity has convinced us of the limitations of unorganized rebellions like Watts; in Detroit in 1967 over forty brothers and sisters were killed and thousands arrested. Stay cool, we tell people. The Party must lead the masses, Huey tells us in a tape, and explain to them that riots are not revolutionary actions anymore. We've got to organize the community. When we see Stokely on television in Washington we're extremely critical: he's waving a .22 around and calling for retribution, urging the crowd to violence.

"Stokeley's acting in a reactionary, adventuristic manner," I tell Eldridge over the phone. "All his words are gonna accomplish are suffering and death."

Eldridge doesn't answer. He's in one of his silent modes, holding his own counsel. When he drives by the office, he's removed, hard to read.

"We got to do something," Eldridge says. "We got to prove we're the vanguard. Everybody's doing something around the country."

"Well not that," I say. I know what he's thinking. The brothers and sisters are moving and the Party's not with them; we must sign our name to what's going on.

"Huey has explained all this in 'The Correct Handling of a Revolution,' I say. "We've got to be mindful of the Algerian revolution. We've got to lead the masses."

Eldridge adopts an enigmatic pose, not stating his obvious disapproval.

"It's time to intensify the struggle," he says. "Now's the time to show people the correct way to do this."

We keep going at it. I repeat Huey's warnings; Eldridge rebuts them with his distant, reserved disapproval.

Then, Saturday morning, Eldridge comes by and gives me the plan. By now rebellions are happening in over one hundred cities.

"All right, we got to get all our shit together. Start organizing, because we're gonna move tonight. We're gonna move now."

This is the plan. We'll transport a cache of guns from my house to West Oakland, catch a policeman on the way, and gun him down. Bobby will stay home. The next day he can explain what happened to the people. We'll set an example of organized violence, establish ourselves as true leadership, show people how to act.

I argue with Eldridge. And fear's not the only reason: I don't feel like sacrificing my life for something I don't believe in. We're not trained guerrilla fighters. Half these guys don't know how to hit the side of a barn. This is spontaneous and absolutely crazy.

"That's totally in opposition to Huey's mandate," I say. "Huey thinks that's crazy—and he's the leader of the Party. The only thing gonna come from that is people getting hurt or killed. Besides, you're talking about doing this in West Oakland, which is insane because I know that area, it's my neighborhood, and there are hundreds of cops there. They're all waiting for something to jump off and they'll destroy us."

But Eldridge won't listen. For him the action will be the revolutionary spark he's been waiting for.

"Well, you're not in charge of the Party," Eldridge answers. "Bobby is. You're only third in command. Bobby is first. And I'm second."

"That's right," I say. "That's exactly right. And I'll do what the majority says. But, Eldridge, you won't get one cop. You'll get hundreds of cops."

It's no good.

And there's no one else to deter him. Melvin's not involved; Bobby Seale stays out of the argument. Eldridge is the leader and the guys he has assembled itch for a confrontation. My only ally is Li'l Bobby. As the day wears on Eldridge's plan becomes inexorable. This thing is really going to happen, I think, while at the same time the possibility that we'll be in the streets, waging our war, seems incredible. I walk around the house. Bud's in the back, barbecuing the meat for the picnic tomorrow. The kids play in the yard, Dorion practicing his march: he's studied the brothers striding up and down at the courthouse and has perfected his own movement, three steps and a shoulder dip—

The revolution has come!
Time to pick up the gun!

Li'l Bobby comes up.

"What do you think?" he asks me.

"I think it's crazy, Bobby. Pigs all over. We talk about guys armed with discipline and ideology, not some crazies going around shooting up the town like a bunch of drunken cowboys. Besides, Huey has said it's wrong."

Even as I speak the words I'm divided because if everyone else goes along with the plan, I'll have no choice. I feel like I'm in a dream, moving against my will to a place I don't want to be.

"Well," Li'l Bobby says, "I'm with you on this. I'm gonna do what you and Huey say. I'm not going along with anything but that."

It's about four o'clock. Warm air, cloudless blue sky. Perfect Oakland day. Cars with brothers pull up around the corner from my house.

My mind is settled. I'm certain the whole thing is pure stupidity. I'm not against fighting, violence, war. That's not me. I've always liked a fight. Fighting clarifies things, resolves problems that can't be put to rest any other way. And I believe that we do need to defend ourselves against the police. The police won't let us alone, let us organize. They want our blood. I know that. But I'm also sure of something else: given the state of our training and discipline this is an inappropriate action, and it's going to get us killed. The cops have surveilled this area for the last month. They know the Magnolia Street house is a Party gathering ground. On the most peaceful nights they have squad cars patrolling the streets constantly, following us; sometimes a van—a portable station house—parks several blocks away. Mao says the guerrilla should lose himself in the sea of the people, and it's undoubtedly true that many of my neighbors sympathize with the Party. But precisely because of our community support the police have infested the area: if one is attacked, hundreds will respond at a moment's notice.

Making a decision that much more difficult is the fact that we can't talk about the plan fully or really put it to a vote. For one, most of the guys present are members of Eldridge's cadre. They're not strong, independent thinkers like Bunchy or Geronimo; these are undisciplined brothers who don't put in hours selling the papers, running the offices. Talking about attacking pigs is their natural language. Plus, we can't be sure whom to trust. Undoubtedly there are informers and provocateurs in the Party and we can't convene a full meeting of the cadre and discuss this openly. So everything is done on the sly, with a preselected group.

"Eldridge," I say, "I think this stuff is really not going to cut it."

We argue again. I can't express everything in my mind. I'm thinking, for instance, that Eldridge is turning his personal vendetta—against Reagan and the California Adult Authority—into Party policy. I also believe he's acting on a need to prove himself: both Huey and D.C. have demonstrated their commitment to revolutionary action, and Eldridge has yet to join their rank. This will give him the opportunity.

But I hold off any psychologizing, concentrating on tactics and strategy.

"Eldridge, this is my neighborhood," I complain.

"Are you coming with us or not?" he answers. This is always his question, a trick bind: he'll talk to me if I answer yes. Agreeing with him is the only way I can continue to register my disapproval.

"I've told you. I'll do what the majority says. But I'm totally against it. First of all there's gonna be a lot of police down here. Not one, but a lot, because that's where they congregate."

Eldridge shrugs off the objection.

"Forget that then," I say and start to repeat Huey's objections.

Eldridge interrupts. He repeats his arguments. People are in motion throughout the country.

"I know that, Eldridge," I say.

A move like this now is the proper timing: we will provide a revolutionary spark that will lift the struggle to a higher level.

"I know that, Eldridge," I say.

We need to make our statement in the street, to strike blows at the oppressor.

"I know that, Eldridge," I say.

"Then you agree with me?" he says.

I feel like my mind is exploding.

"I agree with you, but I don't buy it."

How can I say this to Eldridge? I certainly am not his intellectual equal. But this is not a theoretical debate: my life is at stake. I've been scared before doing Party work, but always I had Huey, whose judgment I trusted; I am instinctively skeptical of everything about this plan.

"It's not what Huey says."

Eldridge relents. Why don't we take a vote?

The cadre crowd around on the street. We stand by the car. Eldridge explains the options. The faces nod. The vote ends before it begins. Without Huey's presence or Bobby's objections no one can resist the power of Eldridge's logic.

"All right?" Eldridge asks me.

No, I want to say. No, it's not all right, it's not all right at all. But I can't. I'm in leadership; I don't want to lose the respect of the comrades. I will abide by the will of the majority. The Party has given me life and I have sworn my loyalty to the organization. The Party is family. You don't pick and choose; you either belong or not. I can't cut myself off from it now.

Chapter

15

WE wait until dark, around seven. The brothers load the guns into the caravan, stuffing them under the seats—wooden-stocked M1s, snub-nosed .38s, semiautomatic M14s. Our arsenal. I look around as they troop from the house, sure the police are watching our every move.

Then it's time.

I get into the lead with Eldridge and Li'l Bobby.

"Captain David, if anything happens, I'm going with you," Li'l Bobby says.

"That's right," I say.

We take off, the other cars behind us, a convoy looking for trouble. We round the corner, down past the Magnolia Street house, then head downtown, the cars almost bumping into one another, jammed together on the narrow streets. We're looking for a cop, Eldridge has said. Where are they? I scan the streets, M14 in my lap, cradled under the window, safety off, bullet clip snapped in place.

We turn onto a side street. One- and two-story wooden shingled houses stand opposite a deserted warehouse and abandoned lot. It's dinnertime. Through the lit windows you can see people at the table. The rockers and chairs on the small raised porches sit empty. Parked cars line the street. Everything's still.

Eldridge says he's got to pee.

We halt. Behind us the caravan stops. Eldridge starts his business. I fidget, survey the road. A car behind us stalls, the lights flickering—a bad battery or something.

From around the corner the car appears.

Keep going, I think—don't be cops.

The car stops. Lights flash. A guy gets out.

"Hey! You!" they call to Eldridge. "Walk out into the middle of the street! Hands up! Quick!"

I turn to Li'l Bobby. He whips out his M14. Noise and brightness flood the street.

We jump from the car. I hold my rifle. The cops are shouting, shooting. Cops pour out of cars on the once-empty road, taking cover behind open doors, emptying their guns at us. Horns blare as guys struggle to leave the cars. In the street one brother falls, already wounded. I lift my rifle; it weighs a lot and seems awfully puny. I point the gun somewhere between the sky and street and press the trigger.

Our windshield shatters. Bullets crash into glass, steel, the wooden sides of the houses. I hear the brothers cursing. There's no order, just abrupt chaos, fear, madness. A cop lies on the pavement, holding his leg. More cop cars swarm to the block, sirens blaring, radios squawking, appearing from nowhere—they must have been tracking us all afternoon.

The trigger sticks. The clip's spent. I have no ammunition; the cops are firing to kill. Our side of the street is a desert: no one lives near the warehouse, and if the cops find us by ourselves they'll kill us for sure.

"This way," Eldridge says.

He takes off across the street. A spray of bullets follows. I follow, running for my life. Thinking Li'l Bobby's behind me, I jump a fence blocking my path. Behind me, the cops direct their fire, rounding people up. But the guns aren't stopping. The fence turns out to be a shed. I look both ways, see an open window, and leap.

I breathe, my heart racing.

Where am I?

A bedroom.

I look around.

No Li'l Bobby.

"Oh my God! What's happening?"

A middle-aged woman enters, a friend of Pat's mother. I try to talk, but my mouth is too dry to form words.

"The police are killing these guys outside," I finally manage. "There's a shoot-out. I just started running! You know me. I'm Pat's husband."

Outside the firing increases. I hear the thud of bullets burying themselves in wood, the barks of the police giving orders.

"You gotta hide me!" I tell her. "You gotta hide me!"

"Where am I gonna hide you!"

She's more terrified than me: the Oakland police are outside and I could be putting her life in jeopardy too.

"The police are gonna come in here looking for me," I explain. "They're gonna think I'm one of these guys. You got to hide me!"

"Get in the closet!" she says, opening the door.

"They're gonna *look* in the closet," I say.

Outside bullhorns echo down the street; the place sounds like a war zone and the cops seem to be preparing for some final combat.

"Get under the *bed*."

I squeeze under the mattress, fluff the dust ruffle so it's over my face.

"Don't you tell them I'm in here, whatever they do!"

The firing keeps on. Under the mattress the air is hot, thick. My heart pounds more powerfully and crazily than ever before. I can't catch my breath and think I might die of fright. You got to save yourself, I tell myself.

She comes back.

"Oh my god! They're never gonna stop shooting! They're just killing people out here."

"What's happening?" I whisper. "I gotta know what's happening."

From outside I smell gas and gunpowder. The shooting is concentrated, very near to us, across the street or next door. Are they shooting brothers? Who's holding out? The gun battle seems like a suspended moment in time, going on and on, the noise and fire getting louder and hotter. All I want is not to die: the real stuff about guns, cops, and war is nothing like the books or movies but deadly, terrifyingly real.

The woman runs back. She's breathless.

"They're burning up the house next *door!*"

"Be quiet! I hear them, I hear them."

Pigs kick and slam against the door, their racket rising over the volleys.

"Open the door! It's the *police!* Open the door!"

The woman's frantic.

"Oh my God! What am I gonna do?"

I plead with her. "Please don't tell them I'm here."

The house shakes with the pounding.

"Open the goddamn door!"

She collects herself. "You just be *quiet,* because they'll kill you."

"I know. I see."

In a moment they overrun the house.

"*Nobody*'s in my house," she's saying. "What do you want?"

"They're shooting through the windows. We got to use your bathroom."

Then I understand: Eldridge and Li'l Bobby are next door, the only ones left. I went one way, Eldridge the other. Li'l Bobby followed Eldridge. They'll be killed by the police. I can't do anything.

From under the bed I see police boots, the woman trailing after them.

"Oh my God! Don't tear my house up!"

"We gotta get them out of there!"

"My God! What are you doing!"

"Set the goddamn house on fire!"

"Don't—"

They push her aside. "Get *back!* Get *out* of the way!"

"My God! What are you doing!"

"You black *bitch!* Get the hell out of the way!"

"Don't hurt me, oh please—"

"We'll kill you! Gonna get those *goddamn* niggers out of there. *Get* out of the way, bitch, before we kill you, too, you black bitch!"

I hug the floor. I want to be invisible. If these murderers find me here alone, they'll shoot me, claim I made a move on them, and if the woman resists them, they'll kill her too. They must not find me! Except I'm breathing—still breathing! And my heart pounds even louder now, an insanely fast, erratic beat: I cover my mouth with my hands, but I can't stop my heart. They must hear it: they've got to hear.

Then a reprieve:

"I think we've smoked them out. They burned up the house."

In a moment the room empties.

"Oh my God!" the woman says. "They've set that house on fire."

Voices scream from the street now, but I don't dare leave my hiding place.

She runs out, comes back.

"I think they killed one of them."

"Which one, which one?"

"I don't know. But you can come out now. They're getting ready to leave."

I climb out from under the bed. Her husband comes in. He doesn't want me there. I have to risk the street.

Outside everything is calm, exhausted. Some police officers talk into their car radios. A little ways down the street a neighborhood woman moans and sobs. A friend or two comfort her. I sit on the stairs; I want to be inconspicuous, but I can't walk down the street yet.

The police notice me.

"Where did you come from?"

"I was in the house."

They stand over me, scared and angry.

"Where?"

"I was *hiding*."

One knocks me with his nightstick. "*Who* are you?" He hits me again, trying to scare me. "Who are you?"

The woman comes out. "Leave him alone!" she says. "He's my nephew."

The police look dubious; the husband joins the crowd.

"*You* know this man?" the police ask him.

The husband tries to kick me. "I don't know him!"

I dodge his foot, scooting away. He's trying to run me off the porch.

"What's the matter with you, man." I say. "What are you doing? I'm your nephew."

"You're not my nephew," the husband says. "I don't know this god-damned guy. Get out of here!"

The police grab me. "Who are you?"

"Get him out of here!" the husband yells.

"He's my nephew," the woman insists.

The cops clear them off the porch, then start on me.

"Who are you?"

"Charles Robinson!" I answer. "Charles Robinson!"

"You know what just happened here?"

"I don't know. I just live here."

All I want is for them to leave me alone or take me to jail. If they find out my true identity they'll surely kill me.

"How did you get here?"

"I just turned up, man. I was hiding! I swear to God!"

"You know the Panthers?"

In PE we've read that when the Vietcong get caught, they never admit their real identity, insisting on their loyalty to the old regime. "What do you mean, 'know the Panthers'?" I say. "I don't know no Panthers. I just live here."

The cops can't figure out what's wrong with my story.

"Get in the van," they say. They're furious. "You're going to jail!"

"That's all right," I say. "Take me to jail."

"Shut up!" they say.

"I want to go to jail. Take me to jail."

"Shut up!"

They push and prod me into the van. Just let me be arrested, I think. Let me get to the station house.

The door slams shut. A fireman hoses down the bloody street. A woman moans: "My God, they killed the young one! They killed the baby!"

I sit there, mortified. Don't react, I tell myself. They'll kill you if you show them what you feel. I remember something I've heard about the LA police. They carry .22s in their boots, along with their standard issue. They shoot you dead, then fire the .22 in the air and lay it beside your corpse, claim that you tried to kill them. Oakland cops will do the same. Kill you. If they know who you are. You're a revolutionary. Get to the station house. Survive. Arrive at the station house alive.

Soon as we enter the station my cover is blown.

"You stupid assholes!!" a sergeant says. "That's David Hilliard! He's a Panther—he's National Headquarters Captain."

My successful trickery incenses the arresting cop. He clubs me. "You motherfucker!"

I twist away from the nightsticks.

"We'll kill you, you motherfucker! You never would have made it here if we had known."

"That's right," I say. "That's right. I know you would have killed me."

A black police officer comes up.

"Lock him up! I *know* him."

I recognize Gwynne Pierson from the job I had at Hale Brothers. He was the officer on the beat and would come in and eat popcorn and hot dogs.

"Lock him up," Gwynne insists.

They put me in the cell by myself. Instantly the sergeant and the investigator walk in. They demand a statement. Some Panthers have talked, they say, identifying the other members of the failed assault; I won't be informing them of anything they don't know already if I simply report what happened.

"Five," I say.

"We know you were there!"

I remain silent. Don't even ask them questions. Now I'm safe. I want to hear what happened, and of course I believe Li'l Bobby is dead, but I must be patient and not question them: anything I say will give them information and violate the rules of the Pocket Lawyer.

"Call my attorney."

The next morning we meet with Alex Hoffmann. He tells us the news. Everybody's been arrested. Eldridge, shot in the leg and butt, has been sent to Vacaville. Li'l Bobby is dead. I listen to the story and imagine the details.

We jump the shed and Li'l Bobby follows Eldridge. They dive into a basement. Surrounded by thin walls already riddled by bullets, they hide behind
a foot-and-a-half-thick cement foundation. For ninety minutes the cops pour
bullets into the place; then they start lobbing tear gas. Finally a stray bullet
ignites the gas, forcing them to flee the heat and flames. Eldridge is naked;
later he says that when he was unconscious, Li'l Bobby stripped him to lo-
cate a wound in the dark, patting him down, feeling for blood. Li'l Bobby is
only bare-chested: not yet eighteen, he's still modest. Eldridge yells they're
surrendering.

Eldridge describes the rest in a written affidavit:

> Little Bobby helped me to my feet and tumbled through the door.
> There were pigs in the windows above us in the house next door, with
> guns pointed at us. They told us not to move, to raise our hands. This
> we did, and an army of pigs ran up from the street. They started kick-
> ing and cursing us, but we were already beyond any pain, any feeling.
> The pigs told us to stand up. Little Bobby helped me to my feet. The
> pigs pointed to a squad car parked in the middle of the street and told
> us to run to it. I told them that I couldn't run. Then they snatched Lit-
> tle Bobby away from me and shoved him forward, telling him to run
> to the car. It was a sickening sight. Little Bobby, coughing and chok-
> ing on the night air that was burning his lungs. . .stumbled forward as
> best he could. . . .

Then, the police say, he reaches for a handgun tucked into his pants. I
know their story is a bold-faced lie: Li'l Bobby was carrying an M14. The
police volley kills him instantly.

"They turned to me," Eldridge later recounts,

> but before they could get into anything, the black people in the neigh-
> borhood who had been drawn to the site by the gunfire and commotion
> began yelling at them, calling the pigs murderers, telling them to leave
> me alone. And a face I will never forget . . .loomed up.
>
> "Where are you wounded?" [the police captain] asked me.
>
> I pointed out my wound to him . . .[he] looked down at my
> wound, raised his foot and stomped on the wound.
>
> "Get him out of here," he told the other pigs, and they took me
> away.

Inside the jail I'm mortified. I've failed to restrain Eldridge and didn't protect Li'l Bobby. I keep the fear and confusion I felt during the shoot-out to myself; I meet the loss of Li'l Bobby with the same fortitude I possessed at my father's death.

The one good thing about the shoot-out is we get a chance to spend time with Huey: cops move us to the "Panther tank," the cellblock where Huey is incarcerated. I am joyous to see him; we haven't spent any unlimited time together since the October shoot-out. But Huey acts distant. He stays in his cell, sleeps, hardly talks. I remember his mood when the "paper panthers" fronted with us before the pigs at Betty Shabazz's appearance. Then he lay in bed for several days, frustrated and discouraged. Now he appears the same.

"Huey thought April 6 was absolutely crazy," Alex Hoffmann remembers. "Afterwards he was very depressed. Terribly depressed. He was upset because Bobby Hutton was killed. And he was upset that you hadn't kept Eldridge in check. Though I think he knew Eldridge was an overpowering personality."

Finally I break the silence.

"Come on, Huey," I say. "We should have a PE class."

I tell him it's crucial he speak to the brothers. These guys have been working for him and most have neither heard nor seen him except on tape or film. He must do something to lift their spirits, transform the jail into a revolutionary college. But I'm also anticipating listening to his clarity and energy again; it's been a long time since our nights at the Bos'un Locker.

He doesn't disappoint. The Party is organizing a memorial service for Li'l Bobby. Huey tells us we'll have our own ceremony in the jail exercise room.

Huey leads the meeting. He reads from the Red Book and talks about death. He's speaking about Li'l Bobby, but obviously he's been thinking about his own mortality — if he's convicted for murder he'll be sentenced to death.

We're afraid of death because we imagine it as the end of life, he says. But death is a part of life. So the question of how you die is really a question of how you live. The person afraid to die is the person who hasn't lived. Even though everyone must die, not every death is the same. Deaths vary in their significance. To die for the reactionaries is lighter than a feather — because you are already dead, spritually dead, stripped of the pride and will that are our human traits. But to die for the people is heavier than a mountain — because then humanity has lost someone who has helped change the intolerable conditions in the world.

We sit at a big square table on steel stools bolted to the floor. A television set screwed to the wall is high above us. There are no windows. Bars enclose the entire space, while the police patrol us, walking on an outer tier. The room stinks of jail: funky old blankets, sweat, stale cigarette smoke. But the acuity of Huey's thinking, the high energy of his voice, the nervous excitement in his face, transports us. We're no longer single individuals, scared and confused, but revolutionaries embarked on a mission of great significance.

Now, Huey goes on, Li'l Bobby died for the people. He was a courageous example. He will live through his spirit and live through us all. This event is definitely not the end. We're all going to get out of here. We should maintain our courage. Li'l Bobby would have been proud of us all. We knew what the Party stood for and we acted appropriately. We are standard bearers in the fight for human liberation.

Later Huey comes over to me. We sit on a bench.

"Tell me everything that happened," he says.

Talking in whispers, sometimes passing notes, I explain to him the sequence of events leading to the shoot-out.

The story infuriates him.

"I told Eldridge not to do this," he keeps saying. "It's lucky more of you guys weren't killed."

"He asserted rank," I tell him. I am anguished with guilt; I let down Huey, let down Li'l Bobby.

"You did right to argue with him," he says. "You did right. Eldridge was wrong. Why did he go against me?"

"He kept saying it was time," I offer. "And then we took a vote. It was a democratic decision. I had to go along."

He senses my self-doubt.

"David," he says, "you did right. You followed the Party's principle. You argued with Eldridge, which was the right thing to do. And you followed the Party. Besides you're the only one who didn't give a statement. Everybody else started snitching as soon as they got in the door. Which is the whole proof of what I was saying—that these guys are really not ready to be guerrillas. Which is why I opposed the whole thing. I always said that if things like this should happen, they should be done by D.C.'s cadre, not Eldridge."

His words exonerate me, lift my spirit.

"Now don't worry. You're gonna get out of here. We're gonna get you bailed out. But I want you to stay in contact with me. From now on you've got to be in charge of the Party's programs. I don't care what anybody says. I'm personally giving that authority to you. You've demonstrated your commitment to carrying out the ideals of the Party, so I want you to keep Bobby in line. That's your job. Keep him in line. I'm giving you a new position. You're now Chief of Staff."

Chapter

16

ON the outside, Pat deals with the Party's administrative duties.

"I called the jail and asked was David there," Pat says.

"Yeah," they told me, "we got the bastard. Too goddamn bad we didn't kill him. We didn't kill but one of them!"

And slammed the phone down in my face.

I got in contact with Garry, and Garry brought his car over. A Thunderbird. A white Thunderbird. I was driving him around. Bobby Seale was with us, having all kind of flashes. He'd see a pickup truck with a rifle rack and hold his head down or holler out. He was really paranoid. Garry said, "Goddamn, Bobby! You're gonna run yourself crazy and me and Pat too." Until Garry told me to take Bobby home and make Bobby stay there.

She also comforts Li'l Bobby's mother, helping organize the funeral and providing the family with financial support.

"Miss Dolly Mae was in shock. She didn't talk for a couple of days. When she did, she said, 'I knew something was going to happen to my baby because he was so hardheaded.'"

Our failed assault sparks no revolutionary upsurge—actually the ghetto rebellions end that week—but the community does rally behind us, protesting Li'l Bobby's murder, upholding our right to self-defense. The shoot-out turns into another colossal event. Telephone calls from BSUs and community organizations flood the office, everybody wanting to start Panther chapters. The reporters and magazine writers demand unlimited interviews. Contributions soar. Suddenly we're celebrities, a cause. After I'm bailed out, I find myself driving around with Godfrey Cambridge and Dick Gregory. Marlon Brando attends Li'l Bobby's memorial service, then goes on a police patrol, sitting in the back of the car, friendly and enigmatic. A few nights later I'm arrested at Bobby Seale's for carrying a weapon, and Brando puts up ten thousand dollars bail. He leaves soon after — a year later *Burn!* is released; we figure he was using us for research; we provided him with a true revolutionary environment — but his presence gets us attention.

The media notice is timely. Our leadership is under siege. Huey's trial — literally a fight to the death — is set for summer. Plus, after the shoot-out, the Adult Authority has revoked Eldridge's parole, charging him with possession of a deadly weapon, associating with people of bad reputation, and failing to cooperate with his parole agent. Garry has appealed, but the odds are against a Reagan-appointed court overruling the Reagan-appointed Adult Authority: Eldridge will be in jail.

Two problems arise.

Eldridge insists on running the Party from inside, exerting his control through messages delivered by Alex.

"Eldridge was *unlike* Huey," remembers Alex.

From the beginning Huey felt he couldn't really run things when he wasn't on the scene. Eldridge absolutely wanted to run things. Both the Party and the contacts with the Free Huey groups and the Peace and Freedom Party, which had been exclusively Eldridge's thing. Kathleen would come back with instructions from him, and the Party would say what she wanted to do was impossible, and then Eldridge would be, "Why isn't it being done?"

He also swears he's not going back to jail.

"There's not gonna be a trial," he says. "Only trial is gonna be a red-light trial, a trial in the streets."

Two months after the shoot-out, in June, a local judge releases Eldridge on fifty thousand dollars bail, dismissing the parole violation charges.

"There is nothing to indicate why it was deemed necessary to cancel his parole before his trial on the pending of criminal charges of which he is presumed innocent," the judge argues. ". . . It has to be stressed that the uncontradicted evidence presented to this Court indicated that the petitioner had been a model parolee. The peril to his parole status stemmed from no failure of personal rehabilitation, but from his undue eloquence in pursuing political goals, goals which were offensive to many of his contemporaries."

We capitalize on the provisional victory. (The state supreme court, unlike this rural county judge, won't dare defy the Adult Authority.) Seize the Time! we say, casting ourselves as agents, not victims, of change: every opportunity should be exploited to its maximum benefit, every contradiction pursued to its ultimate resolution. We run speak-ins, vigils: along with Huey's trial, Eldridge's freedom becomes the focus of our organizing. Two and three times a day, Eldridge and I drive the Plymouth to lectures at which he reviles Reagan—Mickey Mouse Reagan, he calls the governor—with a condemned man's scorn, summoning all his eloquence to denounce his enemies, explain himself. His speeches sing:

> We say, power to the people . . . all people . . . white people . . . Eskimos and Indians, every living ass and swinging dick. . . . You've had government of the pigs, by the pigs and for the pigs. You've had history written by pigs, to edify pigs and to brutalize our minds. We say we have to close the book on [that] history . . . stamp it with a pig hoof and [say] that's pig history . . . put it in the museums and open a new book and let the people write a history fit to be taught to their children: a history that we can all look to and agree that is the truth, that we won't have to be ashamed of it. . . . We need a university of the world that can teach the whole world—all the people of the world—the true history of the world; not a racist history, not a nationalist history, but a history that can enable people to live. And we need a society that will be universal, with no passports, no boundaries, a utopia brought down to earth, a classless society, a society that is not based on capitalistic economics and exploitation. . . . Later for J. Edgar Hoover, later for his mammy, later for the Secret Service, later for all of that because we have to get into a situation where the madmen come forth. When the sane people don't do it, when all the good middle-class people don't do it, then the madmen have to do it, and the madmen say that we're going to have freedom or we're going to have chaos; we're going to be part of the total destruction of America or we're going to be part of the liberation of America. Down with the pigs of the power structure. Back to Disneyland for Mickey Mouse.

I listen, split between my emotions and reason.

Eldridge expresses my visceral feeling. We are fighting for life; we will exact the highest possible cost from those who oppose us. I still honor the gun as the tool of liberation and continue training as though for war: especially since April 6, combat is the only appropriate description of the relationship between us and the police. And I'm quite clear on my commitments: I'll do my duty, risk a personal sacrifice.

But the pain of Li'l Bobby's loss still hurts, while Eldridge's self-styled "madmen" no longer impress me. The fact is I'll be very happy never to find myself in another shoot-out again. Not simply for my own sake — though of course I'm mindful of my own survival — but for my comrades in arms: Li'l Bobby wasn't a friend but a brother. So when members start talking about raising the level of struggle, doing material damage, killing pigs, I set them straight, telling them they'd best go and sell some papers instead, educate the community about our ideology and practice and educate themselves about the community.

With the media attention the Party rises to the top of the political most-wanted list. Reagan and San Francisco mayor Alioto demonize us regularly, stigmatizing the party as Pied Pipers of cultural and social revolution, characterizing us as the essence of violence, chaos, evil. By September, J. Edgar Hoover calls us, "the greatest threat to the internal security of the country. Schooled in the Marxist-Leninist ideology and the teachings of Chinese Communist Mao Tse-tung, its members have perpetrated numerous assaults on police officers and have engaged in violent confrontations with police throughout the country. Leaders and representatives of the Black Panther Party travel extensively all over the United States preaching their gospel of hate and violence not only to ghetto residents, but to students in colleges, universities and high schools as well."

The war between us and the authorities escalates. We call them pigs; they act like pigs. Our lives are subject to a daily attack of FBI visits and harassment arrests. No matter how much money we raise, we constantly scramble to pay someone's bail.

One night I come home and Pat tells me Darryl has almost burnt down his first-grade classroom. He feels mad, doesn't want to play with the other kids. The teacher's punitive, mean-spirited. Besides, maybe she's targeted Darryl because he's a Hilliard: along with the Seales and Newtons the family name is associated now in Oakland with Panther Party leadership. She orders Darryl into the closet and shuts the door. Darryl wants to show the lady he won't be trifled with; even though he's thin as a rail, Darryl's a Hilliard and likes a fight. With a few pocket matches he lights some scrap paper. He means to set only a small flame, teach the teacher a lesson. But the pile bursts into flame. Scared, he tries to stomp out the blaze, but the smoke smothers him. He busts open the door; heat and sparks shoot out. Everybody hollers and firemen are called.

"I told him there was another way of solving the problem of that teacher," Patricia says. She's very concerned about the incident. "I told him he could have come home and talked to me. But that woman shouldn't have locked him up."

I'm starved and my stomach's growling; I've got to eat. "Well it sounds like you said the right thing," I say. I think she's blowing the event way out of proportion.

But her advice isn't what's bothering her. "They're gonna give him trouble."

I grab some chicken; food seems to soothe my aches.

"Patricia, he's a six-year-old boy," I say. "What kind of trouble are they gonna give him?"

"They're calling me, telling me about charges."

"There's nothing to worry about." I stuff my mouth and feel immediate relief. A doctor has told me I'm well on my way to a severe ulcer, but I have no chance of reducing the pressure in my life. "He's a kid. I'm telling you, they won't go after a kid."

But a week later someone knocks on the door.

"Yeah?" I demand.

"Are you David Hilliard?" He wears a suit and tie, hat. Businessman.

"Yeah?"

"Your son's named Darryl?"

I check out the street, looking for other parked cars or suspicious-looking guys. Nothing. "Who's asking?"

He shows me the FBI badge in his wallet.

"We hear Darryl tried to burn down his school."

"Oh my God!" I laugh. In the face of the warfare I'm bracing for, this foolishness strikes me as really contemptible, pathetic. "You gonna bring my boy to trial?"

The man is embarrassed.

"A six-year-old boy? Is that how desperate you are? Worried about six-year-old revolutionaries?"

I'm having fun with the guy until I realize he's not answering; he's using this opportunity to peek into the house.

"What's going on?" I ask.

"There could be a serious charge on your son," he says. He's craning his neck, eager to see beyond the front door.

I stand in his way. "What are you doing? You taking him to jail? A six-year-old boy? For fooling around with some matches?"

The guy backs off. He's my age but tall, light-skinned, and speaks in a bland California accent. My own FBI agent.

"You guys are a joke!" I tell him. I want to run him off, make him flee down the street, like Al, my old boss. But he has the protection of the government; I limit my rage to words. "Trying to intimidate me by using my kid. Get out of here! You guys gotta be kidding."

They're not. In the next two years, the FBI—and the local police, also—use every weapon in their arsenal to destroy the Party. Later experts will conclude that of all the counterintelligence investigations launched against black activists only the attack against Martin Luther King was as ferocious as that leveled against the Black Panther Party. A Senate Select Committee investigating government intelligence operations in 1976 concludes that in its operations against the Party the FBI "engaged in lawless tactics and responded to deep-seated social problems by fomenting violence and unrest."

New members flock to the Party, embrace our revolutionary politics. Losing in Vietnam and at home, pig philosophy—the ideology of Reagan and Nixon—is on the defensive. We answer the attacks on us by strengthening our resolve, tightening Party bonds.

Domestic responsibilities pose real problems. At first the Party fit comfortably into our daily lives; now it dictates our every waking hour. Neither Pat nor I have time to bus the kids to and from one school or another or serve supper promptly at six. At the same time we can't rely on my family anymore; sending the kids to B.B.'s or Dorothy's is like involving noncombatants in a war. Similarly, I rarely visit my mother: I don't want to hand the Oakland pigs an excuse for a midnight raid on her house. Plus, we've outgrown the confines of the Grove Street office. We're busting out at the seams, the piles of newsletters, leaflets, buttons, flags that don't fit in the office overflowing into our homes.

To help with the problem we talk to Arlene Slaughter—a real estate broker who is active in the Democratic Party—and her son, Mickey, who, though white, grew up knowing many Panther members.

"This friend of mine came in to see me and ask for a donation for the Party," Mickey remembers.

I gave her a check. Five or ten bucks. About six months later, at this office that I was working in, the cops came in. They said they had a warrant for my arrest for unpaid parking tickets and took me to jail. I had a file that I kept all these paid tickets in.

I said, "Before you book me, will you *please* let me go through this to see if I can show you that I paid the ticket?"

I pick up the file. There must have been fifty checks in there. Forty-nine hit the ground facedown, and one floats up: the *one* to the Free Huey campaign.

The desk sergeant looks at it and says, "Book him."

Soon after, we started having dialogues with you and Pat about housing situations. You outlined some of the housing needs, which started off with rentals. Just anyplace to house this *vast* number of people that kept swelling the ranks. I had zero political qualms about helping. I would have joined you if you would have let me in.

Another way we try to consolidate the organization is to complete a merger with SNCC. Shortly before Huey's trial begins, we decide to go to New York and hold a press conference announcing the merger and mass demonstrations for Huey. Melvin and I are going to stay at James Forman's house, and I'm looking forward to the visit. I remember Forman's previous valuable advice and I'm eager to stay with the man, to absorb more of his teachings.

But once we get to New York the situation between us and SNCC deteriorates. (Forman has discussed the difficulties in his autobiography. He had championed our alliance, writing a memo shortly before our visit stating SNCC's "legitimate role [is] to assist in the development of the Black Panther Party." But, he adds, "There were . . . tensions between SNCC and the Panthers, between myself and members of the Panthers, created by continuing distrust and suspicion of intentions." Plus, he was under tremendous political and personal pressure — he had just undergone surgery — and the tension took its toll. "I was stretching my own capacity far beyond the limits of the human body," he continues. "I was in a state of near collapse and subsequently forced to take several months of rest.")

From the moment of our arrival, it becomes evident that there are significant differences and little good faith between us and SNCC. They keep accusing us of attempting to take over their organization.

"How stupid can you be?" we say to them. "We're naming Stokely Prime Minister and Rap Minister of Justice. We're voluntarily subordinating ourselves to you guys. Huey's even said that we're prepared to leave Oakland and turn the Party over to you, relocate. So how can you accuse us of trying to take you over. We're asking you guys to spearhead this stuff."

But common sense doesn't seem to work.

Forman himself is acting weirder and weirder. At his house he acts distracted, walking around, picking up and putting down the phone without dialing, annoyed and short-tempered, avoiding me. The whole night's a conspiracy to shut us out; Forman's paranoid, the complete opposite of the patient teacher he appeared to be before. I'm confused by the change, and his peculiar new attitude leaves me a little desperate.

"What the hell's happening with him?" I whisper to Melvin. "It's like he's got a problem or something."

Just before we're to leave for the SNCC office to meet about the merger I get a moment alone with James.

"What's the matter?" I ask. Forman looks a little crazed, suspicious and angry.

"Leave your watch," he tells me.

"I just bought this watch," I tell him. I've recently bought the watch, following Malcolm's advice: he always says he can't respect anybody who isn't conscious of time.

"Don't wear it," he says.

"I bought the watch to wear it," I answer. I'm at a loss. Does Forman think the watch is bugged? But that's crazy. Does he really think I'm a cop? What's happened to him? He's not making sense.

"Don't wear it," he repeats. "I'll buy you another watch."

"I don't want another watch," I say. "I just bought this watch and I'm wearing this watch."

Melvin enters the scene. We face off in the kitchen. Forman's accusation stings me. All we've done is offer our work and good faith to these guys; their only answer has been suspicion. I had imagined SNCC was together, a model to follow, its leaders exemplars who would guide us. Instead they seem to be negative examples, individualistic, manipulative, now seeming absolutely insane. Is this what happens to a political group? Or is this just them?

"Leave the watch, David," Melvin says. "Don't worry about it."

"I don't want to leave the watch," I tell Melvin. "I bought the watch. I'm not leaving the watch."

"Leave the watch," Forman repeats. He's clearly gone now, adamantly echoing his own words over and over.

The three of us go at it, each repeating our position. The whole thing makes no sense. I stand there, looking at myself, telling myself, David, you're arguing about a watch! But the dispute has taken on a life of its own, like the political debates I witness in Berkeley: we're no longer interested in coming to any common ground but simply insisting on our position.

"It's a watch, David," Melvin says. His look tells me Forman isn't the only crazy person in the room. "Give it up," he pleads.

Still furious at Forman, I leave the watch and we continue our discussions. But the conflicts between the two organizations are insurmountable. Our plan for a press conference ends in chaos. The SNCC people are split among themselves; their leaders are eloquent but ineffectual, their organization is falling apart. We must admit to ourselves that Huey's hope that they will provide us with some answers is ill-founded: we're leadership, no one else. For better and worse, we have no one to rely on but ourselves, and we return to Oakland for the start of Huey's trial.

By now we're internationally famous. On the trial's first day, July 15, 1968, the Party and supporters jam the courthouse plaza, more members than ever before, even after all the attacks. Gene McKinney has been away since the October 27 shoot-out, and he's amazed at the change.

"When I left it wasn't too many people who was for the Party. But after I came back, maybe because of the incident down on Seventh Street, everybody you see had a black leather jacket and a tam cap, old ladies and little kids. It was for real. It was live. I said, 'Damn! Everybody's found it now. Right on!'"

Gene's return is part of trial strategy. Garry plans to stand the courtroom on its head. He's going to challenge the jury system, argue that the jury pool unfairly excludes blacks, and insist he examine every prospective juror for unconscious bias. Next he intends to educate the judge and the jury about racism, the court system, and the Party: he wants to make clear the political forces at stake in the trial. Finally he's preparing two dramatic legal surprises. He's going to explode the state's case from the inside, calling Gene — the mystery witness in the car at the shooting whose identity we've managed to keep secret for the last nine months — to testify, and he will put Huey on the stand.

"Oakland's a little old, small, one-horse town anyway," Gene says about his escape from Oakland that night. "So the shooting was the biggest news in town. But I beat the roadblocks."

He went to Philadelphia, living with his brother, an ex–NBA basketball player.

"Nobody knew what was happening. Everything kind of worked out smooth. Kept me incognito. Then, just before the trial was coming up, you and me stayed in touch — on the low-profile side."

Now he intends to plead the Fifth Amendment to any questions about that night. To reach a guilty verdict, the jury must be certain without a reasonable doubt; Garry hopes Gene's refusal to testify will cause some jurors to think he might have shot Frey.

Opening day—and throughout the trial; it's part of our strategy—we pack the courtroom: we want to impress the jury that a movement, not only an individual, is in the dock.

Garry and his cocounsel, Faye Stender, start their attack, calling witnesses who testify to the institutional racism that rules the court. Lowell Jensen, the prosecutor, argues that the legal process is color-blind. But Garry translates the facts of my life—and any Party member's—into legal terms. We're supposed to be judged, for example, by a jury of our peers. But even though most of my friends and lots of my relatives have dealt with the courts, I've never seen a jury of mainly—much less all—blacks deciding their cases. How can whites from the Oakland hills understand our lives? Garry assails the devices that result in the exclusion of blacks. He shows that the voting lists, the source of the master panel, don't fairly represent our overall percentage of the population because blacks vote in fewer numbers. He also insists on broadening the range of questions he can ask to prove prejudice. Jensen claims that people who approve the death penalty don't tend to be prejudiced against blacks. But Garry gets a defense witness to attest that only twenty-eight percent of people who like the death penalty accept open-housing bills and that almost half of all whites would move if a black came to live next door to them. Then Garry goes deeper, asking white sociologists about unconscious racism. "I would think whites should have . . . a knowledge of black history and culture," a Berkeley sociology professor says, explaining how white jurors might minimize their racism, ". . . [an awareness] of their own prejudices . . . [and] some personal experience with minority people, with black people."

Next, Garry quizzes individual jurors. He hopes to overcome the normal anti-black, anti-radical bias of jury trials by forcing the judge to dismiss jurors for cause rather than having to use his challenges. He repeats the same questions: Can they give Huey a fair trial? Do they believe he's innocent as he sits in the box?

"Do you really believe that as Huey Newton sits here right now next to me he is innocent of any wrongdoing of any kind?" Garry asks a middle-aged man.

"No. That I don't believe," the prospective juror says.

"See?" Garry says. "There you are, Judge. I challenge this juror for cause."

But the judge disagrees.

"Well, you see, I will have to explain to you again and see if you understand it," the judge patiently explains to the juror. "From the mere fact that he has been indicted by the grand jury, you are not to infer or presume in any way that the defendant is or must be guilty. Do you understand that?"

The guy—no fool—answers yes. He wants to sit on the jury and be part of history.

So Garry tries again.

"You are not willing to accept the fact that Huey Newton is absolutely innocent as he sits right now, are you, sir?"

"Well, that's a question I can't answer before I hear the evidence," the juror says.

Garry turns to the judge. "I submit the challenge, Your Honor."

But the judge is as persistent as Garry. "No. I don't think that's sufficient. I think that it is a matter of semantics." He leads the juror. "Before you hear any evidence, have you got an idea that he must be guilty or else he wouldn't be here? Is that your idea?"

The juror answers yes.

"Well that is not our law," he explains.

Prosecutor Jensen gets into the act, leading the juror through the dance. No, he would not find Huey innocent. No, he wouldn't find him guilty. Yes, he has no evidence yet about the case. Yes, the fact there's been a charge isn't proof Huey's guilty. Yes, the only testimony he's concerned about is what he will see and hear in court from witnesses and not from newspapers or rumor.

Jensen turns to the bench, his job done. "As Your Honor said, I think this is a semantic problem."

The judge gives Garry one more chance. "You may examine further, Mr. Garry."

Garry stands, pushes the peak of his hair away from his forehead in frustration.

"Again I ask you that same question which you have answered three times to me now—"

But the judge interrupts. "Please ask the question without preface."

Garry takes the challenge. "As Huey Newton sits next to me now," he asks, carefully phrasing the question, "in your opinion is he absolutely innocent?"

"Yes," says the juror.

Then he pounces. "But you don't believe it, do you?"

"No," the man answers, caught off guard.

The duel is done. Jensen sighs. The judge must rule. "Challenge is allowed," he says.

Garry conducts the trial painstakingly. James B. Lucas, the Deputy Sheriff of Alameda County, takes the stand. Garry shows him the card used to take Huey's fingerprints the night of the shoot-out.

"What does it say for complexion?" Garry asks.

"I did not understand," Lucas replies.

"What does it say as to his complexion, sir?"

"'Chocolate,'" Lucas answers.

"Did you put those in there, yourself?"

"Yes, I typed these in."

Garry goes on.

"Now I notice that you have 'descent.' What have you got there for descent?"

"'Negro.'"

"How have you spelled 'Negro'? With a small 'n,' isn't that right?"

"That's right."

"Do you always spell 'Negro' with a small 'n'?"

"I don't recall."

"You don't believe that 'Negro' should be spelled with a capital 'N'?"

"I believe that would be grammatically correct, yes, sir."

As the trial extends through the summer, Garry makes his case for reasonable doubt. Toward the end of August, while Bobby addresses the protesters at the Democratic Convention in Chicago, Gene takes the stand, testifying that he was present with Huey at the shoot-out, then refusing to answer any other questions on Fifth Amendment grounds. Jensen immediately cites him for contempt.

They didn't know *shit* until I got on the stand and it come for me to testify. Jensen? He went crazy. He jumped it! "Who is this here?" Yeah! You didn't know about this one, huh? Who's Gene McKinney? They wouldn't give me immunity. So they gave me contempt of court. Gave me a little punk-ass thing of thirty days. I said, "Hey, nothing to me about going to no jail." You know, you go to jail so much, it don't be no big thing. Plus, you see a lot of people.

When I first got there they was giving me Kool-Aid. Lot of my old buddies show me what's going on. I had this job just handing linen. That lasted about an hour. Then this guard comes by. Says, "Man, I had nothing to do with this here. I got this from upstairs." He says I'm supposed to do my time in a thing they call "Little Greystone." Part of Santa Rita that's like a big-ass warehouse. Got these little cubicles. With wire over the top. It's where the pigs be walking. Where they can see down. Check you out constantly. Everything is concrete. The walls, floor, everything. Had water all around the corner. Floor stayed wet whole time I was there.

Finally Huey takes the stand, explaining, over Jensen's objections, racism, black culture, the Party, and the Ten Point Program.

"Charlie was trying to get Huey's impressive and charming personality across to the jury," Alex Hoffmann says.

He absolutely broke all the rules of how you handle a defendant on the stand. But he was completely unafraid. He knew Huey would do well so he just let Huey ramble on as much as Huey wanted. Charlie made hardly one objection on cross-examination. And Jensen couldn't break Huey at all. Jensen was very bright, and he cross-examined Huey for days, but he could never break him, not a bit.

On September 8, the jury reaches its verdict. We win our first battle in freeing Huey: he is found guilty of voluntary manslaughter of Frey, innocent of assault on the other officer; Huey no longer faces the chair. That night cops drive by the office and shoot out the windows, the gunfire tearing through posters of Li'l Bobby and Huey.

The incident makes us feel our insecurity on Grove Street more acutely. Through Arlene and Mickey we find a house on Shattuck Avenue available for small money. The location is perfect, midway between Berkeley and Oakland. The college-town merchants that surround us provide protection against the marginally more civilized Berkeley police. The place itself is a dream, a half-timbered, stucco, high-pitched two-story house with a back-yard. We can hold meetings, press conferences, and store the paper in the wide space on the ground floor. Upstairs in front we can put out the paper; in back are plenty of rooms, including a kitchen. From the basement we can build tunnels to the backyard of a friend of Eldridge's who lives nearby, escape routes in case of attack. (We dig the tunnels; but the Oakland subway system has backed up the water level and they flood.) The place is a home, headquarters, embassy.

"We should take the kids out of school," I say, looking at the rooms in the back. I speak from my optimism, my enthusiasm. "We can put in bunk beds. They can sleep and go to school here. Shouldn't be learning that bourgeois reactionary culture anyway. This way they'll grow up aware. Socially conscious. Not like us."

We move in quickly, setting up the downstairs, putting in bunk beds, a dining table, telephones on every desk, hanging steel sheets over the windows, sandbagging the supporting walls. The first weekend we're there my brother Bud establishes his dominion over the backyard with his barbecue. I come back from a trip and feel I've lived here all my life. Everything is familiar, natural, right—the chatter of people working, the chaos of last-minute details, some nonsense about the kids upstairs, some members sacked out on the floor in sleeping bags. My comrades in arms. Closer to me because of our shared ideas than my biological relatives. Revolutionaries. In deed as well as speech. My family. My home.

Chapter

17

HUEY's conviction coincides with a new struggle between Eldridge and Reagan. UC-Berkeley invites Eldridge for ten lectures. At Reagan's bidding the Regents immediately try blocking the course. Already booked for a non-stop round of speaking engagements, Eldridge now tours the country taking Reagan on verbally.

The students adore him. It's fall 1968, and everyone is jumping on the revolutionary bandwagon. The San Francisco State BSU — we've been giving them PE, helping them organize — spearheads a strike for black and Third World studies programs controlled by students, faculty, and community; the peaceful demonstrations soon turn into confrontations with the police that reach a level of violence never seen on campuses before. A model for revolt emerges: revolutionary action, rebellion in the black community, support actions in the student/youth areas that surround the great universities, cities coming to a halt, working- and middle-class people becoming radicalized. . . . When Eldridge and I alight on a campus and are greeted by two or three thousand people eager to be led in chants of "Fuck Ronald Reagan!" the notion doesn't seem completely fantastical.

And we don't restrict ourselves to friendly areas. Eldridge wins over openly antagonistic groups, inciting them with an invective toward Reagan that makes the dozens Huey and James Crawford used on each other seem tame.

"We are going to deal with you," he tells an audience in Orange County, addressing the absent governor,

to put an end to your absurd oinking in the faces of the people. . . .
Who the fuck do you think you are, telling me that I can't talk, telling
the students and faculty members. . . that they cannot have me deliver
ten lectures?. . . I don't know what the outcome of all this will be, but
I do know that I, for one, will never kiss your ass, will never submit to
your demagogic machinations. I think you are a cowardly, craven-
hearted wretch. You are not a man. You are a punk. Since you have insulted me by calling me a racist, I would like to have the opportunity
to balance the books. All I ask is a sporting chance. Therefore, Mickey
Mouse, I challenge you to a duel, to the death, and you can choose the
weapons. And if you can't relate to that, right on. Walk, chicken, with
your ass picked clean.

Privately Eldridge says the same. I accompany him, flying cross-country
constantly. Since April 6 we've become closer; the fact that I didn't give the
police a statement has reinforced his faith in me. Not gonna be no trial, he
keeps saying. I'll die in a hail of gunfire before going back to prison. We've
got to unleash the wolves, start a rebellion.
   Listening to him saddens me. His statements aren't about strategy but
life. His refusal to give himself over to the Adult Authority is his birthright.
Whatever I feel objectively about his judgment, I must respect it. We've had
conflicts and differences, but Eldridge has been an invaluable part of the
Party. If he decides on battle we must be loyal. Which means that there'll be
death, more killing of Party leadership.

But in another way Eldridge's possible departure doesn't scare me. The
Party no longer relies on individuals. The organization survives and thrives
on its own, the rank-and-file members publishing and selling the paper, plan-
ning and holding demonstrations, collecting and posting bail—*Juche,* the
North Koreans call this, self-reliance. (We're establishing ties with the North
Koreans; we even put one of their national symbols—the flying horse of
Chulima—in the newspaper centerfold.)
   One aspect of our strength is that we're starting new programs. We begin
a program called Breakfast for Children, collecting donations of food and
supplies from local merchants and offering hot meals in St. Augustine's
Episcopal Church under the auspices of a Party friend named Father Earl
Neil. The program grows naturally from our new lives—Emmett Groggan's
free food baskets, the need now to feed our own kids, our desire to show the
community we do something more than shoot it out with cops. We call the
program a "survival" program—survival pending revolution—not some-

thing to replace revolution or challenge the power relations demanding radical action, but an activity that strengthens us for the coming fight, a lifeboat or raft leading us safely to shore. Plus, the program helps organize people into the Party and provides members with something to do other than worrying about when they're going to off a pig. Bobby talks of initiating many free programs, helping the old people cash their checks, giving medical aid, providing education, all the necessities people do without.

The likelihood of Eldridge's leaving also underscores another Party development. In the six months of our nationally publicized existence we have attracted a cross section of our generation—political activists, warriors, intellectuals. These are the comrades with whom I feel most comfortable, and I rely on their judgment and counsel. I come from the same background as most of them, share their taste and attitudes. They form the second level of leadership—the people who make the Party run—and their experience, more than anything else, reflects the breadth of the Party's appeal in the black community.

One is John Seale. A Party supporter, Bobby's younger brother, John acts a lot like I did before Huey's shoot-out, lending us his car, sometimes joining police patrols, giving us time. Like me, he's married, and he has a full-time job as an Oakland bus driver; and, also like me, as the Party grows he feels increasing pressure and desire to join. Plus, the municipal government gives him trouble:

The word got out that I'm John Seale, Bobby Seale's brother. I was "militant." The FBI came to my house. I closed the door on them. Then they call on the phone and say, "We want to talk."

I say, "What for?"

"About your brother."

Click. I hang the phone up.

Then one of the bosses calls me in the office and asks if I am Bobby Seale's brother. I tell him, "Yes. Sure."

"Well, what do you think about what's going on?"

I say, "I think it's the right thing to do."

"Well, why do you feel that way?" He wants to know all of this stuff.

I say, "Because of how people are being treated."

After that it seems like the supervisor is always out there on me, trying to find me running ahead or behind schedule. "You're twenty seconds ahead of schedule."

I'd say, "Okay, I'll slow down."

Petty little things.

All the time I want to do more. But I can't make up my mind. My wife doesn't understand. She's political — she's the first black to teach Malcolm X in McClymonds High. But she doesn't understand me quitting my job. She's afraid. She never really knows I go on the police patrols. I keep it away from her because it would bother her. Tension increases. We argue about me quitting my job. She doesn't think I should. It's, "What about our family?" I say, "Well, that doesn't have to quit."

Finally I just did it.

It's about five o'clock. Peak-hour traffic. I'm on Telegraph Avenue on the Forty Line, coming out of Berkeley running all the way from Albany to San Leandro, the longest route in the city. I come up Telegraph. My supervisor flags me over because I'm a minute ahead of schedule.

"You're just a general fuck-up!" he says.

Now I'm thinking, Why does this guy keep fucking with me?

I pull into the stop, pick up a few people; the bus is *loaded*. I hit Fortieth, which is a main intersection. My car is parked there. I'm in the center lane. Traffic's heavy. I ease up to about five or six car lengths from the bus stop. I'm still in the middle lane, still haven't gotten over in the right lane to the bus stop, and it hits me: Let me give this shit up! I open the door, pick up my token thing, walk off the bus, get in my car and go home. I'm never gonna drive a bus again.

They call me the next day and tell me I can't.

I say, "What do you mean I can't? It's done."

They don't believe it: "Well, when are you coming to work?"

I say, "Hey! Don't you understand? I've done that already!"

I go to the Party office. "What kind of skills do you have?" they ask.

I was always good with my hands — craftsman, artist, I liked art in school. I see them laying out the paper. I say, "Hey, I can do that!" I started doing the layout and eventually I was the guy in charge of it.

Another is Bobby Rush. Coming from the South — his family moves from Albany, Georgia, to Chicago when he's seven — he's belonged to SNCC for a long time. Like a lot of older, independent blacks his mother has worked for the Republican Party, and Rush — as we call him in the Party — has served in student councils. In 1968, after King's unsuccessful housing campaign and several riots, Rush looks for an organization to mobilize the gangs dominating the black community into political action.

The problem with SNCC was that it didn't have any specific activities. We would attend a lot of meetings, do some fund-raising, marches, stuff like that, but we had no programmatic thrust. Then Stokely became a member of the Central Committee of the Black Panther Party and he asked us to make SNCC here into the local chapter. Later it became clear to me that Stokely wanted us to be his base within the Party because SNCC was disintegrating and he didn't have any base in Oakland.

At the time I had heard of the Party, but it wasn't something I focused on. The only thing I knew about it was that it was nationalist in ideology and militant and spoke about conditions in urban black America. I had heard when Bobby walked into the Assembly, and I might have seen an issue of the paper, but Huey's name didn't necessarily mean anything, nothing that would stimulate me to seek to join the Party. In Chicago itself one guy was running around and calling himself a Panther and trying to extort some money from some businessmen. Nothing impressive. There wasn't anything specific and particular about the Panther Party that said, okay, well, this is it, other than that I could relate to the fact that they talked about armed self-defense.

Stokely arranged for me to go out to California to meet with Don Cox and for D.C. to introduce me to the leadership—yourself, Bobby, and later on Eldridge and Kathleen. My feelings shifted. Panthers in Oakland were different from the ones in Chicago. It was a youth organization. It was very exciting—the discipline, the military aspect, the propaganda, the newspaper, Emory's artwork, the leather jackets. And my conversations with D.C.! This was alive—like the phrase, "Right on!" (I think I actually brought "Right on!" back to Chicago.) It was a style I thought could be successful in Chicago—it represented some of the things that I had been exposed to in the gangs and it had a political message.

You weren't receptive to opening another chapter.

"No," you said, "we already got a chapter out there."

But I wasn't frustrated. You were in California; I was in Chicago. I knew the phonies and the people who were for real, and that it wasn't going to be any great challenge to out-organize the people you had delegated Panthers in Chicago. And I wanted to because I thought the Panther Party would have a bright future in Chicago. I came back with the determination to organize a chapter. I reported to the guys what was going on and started looking for an office: I knew the key to being recognized was to get an office opened, have a base of operations, because none of these other guys had a base. I worked very, very hard and located an office on West Madison, and an

alderman basically rented the place for us and also paid the gas bill and
turned on the phones.

Then we — Bob Brown, the other leader of the chapter here, and myself — got in contact with Fred Hampton. We wanted Fred to be the spokesman for the Party. I had met Fred earlier and we had struck up a friendship.
He was working at the NAACP, which didn't mean a lot, other than the fact
that he could speak. He was a strong speaker. He was a leader; he was an
orator. He moved people based on his own strengths. He had that much
charisma. Which was why I wanted him. Because I wasn't a public speaker.
Also he considered himself a revolutionary — not that he had read Marx or
Lenin: if anybody had told any of us that the Panther Party was Marxist-
Leninist or Communist at the time we probably never would have joined it.
We didn't understand a lot. We had to do a lot of political consciousness–
raising and building and studying in a short period of time.

We arranged to meet at the Afro-Arts Theater, in one of the back
rooms. Fred told me he would think about it and call me back. The next
day he said, "I'm on." We had an office, people we could count on to do
certain things, a telephone, and a spokesman. We represented ourselves as
Panthers, put the sign out, Fred spoke at some anticop, anti-Daley rallies — we were part of the civil rights network, Jesse [Jackson], others —
and so we started to move.

Around the same time, Bunchy, in Los Angeles, recruits Elmer Pratt —
Geronimo, or G., as we call him. G. is raised in "Saint Mary Parish in Morgan City in Louisiana, second-largest swampland in the state."

His father is part Creek. "He was known as the junk man," G. says.

He was a junk man because he refused to work for any white man. He
would pick up junk and when we seven children came back from school we
would go and separate the brass from the aluminum. He raised a family
selling that, and we hunted rabbits, coon, and caught catfish — used to call
them "swimps" because the shrimp factory would pluck the heads off the
shrimp and attract the fish from miles around so that you didn't need no
bait, and you'd get seventy-five or eighty catfish, clean them, sell them for
a dime, and then everybody in the community ate! It wasn't based on no
capitalist thing. You'd better not ask somebody for money. Everybody
worked! A lot of us weren't blood kin, but if you got in trouble there were
lots of people there — a big family almost.

My mother is "Gumbo Creole" — real black. Her ancestors come from

Africa-Haiti. Voodoo. We say, "Hoodoo." My mother's sister is known as a Hoodoo woman. I was brought up with that and the Catholic Church. Once we were coming from Mass and somebody hoodooed our house. Mama got all excited, got some salt and sprinkled it on the house. When we had hurricanes she would light seven candles. The hurricanes would blow everything, but they wouldn't touch the house because we had the seven candles. She used to protect us when my father whipped us: he used to whip us with a fan belt and telephone wires—because he was a junk man he had access to all kinds of weapons. They whip you, but you know that deep down it's love—probably because they don't kill you. But Mama would protect you. She was about the most devout Christian you'd ever want to meet. We were brought up very strict Catholics. We had to go to catechism. I was alter boy for years. Had to go to Mass every morning—Church of the Holy Eucharist, the all-black Catholic church. Went every *single* morning. Do it all in *Latin.* It gave me a sense of serenity—very beautiful.

I grew up with the tradition of refusing to accept slavery, but also not *hating* white people because my mother had taught me to love. But we had skirmishes with the Ku Klux Klan—the Knights of the White Camellia—throughout my life as a child. When I was about sixteen, I was swimming in this water hole and a friend named Calvin Bias joined me. Then all of a sudden these white dudes come and they're throwing rocks, big "railroad rocks," we used to call them. I get out, get out running. But Calvin disappeared. They found Calvin's body the next day.

We were told to spend time with the older men—Aloyisius, Elmo—the old people who just sit on the side, rock back in their rocking chairs, smoking on a pipe. They feel you out and influence you one way or the other. You got them all over. You got women. The Black Panther Party, the US organization, the Nation of Islam—all these groups were superstructures. The infrastructure is a whole different thing. That river—that river flows. It's not to kill white people, it's just a basic preservation that you grow up with and to me it's very real.

I was influenced to go to the service. I took to it like a fish to water because I was a hell of a hunter: I just loved to go hunting by myself; I prided myself on that. So everything came naturally to me. I was on the top of my boot camp and I became what they call "gung-ho." Then my father fell sick and I went to jump school because they give you an extra fifty-five dollars for jumping out of the plane—and I was sending every check, every month, straight to my family. Once I jumped, I got hooked. It's better than an orgasm. That backblast hits you and you're free-falling before your chute opens and you see more colors that you're ever going to see.

All my time in Vietnam was combat. Landed in Saigon and was supposed to be there for a week orientation. That night we were mortared, so the next day we were choppered out to bases, and that night I'm on a bunker pulling guard duty and a dude next to me gets his throat cut.

I was like in a constant state of shock. You conquer fear quick—and since then, fear ain't shit. But it was shock. You went like a robot.

I was a paratrooper assigned to a nonparatrooper outfit, the First L Cavalry. I didn't see any racial stuff. I never heard no one call anyone a racial name. You didn't have time. You were preoccupied with staying alive instead of preoccupied with the ignorance that brings about racial bigotry. I got real close. Schultz, Maddox, Coons: they were all white, white like white bread. Maddox was like our father. He had been in about twelve years. He was a platoon leader. We all really looked up to him. We were in recon, a vehicular patrol, scouting out, mapping out. Military word they use was "close with the enemy and make initial contact" so they can fire on you so the division knows, "Yeah, here they are." Because there was no front lines. It's two of us in this squad. Maddox and Coons is the lead vehicle and I'm in the trailer. And I'm not more than thirty meters behind him. He got blown up. I could feel the heat and saw him go straight up. Maddox was just burnt. Coons, the driver, had his eyeglasses still on. A young white kid from Nebraska. He landed with his eyes open. When we went to pick him up, all his back was out.

I stay until '67. I'm a sergeant now. After a few months at home base in Carolina, the riots jump off in Detroit and we're sent there. The next thing I know I'm standing next to Lyndon Baines Johnson at Fort Bragg—I want to say something to him but he doesn't shake my hand. Then I'm on my way back to Vietnam going to Hue to retake the city. We get there and the dead are everywhere. They give us a parade down the streets. It was like something out of a movie. Thousands of people. A weird feeling, just coming from the situation in Detroit. But I survive all that and now I'm a sergeant, making money, sending it home to Mama, got a girlfriend, got another woman, got a trailer I won shooting dice, got it made in the service, and it's April fourth, 1968, and I'm about thirty miles south of Hue and I'm on the bunker and on the radio I hear Martin Luther King is assassinated. Everything got quiet. I never will forget that feeling—standing on top of that bunker, looking over the country and feeling as though I missed my calling, and within a month I'm out of the service.

I go to Louisiana and my sister asks me to drive her to California—

she's going to UCLA in the fall. In Los Angeles everything is different—
all the conversation during that period was very political and there was
never a dull moment. I have every intention of going back to Louisiana
but I let my sister talk me into looking into a program they were starting
at UCLA.

Meantime, I meet a partner from the service—actually I was really
looking for his sister because I used to write her from Vietnam. He tells
me what's happening and the situation with the militant movement since
King is dead. And he starts talking about this guy named Bunchy. Like
he was a god or something.

Meanwhile my sister signs me up and next thing I know I'm enrolled
in UCLA in a program that Bunchy and John Huggins and some other
people from the ghetto area are in.

The students flock around Bunchy. He's this dynamic individual who
can relate. He was originally from Shreveport, Louisiana, and when he was
a kid he had polio and he was a success story, a hell of a dancer, growing
up in the gangs, coming to prison, and becoming transformed in prison.
Abdul Jabbar was on campus then, but Bunchy was more charismatic.
When he got out of prison he went to all the gangs and told them that
they had to transform their way of thinking from a gangster mentality to
a revolutionary mentality.

We would have conversations. He always comes to me after the little
classes were over and says, "Man, could I ride back to the city with you?"
I think he targeted me to join the Party, but he never talked about it, just
seemed to be guiding me to join the BSU that was just formed. He was so
clear. One day we're coming from campus and I pick up a brother named
Wolf—Wolf's dead now; he killed himself not too long ago. Bunchy talks
about the necessity of joining together and protecting the community. And
Wolf listens to Bunchy like Bunchy has some natural command over him.

So I go to political education classes, work in the community, pass out
programs, clothes, drive people back home. But I'm not known as a Panther; I don't consider myself a Panther.

Eldridge must surrender on November 27. He has not budged. He's not
going to prison. He'll either go into exile or there will be a "red-light" trial.

We—Bunchy, myself, Emory—plead for exile.

"Go underground for a while," we say. "You can do stuff from foreign
shores. You get into a shoot-out everything will be over. This won't be a
final departure. We can build pressure. Mount a campaign. Make them bring
you back. In the meantime we'll be able to keep contact."

Eldridge keeps his plans to himself. A few days before the date, we hear the police may arrest him momentarily. We organize a vigil outside his Pine Street house so they don't kidnap him. For twenty-four hours we wait inside armed with shotguns, ready to resist, white supporters clustered in front. The day is nightmarish and liberating. We share the comradeship of people waiting for approaching battle. We post ourselves at windows, watching for the cars, get rumors over the phones. No one knows whether the police will attack. If they try to take him we are sworn to resist. We hold constant meetings, eat; no one sleeps.

Finally Garry assures us there'll be no attack. Later that afternoon I speak to Eldridge. We talk about the future and he tells me not to worry, whatever happens he's made sure the Party will continue to receive royalties from his book—and besides, the book will sell even more once he leaves.

"We'll get you back," I say.

He too expects something to work out.

"So long," I say.

There's nothing more.

"Power to the people," I say.

"All right. Later."

Next day he's gone.

Chapter

18

SO Bobby and I take charge.

The Party's only charismatic speaker, its best-known, most sought after public representative, Bobby's always on the go. His stays in the office are visits; he gives a PE class, attends a Central Committee meeting, proposes some ideas, and then he's got to leave.

I'm responsible for the Party's administration. I read the weekly reports submitted by the thirty operating chapters and consult with their leadership—visiting them if necessary—supervise the Free Breakfast programs and coordinate donations from local merchants, answer correspondence and maintain press contacts, advise about personal problems, and oversee newspaper production. Plus, I make sure we—the national headquarters—schedule at least two PE classes a week as well as an all-afternoon Sunday Central Committee meeting. As leadership, we must set the standard for how a chapter should function.

To ease our load, we name June Assistant to the Chief of Staff and put John Seale in charge of laying out the newspaper; we also rotate the editorial staff, everyone learning all aspects of production, a precaution against the paper being crippled by future arrests.

Still, there's no time to rest. The war intensifies every day. In the next nine months, the police are involved in the deaths of between ten and twenty members, bust four hundred others, and raid fifteen offices. Panthers become an endangered species.

The FBI leads the attack. "None of our programs have contemplated violence," an FBI official later tells the Senate Select Committee. But FBI memoranda show that the bureau intentionally created situations they hoped would do just that. "We have been able to establish beyond doubt . . . that high officials of the FBI desired to promote violent confrontations between BPP members and members of other groups," the committee writes. The police don't simply monitor our activity—which they would have had dubious constitutional right to do. Instead, they set out to sabotage and destroy us. They employ every kind of deviousness to put us at one another's throat, make us appear like gangsters and thugs, niggers killing niggers.

Reacting to the demands of the increasing pressure, I further distance myself from my family. The kids become strangers. Spending little time with them, I hear about them from Pat. Dorion's always eager, energetic, full of goodwill, and Darryl seems to be always in trouble; Patrice wants to be a model. They live full-time in the Shattuck office, go to classes we establish at the headquarters. We even create Panther outfits for them, blue shirts, black pants. Panther Youth.

Pat and I see one another less frequently too. She has her own obligations to the Party.

"I did everything that a housewife or a mother does for her children," she says.

I used to go to New York and walk the streets with a list of the sisters' sizes, getting everybody what they wanted—because a lot of the sisters were from back East and would tell me where to get clothes. Plus, I had always been a bookkeeper and cashier so I also took care of the money. I couldn't have anything on paper because they had started breaking into offices, killing Panthers. I had a little tablet and my own codes for six running accounts in my head: two bank accounts for the newspaper, the Huey P. Newton Defense Fund, the Black Panther Party fund, a bail fund, and one more. I did no business over the phone. If they started talking business, I'd take the conversation somewhere else.

At the same time my sexual loyalty to Pat is tested by the practice of members and Party ideology. A lot of members are younger than I and single; they seem to be playing romantic musical chairs, practicing to the extreme our principle that people are free to choose their sexual partners. Not that any brother forces a woman to sleep with him; we incessantly instruct the men that every Party member has the freedom to choose his or her lover. But sisters often complain that the men take advantage of our commitment to create a different kind of personal life, something beyond the well-defined limits of bourgeois morality.

"You got people from different backgrounds," Emory explains.

When they came in, they brought their luggage with them. You had pimps, prostitutes, dope dealers, and some of them thought they were slicker than others. There was an underground thing of brothers saying—because they were giving their lives for the revolution—that they should be given sex. But Party policy was that if a person didn't want to relate to you, they didn't have to—you couldn't disrespect them, harass them, or intimidate them. But people had to grow to understand that policy, cleanse themselves and become disciplined. And that was a process that went on throughout the whole duration of the Party.

Yet I don't stray. I'm too busy to mess around, and many of the women—better educated, middle-class, college graduates—intimidate me. Plus, for me, Pat remains the essence of womanhood. A lot of craziness has passed between us; but there's no one I desire as much.

Then one afternoon I walk into the liquor store, Big Dee's, down the block from the office. I reach for the port to make my Bitter Dog—Panther Piss, the Chicago comrades call it—

—and—

—I'm in another world, fragrant, musky, warm, filled with scents of flesh and flowers.

I look and there's Brenda.

She's been in the office, working on the newspaper. Sam Napier has recruited her. He's walking down the street in the Fillmore. Hey, sister, he says, you heard of the Black Panther Party? We're putting out a paper and need your help typing something up.

Brenda knows about the Party. She's participated in an African dance presentation at Huey's birthday party. Still, she's never committed herself politically—she's grown up in the isolation of Alaska—and this strange-looking guy's request is an uninviting introduction to revolutionary politics.

But Brenda's neither scared nor insulted.

"He showed me something he had tried to type and it was *terrible*," Brenda remembers.

"He said, 'I can't do it, and I don't want this going out to the masses looking like this.' Not, 'Sister, you come in here and type because you're a woman and you can do this.' It wasn't from that point. If it had of been, I wouldn't have done it. So, it was like, okay."

After her first visit to the office she keeps coming, rearranging her schedule to help with newspaper production, an increasingly devoted worker.

Now she stands before me, the sweetest, most enticing-smelling thing I've ever encountered.

"Oh my God," I say; her soft scent surrounds me; I don't want to leave. "You sure smell good. What is that?"

"Follow Me Boy," she says, meaning the perfume's name.

We talk a little and I watch her go back to the office, sexy, willowy.

Follow Me Boy.

The next day I wait for her on the second floor, keyed up, anticipating her appearance. No woman has excited my imagination as powerfully since Pat stood outside my mother's door.

We start talking immediately.

"How come you don't smile, Chief," she says, calling me by my new Party nickname. "You never smile."

We arrange I'll drive her to her house. There's no need to tell Pat anything: I'm away more often than at home.

Brenda doesn't say anything when I stop at the motel. I sign the card in the office, wondering whether she'll remain in the car. Through the window I see her staring at me. Before I'm back at the car, she slams the door shut, slings her pocketbook over her shoulder, defiantly striding toward the rooms.

I don't hesitate or think of Pat. Going with Brenda no longer seems a betrayal but natural, an extension of myself. My relationship with Pat isn't bound by the Party. The Party didn't bring us together; it can't separate us. Besides, I don't accept the concept of romantic love. Love relationships, like anything else in the universe, are a constant struggle. Even in the best circumstances the idea of a perfect match between a man and a woman is idealistic. There's no single person who can satisfy all my needs and desires absolutely. I've never bought that.

I follow her.

Brenda's at Shattuck because we've moved newspaper production to the office. *The Black Panther* is the voice of the people, we've said, and cadre now rely on the weekly shipments. When the paper is late chapter representatives flood the office with calls: "Hey, where's the paper? When's the paper coming out?" The paper is synonymous with our invincibility, and its publication is one of our top priorities. No more once-every-two-or-three-week issues like we used to publish with Eldridge. Now the paper will appear like clockwork, every Thursday, our lifeline to the chapters and community and a visible sign of our defiance of the pigs.

To facilitate production we transform the front-second-floor room: drafting tables, desks and typewriters, two Linotype machines, a mimeograph machine, and several tape recorders to take testimony from people harassed by the police. Bobby, Masai Hewitt—our new Minister of Education—John, June, myself, Emory, Brenda, and other staff oversee the editorial content, discussing and deciding on articles and the cover. Sometimes we give attention to a bust or an article Eldridge sends from Cuba.

We even put international events on the cover. We're so keen on the Red Book that we feature a border confrontation between the Russians and Chinese. We also champion the North Koreans, presenting them as the precursors to the Vietnamese, the first communist people to repel American aggression.

Our emphasis on foreign events drives Huey crazy.

"Who are we selling papers to?" he asks us in one his tapes. "The black community, or the Chinese or the Koreans? I think that they should give us some money to print it."

"They would give us money, if the government didn't intercept the checks!" I answer.

But Huey's not fooling around.

"What are you guys doing?" we hear him say in his next tape. We're sitting around the table in the kitchen, playing his comments to the newspaper staff. "What's wrong with you guys out there? People buy the paper because the people see their faces in the paper. The paper echoes the will and aspirations of the people in the community. All they see when they open the paper up is Koreans, and 'Long Live Chairman Mao.' You were wondering why the paper sales are going down. Look at your paper. Can't nobody read it. You're sending them all to China."

Huey's funny; he has a way of saying things. We put the Koreans and the rest on an international page.

Since Eldridge's departure we've increased the democratic procedures in the Party. Without any single dominant personality in leadership, we now decide everything collectively, gathering the opinions of the local chapters and arriving at a decison jointly.

"I don't know what's going on here," I explain to the Chicago people on one of my first visits to the chapter. "All situations are different, and you've got to make a concrete analysis of concrete conditions. We're dialectical materialists; we're not mechanical, applying one solution to every problem. So let's work it this way. I'll tell you how the Party does things in Oakland and what Huey and I talk about. Then you tell me your problems and how you think you should deal with them. Then we can take this stuff back to California and deal with it in the Central Committee."

Within a month we're on a merry-go-round of flights back and forth to O'Hare and the "fascist lake," Fred Hampton's name for Lake Michigan.

The growth of the Chicago chapter adds to our national importance. The organization has expanded almost as rapidly as the national Party, recruiting several hundred members and setting up satellite chapters as far south as East St. Louis and as far north as Detroit.

The change from unrecognized chapter to Party center comes by a coincidence involving Masai.

"Masai was eccentric," Geronimo recalls.

His brother was a genuine thoroughbred in the Slauson. But Masai was what we would call a "Blippy"—a black hippy. He used to dress like the hippies, the flower-children type, and would be out chasing girls and dropping acid.

One day I pick him up on the way to Bunchy's mother's house—I was adopted in their family. Masai's barefooted; he's got cutoff jeans. We're talking. I'm just beginning to study Maoism. Because we've got to study so we understand politics. And I'm listening to this man, because to study Maoism, you have to know Marxism. He's spieling this dialectical materialism like he's a *machine!* I see something. I ask him to come around.

"No, man!" he says. "The Panthers, they're too macho, man! I'm more inclined to some socialist group—like the American Trotsky Party or something."

I say, "Well, could you at least come and talk to a few people at one of our classes?"

To make a long story short, he ends up being one of the best educators—he has a very deep, resonant voice—and the more he teaches, the more I like him, because I'm learning. Because I've never had time to go deep into *Das Kapital,* or any of the other esoteric books. He's making sense of the economy, of fascism, of slavery, socialism—all this economic analysis.

But he was still a nut. He was just so much like a kid! He was unable to *relate* to the "lumpen proletariat." He could relate to an Angela Davis, who was a *giant* in that same field, but to us regular folks he'd get very technical and very snotty-nosed. He would criticize the lumpen in a haughty, condescending way. He would get down on them and say, "Well, Marx wouldn't have liked that. That was the scum of society." And that would cause problems.

Anyway, I bring him up to Oakland, and get him with Bobby Seale. Bobby loved him right away, because here is a walking *computer* who knows all about Marxism and Leninism, and where it comes from, dialectical materialism.

So I left. The next thing I know, they got him as the Acting Minister of Education.

Masai travels across the country, giving PE to new chapters. On one flight he and another Party member ask the stewardess if it's the same number of miles from New York to Oakland as from New York to Cuba. The question — actually, the pair asking it — worries her: they're black males, hip looking, and she figures they must be skyjackers. She tells the captain; he radios O'Hare, where the plane makes an unscheduled landing and the police arrest Masai and the other brother. In the Cook County Jail Masai has no money, no lawyer. When he calls us at Central Headquarters I don't know what to do. My only Chicago contact is Bobby Rush, the guy we rebuffed as a chapter organizer. So I call him.

"We went in the county jail and got them out," remembers Rush.

Masai stayed around for a week or so, helped us get oriented, held a couple of PE classes. We became the official Panthers. We started getting newspapers, material, had direct lines of communication with the leadership. The press started relating to us — all seven local TV stations covered our first major speaking engagement at the University of Illinois Circle Campus. The word was out that the Panthers was in Chicago. We just took off. We set out to be the best chapter and we started dealing with that, opening up new chapters, setting up Serve the People programs.

Their association with the national Party has two important effects. The Party distances itself from Stokely ("I began to move more and more away from Stokely," says Rush, "because he was becoming more of a superstar as opposed to a person who was actually leading something"). And the media exposure calls attention to Fred. In very short time he emerges as a natural leader, as tenacious and energetic as Bunchy, though with Chicago style, priding himself on a proletarian look: scruffy beard, floppy hats, sweatshirts, and sneakers instead of waistcoats and fine leather shoes worn as slippers.

He's also a born orator. He's a feel-good preacher, like the ministers I used to hear down south. He can get the church jumping, clapping. He speaks in rhyme and rhythm, breaking down ideas with Eldridge's wit and clarity, but using images that community people can understand.

I hear him one night at the People's Church. Community people and white radicals pack the place. Bobby Rush—thin, with wire-rimmed H. Rap Brown glasses—introduces Fred quickly, talking about the pigs' attempt to get him off the streets with a charge of stealing seventy-odd dollars' worth of ice-cream cones.

> *Fre-eee Fred Hampton!*

The audience starts to sing to the melody of the spiritual "Wade in the Water."

> *Fre-eee Fred Hampton!*
> *We need our warriors beside us!*

Fred steps up to the podium, slapping his hands together, a DJ bringing the people together, getting them high off their own energy.

"Can you hear the beat?"

Everybody pounds the floor with their feet and claps their hands like at a spiritual revival.

"That's the beat of the revolution."

Fred's nonstop.

"You can jail a revolutionary, but you can't jail the revolution.

"You can run a freedom fighter around the country, but you can't run freedom fighting around the country.

"You can murder a liberator, but you can't murder liberation.

"Because if you do then you've got answers that don't answer, explanations that don't explain, and conclusions that don't conclude."

He tells a story. An old lady comes into the People's Church. Fred asks her if she likes socialism. She hates socialism. But she loves the Free Breakfast program. This is what happens, he says. First you have free breakfasts, then you have free medical care, then you have free bus rides, and soon you have—FREEDOM!

"Socialism is the people!" he exhorts.

"So if you're afraid of socialism you're afraid of yourself!"

He works up the crowd as he nears the end. He throws his chest out, a rooster bursting out of his sweatshirt, revving up the crowd:

"Now before you go to bed tonight I want you to say one thing: I am—"
The crowd's on its feet, everyone repeating.
"I am—"
"—a revolutionary!"
"—a revolutionary!"
"And I love—"
"And I love—"
"—all the people!"

Rush and Fred employ the same strategy Bunchy uses in LA. They try to forge an alliance between the two largest concentrations of black youth—the campus and the streets.

Their biggest challenge is to politicize the gangs that dominate the black community, Blackstone Rangers on the South Side, D's—Disciples—on the West. They seem to have some success with the Rangers at first, an uneasy rivalry emerging between us, the Party, and them.

Then the FBI sabotages the newly developing coalition. In later years, the FBI and local police deplore the violence of youth gangs, especially the infamous Crips and Bloods. But now, when we are actively trying to politicize the Rangers, give them an ideology, introduce these guys to serving, rather than smashing, the people, the FBI encourages the Rangers to remain gang-bangers. Instead of acting to constrain Ranger violence, they try to capitalize on the guns. As the Select Committee report reveals, the FBI proposes telling Jeff Fort—leader of the Rangers—the Panthers are disparaging him for "his lack of commitment to black people" and reasons that "if Fort were to be aware the BPP was responsible [for these remarks] it would lend impetus to his refusal to accept any BPP overtures to the Rangers and additionally might result in Fort having active steps taken to exact some form of retribution towards the leadership of the BPP."

A meeting is arranged between us and the Rangers. That morning Rush and Fred organize their cadre, hand out guns. Fort really prizes discipline—he's dissociated himself from the Disciples because the group was too erratic—so Fred and Rush spend the day getting the Panthers' act together, making sure the cadre are sharp, practicing leaving their cars in formation, marching down the street in cadence. After some mess-ups, the Panthers finally parade to Fort's office, everyone wearing blue and black, berets and jackets, guns strapped or slung over their shoulders.

The Panthers enter the abandoned church that serves as the Rangers' HQ. No light inside; a staircase twists up into darkness. A lone sentry motions to them. Rangers carrying walkie-talkies patrol every landing, telling unseen people the Panthers' exact location. By the third floor the Panthers can't see the bottom. They're cut off from escape but not breaking formation or showing fear. Finally they reach Fort's office and are told to wait.

Fred turns to Rush.

"If something goes down, Rush," he says, touching the .45 stuck into his pants. "Fort's mine."

The door opens. Fort greets them.

"You showed me your hardware," he says, "I'll show you mine."

He claps his hands. Doors open, guys start coming out, displaying armaments like models in a fashion show. "Two men appeared carrying sawed-off carbines," an FBI informant reports later on, "then eight more, each carrying a .45 calibre machine gun, clip type, operated from the shoulder or hip, then others came with over and under type weapons. . . . After this procession Fort had all Rangers . . . approximately 100, display their side arms."

The meeting ends with an uneasy truce. Both Fort and Fred declare their common cause but vie for control, Fort saying the Panthers should join the Rangers, Fred insisting the opposite. Whether any alliance could ultimately have been created is questionable. But certainly the FBI does everything in its power to prevent it. It sends the following letter to Fort, for instance:

> Brother Jeff,
>
> I've spent some time with some Panther friends on the West Side and I know what's going on. The brothers that run the Panthers blame you for blocking their thing and there's supposed to be a hit out on you. I'm not a Panther or a Ranger, just black. From what I see these Panthers are out for themselves, not black people. I think you ought to know what they're up to, I know what I'd do if I was you. You might hear from me again.
>
> A black brother you don't know.

The Chicago chapter also tries to put together other coalitions. A Puerto Rican gang leader named Cha-Cha Jimenez models a revolutionary Puerto Rican nationalist group named the Young Lords after the Party. Meanwhile a group of poor whites who have been organized by SDS—there's a large community of Appalachian immigrants in Chicago at the time—form the Patriot Party, led by a white seminary student named Preacherman. Both go around speaking with Panthers. "We got blacks, browns, and whites," says Fred. "We've got a Rainbow Coalition!" (Lots of Jesse Jackson's best lines come from Fred.)

The Party inspires other groups also.

"We started with the Panthers as a frame of reference and then figured out how to adapt the Party model to our situation," remembers Steve Tappis, a founder of Rising Up Angry, a revolutionary white working-class organization that comes after the Patriot Party.

> We didn't know what to do with neighborhood people, so we would bring ten, fifteen people from some different gangs to the Panther rallies sometimes. They'd be nervous. They'd think it was a trap. But we'd bring them down to a Fred Hampton speech or show them a movie about the Party and maybe get a Panther to come talk in a church in one of the neighborhoods — all just to show them that Panthers don't hate all white people. Or if somebody got arrested in the neighborhood we would say: "The Bellaires have taken enough shit from the racist, oppressive police, and we're gonna stand with revolutionaries of Mao and Huey Newton around the world, and fight the fourteenth district police as well as all other oppressive armies," or something. And then they'd hang that picture up on their garage or something.
>
> Plus, we used the Panther paper as a model for our own. They had Emory's thing on the back page; we had our own Rising Up Angry funnies. And they were a model in a more fundamental way. I've always been obsessed with nuts and bolts. That's what I was gonna write a dissertation on when we were finished. Who took out the garbage? Who cleaned the office? Who's the janitor? And we had no guidance at all. The *old* left was from a whole different era — I couldn't find some old communists and ask them what you did to get people to hand out leaflets or something like that — and the white movement types really didn't do any *organizing*. It seemed like the only ones around that did what we wanted to do, and did it well, were the Panthers. So I used to go and talk to one of their members, ask all these organizational questions. Real simple stuff, like, What do people have to do to get thrown out? What do you do when people don't have money or want to go back to work?
>
> Still there were differences — big differences. A good chunk of our community didn't hate the cops. They wanted protection from the kids as much as from the police. Plus, the cops weren't as indiscriminate in beating whites as in beating blacks. We had one kid who was our Li'l Bobby Hutton. He couldn't see a cop without throwing something. I spent half my time bailing him out of jail. But his mother was a receptionist in Mayor Daley's office and his grandfather was a big shot in the fire department. And *that's* the difference. The cops killed Li'l Bobby Hutton. But you couldn't kill this kid. You'd get a bunch of firemen pissed off. So that was the big difference there.

Same thing was true about the programs. When the Panthers started the breakfast program another white guy who was devoted to the Party started a breakfast program in the poor white neighborhood called Uptown. We thought the idea of serving-the-people programs was good, but the breakfast program wasn't really the most appropriate thing for white working-class people. They really didn't feel like they needed a free bowl of cereal. They didn't consider themselves poor folks.

On the other hand, free legal services — a lawyer cost a few hundred dollars — were very attractive. So we started a free legal program. We went around to the street-gang kids and said, "If you get arrested, we'll get you a good lawyer." We virtually didn't lose a case.

There were other differences too. We used to have "educational sessions" with Fred. You'd go in the first door and get buzzed in. Then there was a steel gate and they'd look to see who it was. You'd walk up this dark hallway one at a time. Five guys would be at the bottom of the stairs. When you'd get up to the top there'd be three guys in berets. You'd put your hands up and they'd search you for weapons. This was when you already had an appointment and they knew who you were and everything. They were really into the military thing.

I remember one day I was sitting in a meeting and a young kid walks in.

He said, "Chairman Fred, I'm going to the meeting at the Black Student Union at Roosevelt College tonight. We're gonna speak there."

He says, "Did you sell your papers this week?"

The kid says, "Well, no, Chairman. I didn't sell them all."

He says, "You don't go. You go sell papers!"

I was impressed that people listened to him. We had discipline too, but nobody ever listened. It wasn't like SDS, where a leader like Mark Rudd would say, "Did you hand out your leaflets?" and you'd say, "Ahh, shut up," or where there was a meeting and Mark Rudd would walk in and everybody would say, "Big deal!"

At the same time, we were frustrated with the Panthers. I admired the fact that they weren't much interested in the white movement, that they didn't want to play the role of "wise advisers," *didn't* quit organizing their own community and fall into the trap of speaking to the white left, that they decided to do breakfast programs instead of merging with SDS and Yippies. But still, we wanted them to like us. It's sort of like the first date. You want a girl who doesn't sleep with anybody except you. We wanted to be their favored whites.

But I related to them as leadership. Ultimately, I thought the Panthers would *expand* into a communist party and lead the revolution and I would be part of it. I mean, in 1965 there was no Panther Party, only isolated campus protests, a small antiwar movement. By 1969 the Panthers had thirty chapters and maybe five thousand members, ten to twenty percent of the country's campuses were shut down, and you had antiwar organizations in every city. So I really thought that if you extrapolated what had gone on from '67 to '70, and multiplied it into the future, by '78–'79 we would have had a revolution and just take over. The Black Panther Party would be, let's say, fifty percent of our newly formed revolutionary communist party. Then you'd have other Third World–type groups and a handful of white groups. And when the Central Committee was formed, I'd be the *one* white representative from Chicago. I don't know. It turned out there was some fallacy in that logic, but *logically*, it made sense. It just didn't work out that way.

When I'm in Oakland, I spend most of my time with Brenda. We stay at her grandmother's house, in San Francisco. We get to know each other. Brenda's California. Back rubs and politics. Tender and spunky. She's only a few years younger than Pat, but she seems from a different generation; she's hopeful, independent. Pat belongs to the Party because I joined. An independent spirit, Brenda has joined on her own. A hard-working comrade, as we say. One night she tells me about her family. She fought kids who teased her younger, handicapped brother, making sure no one would bother him. When the Party women criticize her clothes, she answers back. I enter the office at one in the morning and she's laying out the paper with John, Emory, and other comrades, joking around. She's passionate, but she hugs by patting my back, soothing me. And she always smells good.

I seem to do well in her presence; we share our loyalty to the Party. The time I spend with her is quality, not just lost in passion, but talking about politics and the state of the Party.

One night she calls.

"David, you've got to get over here. The printers won't do the paper."

The situation has been building. The San Francisco printers, another contact through Eldridge, publish all the movement papers. But the FBI hounds them. "The Black Panther Party paper was the subject of a number of actions," says the Select Committee report, "both because of its contents and because it was a source of income for the party." Now the printers say they must refuse our job because the Feds promise to bother their regular clients.

"They're going to take away our business," the owner explains.

The plant smells of ink and rolls of paper. The man is abashed, not wanting this confrontation.

"Well, you don't print us and we'll boycott you," I say. "Get the whole left to stop using you."

Brenda and the other cadre stand on the side, waiting for me to do something.

"I can't let my guys print you," he says.

"Well, I'll tell you what. You teach us and we'll print ourselves."

"I can't teach you," he says. "I'm a union shop. You guys don't belong to the union."

"Chief, we got to get the paper out," Brenda says.

"I know what we got to do," I tell her. "I know exactly what we got to do. Just wait a minute."

I turn back to the owner, remembering something I learned at Del Monte: the Taft-Hartley Act ensures your right to work for thirty days before joining a union. Now I use the strategy for our benefit.

"I'll tell you what we do. We have the Taft-Hartley Act. So you can teach us and we can join and then you can tell the FBI you had no choice. You were just following the law."

The owner looks stumped. He has no answer, doesn't want trouble.

"All right," he says.

Brenda laughs, charmed by our victory.

"Chief, where'd you get that?"

"I just seem to find a way," I say. "Now let's get the paper out."

Chapter

19

THE Los Angeles chapter is also growing, appealing to brothers and sisters from both the Slauson and UCLA. But there are internal and external problems. Flux, flux, flux, Huey always says, everything is flux. Flux: revolutionary organizing is a process of solving problems and confronting new ones.

One of LA's problems is discipline.

Bunchy is a master controller. When someone's angry, he tells me, the thing to do is sit them down. Fifty percent of the time that will stop a fight. But when a struggle becomes physical Bunchy doesn't equivocate. He doesn't call himself the reincarnation of Genghis Khan idly: he conceives of himself as and acts like a warlord. His partners listen to him because they fear him. He runs the Party the same way, "mud-holing" guys when they get out of line—gangster stuff, putting the victim in the center and stomping him down.

Two main problems demand discipline: unreliabilty and the abuse of women.

"A lot of people that came into the Party brought a lot of violence with them," says John Seale.

But violence committed by the Party was because somebody had done something wrong to someone else or something that violated a Party rule or principle.

One rule was, "You never hit or swear at another Party member." But a lot of guys still had that chauvinistic attitude. A guy'd pop a woman in the eye and bruise her all up. That was wrong.

We would mud-hole guys—that's an old term that means "beat your ass." It came out of the streets; if there were fights and a person fell down, he'd get stomped—"mud-holed," you're in the mud. We'd have a trial: "We're gonna mud-hole you." In other words, "If you go beat someone, we have a right to beat your ass." We extended that to stop people from doing that. We felt that that would stop that from happening. And it did. God, yes! It sure did!

There was a cadre of people who did it. They just beat them up. Nothing that would break any arms or bones or anything like that. You figure four or five guys beating a guy in his ribs and his chest. Popping him in his face. He'd get bruised. I didn't think there was anything wrong with it. It wasn't like when I was kid and my dad beat my ass. I didn't do a lot wrong when my dad beat my ass, as I remember.

The violence of men toward women even affects leadership.

"He used to beat his wife up all the time," John remembers about one Party leader.

She'd always come out with sunglasses on to hide the bruises and stuff.

One time she called me and asked if she could come over. I say, "I'll come and get you." Because I never condoned that. I went and picked her up, took her to the house I was in charge of—certain people in the Party had houses, and you had a certain cadre that stayed with you.

He came that night to get her.

I told him, "The lady's gonna *stay* here. You done beat the woman up. Leave her alone! You're not coming in the house. This is *my* house!" Told him I'd blow his brains out if he tried to come in. I was sure I'd get the better of him in a fight. I'd kill him. I knew how to use weapons. But I didn't think we would fight.

So he finally left, called back later that night saying that's wrong for me to take sides, or what have you. You know, "This is my problem!"

I said, "No, this is a Party problem. That's not what we do."

What had happened came out in discussion. But nothing came about it. Bobby says I should leave it alone. I say, "Hey! I'll leave it alone, but he's at my house; she asked if she could come there because she didn't want to be beat up anymore, and she's got a right to be here."

In the Central Committee, we talk about "mud-holing," Bunchy and G. flying to Oakland so we can sit around the table and figure things out.

Bunchy has a strong argument. Cadre must follow orders. Undisciplined brothers disrespect themselves and others; they jeopardize the Party. Plus, the LAPD are mean cops, spawned in the absolute belly of the beast. The Party doesn't have the luxury of taking chances. We've got to operate on the "greater fear" theory: make the rank and file more frightened of the Party than of the police.

We agree. My own experience tells me you can't always talk sense to people. But the issue concerns consciousness as well as obedience. We don't want people to obey out of fear: intimidation creates weak cadre. We want brothers and sisters to understand the errors of their ways, to be new men and new women.

The debate remains unresolved. Then one day we get a call from Chicago. Their head of security — who later turns out to be working for the FBI — has taken the issue to a higher level. In the basement he's wired up an electric chair he's managed to get, and they plan —

No, we tell them. Things have gone too far. No physical discipline. Instead we establish a "people's jail," the adult equivalent of quiet time when you stand in a corner and consider your behavior, a room with a chair and light where people can read the Red Book or an appropriate essay.

Brenda's one of the first to use it.

One night no one meets me at the airport. I'm exhausted from a New York trip. The chapter there has moved to Harlem, taken over by some veteran movement people and a family named Shakur. With their confusing African names and peculiar New York manner, I can hardly keep track of them. Besides, I never feel comfortable in New York. Chicago has the nation's biggest housing project, the Robert Taylor Homes stretching like tombstones for over a mile. Yet the city feels like a small town. Other than the projects, one-family houses and Oakland-like shacks and working-class homes line the streets. The smell of barbecue permeates even the freezing air. The people speak in the accents and with the assumptions of the South: recognizing these types from my early years, I can tell who's for real. But New York feels foreign. I don't seem able to read the people. My uneasiness isn't a matter of personal discomfort but organizational security. We're worried about infiltrators, provocateurs who use revolutionary militancy to encourage a chapter into a jackanape action. (We guard against this by printing pictures of suspected pigs in the paper, urging community people to let us hear what they know about them.) My uptightness with the cadre damages us because New York should be an important chapter and they're going to need attention; the cops and New York Red squad have already targeted them.

My pickup—Charles Bursey—doesn't arrive. I'm burnt-out and leery. I'm used to constant surveillance, cops parked in front of my house and the office, FBI sitting behind me on planes, following my every move. (Sometimes I'll get up and down, pretending I'm about to go to the bathroom, then change my mind, only to annoy them.) But I don't like being alone. Isolation gives the pigs an opportunity to grab me with impunity. I jump into a cab, and after the long ride—the driver isn't going to protect me if the cops stop us—I chew Brenda out soon as I'm inside the office.

"What happened to my message!" I ask her, addressing her as a cadre. In public our relationship is carefully prescribed by our Party roles.

"You didn't tell me!"

"That's it! You're going to jail!"

"I didn't do anything wrong," she answers.

"You're going to jail," I repeat, even as I realize I'm wrong to take out my frustrations on her.

She's already marching off, showing me her back.

"Read the Red Book on Party discipline!" I say.

Later that night we're together.

"You weren't angry with me," Brenda says. "You exploded because you're under so much stress. And you keep it all inside."

Her understanding touches me. She demonstrates a kind of love I've never experienced before.

"You're right," I say. "You know, you're really right."

Then I have to face my nightly question: Do I go home or not? I lie in bed.

"It's my turn tonight?" she teases me.

"Shut up, Brenda," I say. I hate when she jokes.

"I'm kidding," she says. "It doesn't bother me. Really."

I believe she means this. Brenda has no intentions to steal me from Pat; she's content simply to continue the relationship. I'm too exhausted to drive home. I stay the night.

Meanwhile, LA's external problems have increased: the chapter is a special target of the LAPD and also at war with US, which is threatened by Bunchy's success at organizing students at UCLA. (US considers the campus its home ground.) Throughout the fall there have been incidents between US and Party members in both Los Angeles and San Diego, including a rumored plot on their part to assassinate Eldridge before he goes into exile.

Wanting to capitalize on the situation (as in Chicago), J. Edgar Hoover himself instructs local field offices to "submit imaginative and hard-hitting counterintelligence measures aimed at crippling the BPP."

In the winter the UCLA BSU—where Panther sympathizers and US members vie for appointment to a community and student program—becomes the struggle's focus.

"Bunchy and I met with Karenga and Jumbo—he was the head of the Simba Wachukas," remembers G. "Bunchy had a good rapport with Karenga and Jumbo."

> After we left Karenga we went over to John Huggins's house. Bunchy told the people in favor of the Panther-oriented program: "No violence, no problem. There's a contradiction here, but it's nonantagonistic. If the vote goes the cultural nationalist way—the Karenga way—we're gonna support it. This is a nonantagonistic situation." Bunchy was *very* clear about that. He didn't want running violence with no black people. We could sit and talk with them. He was very, very good with that.

At Shattuck Avenue it's close to dinnertime. Kids run underfoot while some cadre quiz Masai at the table about the meaning of quantitative into qualitative change. In the front Emory, Brenda, and some others work on the paper. The phone rings. (I start hating the phone, late-night and early-morning rings especially; people only call then to announce busts and deaths.)

"Chief, they killed Bunchy!"

"That's crazy. Give me the phone."

I listen to the story. Nothing's clear. Bunchy and John have been ambushed on campus by US members, shot at point-blank range. Brothers from the gangs want retribution; G. is telling them to wait a moment, not to avenge the deaths. The chapter is putting out a special issue of the newspaper. What should we say? We've got to deal with cultural nationalism and the police story that the murder proves we're not political activists but gangbangers.

We work out the statement over the phone, employing Eldridge-style rhetoric.

> The narrow-minded breed of nonthinking so-called sounding-revolutionary, sell-out politics that have historically aimed and fired guns only at Black people can best be described as . . . "Pork Chop Nationalism." . . . Pork Chopism killed two beautiful Black brothers in the prime of revolutionary life of serving our people. Pork Chop National-

ism is as guilty as Cain, as scurvy as Brutus, as low-lifed and trifling as Judas. Pork Chop Nationalism may at a casual glance seem comical and even lovable but if allowed to run amok it can speed the racist journey to Black genocide that the pig power structure has planned for all of us. . . . The issue of control of UCLA's Black Studies Program is not an objective of the Black Panther Party. The Black Panther Party would not trade one block of Central Avenue for the whole city of Westwood, because the Black Panther Party is based on the masses of Black people. . . .

Bunchy's murder terrifies me. Bunchy isn't simply a beloved brother. He's Bunchy—invincible, beyond death! I've seen him control gangbangers, dominate people who would normally scare me. If this can happen to Bunchy, what will happen to us?

But Bunchy himself forbids me to retreat. I remember his challenge: "How come you don't talk that much? You've got good words. Good words. I demand you talk more." We must move on, redeem his sacrifice by advancing the struggle to a higher level.

We appoint G. to take Bunchy's place.

"I almost fainted," says G.

Can you imagine the state of mind I was in? I felt very close to Bunchy. I looked to him as a leader. And here's me—little old me—taking a spot like that. All this is confusing.

I said I'd get back to you. I had to figure things out. I don't want to be here; my heart is in the South. It was too much happening too quick.

I flew to Louisiana from Oakland. I went out to the swamps and did a lot of soul-searching. I talked to one of the elders—Thibadoux. He's about forty miles from Morgan City. Because the thing was that the southern movement was not supposed to supply any people with my education, my training. It's supposed to be indigenous. Like LA. What do I know about LA?

I came back, talked to you, went back to LA. We made the programs our priority. The military was second. All of it was based on an effort at socialism. We were going to show the community how to survive better by using socialist ways and thinking and economics. At the same time we went and talked to the merchants and tried to talk them into supporting these programs. We were trying to create a new reality based on independence, self-reliance, self-struggle, and autonomy.

We also appoint G. to ensure the members' physical security; in the coming months, we emphasize G.'s martial spirit and promise to avenge Bunchy's and John's deaths while also attempting to establish a truce with US. But FBI sabotage—including racist cartoons drawn by the government employees and distributed as the work of either the Panthers or US—destroys any possibility of peace. "Shootings, beatings, and a high degree of unrest continues to prevail in the ghetto area of southeast San Diego," one FBI report reads. "Although no specific counterintelligence action can be credited with contributing to this overall situation, it is felt that a substantial amount of the unrest is directly attributable to this program."

Still, we keep growing. Soon after the killings, Elaine Brown, one of the leaders of the LA chapter, and Ericka Huggins, John's widow, go to Bridgeport, Connecticut, John's home, and start a new branch.

Two sisters, Peggy and Frances Carter—Frances later marries June—are among their first converts.

"We—me and Peggy—grew up on the East End of Bridgeport, which was a mixed neighborhood," remembers Frances.

Italian, Polish, Puerto Rican, black. My parents ran a barbershop.

We went to an almost all-white high school. There was only about five blacks in the entire high school of about maybe eight hundred. We were continually harassed by teachers, by other students.

"What are you doing here?"

"Well, we don't want to be here no more than you don't *want* us to be here!"

Our uncle—he's a Republican, an alderman, and has always been involved in politics—took us to the March on Washington. At the time it was like, "I want to hurry up and get back home, so we can go party." Our whole thing was having a good time, socializing with our friends, parties, doing each other's hair, buying nice outfits and clothes, going to New York, going to Boston. Whatever. But never anything like doing something for somebody.

Still the march was a very great experience. It made an impact. We couldn't fully understand everything various groups said, but we noticed the whites and blacks and Puerto Ricans and Jamaicans all together. Then we come back to school, that following Monday, and were totally alienated *again*.

So, Peggy and I, we decided we weren't gonna have it. We started resisting at every turn. They start suspending us, throwing us out of school.

My parents would have to come up to get us back in. If the history teacher would say something about black people being "heathens," I would stand up and tell him, "I take exception to that, because you're not correct." But every time we *said* that, we would get thrown out.

Our parents didn't sympathize. They wanted us to participate in the cotillion and the yearbook staff. Their intentions were very good, but they weren't for us, because to be at the school and not effect any change didn't help us at all. If anything, it kept tearing down our self-esteem.

Finally Peggy became pregnant. We were trying to keep the news from our parents. But the gym teacher saw her undressing and told her to go to the office. They asked her if she was pregnant. She said no, she was just getting fat. I wanted to tear out the gym teacher's eyes. Peggy got kicked out of school—which left me there alone—and we were separated because our parents put her in an unwed mothers home. I tried everything to get placed with her, but I couldn't—even after I had become *really* very rebellious in school.

Then right after John and Bunchy were killed, my uncle—the same one who took us to Washington—came to us.

He says, "You know, one of the young brothers that got killed was named 'Carter.' Which is *our* last name. I went over to their office in Bridgeport and I wasn't readily received."

He figured the cool reception was because he was older. He guessed they were thinking, "Who is this? The police or something?" He suggests we go check them out. And we were interested ourselves. We wanted to know, What kind of political organization could there be in 1969 that you get shot from being a member of? What is this going on there? Because the media out here didn't have much about it.

Peggy and I went down to the office on East Main Street, in the Bridgeport Spanish-American community. We dressed in our *finest* because we were very meticulous. My sister worked in a specialty boutique and we got our clothes at discount. We didn't walk out of our house unless our hair, nails, pedicure was meticulous. We had the big naturals. The fur jackets. Everything matching.

There were about thirty people in the meeting—street people, no revolutionaries, other than the organizers. I don't remember exactly what they spoke about—racism, capitalism, the conspiracy on the part of the white power structure to destroy the black family. They said we needed to bring all power back to the people—the regular *people.*

The Panthers were dressed in fatigues and looked like guerrillas. Urban guerrillas. That led to an immediate class distinction between us and them because Elaine Brown made reference to these "little china dolls, little kewpie dolls." We answered back, told her not to put any distinction between herself and us, that we were black women, not kewpie dolls, and that we would not be categorized as china dolls, and assured her that if we wanted to come next time in a Oscar de la Renta we would come through that door and be totally accepted. We even invited her to come to our little boutique across town. One of those-type things.

We went to the memorial service. There, Ericka asked us if we'd come back around, because Elaine and some other sisters were leaving, and she was gonna stay on. She seemed really genuine, spaced out, but genuine.

We went to several PE classes. The way they talked was foreign—even colloquial words were different—but we felt sympathy for Ericka and believed the Ten Point Program would really do good down in our community: the breakfast program, determining your own destiny. Plus, working with the Party would be a good excuse to get out from the white community, *back* down into our community. So we kept going. And each time we're going, we're seeing more and more people wearing all these clothes and we're feeling like, "Well, there's still just a little distinction going here."

Finally we went to the Army and Navy surplus store.

We dashed in. "Give us everything you have for the urban guerrilla!"

They looked: "What the hell are you talking about?"

Peggy grabs some combat boots.

"What do you think?" she asks me. "Should I take off my stockings before I put them on?"

We're pulling everything down, putting everything on the counter. It was like we were in a candy store. Everything we'd seen anybody ever had on, we're gonna get. We even had belts you put bullets in with a canteen on the other side. I took this little helmet that looked like a little spittoon. I thought I'd seen somebody with one. Then we got the tams to put on and had to stuff our hair under them. Plus everything had to match. Olive green.

The guy thought we were just playing, that we weren't gonna buy all that stuff. He says, "How are you gonna pay for this? Credit card or cash?" Like it's all a joke.

"Cash," we say.

We pay him, jump in the car and drive to the office. We walk up and everybody starts laughing. We had to laugh too, because everybody was old and dirty and stinky and here we are, big, shiny guerrilla boots, all our clothes really pressed, clean and green, the tags still on. We looked

David

Huey Newton

Bobby Seale

Stephen Shames

Eldridge Cleaver

Stephen Shames

Kathleen Cleaver

Gene McKinney

Melvin Newton

Alan Copelana

Fred Hampton

Geronimo Pratt

Li'l Bobby Hutton and Bobby Seale storming the California State Capitol at Sacramento, May 2, 1967

Bobby Seale (*left*) and David during press conference at Shattuck Avenue office

David speaking at a mass meeting at Yale during the New Haven trial

Bill Crawford

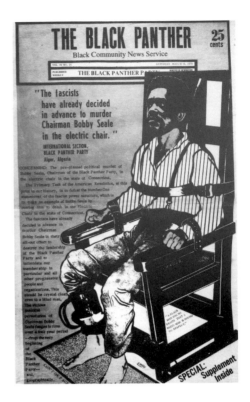

Emory Douglas working on *The Black Panther* newspaper

The Black Panther Youth—Ralph Hilliard, June's son, left, calling cadence; Dorion Hilliard, front, center

Sickle-cell anemia testing at De Fremery
Park

People receiving free food at the Black
Survival Conference at Bobby Hutton Memorial Park

Supporters hold posters of Huey Newton outside the Alameda County Courthouse during his trial

David and Huey upon Huey's release from prison in 1970

like little kids because the clothes were big and bulky and we were small. Ericka had tears in her eyes, she was laughing so hard.

Peggy said, "Now, ain't no difference between none of us anymore, right?"

Everybody hollered, "Right on!"

Well, soon we changed our way of walking and talking, doing things. My mother and father got upset, extremely upset.

We tried to politicize them: "You don't understand. These folks say they're gonna effect some change. We're gonna have a revolution."

My father goes, "BULLSHIT! What do you MEAN?"

Here's this man who moved into the white community to be accepted, and we're talking about tearing that down.

He says, "You're being brainwashed" and everything. He wants us to go lay on a couch somewhere. "Helen, call the doctor. These girls have gone *crazy!* What's wrong with them, Helen?"

I said, "Wait a minute. We really believe in this. We're gonna keep on going."

Then he gave us an ultimatum: "Either you stay here, or you leave and you go with them."

Peggy said, "You know, I wish you didn't say that."

He answered with something angry.

So we got our little stuff and left. We were just learning to believe in different values and were willing to make sacrifices. It hurt a lot, and it hurt them.

We went to live with Ericka. We had Peggy's kids with us—she had three by then because she had been married and then split up. We stayed in various apartments. We always had access to money, from our friends and stuff, and from my mother—my parents tried to take a heavy stand, but they weren't gonna see us suffer out there in the gutter.

At this time the Party had already moved from Bridgeport to New Haven—the area in Bridgeport was more Latin than black. We worked every day. We would do the paper, sit around and have classes. Sometimes Peggy and I would go the bars and politicize over the booze. There was never any kind of negativity from the community itself. Their reaction was to stop and listen to us.

The chapter started to grow. We were going over to the different colleges, talking to the high school students. We gave our interpretation of what we heard in the Party in real street. Because that's the only way we knew how. When we got back Ericka or Lonnie—McLucas, the other leadership; he was *fantastic*, grass-roots—would say, "When you were saying this, you actually should have explained it this way." Or whatever.

It was *fun!* Totally different. We felt a camaraderie, kinship. We had no idea of where we were *going,* what we were doing. We were learning more and more every day. We were gonna *make* it.

Then the money started dwindling. I wanted us to have our own apartment and everything with the kiddies.

I went to Remington Gun Company. Because my mother had contact with a foreman there. They made guns and everything. All these bullets. The bullets smelled terrible and the plastic made me nauseous.

I made two hundred and fifty a week.

"Two-fifty a week!" Party members said. "Do you know how many children that can feed? Do you know how many clothes we can buy for the breakfast children?"

I'm thinking, "Great!" Gave me more incentive to go in there. Little did I realize I was *pregnant* during that time, and that's why I kept getting so nauseous and feeling so *bad.* I really felt that I was working for a purpose.

Brenda and I spend all our time together. We're lovers, buddies, comrades. We drive endlessly through the Bay Area. I can stay silent with her or unload, getting everything off my chest. With Pat I'm never free from the demands of husband and father. With Pat I'm always anxious, worried for her, the kids. Even at rallies I feel torn, as though I have another pair of eyes watching everything I do, another pair of ears hearing everything I say: Pat's eyes and ears. With Brenda I have fun. Brenda's calm when Pat's frantic, loving when Pat's scared; she listens when I speak, soothes me when something goes wrong. She makes me laugh. She says she hates Emory because he's stolen her secret stash of candy; she doesn't bat an eye when we return to the office late from an airport run and Charles Bursey answers the door butt naked. When I go around the country during this time I am overwhelmed by the affection and regard of chapter members. Brenda embodies this. When I make love to her I don't only embrace her warmth and smell; I'm making love to the spirit of the Party itself.

My only worry about the relationship is Pat. I still haven't told her. My silence violates Party principle, but I'm not so honest that I can tell my wife I'm sleeping with another woman. We've pledged to make ourselves new men and women, but I'm not that advanced yet.

Plus, there's always something happening to distract me from the problem.

One morning the officer of the day says there's someone out front wanting to talk to me. I go downstairs; my own FBI agent waits there, dressed in jacket and tie, hat.

"I've got no time," I say.

"I've got a proposition for you and Bobby," he starts.

"Bobby," I say, "this fool wants to talk."

He stands, taller than both of us, enticing us — a seducer, corruptor.

"I believe in what you're doing. But you people are going to hurt yourselves. You don't have the firepower. And we know you don't really mean it. So abandon the rhetoric about guns and violence. We'll give you a million dollars."

He speaks with perfect calm, unembarrassed. He expects us to take the offer, appealing to our reason. A salesman. Meanwhile I'm thinking, Why do these guys always come after me?

"You guys are smart. We know there are differences. You're not like Cleaver. You care about people. You're not a con. We feel we can talk sense to you."

"Hey, we're not talking," I say. "And we're definitely not talking to you!"

"Get out of here, man," Bobby says.

The agent peers into the office, the epitome of self-assurance. "You know what you're up against. And the real stuff hasn't even begun yet."

"Get out! We're not for sale. You can't buy us for a million dollars!"

"Don't get into a situation you can't get out of."

We slam the door.

"A million dollars!"

When we tell Huey about the incident he criticizes us. You should have taken the money, used it to develop the Party's programs, he says: that would have really been manipulating the system to promote the Party. Then he adds another, strange request, asking me to give Melvin eleven thousand dollars from the defense fund. He doesn't say what the money's for, but I don't question him: he's the leader.

"Thank you very much," he says over the tape after Melvin reports receiving the money. "I'll let you know later on what this is all about."

Chapter

20

EVERY time Bobby and I look around during that spring of 1969 someone's opening up a chapter. The paper appears like clockwork and new Serve the People programs start everywhere: free clothes, food distribution centers, medical and legal clinics.

"Sixty-nine and '70, there was a brand-new branch cropping up every day almost," my brother June remembers.

> New Orleans, Winston-Salem. Somebody had to go out and try to give them directions on how to put it together, make sure they were structured correctly. I was Assistant Chief of Staff. I would go to the new chapter — you and Bobby both definitely had your hands full, on a daily basis — and have a copy of the Black Panther Party Ten Point Platform and Program and the Party's rules. I would tell them, "Here's how you have to structure the Party. Everybody has to memorize and know the Ten Point Platform and Program. You have to maintain contact with Central Headquarters weekly. According to the size of the branch you're expected to sell so many papers on a weekly basis. There's also certain posters and paraphernalia that you're charged with selling to help raise money to sustain your own operation and also send a certain amount to Central Headquarters for the overall Party functions." I would stay two or three days, sometimes a week. I had nothing to do with the military education — though our credo was that every home should have a shotgun — and the responsibility of the PE classes was left to Masai or to Bobby.

My presence was just a matter of contacting them, letting them see there really was someone from Central Headquarters in the flesh, someone they could *see,* who actually existed.

The Party branches out in other ways. Eldridge has left Cuba and set himself up in Algeria, creating an international section. Through him we contact representatives from Third World socialist countries, including the Vietnamese.

Until this point the Vietnamese haven't been a major Party influence. The Red Book has served as our bible, a practical handbook on personal remolding and problems of organization and discipline. Fanon — and the Algerian Revolution — has provided us our most important theoretical model. And the Koreans, who want to ally with us, have offered us money and support.

But when we see representatives of the National Liberation Front that spring in Montreal, we are mutually impressed. Their resilience and ingenuity in defeating American military power awes me and proves the correctness of Huey's maxim: The spirit of the people is always greater than the man's technology. They seem equally amazed by us. Elbert Howard attends the conference with us, an original Panther whom we call Big Man because of his six-foot, three-hundred-pound size. "Big Man!" the Vietnamese say. "He's a big man! He's Panther! He Black Panther, we Yellow Panther!" We say, "Yeah, you're Yellow Panthers, we're Black Panthers. All power to the people!" They give us books on General Giap and Ho Chi Minh; while they support and applaud the mass antiwar movement, they are unstinting in their respect for us, saying in no uncertain terms that they think we and they are the Third World revolutionary vanguard and that together we will eventually destroy imperialism and free the people of the world.

We've also expanded our college student base. The San Francisco State strike has become a model of campus insurrection; Panther-inspired BSUs and Third World liberation fronts appear on campuses nationwide. The groups not only provide future cadre but create the possibility of community-campus actions and also a realistic Third World–white alliance.

"At the Berkeley campus during the winter of '68–'69, we went through a Third World Strike," recalls Dan Siegel, a white campus leader, of the strike closest to us.

It was very violent. We had had police on campus a lot since I arrived in September '67, and they were *rough,* but they were much more violent towards the minority students, as compared to the white students. The first week of the strike the Third World students were literally just picketing back and forth in front of the Telegraph Avenue Sather Gate. It was a symbolic picket line. If you wanted to get on the campus, you could walk around them, or if you were macho and wanted to make a point, you could even push through them. They weren't looking for a fight. Yet they were attacked by police. They hit them on the head instead of on the back; and it was the first time I'd ever seen cops drawing their guns.

So some of us, as whites, did things designed to be supportive. For example, the university suspended noontime rallies, which had been a well-accepted part of campus life ever since the Free Speech movement. So a group of us law students held an illegal rally, basically, to test the university prohibition. And we were not expelled—of course we weren't; we were a bunch of white, middle-class law students—and that then created a context in which the Third World students could continue to have noon rallies.

Things like that really cemented positive relations among activists of different races.

Our influence is felt everywhere. We've become recognized leaders, setting the philosophical and political agenda of the left. We're even denounced—only six months after being exalted—by segments of the white left. The Panthers are only part of the vanguard, they say, not *the* vanguard. Later for that, we say. We don't need to be told who we are. We know: the people creating revolution, the main targets of the state.

The rapid growth doubles the problem of infiltration. On April 2, 1969, the police bust twenty-one New York members, charging them with conspiracy to lob mortars at police stations and blow up department stores and the Bronx Botanical Gardens. The perpetrator of the so-called conspiracy is an undercover pig named Gene Roberts who has tried to convince Party members to engage in his ridiculous schemes.

Roberts has counterparts throughout the Party, guys who present themselves as security specialists, elect themselves bodyguards for leadership. We have little trouble with this in Oakland; the area's fairly contained, and besides, between the Hilliards, Newtons, and Seales, we know everyone. But in larger cities and new chapters guys bully their ways into positions of trust. (Later on we find that the head of Chicago security, William O'Neal, works regularly for the police.)

We become victims of our own fears, and a catastrophe occurs. George Sams—a weird-looking, crazy-seeming guy I've met once or twice—is introduced to us by Stokely. Sams insinuates himself into the Party, traveling from chapter to chapter, claiming he represents the Central Committee. He arrives in New Haven—where the old Bridgeport chapter has transplanted itself—in late spring.

"Then George Sams jumped on the scene," remembers Frances.

The biggest fool, the ugliest bastard I'd ever seen. Talking crazy, his eyes deep, beet red. Black skin, lips—way, way out. Just stunk like ten dogs. Foamy when he talked. Almost like a Halloween character. Scary! Wanting to walk around using all this power and fright.

Peggy said, "Who are you? What are you doing?"

"None of your business! Don't mess with this! You just do what you're supposed to do and don't ask me about nothing! You start questioning me like that, it makes me think you're the police and everything!"

Peggy said, "Well, the way you're walking around here acting, you might just be the police!"

I said, "Right on! You know, he just might be."

He was sick. Sexually perverted, always trying to work his will and wanting to forcibly have sex. One evening he pulled me up into a room. "All right, now. We'll put you on report."

I said, "Fuck you. Something big and nasty and ugly and stinking like you?"

He stayed a week, maybe a few days. But it seemed like a lifetime. He was the kiss of death. I can recall him wielding this big old billy club–type thing. The whole family cohesiveness camaraderie we were experiencing stopped. Ericka was submissive-acting. Clearly frightened. She would never even try to say anything. Only Lonnie was standing up to him. Sams never liked that: here was somebody he really had to tear down. But Lonnie would never allow it.

Later me and June talked about how there were situations where if people had had the time to be listened to, a lot of things may not have happened the way they happened. I wish we'd had more of an insight into more things during that time. We wouldn't have been so naive. It comes back to you. Me and June, sometimes we sit up going over all kinds of stuff that happened and how naive some of us were—how we should have questioned more, should have *felt* more. If we felt that much of a group, then why did you feel hesitant when it came to asking about a fool like George Sams? It just leaves a whole emptiness and sadness within you. You know something's happening, but you don't know what it is. Then you don't choose to know, because, again, it's no longer fun and challenging— it's ceased being that. And then this whole nightmare broke out.

Sams focuses on Alex Rackley, a new Party member. He casts suspicions on him, then claims Rackley is a police agent. At the same time Bobby goes to speak in New Haven. When he calls me from there, I can sense something's wrong.

"Get out of there, man," I say. "Something bad's going on."

Later we find out what happened. Sams and other members interrogate Rackley. Then Sams and another Panther torture Rackley—shackle him to a bed, scald him with water—and kill him. They dump the corpse in a swamp. By the time the cops find it, Sams has disappeared. Local police and the FBI search for him, using warrants as excuses to bust into offices in Chicago, Detroit, Denver, and Sacramento.

"The FBI and Chicago police raided the office, looking for Sams," remembers Rush.

They had arrested some Panthers before, but this was the first actual raid.

We weren't surprised. A shoot-out was always imminent. The Chicago police have always been part of the political machine, used to protect the political status quo, and this was *Daley's* police force, so we knew the police department was out to destroy us.

But we had committed our lives; we had adopted a political philosophy and were defending our rights. We wanted to show people that they should defend themselves against unlawful, illegal acts by the police. We viewed ourselves as the vanguard and accepted the responsibility for that. We knew we would have battles with the police, and we fully expected to be killed. We had all committed ourselves to that.

Meanwhile we are meeting in Oakland. The success of the local chapters has created a new problem. Confused about the Party's structure, members turn local leaders—deputy ministers—into national officers. People call Fred "Chairman Fred" and rumors claim he's the Party's chairman—which of course is not true, since Bobby is the only chairman.

"It didn't bother us that we hadn't been asked to be on the Central Committee," says Rush. "We had our hands full dealing with Chicago. I don't think anybody had ambitions of being on the Central Committee. Obviously if it had opened up to [Fred Hampton] he would have accepted it, but he never talked to me about it. We loved Bobby and you and Huey and Masai. Had a lot of respect for you—and the fact is, you had a lot of respect for us."

The confusion weakens us, and Bobby—who plays a key role in amplifying and detailing the Party structure—wants to meet to clarify titles and the different levels of leadership and to emphasize that there's only one Black Panther Party *Chairman,* with me next in line and Huey at the top. Afterward, we plan to celebrate: Masai is getting married and we'll hold a party at the national headquarters.

The morning before the meeting, I'm lying in bed with Brenda in the one-bedroom she shares with another comrade. I've been ducking Pat constantly, lying, making excuses for coming home late or not at all. I've assured Pat nothing's going on between Brenda and me; but my wife is no fool: sensing the truth, she's been asking Party women whether I'm relating to anyone.

The doorbell rings and someone walks though the living room. I don't worry; in Panther pads people come and go at all hours.

I turn over to sleep—my ulcer pains me frequently, and I really appreciate any peaceful hours I can steal—when the bedroom door slams open.

"You motherfucker!"

Pat stands there. The sight of me and Brenda—confirming every rumor Pat's heard in the last weeks, rumors that I'm sure she has wanted to disbelieve until now—puts her completely out of control.

I jump in the bed. I'm mortified. Why haven't I dealt with this before?

"I'm gonna kill you and the bitch!" She points a nine-millimeter straight at my head.

"No, Pat—"

"Goddamn you!"

This is an absolutely insane way to die, I think: I'm the Chief of Staff of the Black Panther Party, not Stagolee.

I'm terrified. I try to stay calm, remember Bunchy's dictum: Sit them down, get them in the chair. I've got to get the gun from her hand, not let fear make me panic.

"Give me the gun," I say.

Pat cries and rages, cursing, insane with grief. The way my generation deals with marriage is to hang in until one or the other gets killed. I promise myself if I stay alive, I'll never lie about this stuff again; love isn't worth it.

"You lying son of a bitch!"

"Put the gun down."

My biggest fear is that the gun will go off accidentally. Brenda lies by my side, still as death.

"I see you!" Pat says. "I'm gonna kill you!"

I know my chances for survival increase the more she talks. I hate seeing the way humiliation twists and makes hideous her beautiful face; at the same time, for my own sake, I hope her shame is stronger than her fury.

"This is not the thing to do," I say. "The Party will kill you if you kill me. Besides, you say you love me. How can you do this crazy stuff?"

Pat raves with jealousy and hurt. Her words speak the truth. I've crossed a boundary, trashed the sanctity of our vows; I haven't hidden my intimacy with Brenda, and I've let Brenda usurp Pat's place and become central in my life.

"Put down the gun," I repeat. "Let it go."

I must make a move, risk her shooting at me, try to get the gun.

I reach out.

Pat wavers, calling me names.

I get up from the bed. "Let it go," I say.

Pat sobs and curses, but the threat is past. I remove the piece from her hand. Soon as I feel the weight, I breathe again.

"Patricia," I say, my voice gaining authority, "go home. I'll meet you there. Go home."

A little later I approach our house. I'm still not sure what to do. In the old days, all this would have passed over. I'd apologize to Pat, tell her I love her, give up Brenda, go out and drink with the guys on the corner.

Now things aren't so easy. My membership in the Party demands I acknowledge the truth: I live with death every day; surely I can admit the vicissitudes of my love life. That's one thing the talk of remolding from the Red Book is about: resolving conflicts in a more humane, rational way than the brutal, desperate ones we've been given and taught. I must do something with Pat other than settle our problem barroom fashion, man and woman slugging it out. I've got to elevate, as we say, this part of the struggle too.

Well, what am I going to do? First, I don't want to fight with Pat. Arguments with Brenda resolve themselves; fights with Pat are interminable and pointless. Second, I'm not prepared to stop seeing Brenda. Third, I don't want my behavior to sink to the madness of this morning. I'm not balancing one woman off another here. I haven't simply been cheating. This relationship—I love Brenda—is more dignified than that, and I must honor that quality.

But Pat has also been my lover, comrade, and friend. I can't simply cut her loose now. I face this logical conclusion. If I stay with Pat and remain Brenda's lover, I must grant Pat the same freedom I claim for myself.

"I'm not playing with you," I tell Pat. "You can't keep acting like this. If you want to be with someone else, then go ahead. You have the same right as me. But you can't keep acting like this: it destroys Party unity and it's crazy."

*   *   *

The busts begin.

"My mother drove me to work and dropped me out," Frances remembers.

I'm walking in the gate.

All of a sudden, police are jumping out of everywhere.

"She's armed and dangerous!!"

All I see is guns.

I'm thinking, "Is this some kind of game or something they got going?" I seriously did not think they were all there for me! "What do you want me for?"

They surrounded me. They had cameras, guns, shotguns. It blew my mind.

"You're coming with us."

I said, "Wait a minute!! Ma!"

But she can't hear me. She's driving her little Fiat down the street. "MAAAAA!"

They took me to Bridgeport. Threw me in the back of the car. I'm spouting this rhetoric: "Wait a minute! You're not supposed to do this! What the hell's wrong with you? I gotta call somebody!"

It was very frightening.

They put me in this little old small cell. Dirty, nasty place.

I'm still saying, "What's *wrong?* What's going on? You only arrested me because I'm a Black Panther Party member. You're harassing me and you're gonna be sorry!" All I kept thinking was, "Don't act scared." Because I was scared shitless.

Then a bunch of them rush in. "Okay, it's time to take her."

"Take me *where?*"

"Just get in the car. You're coming with us."

They have me with handcuffs and leg chains and put me in the car, even chained me down with the seat belts.

They take me to the New Haven jail, pushed me into this room. There's about ten or twenty of them standing around.

"Okay, Okay!! Who killed him?"

"Who killed who?" Back then I used to have migraines real bad whenever I got nervous. So my head's aching.

"We know all about it! We know all about it!"

"What are you talking about? Wait a minute! I gotta call headquarters. I gotta call the *office!*"

"There *is* no more office. Everybody's dead!"

The only thing I focus on right then is Peggy and the kids.

"What the hell you mean, 'Everybody's dead'?"

"You all kill people."

"What do you mean they're dead?"

"They're no longer around."

"Where's Peggy? What did you do with Peggy? I've got to have a phone. I got to call Peggy!"

I'm talking about Peggy more than calling an attorney! But I've never been arrested before in my life. Although we always talked about it: you call an attorney, you give your name and address and whatever.

Finally they gave me something for my migraine. Mescaline or something — that was the effect.

They kept saying we were charged with first-degree murder: "You will be in an electric chair."

I just kept asking for my sister. Then, after a while, I could barely speak. And my head felt even worse than how it felt prior.

There was one white woman, a police lady. I said to her, "Look, I just need to know where my sister is. And the baby."

They were saying, "Don't talk to her! Don't tell her nothing! As far as she's concerned, they're all dead."

She says, "Let me get you some cold water."

I remember being soaking wet — all kinds of sweat.

She brought me some water and I threw it over me.

Then she whispered, "Peggy's fine," and I passed out.

In Oakland, we prepare to celebrate Masai's marriage. Bobby has been ordained by a local minister — instant ministers' licenses, we say — and will perform the ceremony at the Berkeley Free Church; then we'll reconvene at the national office for a party.

We drive to the church in a convoy of six or seven cars, maybe thirty of us altogether. Before we go I leave Bud at the barbecue pit; we'll come back to Shattuck to have the reception. I'm looking forward to the celebration. The only times we've gotten together socially like this have been at funerals or after court appearances.

Bobby reads the vows — he talks about the new man and new woman; Pat gives me a bad look — and we drive back. We ignore the helicopters overhead: air surveillance is normal after the radical activity on campus the previous spring.

June's at the wheel. We stop at Ashby, a few blocks from the office. Suddenly a sedan pulls ahead of us and we're surrounded. Guys rush out, guns drawn, ordering us out. There won't be any shoot-out; we're completely outnumbered. They slap handcuffs on Bobby, squash him into the car, drive him away. We hear the charges later: unlawful flight and, still later, murder and conspiracy to kidnap and murder Alex Rackley. There's no bail. Except for me, all the original Party leaders are jailed or in exile. I'm alone.

Chapter
21

BOBBY'S trial begins in the fall. Along with seven other defendants from the antiwar movement—Tom Hayden, Rennie Davis, Jerry Rubin, Abbie Hoffman, Dave Dellinger, Lee Weiner, and Jon Froines—he's charged with crossing state lines to incite a riot, the demonstrations the previous August against the Democratic Convention. Actually Bobby spent only one night in Chicago, to deliver one speech—the real purpose of his visit was to support striking bus drivers. But the government uses the case to eliminate him: Chicago is the first stop on the way to the New Haven electric chair. Years later, the Senate Committee will determine that Attorney General John Mitchell wanted to "hang" the "Chicago rioting business" on Bobby.

The white defendants differ among themselves about how to handle the charges, Abbie and Jerry, the Yippies, making fun of the creepy older judge, Julius Hoffman—Abbie calls him "Julie"—while the others treat the proceedings solemnly. But for all the antics and strategical talk, Bobby quickly becomes the center of attention. Bobby wants to be defended by Charles Garry, who has requested a postponement—Charlie's in the hospital for a gallbladder operation. Judge Hoffman refuses the motion and insists Bobby accept Bill Kunstler and Lenny Weinglass, the lawyers for the other defendants, as his own counsel. Refusing, Bobby represents himself, and when he is declared in contempt he takes the struggle to the highest level, trying to speak out even when the judge orders him bound and gagged. Finally Hoffman sentences Bobby to four years for contempt and severs his case from the others'.

Bobby's incarceration and trial cripples us, depriving us of his organizational and inspirational talents (besides inflicting physical and psychological pain on him). The trial also brings home the failure at creating a solid alliance with the white left. Since Nixon's election, the antiwar movement has changed. New, mainstream forces who don't give a damn about the Panthers and the black community have taken over the peace movement. Meanwhile, traditional friends among the white mother country radicals are frozen out and fighting among themselves. In the confusion, the white left almost completely ignores Bobby's presence, focusing instead on the other defendants. When they finally do relate to him, they separate him and us from the antiwar struggle, acting as though we're competing against the Vietnamese for their attention. Their attitude infuriates me. Later for the antiwar movement, I want to say. The Vietnamese will take care of the war. They're beating the American Army without your help. Why do you have to go find a war ten thousand miles away to relate to? We're the guys you should be dealing with. We're right down the corner; the police are killing us and you're standing around. We're proceeding with revolutionary urgency, sometimes not knowing whether we'll survive the night, and you're debating whether to let us speak at your rallies!

The more radical elements of the white left aren't much better. I have no problem with Abbie and Jerry as individuals. But politically Jerry and Abbie engage in theatrics. We don't take them seriously. They have no revolutionary agenda. The way they organize is all right if you want to run a pig for president and throw money into the stock exchange. But we're not about such pranks; we're not jesters.

Tom's another matter. He takes himself seriously enough, but his groups never come through. You must intensify the struggle, we've told students after the violent police attacks against the Berkeley strikers; you must take things to a higher level, not suffer, as blacks have done following Martin Luther King's nonviolent strategy, but organize for self-defense. Finally — after the police bomb the campus with tear gas — the students seem to hear us. Tom and some of his comrades ask us where they can obtain ordnance to shoot down helicopters. (Bursey offers to do it for them with an AR-15, as long as the Party agrees.) We figure they've finally come to their senses, realized there's nothing honorable about losing, nothing revolutionary about a banged head. But no craft are ever downed.

We like SDS, the largest, most important national radical white organization, even less. That summer SDS splits into several factions. Weathermen — the one presumably most ideologically compatible to us — spites us: You're not the vanguard, they tell us, then announce a demonstration in Chicago —

the city is their national headquarters — called the Days of Rage, scheduled to begin right before the trial.

"Fred was against the demonstration from the beginning," remembers Steve Tappis of Rising Up Angry.

> He gave this speech. He told them to go off and organize breakfast pro-grams or something. He certainly didn't want them to be getting the cops mad, so that the cops could then turn around and kill some Panthers in re-venge. He called them "adventuristic, Custeristic" — which was a word he made up. I don't know if he meant to be funny, but he was. He really had a tremendous sense of humor. He said, "They come into town, you'd think they'd stop in, say 'hi' to the vanguard? We're the vanguard. You don't have revolutionary demonstrations and rallies without checking in with the vanguard. That's what the vanguard *means!*" He said it with a straight face. But what were the Weathermen gonna do? They weren't gonna change the program. And so they did it anyway.
>
> It's kind of ironic, because the whole ideology of the Weatherman was that Fred *was* the vanguard. They believed blacks could bring down the empire. Blacks and the Third World could bring down the empire alone, they used to say, but the cost would be high. Maybe even too high. That was the purpose of the Weathermen — to lower the cost by making sure that when the race war starts there were some white people out there *dying* alongside blacks. I remember Stew Albert wrote an article in the Berkeley *Tribe* halfheartedly defending the Days of Rage, saying, What if you had read that during the Warsaw Ghetto Uprising a band of twenty Germans went out and joined the Jews protesting the Holocaust? As ineffective as that might have been at the time, history would absolve them, saying that at least there were a few good Germans.

The demonstration proceeds as Fred predicts — after busting Weathermen for trashing the fancy downtown lakefront district, the cops invade the black community and kill two kids — and the gap separating us and the white left in-creases. By indicting these defendants the government has inadvertently laid the foundation for a strong alliance between the black, antiwar, and student movements; instead we remain resentful and suspicious. And the war between Panthers and cops in Chicago intensifies: two raids in the summer, the murder of Larry Roberson, the chapter's breakfast coordinator, in early September, then another attack against the office in early October during which we return fire and defend ourselves, and a month later a shoot-out in which the cops kill Spurgeon Jake Winters, one of the office's defenders.

Because of the trial I constantly visit Chicago. The Chicago chapter continues to excel. Irving Thalberg, the son of the famous Hollywood producer, has donated a bus to them, and soon they plan to open a People's Health Clinic headed partly by Ron "Doc" Satchel, a Panther who was a medic in Vietnam. Fred's spirit and Rush's organizational clarity pervade the chapter.

But Fred's still naive; he's never been outside Chicago and wants to visit California.

"Let's go," I tell him. "I want you to see Oakland and how the national headquarters operates. And I also want you to visit Los Angeles. Get a sense of the rest of the country."

In late fall we take our trip. I'm especially excited to bring Fred to Los Angeles. Between the LAPD and US, the chapter lives under siege—US people have killed at least two Party members in shoot-outs. We try to steel their resolve, Huey sending them messages regularly, encouraging and fortifying them, and G. creating a military cadre to provide the branch protection and confidence. And even under attack, the chapter has kept growing, operating several community centers and survival programs. But Bunchy's loss still undercuts them. Fred will give the chapter the final spiritual boost it needs: a powerful spokesperson and a strong leader effortlessly combining love, determination, and anger, he seems almost the reincarnation of Bunchy. After he spends time with them, the LA members feel a renewed faith in the Party; we have produced a hero to take the place of the fallen.

Fred's so much like Bunchy that he even targets the same weakness in me that Bunchy attacked.

"You know, you're much more effective when you get emotional," he tells me after hearing me speak. "Don't try to be so controlled. You should accentuate the emotional aspect of your speaking style—because you're much more effective when you speak from the heart. And it's important you develop your own style because you're the leader, and whether or not you like doing this stuff, you're gonna have to."

Soon I get a chance to follow his suggestion. I'm scheduled to address a huge Golden Gate Park antiwar rally on November 15, the second phase of the national Moratorium, a new countrywide antiwar effort.

For the organizers, the previous Moratorium has been very successful, every town in the country seemingly holding some demonstration. But for us the demonstrations are a reason for anger, not satisfaction: no one has mentioned the Panthers, the antiwar movement treating us as anathema. Even the Bay Area mobilization committee — of which we're part — ignores and insults us, debating whether or not to let us speak, afraid of alienating protestors. And I'm constantly coached in what to say and how to appeal to these people, though from my perspective they should be eager to defend us, take up arms with us. Why should we have to be so worried about them? We have pursued very ordinary goals, only asking for what other people already have.

Things get really out of hand shortly before the speech. Jean Genet, the French novelist and playwright, has come over to help mobilize support for us. Genet's an ex-inmate himself, a rebel and homosexual; although I don't understand a word he says — and he claims not to know English — I feel we are completely and easily accepted by him, that this world-famous writer is a comrade in arms.

Because of Genet, we hold a fund-raiser at Jessica Mitford's. Tom Hayden plans to address the large, influential group. Before the meeting, D.C., Masai, and myself tell Tom not to upstage us. This is our event, we say to him. Don't concentrate on the war but on Bobby and the defendants in the New Haven trial, and use your influence to move the people here to support us.

Tom starts.

I'm standing across the room, next to a refreshment table. My fuse is already short, but I'm sober and hoping Tom does what we want. Instead he double-crosses us, talks about the moratorium and Vietnam. My anger builds. This is our function and we've invited him here. Moratorium organizers don't know us or consider themselves radicals; Tom calls himself our ally, but he has calculatedly, intentionally betrayed us.

I pick up a half-gallon glass wine jug and fling it across the room. I aim for Tom's head, but he ducks and the bottle glances a kid's leg. The room erupts. The kid's father screams; the kid cries; I charge — some people hold me back — and Tom flees.

"I'm not apologizing for my violence," I say later, once things have calmed down. "Tom is the one who ought to apologize. Bobby is being brutalized in that courtroom, Bobby's facing the electric chair, and I'll be damned if I'm gonna say I'm sorry for trying to rectify somebody who's betraying legitimate comrades. We're not going for that. We don't need those kind of friends. We're looking for commitment, especially from people who call themselves our comrades in arms. If it's gonna be a commitment to us in funds or whatever, it's greatly appreciated. Other than that, back up, get out of the way. Because our lives are on the line, and we're not gonna take half measures. We're very serious about that."

Insecurity also fuels my anger: Can I meet all this responsibility?

Sometimes at night, when I'm with Brenda, she'll make me laugh, replacing my worries with love. But then I'll startle later, feeling swamped by the tasks ahead; if I don't telephone someone or wake up Brenda I'll drown under the flood.

One night I confess my doubts to Alex Hoffmann.

"How am I supposed to do this myself?" I ask him.

I've come over for dinner. We haven't seen each other for a while. Since Huey has been transferred to San Luis Obispo Alex has dropped out somewhat, visiting Huey less regularly. But he's kind and without any political agenda; I can trust him completely.

Alex reassures me. I appreciate it; he's tasted my impatience himself.

"The Party wanted to put Stalin's picture on the cover of the paper," remembers Alex.

Meanwhile Huey was reading Isaac Deutcher's anti-Stalinist life of Trotsky. Talk about problems of running an organization with leadership in different jails. He said, "No, you should not put Stalin on the cover."

You called and there was this meeting. Clearly what was going on was resentment over losing contact with Huey, because while he was still in the Alameda County Jail people could go up and see him, even if you couldn't really talk. But here he was at a distance. You were real upset.

Somehow we got back to the nonsense about Stalin, and there was a Stew Albertism about killing forty thousand horses in order to mechanize farms — some wild story that I'd never heard of before or since.

I said, "All this talk about Stalin or not Stalin is really not the point. That's all academic now."

You had been really seething and you blew up, with a total misunderstanding of the word "academic." You thought I was saying that you didn't have enough education.

What really pissed me off was not so much you're going off — you obviously were upset, and didn't know what you were talking about. But the next time I had the chance to talk to you, I said, "You know, you misunderstood me. That is not what I meant by 'academic.'"

You said, "Yeah. Well, afterwards Masai told me that."

I really got pissed off at Masai, because I knew Masai knew. And why didn't Masai, at that point, say something to you before letting you go on about "intellectuals."

But I always liked your personal and political instincts. I thought you underestimated yourself. You had a tendency to defer to Bobby and Eldridge.

On his next visit to Huey, the incident with Tom at Jessica Mitford's comes up.

I or somebody had already told Huey about the story, or he had read about it in the paper.

Huey said, "David has this evil side. Tell David to stop being evil."

I said, "I never noticed that. I think David's sweet."

He said, "Ahhh, I've known David since he's seven years old. If you cross David he strikes out."

November 15 arrives. John Seale and I drive to Golden Gate. In my pocket I hold a speech with the correct antiwar position, including a suggestion of Eldridge's that we negotiate with the NLF for prisoners of war. The Party discipline is clear: Say what's right and don't curse — Huey keeps admonishing us that our dirty language alienates us from the community.

But discipline is hard. I tense as we drive. The day is gray and rainy, unwelcoming. The prospect of addressing such a large crowd makes me uptight, and Judge Hoffman's hog-tying Bobby in court — he keeps speaking, even with tape over his mouth and guards holding him down; Jerry, Abbie, and Dave try to help him; Tom doesn't — makes me even angrier than usual at the antiwar movement's refusal to recognize and relate to our persecution.

So I don't feel good about the speech.

I want to say what I think.

"John, what the hell am I gonna say here?" I ask. "All those people are gonna be there."

I study the paper. The words contain none of my rage about their attack on us, on Bobby.

"I don't know what I'm gonna do," I say.

We near the park. The place is jammed. We maneuver through the stop signs, following the monitors waving us on, telling them we're invited guest speakers. Cars and buses fill the field; people wander in the mist. My stomach tightens and burns. There must be over a quarter of a million people. But if we had a rally for Bobby and the Party there would be only ten, fifteen thousand. How can that be? They'll come for Vietnamese but not for us? We're citizens of this country. And the police are killing us because we're demanding the same rights white people have. Because that's what's being displayed in Chicago: that black people like Bobby have *no* rights white people are bound to respect.

Exactly like slavery.

You can't read.

Can't marry.

Can't raise your children.

Can't work where you want.

Can't do what you want.

Can't think what you want.

And for asking slavery to stop we're hunted like criminals and must beg people to support us.

The wait for the speech is long. I stand on the platform looking at the audience. White faces. Practically no blacks. Lots of American flags. Why American flags? The flag symbolizes the government killing Vietnamese and beating up Bobby. The crowd's desultory, no revolutionary enthusiasm. Even when the speakers say good things the ideas float away in the big field. Besides, there's a fundamental difference between me and these people. They want peace; they believe in peace; peace is their program. But peace isn't my program. I want our Ten Point Program. Achieving those goals—peacefully if possible, but by any means necessary, like Malcolm says—matters to me. Demonstrating *for* peace strikes me as unrealistic and beside the point: the point is to let the Vietnamese determine their own destiny, let us determine ours. Later for peace.

I'm introduced.

Perfunctory applause fades over the vast field.

Well, I'm not completely a wild man. I take the speech out of my pocket. I remember the coaching of my mentors, Forman, Bunchy, Fred—speak with passion, make contact with someone in the audience, say what you know.

I start out well enough.

I tell them there are too many American flags in the crowd because the flag is the symbol of fascism.

"Do you want peace in Vietnam?" I ask.

The crowd shouts back a soggy yes.

"Do you want peace in the black community?"

Again, yes—maybe this time with more conviction.

"Well, you sure can't get it with no guitars. You sure can't get it demonstrating. The only way you're going to get peace in Vietnam is to withdraw the oppressive forces from the black community right here in Babylon."

The reception is less hostile than I thought it might be, and I go on. I tell them the black community is occupied territory where the pigs of the power structure kill black people with the same lack of compunction, the same sadistic racism with which our soldiers slaughter Vietnamese, and that if the soldiers weren't raised on racist values at home they couldn't even imagine the vicious napalming and wholesale destruction they're perpetrating.

"We're not going to let you get around that," I say. "We're not going to let you talk about waging a struggle in support of people ten thousand miles from here, when you have problems right here in fascist America."

The reception builds. I feel more comfortable, more confident. My words are reaching the crowd, bringing them together.

I offer our proposal: Eldridge will negotiate to exchange POWs for Bobby and Huey and other political prisoners.

"We say down with the American fascist society!" I shout. "Later for Richard Milhous Nixon, the motherfucker."

A muffled chorus of boos comes from the back. I've stepped over a line, spoken impolitely.

"Later for all the pigs of the power structure," I say.

The boos gather strength. In my mind I know I shouldn't answer them. Go on with what I'm saying. Follow Forman's formula: Say what you know. But the boos ignite my anger. Who are they to boo me?

"Later for all the people out here who don't want to hear me curse because that's all that I know how to do."

More boos.

I stand at the microphone, staring out toward the far corner of the crowd; the boos come from there.

"I'm never gonna stop cursing," I tell them. "Not only are we going to curse, we're gonna put into practice some of the shit we talk about. Because Richard Nixon is an evil man. This is the motherfucker that unleashed the counterinsurgent teams upon the Black Panther Party. This is the man that's responsible for all the attacks on the Black Panther Party nationally. This is the man that sends his vicious murderous dogs out into the black community and invades our Black Panther Party breakfast programs. Destroys food that we have for hungry kids and expects us to accept shit like that idly."

My anger quiets them for the moment.

I know I should stop. But I don't want them telling me what to do, controlling me.

Let them hear the truth.

"Fuck that motherfucking man!" I say. "We will kill Richard Nixon."

The boos start again. Louder than before. They really don't like what I'm saying. So I address them *and* Nixon.

"We will kill any motherfucker that stands in the way of our freedom."

They answer immediately. "Peace! Peace! Peace!"

I lean against the podium, looking at them as the chant builds.

"Peace! Peace! Peace!"

What am I going to do?

"Peace! Peace! Peace!"

Why not? I'm not against peace. Not worrying about the police coming through the door—that would be peace. I'm just not prepared to buy it at any price.

"Peace! Peace!" I say, joining them. But they don't want reconciliation; what I stand for scares these people.

I observe them silently. A sad, exhausted anger fills me. I'm tired of fighting this battle to win their approval. I think of Bunchy, John Huggins, other members I've never even known, all the hours and days we've spent working; the chants seem pitiful, the most pathetic example of a lack of humanity and understanding I've ever witnessed, even more contemptible and disheartening than the most doggish action of the worst pig.

I speak my mind again:

"Yeah, peace," I say. "Well, we ain't here for no goddamned peace. Because we know that we can't have no peace because this country is built on war. And if you want peace you got to fight for it."

Chapter

22

THE speech creates the normal controversy: Mayor Alioto hypocritically complains I spoiled the rally, pretending he's the antiwar spokesman and I'm the imposter. Garry expects the police will arrest me — my record is lengthening now — but it's two weeks before the bust comes.

Brenda and I leave the San Francisco office and are driving toward the Bay Bridge when cars converge out of nowhere, guys streaming out, guns in their hands.

"David!" Brenda shouts.

Walk, I want to tell the cops, don't run! One of these guys trips, he'll start a war by himself. But these guys need the action; this stuff excites them; they think they're Marines hitting a beachhead.

"Are you David Hilliard?"

"Yes," I say. As long as they don't kill me, I'm relieved. The cops shoo back the crowd that forms around the car, but passersby push up, demanding to know what's happening. Good, I think, the cops won't be able to pretend I resisted.

"You're under arrest."

"What for?" No matter that I know; it's important for the people observing to see I don't break form.

"You've gone too far. You threatened the life of the President."

I'm out of the car immediately, saying, "No gun. I've got no gun." I don't want to give the cops any excuse.

The agents point pistols and shotguns at me, as though I might go crazy and start shooting. I make sure to hold my hands by my side. "I wish you'd lower your rifles," I say. "One of them could accidentally go off and shoot me on purpose."

Instead of answering, they force me against a car and frisk me, then push Brenda and me into one of the sedans. Already they're calling Brenda by her first name, a ploy to show her they know everything about us, that they're all-powerful, all-seeing.

"How'd you get mixed up in this?" My own FBI agent woos her. "You're a nice girl."

Brenda's staunch. "You seem like a nice guy," she answers. "How'd you?"

At the San Francisco County Jail we go up the back way. I'm in handcuffs. As I walk through the halls there's a buzz of excitement: We got him, we did it. The judge sets a fifty-thousand-dollar bail that needs to be given in full and they transfer me across the bay to the Panther tank, the hole in the Alameda County Jail, a closed, claustrophobic four-and-a-half by six-foot cell without a bed—every morning the guard takes away the mattress— washbasin, or faucet. This was Huey's home for seven months. One of the inmates sends me a dog-eared page from a copy of *Wretched of the Earth* that Huey had left behind: "To educate the masses politically," I read, "does not mean, cannot mean making a political speech. What it means is to try, relentlessly and passionately, to teach the masses that everything depends on them; that if we stagnate it is their responsibility, and that if we go forward it is due to them too, that there is no such thing as a demiurge, that there is no famous man who will take the responsibility for everything, but that the demiurge is the people themselves and the magic hands are finally only the hands of the people."

The words are no longer foreign to me. Earlier this fall I have actually visited Algeria, a guest at the Pan-African Cultural Festival—organized by Julia Wright, the daughter of Richard Wright—where we were displaying Emory's artwork. I've gone through the cobblestoned streets of the Casbah with a guide showing us the houses where Ali La Pointe—the hero of the great film *The Battle of Algiers*—actually hid out, met some of the revolutionary leaders who knew Fanon. My stomach clenches with its familiar ache. We've come a long way since Huey was first here; we've become a part of history.

*   *   *

My arrest coincides with what seems to be a national attack.

"We had a week-long retreat in Chicago," remembers Rush,

and had brought all the branches here. The first evening we held a PE class and after that the Central Committee was supposed to meet at Fred's. After the Central Staff meeting, which ended early, there wasn't enough room for everybody to stay there, and a member dropped me off. It must have been about two-thirty.

Between four and five that morning I got a call from a member who had gotten a call from a woman who lived down the street. They said there was a shoot-out at Fred's house and the cops had cordoned off the streets. So I had somebody come by and pick me up, and went over to the woman's house.

Her apartment was in the basement. We stayed there, listening to the radio. I guess it must have been about six, six-thirty. And they — they had said, you know, that there was a shoot-out — but they said Fred Hampton had been killed. He had been taken to the Cook County Hospital. I don't know what other persons they had announced. I don't know if they announced anybody, but they said Fred Hampton was killed. That's how we found out about it. On the radio.

It was very...I mean it was something where you...I mean I broke down and cried.

I guess the next thing I remember was that I hoped Fred took someone with him. They didn't say, but I knew that Fred was...that taking someone with him was what Fred was gonna be about.

I guess maybe we stayed down there till eight, eight-thirty, nine o'clock. I'm not sure what all was going on. It's almost a real blank in terms of what was happening. People calling in, us calling folks, things like that. I remember Eldridge. He called from Algiers. Tried to tell us how to deal with the situation. Something to do with retaliation and that kind of thing. What was he doing calling from Algiers, some *villa* in Algiers, telling us how to deal with something here in Chicago?

Not to say retaliation wasn't on our mind. We were gonna retaliate. I had given some specific directions about what should have happened and where it should happen. But certain things didn't get carried out. In retrospect it was good that revenge didn't happen militarily, but politically. The *political* development and consciousness of the people of Chicago would never have occurred, the whole thing would have been blurred and obliterated, had we gone out and killed some policemen.

We went over to the house and saw the bullet holes. Then we dealt with the attorneys, dealt with the media, dealt with trying to find out whether or not somebody else had been killed, trying to find out *what* had really happened. It was then that we found out another member, Mark Clark, the defense captain of the Peoria branch, had also been killed.

I remember going to the morgue . . . you know, identifying Fred's body.

They didn't cordon off the apartment. So we had people walk through the apartment. Twenty-five thousand people came through that apartment to see what was going on. That was the biggest thing in terms of making sure that our version of the story was at least *heard* and also accepted.

The next thing was this guy who used to be a producer of the NBC midday news. He invited me and another Party member and Hanrahan, the state's attorney, to be on his show. Hanrahan refused. We went on the station and told him that Fred had been murdered. That's how the word really began to get out that Fred had been murdered. One reporter, named Phil Walters, took the side of the Panthers. He called it murder. He almost got fired. But then a couple of days after, the *Tribune* came out with this big article questioning who did it, who shot, how many bullets were fired, and was it a real shoot-out, or was it murder, just cold-blooded murder?

Two days later, Los Angeles is hit.
"The police had made a dry run at the end of November," remembers G.,

during a regular community night, at which you had parents and people in the community coming to the library and stuff. They went through terrorist tactics for fifteen minutes and then it was over.

Then we got the word that they were hitting us on December 7. So I stayed there. Had everything prepared, sandbags at the location, weapons and stuff laid out. And they didn't come.

Instead they came the next night.

At the time I had been up like two and a half nights: Fred Hampton had been very very close to me.

I figured they would hit the central office on Central Avenue. Around three-thirty that morning the other Panthers said to me, "Brother, you got to get some rest." It was looking like they might not do it. We were hoping our information was wrong.

So I say, "Okay."

We have a bunch of different houses. I go to Fifty-fifth — a community center — and I just fell out, sleeping on the floor like I always do because of Vietnam.

I'm in a deep sleep. I might have been drugged. Or it could have been from me staying up so many days and nights. I don't even hear the first boom from the front door. Then they're shooting everywhere. But they miss. Because it's completely dark and because I'm sleeping low.

They bust in. I see the shots. My wife, Sandra, goes, "Ahhh!" She throws herself half on top of me. She's screaming and hollering at them — screaming at them the whole time. She was a very audacious woman.

I'm still trying to focus, trying to figure out whether I'm in Vietnam or here, and what the hell is this? The detectives come in. You can tell something is wrong because they look surprised to see me there still living. They swing me over to handcuff me and I see them take a gun out and put it under the bunk. To justify the shooting. Because there wasn't a single weapon in that building. That was a community center.

The murder of Fred and Mark Clark quickly becomes a scandal. Edward Hanrahan, the Illinois state's attorney, issues a statement. "We wholeheartedly commend the police officers for this bravery, their remarkable restraint and discipline in the face of this vicious Black Panther attack, and we expect every decent citizen of our community to do likewise." Directing a public relations campaign to sell the official version, he publishes pictures of Fred's apartment and prepares a twenty-eight minute reenactment of the raid in a plywood reconstruction of the unit.

But the Panthers easily prove the discrepancies between the physical evidence and the police account: on examination of the bullet holes in the apartment, the "vicious attack" proves to be two shots going out — fired by Mark Clark — and close to ninety going in. Other circled holes that the police point out in their pictures turn out to be nail heads.

In time — the survivors win a suit thirteen years later — details of the murder emerge. The cops justify the raid, claiming illegal guns are stashed in the apartment. The source for this information is William O'Neal, a party security captain and FBI informer paid about thirty thousand dollars by the bureau over three years. O'Neal — the member who brings the electric chair into the Chicago office — offers his condolences to Hampton's family shortly after Fred's murder and a few days before he picks up an extra three-hundred-dollar bonus for his work. Although police acting under Hanrahan perform the raid, the attack is directly linked to the FBI. O'Neal provides them with a map of Fred's apartment that they later give to the police; plus, later evidence proves that the FBI "had tried to persuade the Chicago Police Department to conduct the raid before State's Attorney Hanrahan finally agreed to do it." Finally, even by their own records the police explanation for the raid is bogus: O'Neal's last reports say the Panther guns are legal and registered.

But the real purpose of the attack is clear: it's death. The fourteen cops on the assault squad—led by a black sergeant named "Gloves" Davis—carry twenty-seven guns, including five shotguns and a submachine gun. At the time, Hampton may well be drugged; plus, circumstantial evidence indicates he's shot—after the initial blasts—at close range with two .45 bullets to the head. Although all this is still unknown then, the circumstantial evidence alone makes the police version extremely dubious, casting Daley and the Chicago machine as cold-blooded killers. The verdict haunts him the rest of his political life and eventually contributes to his overthrow.

The LA shoot-out backfires against the police in another way. Simultaneous with G.'s arrest, the police attack the Central Avenue headquarters. (As in Chicago, the LAPD unit that carries out the raid works closely with the FBI and the assault is justified by a warrant for illegal weapons.) While destroying the Panther office, the raid backfires on the police. The Panthers defend themselves for five hours, wounding three cops—G. has so expertly fortified the office that even dynamite charges dropped on the roof fail to dislodge the Party members. Their resistance terrifies cops across the country and inspires the black community and other revolutionaries.

The violence and viciousness of the raids brings the Party once again to national attention: another colossal event. As soon as I'm out of jail, the Sunday-morning national television show "Face the Nation" asks me for an interview. My appearance provides the Party with important national exposure. With the various charges against me, I must notify my parole officer that I'm flying to DC. The night before the show I stay in my hotel room entertaining bellhops who take the night off as I buy them liquor and give them exorbitant tips on CBS's tab.

The next morning I meet my three interviewers at the studio. The trio represents the range of the press's attitudes toward us. CBS's Ike Pappas is the good guy, paunchy, friendly. George Herman, his colleague, wears his hair slicked back and apes Mike Wallace's no-nonsense, tough style. Bernard Nossiter has a sour smile and a high-pitched nasal voice.

"When we get out in front of the cameras, we're going to destroy you," he says.

"That's all right," I answer. I know his plan: he wants to provoke me, get me to say something outrageous that will make news for them. But I'm concentrated on my task: I'm going to say what I know and explain the Party's program and tactics.

"I'm armed with an ideological, spiritual, hydrogen bomb," I tell them.

"What's that?" Pappas asks in his mild voice.

But I don't trust any of them. They hope to ridicule my organization, expect I'll give them the opportunity.

"It's called the philosophy of the Black Panther Party," I say. I check myself out for a second in the mirror opposite; the blue turtleneck looks fine against my skin and my eyes are clear. I turn to go.

"And I will annihilate you with it in the next hour."

"Mr. Hilliard, don't the Panthers stock and collect guns," Nossiter begins. His head bobs up and down, a turtle coming in and out of its shell, a mix of caution and arrogance. "Isn't that an invitation for the police to take action."

I sit in the chair, under the bright lights. I'm nervous, but not as worried as I was giving the Golden Gate speech; I'm more confident in one-on-one sessions.

"The Panthers do not stock guns," I answer. "It's not our purpose to assemble large caches of weapons. If we have weapons, we would distribute them to the community for self-defense."

Then they start on my speech. Did I say the quote? Did I mean the quote? The whole thing is absurd. Any number of tapes will prove I spoke the words. But it's equally clear I'm not about to kill the President. What do they imagine—I'm going to order some ICBMs to bomb the White House? I regret the statement because these fools can now focus on the five words—We will kill Richard Nixon—rather than our programs and philosophy. But I also won't back down. I talked the language of Nixon and Attorney General Mitchell. These men pretend to be lawmen and statesmen who are above the battle. The fact is they are tyrants, paying professional gunmen to kill my comrades in early-morning attacks; their only legitimacy is that they pack more guns than we do.

"You say that you do not favor violence," Nossiter goes on. The man drives me crazy: he closes his eyes as he imagines himself phrasing a particularly clever question. "And I gather that what you are suggesting is that you use your weapons in your view only for defensive purposes. Is that correct?" Why can't he ask the question simply? Why is he always mending and proving?

"That's right," I say.

"Then why do you have cartoons in your paper saying 'Kill the Pigs'?"

Does he think I'm a simpleton they can put in front of the camera and make a fool of for the audience's fun? I relax further into the chair. Their arrogance and contempt builds my confidence; these guys really don't know what they're talking about.

"We don't have anything in the paper saying 'Kill the Pigs.' We talk about defending ourselves and targeting the enemy—"

George Herman—straightforward, slicked back, not like Nossiter's nerd—now tries cornering me with a quote.

"But without trying to put my own interpretation on it, let me ask you your interpretation of this quote. 'We advocate the very direct overthrow of the government by way of force and violence because we recognize it as being oppressive. . . .'"

I answer by quoting the Declaration of Independence.

". . . when a long train of abuses and usurpations, pursuing invariably the same Object evinces a design to reduce them under absolute Despotism, it is their right, it is their duty, to throw off such Government, and to provide new Guards for their future security."

Their blows keep missing.

"How can this small group—five or ten thousand people—really represent the masses of black people?" Ike Pappas asks.

"I'm saying that the ideas spelled out in our Ten Point Program represent the basic desires and needs of the people," I say.

"How do you know that?" he asks.

"Because these are ideas taken from the masses," I say.

"But aren't some of these ideas you have—aren't some of them paraphrases of Mao Tse-tung and Che Guevara?" George Herman asks.

"Nothing here paraphrases Mao or Che Guevara," I say. But I go on. What's wrong if the ideas are the same? Why shouldn't they be? The gap between us becomes clear. They think I'll want to cover up, that I'm ashamed or frightened to admit things I'm proud of.

"Mr. Hilliard," Nossiter starts again. "Is your back really to the wall? Here you are on national television."

I lean back. "I don't think television is the big payoff. We could ask for a lot of other things. More than being on television, I would rather be in our communities feeding hungry children, trying to erect institutions that would educate the people so that they would not have to wage war in your name."

"At what stage is the revolution, in your evaluation?" asks Pappas.

"Educational," I say, and explain that we're trying to show people the truth.

"I'm sure people would agree that giving children food or medical aid is good, but don't you also indoctrinate them?" he asks.

"We teach them about the real conditions of their lives," I say. "We teach them not to travel ten thousand miles away to shoot someone who has never called them 'nigger.'"

There's time for only a few more.

"Given the jailings, does your organization have any future?" asks Nossiter.

"It has more of a future than this country," I answer.

I believe this. We can turn this around, I think. Just as I've turned around this program. They brought me here to humiliate me, enlist me in my own self-destruction. Instead I walk away more confident than ever before.

I return to Oakland in time for New Year's.

"I'm gonna make hog-head cheese," I tell Brenda.

"I hate hog-head cheese," she says. "I grew up with that madness. My mama and grandma would do that."

"In Alaska?"

"Yeah. All six black families in town would get together and do it. But my mother knew to make me something else. Because I never ate it. And I'm not gonna eat it now."

She walks off. Her defiance drives me crazy. Besides, lately she's been acting a little strange, distracted and tired.

"I don't care," I tell her back. I won't let her mood deter me. New Year's is coming and hog-head cheese is what we made in the South. We'll make some now. Besides, I like to cook big family meals when I'm feeling good, and sometimes making turkeys, ham, ducks, gumbo revives my better spirits. "I'm making hog-head cheese and you're gonna eat it."

I take over the kitchen, boiling the pig's head in the largest pot I can find. The members are all talking about it.

"The Chief's making hog-head cheese! The Chief's making hog-head cheese!"

Throughout the day, Brenda remains adamant. Her refusal becomes a joke.

"You're gonna eat it," I torment her.

"Oh no, I'm not," she says, shaking her small head with a smile.

"It's just hog-head cheese."

"I know hog-head cheese and I think it's disgusting and I'm definitely not having any."

"But I'm making it," I say.

"I know," she says, laughing. "You think you're happy, everybody gotta be happy. You're sad, everybody gotta be sad. Everybody gotta participate. But this is one thing I won't do. I don't care who makes it."

Around ten that night the cheese is ready. We gather in the kitchen, members hovering near the door, keeping their distance from the table, shooting glances at one another. Meanwhile one of the comrades goes around talking up the cheese. Cautiously, the members come up, accepting and tasting little slivers.

Brenda doesn't budge from the doorway.

"Brenda's gonna eat this," I tease her.

She just shakes her head. Her eyes sparkle at the private joke between us: who's got power here?

"I told you," she answers. "Not my mother's. Not yours."

"Oh yeah, you're gonna eat this!"

She backs away, laughing. "I'm not eating any hog-head cheese."

I come after her. "Brenda, you have to!"

She runs and I call out to somebody. "Hold that woman down. She's gonna eat some of this cheese!"

The cadre is a little too zealous. He acts as though the joke between Brenda and me is a solemn order, cornering Brenda and forcing her down on the floor.

"I got the cheese, Chief!"

We laugh as Brenda struggles under him, giggling, covering her mouth with her hand, her lips shut tight.

But the cadre doesn't give up. He pushes the cheese at her mouth, the jellylike stuff dribbling over her face, the cheese smearing her nose as she squirms.

"David!" she yells, trying to tell me to call off the guy.

But she can't say too much because opening her mouth gives him an opportunity.

He pins her. Kneeling over Brenda, he tries to pry her mouth open. Brenda bucks like a horse, pushing him away, shaking her head.

"You fool!" she yells at him.

The next morning in the office she comes up and tells me she has something to say.

"I went to the doctor to get a checkup," she remembers,

and he told me I was pregnant.

I was like, "Oh." Because this wasn't anything we had planned or even talked about. I was taking birth-control pills.

My first inclination was to get an abortion. Then I came to the office, told you. I can't remember what you said, but it pissed me off. I think all pregnant women feel this way, especially if they're not married. You have to say the *exact* right thing—otherwise. . . And it wasn't the *exact* right thing. I think you were a little nervous about it.

Then sometime in the midafternoon I talked with June. He said, "David told me, you *mommy!*"

I said, "Yeah. Well I don't know about being a mommy because I don't think I'm gonna have the baby."

He said, "No. You should have the baby. We need some Panther cubs, and you'd make a good mommy."

I was glad he said that, and I thought about it for a couple of days and just decided to go ahead.

Chapter

23

AFTER Fred's sacrifice previously hostile liberal black organizations offer us legal support and financial aid. The Chicago Afro-American Patrolmen's League denounces the police version of the attack. Ralph Abernathy, head of King's Southern Christian Leadership Conferences, declares, "If the United States is successful in crushing the Black Panther Party it won't be too long before they will crush the Southern Christian Leadership Conference, the Urban League and any other organization trying to make things better." The NAACP's Roy Wilkins telegrams the Justice Department calling for an investigation. People adopt a more skeptical view of the New York and New Haven conspiracy charges. Plus, we use Fred's death to emphasize our political point: his assassination isn't simply the action of a particularly fascistic police force but part of a *national* search-and-destroy mission against the Party.

The black liberal support gives sanction to greater sympathy in the white community. But this time we stay away from any grand alliances between organizations and concentrate on working arrangements with individuals dedicated to defense work.

Two of the most valuable people are Marty Kenner, who heads the national defense committee effort out of New York, and Donald Freed, a playwright who organizes a Panther support group in Los Angeles and later works on the New Haven conspiracy trial.

Marty becomes as valuable a confidant and adviser to the Party as Stanley David Levison was to Martin Luther King's SCLC. Coming from a liberal household, he leaves his suburban home and goes to Berkeley in the late fifties.

"Eleanor Roosevelt was the hero in my household," he says, describing the path that eventually led him to Panther support work.

My parents weren't communists, but they had no fear in speaking out against McCarthyism. When we had demonstrations against the House Un-American Activities Committee — in the early sixties — these former lefties from City College like Seymour Martin Lipset came and said it's fine to demonstrate against HUAC, but you should also say that you're not communists. Their attitude boggled my mind, because the whole point of demonstrating against HUAC is that you shouldn't have to have loyalty oaths.

I went off to Berkeley — which was unusual at that time from New York — in 1959. There were a particularly brilliant group of people there then — Robert Scheer, Maurice Zeitland — who were just slightly older than myself and were involved in a lot of struggles — around Cuba, HUAC, capital punishment.

We debated things all the time. A right-wing Social Democrat would say Cuba wasn't a democratic country because there weren't elections. Bob Scheer would answer, "Everybody has a gun, so there's an election every day." We took democracy very seriously. It was one of the differences between us and the radicals who came along later. Some of them assumed democracy was unimportant; we wanted to make things more democratic. Similarly we were very happy to get twenty people out to a demonstration; but they were used to mass demonstrations and felt that if they hadn't stopped the war yesterday, what was the point?

I came back to New York. My politics — if I had to characterize them — were anti-imperialist. We were doing evil abroad and I wanted to try to stop it. I wasn't worried about programs. I thought that if you got a mass movement going, programs would evolve. Sometimes Malcolm would come and speak to the groups I was involved with. He was pursuing and working with white groups, and was very accessible. It wasn't like Louis Farrakhan being paid fifteen thousand to walk in with twenty bodyguards and harangue a hostile student union. No, Malcolm spoke to people whom he viewed as comrades, and that was very thrilling.

I started teaching at the New School for Social Research. There was a young dropout who was a janitor there named Steve Tappis. The local SDS chapter put people like Steve and myself down as being liberals, because we were only fighting imperialism, but they were fighting really to overthrow capitalism in all of its oppressive manifestations, including the way commodities oppress people.

Later—in the spring of 1968—I got involved in the Columbia strike. The same conflict arose. Some of us were anti-imperialists. But other strikers were more concentrated on themselves. It wasn't that they were middle-class—I never pretended I was anything but middle-class—but their concerns were around their own liberation. One of the lines at that time was that we have to advance from just fighting for *other* people's liberation to fighting for our *own* liberation. I never understood this. I never felt it demeaned me to fight against the war in Vietnam. I felt I was fighting to live in a humane society that didn't kill and oppress and napalm other people and that would make my life better too. These people somehow felt that they had to become the center of the liberation, and that focusing on the Vietnamese smacked to them of humanitarianism and not really being radical: charity work. That always truly offended me.

At the end of the strike I faced serious legal charges, but I didn't slow down my political activity. I really believed that within three years we'd see red flags flying in the White House, and some of us would be there with our feet up on the desk. We were on a winning streak, and I thought we'd keep on winning. How little did I know.

Through friendship and a shared political vision, I got involved with Weathermen, who took over SDS in the summer of '69. Soon after, I went to Chicago to help Weathermen set up educational programs. Ironically Steve Tappis, who had been on the Central Committee of Weathermen, was leaving them—he was the first to quit—just as I was arriving.

It didn't take me very long to become deeply disillusioned with the characters in Weathermen. They were extremely immature. They felt that to gird themselves as this revolutionary vanguard they had to live in communes, cut off their associations with everybody they knew; everybody sleeping with someone different every night became very important. Mark Rudd told me one night, "We're here to smash monogamy." I said, "Mark, I'm here to smash imperialism, and quite frankly, if my girlfriend wanted to live with me, I'd be very happy." Shortly before going underground Mark Rudd, Jerry Lefcourt—the lawyer who represented me on the Columbia charges and got me involved with Panther work—and I had some drinks. Jerry said, "Mark, you don't understand. For me monogamy would be a progressive step." Weathermen had a weird combination of guilt and personal self-liberation, which I felt was taking them away from the principal struggle, which was for black liberation and an end to the war in Vietnam. One day some black kids attacked an SDS worker — the headquarters was in the middle of a black ghetto. I came out to help her and was gonna slam one of the kids with a door. She accused me of being a racist. I said, "Someone's attacking you. If we shouldn't be in the black ghetto, which I agree with, then we should move. But I don't think people should hit you. And if someone's gonna hit me, I'll defend myself."

As their base shrunk, their shrillness about being leaders intensified. This even extended to the black movement. Weathermen was often anti-Panther. They never wanted a black group that had a real following. They were like pretentious people whose favorite movie must always be something no one else has ever seen. With them, the more obscure and nationalistic the group, the more they liked it. They were completely into their own exclusivity and their own elitism. They reminded me of some graduate students whom Stew Albert used to call "Eureka Socialists." They would never participate in struggles, but would spend all their time studying, until suddenly they would say, "Eureka! This is the answer. This is how we'll create socialism!"

I quit, tried organizing another group, and around October or November Jerry Lefcourt came to me. He said, "Martin, can you please help me a little. I've got this case of the Panther Twenty-one and it's very much like a modern version of the Rosenberg case because what they're doing is accusing them of heinous crimes with which they hope to smear a whole movement. What I'd like you to do is raise a little money, or bring a little attention. Get a little support going."

We — myself and a cousin of mine named Betty Shertzer — set up an operation in the law office of Jerry Lefcourt and some of the other Panther lawyers. The journalist Murray Kempton was working there at the time, writing a book about the upcoming trial; he seemed to be the only person in the white liberal intellectual community who even knew about the Twenty-one — the Party members had been busted before they had started organizing and had almost no support. But nationally the Panthers were getting lots of attention because this was early November when Bobby Seale was being chained and gagged in Chicago.

Soon after we started I got a call from Hannah Weinstein, an old leftie who had gone to England during the witch-hunts and had helped support a lot of blacklisted writers in England by doing a television show called "Robin Hood." Hannah called up to ask was there anybody in New York doing anything about Bobby Seale. We said, "There's the Twenty-one in New York, it's part of the same party and struggle, and we've got to get them out of jail and all of that." So she said she knew some people who wanted to get together.

I, then, had this very interesting meeting with Hannah, Judy Bernstein—the wife of Walter Bernstein, a screenwriter—Gail Lumet—the daughter of Lena Horne and the wife, then, of Sidney Lumet—and another very attractive black woman, who I figured was the wife of another movie star or a movie star herself and who turned out to be Iris Moore, the wife of "Dharuba" Moore, a member of the Panther Twenty-one. It was quite a cultural switch, to be sitting around with these well-dressed, well-to-do wealthy women talking about politics, but it was still a helluva lot different than sitting around with Mark Rudd in Chicago, talking about smashing monogamy.

Hannah then planned out a campaign, saying, "What we really have to do is get the Panthers out of jail. To do this we have to go through a whole series of steps. First of all, we have to create it as an issue. And we have to raise money. So, the first thing we're gonna do, since Gail Lumet is here, is have a little party at Gail Lumet's house. We'll have some Panthers speak and we'll arrange to have Felicia Bernstein—the wife of Lenny—at that party because the goal of this party is very simply just to get Felicia Bernstein to want to agree to have another party. And the goal of Felicia Bernstein's party is to have a lot of opinion makers there— Tom Wickers and others. And even *that* party's goal is not to raise money, but to convince the opinion makers that this is an important issue. Then we'll go on to a whole series of parties to raise money."

We had our first meeting. Felicia Bernstein showed up. Masai Hewitt— who was absolutely wonderful—spoke. Afterwards Betty and I went out with some of the Panthers. It was the first time we had met most of them. For some reason one of them was critical of me and Betty. He was a big guy and I was slightly intimidated by the whole thing. But little Betty—I mean literally; she's quite small—wagged her little finger in their face and stood up to these guys. I'll never forget that. It set the tone for all the work we were going to do. We were equals and it was fun.

Shortly after, Fred Hampton was killed and the LA office was attacked. We ran an ad for the defense of the New York Panther Twenty-one or just the Panther defense committee, and the money started coming in unbelievable amounts—unsolicited, thousands and thousands of dollars. At least one hundred thousand dollars. We had people opening up envelopes all day long. Later on I gained this reputation in the movement as a great fund-raiser, but all I did was hold my hat out and gold fell in. The only thing I did have — and this is what led to my very close relationship with you and Huey, later on — was that neither Betty nor I in any way tried to dictate to the Panthers what they should do with the money. We had no agenda. We were simply raising money for the Twenty-one and the legal defense of the Party nationwide — two things we saw as one because it was impossible to separate out whether people were sending money in protest against Judge Hoffman's abuse of Bobby Seale, the murder of Fred Hampton, the LA raid, or only for the Twenty-one defense. The distinction later on turned into real trouble because the Panther Twenty-one said they felt neglected, and I was horrified by this because I knew how strongly you had fought for them, and I also knew the origin of where their support came from, which wasn't from their own: if it was just the New York Panther Twenty-one we wouldn't have been able to do anything.

Anyway, around this time a liaison in the Party said, "The Chief wants to see you. Get on the next thing smoking."

So that, then, became my life for at least the next two years. Catching the next thing smoking. Later I often flew with you or other Panthers, and I remember very well your briefcases: Samsonite briefcases always with three things inside — a Panther newspaper, a bottle of Maalox — which is something I hadn't been familiar with, though everyone had ulcers — and a .357 Magnum. As my buddy Stew Albert once said to me, ulcers and Magnums go together.

I took the night plane and got picked up by a Panther member and taken to your house. I was very flattered and thrilled that you wanted to see me, because we had not raised *that* much money yet.

Now, part of meeting with Panther leadership — and this was true the entire time, though the settings changed — was hanging around a lot: going out, sitting out, and waiting. For a two-hour meeting, you could spend two days. But you'd eat well. There'd be communal cooking. These visits served a very important function. It wasn't just that the phones were tapped. People's lives were on the line, and the time spent in Oakland provided a bonding experience for people. They also gave people a way of knowing who they were dealing with. In my case, I felt very good, because very quickly I felt you trusted me completely, and of course that only made me work harder.

I also got my first impression of you — the "Chief." You were always busy. You'd be darting about, and would always look very elegant — it's a funny thing with you, because you're not vain at all, but you always seem very put together. I'm in business now, and once in a while have to wear a fancy suit, but even with my fanciest pinstripe I somehow never quite look as put together as you.

The other thing I remember about that trip is seeing you with your comrades and the warmth that all of you had for each other. Six months before I'd been with these crazies in Chicago, talking about smashing monogamy. But here comrades were getting killed, and people were dealing with each other in an honorable and dignified way, without any self-consciousness whatsoever. I was just overwhelmingly impressed.

I went back to New York and we had the Bernstein party. First there were cocktails; then all these people gathered in a room with seats to hear D.C. speak. Suddenly Leonard Bernstein—who hadn't been part of the discussions and wasn't supposed to be there—came up and started acting crazy, kissing D.C. and saying D.C. was his brother. A couple of people asked these baiting questions like, "Why did you go to violence?" The person we had the warmest feelings for was Otto Preminger. He spoke about having been a refugee and how he could identify with the Panthers and also came through with his promise of a thousand dollars, which was then a big contribution for us.

We did succeed in one of our goals. The Panthers, with that notoriety, got to be put all in one cell together and aspects of the Twenty-one case— which were outrageous—were publicized.

But the rest of the fallout from the party was bad. Charlotte Curtiss was then the women's page editor of the *New York Times*. Charlotte had participated in some of our early discussions and in getting people to these parties and seemed very sincerely committed to the cause. Then, the next day, she wrote a devastating account. The article set the stage for the liberal backlash against the Panthers. It was followed by a *New York Times* editorial about radical chic saying, "What are people on Park Avenue doing raising money for the Panthers?" Like it shouldn't be any of their concern. (We apologized to Felicia, but she seemed inconsolable.)

In reaction we set up meetings with *Time* magazine and the *New York Times*. D.C. and I went. At the *Times* we met the education editor, named Fred Hechtinger, who spent the whole time lecturing us about Hitler and Social Democrats and ultra-leftism and how we were bringing fascism to America. At *Time* magazine we met with a guy named Dick Clurman who just asked us very hard questions, which was the purpose of the meeting after all. Such was our state then: when you met a guy who asked you intelligent questions rather than just attacking you, you felt that was a step up.

That winter and spring we were kept frantically busy by the pace of police activity: raids in Winston-Salem, New Orleans, meetings in Atlanta

with SCLC, meetings in Chicago at a national conference of lawyers organized by Arthur Kinoy, a constitutional scholar and activist. The whole
winter and spring it seems to me was spent flying around the country with
you and G. and Masai, or just alone, assisting in setting up legal defense
operations.

But there was no doubt that the negative press had its effect. Sidney
Lumet met with us. He started lecturing us again: "Remember the witch-
hunts," as if we shouldn't do anything. For me "Remember the witch-
hunts" means you stand up to the witch-hunters. Other people who had
agreed before that to throw fund-raising parties now backed out. Andy
Young, who was later President Carter's UN ambassador, came up and
gave a press conference, really critical of the *New York Times.* But the
press had its effect. The smaller fund-raising parties didn't happen. Except for one — there was one fund-raising event that was completely successful. Zayd Shakur — the one family member still free — and black
jazz musicians came and we had a twenty-four-hour jazz concert in
Brooklyn where we made a lot more money than we did at the
Bernstein party.

In the Party we debate what to do. I speak to Eldridge every day and am
mindful of the cadre who want to pick up the gun. But the concept of the
Party as a liberation army overthrowing the American government is not realistic. When we begin our attack who's going to join us? Party comrades
will jump off the moon if Huey tells them to. Our allies won't. Plus, with or
without them, I really don't think we're going to get very far. We've waged
as stiff a resistance to the police as any American revolutionary group, but
the fact is that we're not very effective as fighters: we're the victims in most
of the street encounters with police. I know because I get the telephone calls.
East St. Louis. New York. Boston. New Orleans. Topeka. Wherever we open
an office, the police gather right behind us, busting us, making sure the Party
expends all its energy, resources, and finances on staying out of jail — if
we're lucky; often it's staying out of jail *and* the hospital — rather than pursuing programs.

And programs were our original purpose.

Even patrolling the police.

But no one gets this point. The police dominate what we do, how we're
seen. We wanted to create a party that would let us — and the black community — determine our own destinies. But now, because of the Party, the state —
FBI, police, Red squads — is deciding our fate.

*   *   *

And the media. After Chicago and Los Angeles, Charles Garry claims the police have killed twenty-eight Party members in the last year. Journalists insist
the number's too high. Panthers are dying, being sent to jail, arrested for all
sorts of major and minor infractions. But all the reporters can focus on is
whether the number of Panther victims of police attack is twenty-one or
twenty-eight. "The theory. . .that the Nixon Administration had, through the
statements of public officials, at least contributed to a climate of opinion
among local police. . .that a virtual open season has been declared on the
Panthers, seems historically inaccurate," writes Edward Epstein in *The New
Yorker.* Later on we learn the FBI encouraged the police to attack the Party, as
in Chicago, and that Hoover reported that Nixon himself promised the FBI
director to ask the Justice Department "to move against the Black Panthers."
But back then Epstein's article is taken as gospel.

"Every important newspaper in the country quoted Epstein's piece," remembers Donald Freed.

Charles Garry debated Ed Epstein on "David Frost." Frost was supposed to
be the mediator, but he and Epstein just went for Charles. Everything they
were saying was out of context. Charles would give an example and they'd
say, "Oh no! That was a shoot-out! The Panthers fought back. There was a
policeman wounded. That doesn't count." Charles was tough and didn't realize how bad he looked, didn't realize how devastating was the damage.

Then there were articles that attacked supporting the Panthers by
charging them with anti-Semitism, stealing money, and ideas of liberal
guilt. Well, the Panthers were not Martin Luther King. They were not just
feeding hungry children. They were fighting back. And not always fighting back in the most coherent way. But the liberal intellectual magazines
and writers, who might have intervened to try to give these events a context, to help explain them to other people without apologizing for them,
instead weighed in completely and in the most nefarious way on the other
side and made it respectable to turn against the Panthers. They demonized
them. Genet was writing a pamphlet, "Here and Now for Bobby Seale,"
and at the same time, Norman Mailer was saying, "I'm starting to get
bored with the Black Panther revolution, and if I'm starting to feel that I
tremble to think what's coming." It's a typical Mailer statement—an
honest confession of his own narcissism, and then a second clause that
passes judgment back on himself and everyone else.

Donald is a government target himself—"It is felt that any prosecution or
exposure of Freed will severely hurt the BPP," reads a memo from the LA

bureau to FBI headquarters. "Any exposure will not only deny the Panthers money, but additionally, would cause other white supporters of the BPP to withdraw their support. It is felt that the Los Angeles chapter of the BPP could not operate without the financial support of white supporters."

Freed comes to the Party after working with a group called Operation Bootstrap.

"Operation Bootstrap was a place to get people from the Valley into the ghetto," he says.

To help young black people get jobs, education, what have you. Trying to set up a dialogue.

Once in going to raise money in the ghetto I parked my car across from a church, just barely *touching* the front of the car behind me.

These black kids came up. Cassius Clay had just knocked out some white English boxer that night, and they were *full* of that.

"You touched the *car!*" Very threatening.

I said, "Look, I'm going to the barbecue across the street. We're raising money for Bootstrap. Why don't you come over?"

"No, no, no. You touched that car." Very menacing.

I went to the barbecue. I said, "There's a bunch of teenagers over there, very angry, very upset. This is what it's all about, isn't it? Why don't we have them over here to the barbecue?"

But the black minister didn't want any part of these kids. There were nice, respectable people there.

When I went about an hour or so later, the kids were still there. They surrounded me. "The car, the car! You touched the car!" and "Muhammad Ali." That's all they had. Cassius Clay had knocked out a white man. They'd seen it on television and they were hungry for a chance to be somebody.

One hit me in the stomach. I have some training in nonviolence, so I simply presented a mute, immobile form and sank to the ground.

Then they crowded around me. I heard one say, "Oh, *fuck* him! Leave him alone."

When I got in the car, the adrenaline was so powerful and the trembling so great I could barely put my leg on the gas. Fear had wiped out everything.

But I knew as I drove home that I either had to come out on the other side of this or I would drop out of the whole movement. I had to find some way of being able to handle the fear.

I kept it to myself and wrestled with it, and in about a day or two it hit me. I couldn't just pick the black people from Central Casting that I

wanted. These black teenagers with their Muhammad Ali mythomania—
that's what it was all about. *They* are what it's all about. I realized that if
you were to continue doing what your impulses led you to do, you were
going to have to accept this risk or otherwise bury those impulses in
yourself. I might get a knife next time. And I couldn't control that. This is
America; it could happen. But I also realized there's no hiding from it.

Later I set up these dialogues with the Panthers—John Huggins and
Bunchy Carter and Ericka Huggins and Masai. They were all very formi-
dable, remarkable people, leadership people. They inspired me. I had never
seen anything like it. We formed a group called Friends of the Panthers.

Soon we were marked by the police. Our agent provocateur came from
the Green Berets, went into the Los Angeles police force, did not go through
the academy—went right out into the street. He posed as a Vietnam vet
who had turned into a rebel. You know the type: "You fucking people aren't
doing enough! Get guns!" He was teaching akido and judo and bringing
guns around, talking about, "Well, let's hold up a gun store." He always
had to be discouraged.

We said, "Look, he's a crazy veteran, but you can't just turn your back
on everybody who's white. Everybody can't be a policeman. He's a different class than you, a different style."

Then a woman was raped and threatened at the John Brown Bookstore,
down in the San Fernando Valley.

This guy said, "I can get guns, I can get bombs, I can get whatever you
want."

Everyone was saying, "We don't want anything."

I said to him, "We could use some of this Mace. I think we could use
something."

So, okay! That's that.

That night at a meeting I got a call.

"Hi," the guy says. "Now, what do you want again? You say you
want—"

I said, "I want this for self-protection at the John Brown Bookstore."

He's asking leading questions. I'm saying, "Well, just as I said. Just
something that can be used for protection."

"Okay. It'll be a hundred dollars."

I told him I didn't have the money and that he should pick it up from
another member of our group—Shirley Sutherland. He agrees.

At four o'clock in the morning I get a call: "I don't like this! I'm not
going up to Shirley Sutherland. Fuck these people in Beverly Hills! I don't
trust 'em! Fuck 'em! I'll get the money from you!"

I said, "I don't have any money. I'll write you a check and Shirley can pay me back, but I'll have to postdate it."

"Well, okay," he said.

I go back to bed. He arrives about four-thirty, brings in a box wrapped in brown paper. He sits down. He was wired, of course—I mean wearing a tape recorder. I'm sitting there beside the bed in my pajamas.

He says, "Now what are these for, again?"

I said, "It's for the John Brown Bookstore."

"So the browns and the blacks?"

I said, "John *Brown* Bookstore. Here's the check."

I write it out to him, "for Mace," one hundred dollars, and postdate it. This was a big joke among the lawyers, that the government was gonna try to prove a case with this check.

He says, "Okay."

He takes it, and I go back to bed.

About ten minutes later, there's a knock on the door. I opened it—it had a chain—and a hand comes in with identification, and he says, "Don."

"Who's there?"

"It's me."

"What is it?"

Hand comes in. "LAPD, Don. Open up."

I opened the door, and there were Treasury agents with shotguns.

In they came and started saying, "What are these books by Sartre and Camus, and what's all this *shit?*"

I'm standing there.

The guy is standing there.

And the package is sitting there. It hasn't been unwrapped.

An FBI man sits down. "Well, Don," he says. "Do you want to say anything? Of course you're a teacher—do you want to talk?"

I said, "You have a *very* disturbed man as your agent here, and you are going to pay a heavy price for it. May I get dressed?"

The package contained grenades. Judge Ferguson, a well-known federal judge here, said to the government, "Did your agent go to the naval base in San Diego and get these grenades?"

"Well, yes."

"And he got them in order to bring them to someone, not knowing what they were? What if they'd blown up the apartment building? *Out!*"

Then the government reinstated the case. But it never went to trial, because it turned out that the government had stolen the tapes of the defense lawyers and private investigators.

*   *   *

We gather more and more support. In Berkeley we discover full-scale war plans to attack the office, including helicopter bombings. We publicize the terrifying plans at a press conference and the student and liberal community come to our defense.

"We went to the Panthers and said, 'We think we should form a support committee to try to help you put pressure on Berkeley city government and others to avoid an attack,'" remembers Dan Siegel, elected president of the Berkeley student body that year.

> You thought that was a good idea, so we formed something called the Committee to Defend the Black Panther Party, formed a steering committee, issued press releases, and went to the Berkeley City Council demanding they pass a resolution that they were going to forbid their police to attack the Party headquarters. When things were really tense we organized all-night vigils at the Panther headquarters on Shattuck, and had crowds of people standing in front of the building or sitting in the lobby all day and all night. I remember you coming down the stairs every night with your Red Book and giving little lectures, applying the Red Book in a very rational and realistic way to some situation in Oakland or in the United States. People like yourself, June, another Panther named Fred Bennett, were the ones we really had the greatest respect for as committed political activists and fellow revolutionaries, black working-class guys whose ideals and attitudes and approaches to doing work epitomized our view of what the professional revolutionary was: a black American version of the Cuban or Vietnamese revolutionaries.

The peak of our popularity comes that spring. A leaflet put out in Boston announcing TDA—The Day After, the name for demonstrations planned to begin after the verdicts in the Chicago conspiracy trial—suggests the general attitude. The top is a fake Western Union telegram that reads:

EMERGENCY MEETING OF NATIONAL SECURITY COUNCIL CEDES DEFEAT STOP VIETNAM TROOPS WILL BE WITHDRAWN IMMEDIATELY STOP ALL POLITICAL PRISONERS WILL BE FREED STOP THE TRIAL IS OVER STOP JUDGE HOFFMAN TO BE DEALT WITH APPROPRIATELY STOP CORPORATE AND GOVERNMENT LEADERS AGREE TO IMMEDIATE WHITE HOUSE MEETING STOP WILL DISCUSS TERMS OF IMMEDIATE TRANSFER OF POWER TO PEOPLE WITH MR.

HUEY NEWTON AND REVOLUTIONARY GOVERNMENT STOP
WHATEVER GOES UP MUST COME DOWN.

(The rest of the leaflet went on to say that change didn't happen that way,
telling people to fight back.)

Bobby's trial now becomes paramount. The dangers of conviction are
very real. Garry warns us New Haven's legal system is no more progressive
than Oakland's. We know the Party has much less of a presence on the East
Coast. Plus, the state has been employing all its power to destroy the political and spiritual conviction of the defendants.

"I don't think I saw Peggy until the next day," Frances remembers about
her first day in jail on the charges stemming from the Alex Rackley murder.

We all ended up in Niantic together. We just embraced and cried and re-
joiced at the same time that we were all very much alive. Ericka kept saying to us, "Look, just don't talk because this whole place is bugged." We're
like, "You don't talk?" Because if you didn't your whole head would split
wide open.

And we wanted to know what had happened.

I personally wanted to know because I knew I wasn't there.

Anyway, Ericka didn't want to talk about it.

We were like, "Let's hope that Mom and Dad didn't find out." That's
the last thing we wanted. "Oh, Mom and Dad can't find out. Maybe they'll
just realize they made a mistake and we'll be able to leave here."

Then the days went on and we realized this was some serious stuff. A
guy had been killed.

At that point there was the divide-and-conquer tactic — Who said what?
Who did what? How was it all initiated?

They would take us down separately. Sometimes Ericka would be down
there for a long time. She would come back and we'd say, "We know what
you were doing, Ericka. You were up there running all that damn rhetoric,
trying to change these FBI and CIA around."

"Oh yeah," she'd say. "I told them that they're part of the structure."

We *had* to do something to try to make light of our situation, because
when we realized and internalized exactly where we were, that was very
scary in itself too.

They would take us back and forth to court. Peggy was always the
smallest of us. She'd slide out of her handcuffs. Then she'd go, "Oh, it's
such a *beautiful* day! Oh, I just love it!" The police would *screech* to a
halt — this big, huge caravan of all these state police.

Another thing was that they said we couldn't smoke either. Peggy's natural was still real, real big and wide—she was the most beautiful person! So when we would come from court, different people would give us cigarettes, weed, and whatever. She'd stick them in her hair. Then she'd slide out of her cuffs and stretch a little bit and light a cigarette.

One night they got tired of that happening. When we were coming back in from the court, the matrons and the guards were all lined up by our area, because they put us in punitive isolation. We had all of our letters and, again, our weed and our cigarettes in our hair. They stripped and searched us right then and there. We didn't want that to happen. So there was an all-out free-for-all. There were about three guards all on top of each other, and one matron. The other women in the prison could kind of see and they were saying, "Kick their asses again!" Even when we had the worst of times, we had the best of times.

Out of us all, Ericka went through the hardest time. She had already lost her husband, John. Now she was pulled away from her daughter. Sometimes she would be up in the corner somewhere, in a fetal position, crying and pulling her hair out.

We would go over, say, "Hey, come on. We're gonna get out of this shit. We're *revolutionaries.* You pumped us up, saying we're invincible and nothing's gonna possibly happen to us. So you can't do that. Because if you do, then you won't be any help to us. So, come on, let's get it together." Then Ericka would rise to the occasion.

Peggy was the main one. She would start something. "Oh, Fran, let's tell her about what happened one night when we went to Boston and ended up in the damn X-rated district, and we're walking up and down, and pretended we were soliciting."

We would tell these stories, and Ericka would be laughing hard.

Peggy was just so up. Bubbly—had so much life, so much strength. I always drew my strength from her. I don't think I would have left home if it hadn't been us leaving together. I never wanted to be separated from her anymore, like I was when she was younger and had to go to that home. From now on, we were going together, and we had made a pact that would never happen to us again.

Then they checked me—I kept getting sick, complaining—and told me I was three or four months pregnant. My first emotion was anger—I felt my pregnancy would be something else for them to use.

Which it was.

First they had a lot of FBI in the delivery room. Then, afterwards, they came, said, "Well, you got a choice. You just had this little baby, and I know you want to be home with him. So what are you gonna do? Tell us about Ericka, tell us about this one, tell us about that one."

"Tell you *what?*" I said. "I don't *know* what to tell you!"

"Oh, yes, you do, yes, you do."

I had gotten very, very sick so my mother got the baby and they sent me back to Niantic—the medical wing. They didn't change my bandage. I had gangrene, stinking like I don't know. They would not wash me. I was full of crabs and everything. I told the girl who came around putting food through the door, "Please get to Peggy. Tell Peggy to call my lawyer right away."

As punishment for communicating with someone they put me in solitary confinement. They had sewn my stomach, but it was kind of open and still seeping, the nastiest thing anyone would ever want to see.

They would open up the door, and I would go out for maybe about ten minutes. I would say, "Any water, or something? Can I wash or anything? This thing is getting worse."

"Oh, fuck you. We don't care if you die."

But when it came time for pills and medication, they would force it on me. Half the time I would just stick the pill under my tongue, but then they'd throw the water down and I'd drink because I was so extremely thirsty.

I went down to like about ninety pounds. Dehydrated and stuff, full of Thorazine and Librium, Pentothal—I was trying to remember everything I heard them say about giving me medicine so I could tell my lawyers exactly what I was ingesting. Every day I'd say to the guards, "Yeah, that's all right. You can kill the revolutionary, but you can't kill the revolution." All that kind of stuff. "Oh, they will tear this whole place apart. There will be bombs all over the place! The skies will light up." I was still trying to get to them, instead of their like getting to me.

Then one day I hear a noise above me. Well, when I had been with Peggy and Ericka we always used to walk around the grounds, and sometimes we would take off and run and the guards would try to chase us. When I heard this noise I thought it might be Peggy and the others running. So all of a sudden I started hollering. Sure enough it was Peggy and Ericka. They hollered back to me and everything. I told them where I was and what was happening. Then they were able to get my lawyer back up.

My lawyer got a writ of habeas corpus. I didn't want to get out, didn't want to be separated from Peggy. Because by this time Peggy's health was deteriorating very fast. She had always been sickly—she had pneumonia, and was very small—and what would happen was that they would keep the doors closed to the room, and all we had was the damp concrete to sit on. Sitting on the concrete continually, the wetness got into her bones, and her system, and brought about the arthritis in her joints and stuff. She started becoming very crippled. We protested and got some medical treatment for her. But when the whole habeas corpus thing came up I said, "I'm not leaving you in here. I don't know what they might do to you and Ericka."

She said, "No. You go on out there and you let them know exactly what is gonna happen. What's happening with us in here, and what you've been through."

I came out. I felt that they weren't gonna do anything but turn right around, and I'm gonna go right back. Because they're saying the next day they want me to show up in court and testify. As a hostile witness or something.

I said, "You're damn *right* I'm hostile. But I'm not going along with your game."

They wanted to use my baby to get me. But I didn't have that bond with him anyway because I hadn't spent no more than maybe two days with him, and was too weak to even hold him, after going through all that twenty-four-hour ordeal. So it wasn't that I didn't *love* my child, because I did, but I knew he was going to be taken care of by my parents, so for them to want to use *that* didn't mean that much to me.

But I called you and told you what was happening. That they wanted me to come in the next day. I wanted to know from you what you felt about what I should do.

You said, "Whatever you do, it's gonna be the right thing, and in the best interests of all. Please know and understand that we love you *and* your sister, as well as Ericka and Bobby. We're concerned about each one of you."

You were saying that you knew I would do nothing or say nothing that would hurt, but also that I shouldn't fall prey to any of the strategies that the police were using, because the Party would be there supporting us and supporting me. It just made it *great!*

So the next morning, when it was time to go to court, I felt really good, really refreshed.

We got there, and I got on the witness stand. It was already laid out as to which questions to answer, which ones to take the Fifth. For the majority I took the Fifth; on the other ones I went into the whole thing about the birth and the dope and the medication. "You know these fools sat up there in this room, when I was delivering my child, looking at me wide open and everything."

They would strike that down: "Don't answer the question any more than what we're asking you. That ain't relevant to nothing."

The judge is saying, "Stop—"

But I'm talking. "Look, if you don't want me to talk, what am I doing here?"

"Take this woman away! She is held in contempt, and she is a hostile witness, and she has gone over a hundred-some questions and taken the Fifth, and I don't want to hear this no more!"

I'm hoping to go to Niantic. Be with Peggy. Instead they put me in this part separated away from them. I raised so much hell about it, so then they put me back in there. My father came and visited. We all embraced. He didn't have that "I told you so" attitude anymore. Finally I got out. There was work to do, and I was going back out there to make sure I did it— work for Peggy, and Bobby, Ericka, for all of us, really.

We call for a May Day demonstration in New Haven to support the Panthers. Expecting the revolution to start on their campus, the Yale Corporation panics. All we've announced is a mass gathering, nothing more, but they act like they believe Yale will be destroyed. The university debates what to do. Yale's president, Kingman Brewster, finally makes a comment. He says he thinks black revolutionaries can't get a fair trial in America. The statement makes the front page of the *New York Times*.

By May 1, there is a groundswell of support for the New Haven defendants. Come See About Bobby, we say, Because Bobby Came and Saw About Us. Thousands turn out for the demonstration. Everyone speaks—Genet, myself, Jerry, Tom (who actually ends his—this time very good—speech with the line that this is going to be the last public speech he will ever make). The weekend is completely peaceful. Even a harassment arrest of me and Masai a few days before the weekend doesn't provoke us. But the demonstration does have its effect, putting the judge and prosecutor on notice that they had better bend over backward to give Bobby a fair trial, and Brewster's comment helps to ensure that the judge will give Garry a broad hand in his jury selection. We're hopeful.

Then America invades Cambodia and the students at Kent State and Jackson State are killed. It seems every university in America, every college, is shut down, all inhabited by revolutionaries, all at least vaguely sympathetic to us.

And the best news is last: Garry tells us that his appeals seem to be working. The long wait is over; Huey will be getting out of jail.

Chapter
24

AS early as seven that morning, people start waiting outside the county court-house for Huey. By two, when Melvin, myself, G., and Masai meet him up-stairs, we warn him about the crowd.

"I'll stay here," he jokes. "I don't know what's going on out there anyway."

On his tapes these past months he's said he feels removed from the Party, puzzled and delighted by my own political development and the Party's growth, the enormous change that has occurred in the guy who asked him questions about *Doctor Zhivago* and the gang that first patrolled the police. "He's scared to death of getting out," Alex Hoffmann likes to joke: "He's scared of getting married."

Actually LaVerne, his old girlfriend, has been off the scene for some time; but the joke—Charlie Garry's invention—contains some truth: Huey's apprehensive about the future.

First there's the problem of what to do with him. The past three years we've struggled to get Huey out. Now that he's free where are we going to put him? We'd be crazy not to take precautions against some cop taking a retaliatory shot.

Huey has partly provided for his own safety. In prison he has befriended an inmate named James Carr. A bodybuilder—Jackal Dog's his nickname—Carr belongs to a circle of longtime, radicalized prisoners; the group's leader is George Jackson, an inmate renowned in the California jails for his discipline and strength, a master of thought and deed, a karate expert and communist whose collection of letters entitled *Soledad Brother* is soon going to be published. "I was accused of robbing a gas station of seventy dollars," George writes in the introduction to the book, explaining his revolutionary lineage,

> and accepted a deal—I agreed to confess and spare the county court costs in return for a light county jail sentence. I confessed, but when time came for sentencing, they tossed me into the penitentiary with one to life. That was in 1960. I was 18 years old. I've been here ever since. I met Marx, Lenin, Trotsky, Engels and Mao when I entered prison and they redeemed me. For the first four years I studied nothing but economics and military ideas. I met black guerrillas, George "Big Jake" Lewis, and James Carr, W. L. Nolen, Bill Christmas, Tony Gibson, and many, many others. We attempted to transform the black criminal mentality into a black revolutionary mentality. As a result, each of us has been subjected to years of the most vicious reactionary violence by the state. Our mortality rate is almost what you would expect to find in a history of Dachau. Three of us were murdered several months ago by a pig shooting from 30 feet above their heads with a military rifle.

Recently he and two other inmates have been charged with a guard's death, a retaliatory killing, the state claims, for the shooting of W. L. Nolen, one of the three murdered inmates George mentions. Jackson is represented by another lawyer in Garry's firm through whom Huey has established contact with George and asked us to start a defense committee. In thanks George promises to organize for the Party in prison, sending us his warriors.

Jackal Dog's the first. A mix of brains and brawn, he's an impressive example. Eldridge's prison cadre are brave but lack both intellectual and political discipline. Jackal Dog's different. George has taught him dialectics, coached him not to overreact but to cultivate patience and gauge the right time to strike. There's no discernible jackanape tendency in him. Plus, he seems completely loyal to Huey, the epitome of a personal bodyguard.

A harder question is where Huey will live. He can't simply stay with us. He needs his own place. But he must be safe.

At first we check out the home of Sonny Barger, ex-head of the Hell's Angels. It's a fortress with video cameras and alarms protecting every window and door. We drive out there with Mickey Phillips, Arlene Slaughter's son; a police helicopter follows us the entire way, convincing us the place won't provide Huey the protection he needs.

"Huey," I tell him in a tape, "we're having problems finding a place to put you."

"No problem," he answers, repeating his joke. "I'll stay right here."

We decide he'll stay with Alex Hoffmann and Elsa Knight Thompson, the head of public affairs for radio station KPFA; they share an apartment in North Berkeley, and the police are unlikely to stage a raid on them. A month and a half later we find a permanent address. Opposite the courthouse is a high rise right on the lake, 1200 Lake Shore Drive, twenty-four-hour doorman, top security. Plus, Charlie Finley, the owner of the Oakland A's, lives there: he certainly won't abide midnight helicopter flybys. A penthouse is available for $650 a month. Huey visits the place and we find a contributor for the payments so the money doesn't come straight from the Party's coffers. The Throne, we later call it, and Huey stations a telescope in a window to check up on his old home across the way.

Other complications are more subtle, more difficult to solve. The biggest is defining Huey's future political role.

What is his political role going to be?

Huey has always said he's not the figure in Eldridge's poster. But Huey's now established as a movement leader, proven in both action and thought, a thinker and doer who has changed history. Except that Huey doesn't picture himself a leader. He's not a speaker like Fred or Bobby. He's Huey.

The pressures are greatest in the Party itself. My experience after April 6 will now have to be repeated on a national level: then I had to introduce Huey to a couple of guys in jail; now he'll have to meet the entire Party — then the general movement.

We leave the courthouse, head into the hot midday glare.

"Power to the people, everybody!" Huey calls as soon as he steps outside.

People cram the plaza wanting to see and hear Huey. Their desire doesn't come from hero worship. Their work and struggle has accomplished a remarkable thing. His release demonstrates the power of the people. Two years ago the idea that Huey might be free, walking the streets, seemed completely unrealistic. Next we'll bring back Eldridge, then spring Bobby. For once we'll all be together and the Party will be able to reach even greater heights.

The police hate the moment. I see them massed behind the crowd, helmeted, tense, nightsticks already unsheathed. We turn around, going out the back.

"Where's your car?" Alex asks me.

I've parked two blocks away and we've got to get out soon.

"I'm parked around the corner," Alex tells me and we make a beeline for his car.

A new sea of people meets us when we get there. The police have also moved; they're waiting for an excuse to wade in, and this crowd will fight. I remember a scene from the Party's early days. Huey and I were driving around in LaVerne's Volkswagen, selling weed to raise money for the Party. Campus Club—a nightclub owned by an Italian guy and frequented by the fast-life people—was on fire. There's tension between the cops and the people; Huey and I both know its only moments before a riot will break out. Huey stands there, trying to turn the crowd around, cool things out. I walk back and forth, touching people, getting their attention. Listen up, people, I say. This is Huey Newton, leader of the Panthers. Listen to what he has to say. Huey speaks and the situation's defused.

We need something like this now.

We climb on Alex's VW to make Huey visible. I stand behind Huey; G.'s to the side, checking the crowd. Huey waves, raises his fist; he's ecstatic. He takes off his shirt, thanking them, saying that if they liked what they did for him, then they should do the same for Bobby and Ericka and the other New Haven defendants.

"We gotta get out of here. Tell them there'll be a rally at Bobby Hutton Park," I say, using our new name for De Fremery Park.

The police push at the fringes of the crowd, trying to provoke something. G. looks worried.

"I can't do that," Huey says. "I can't lie to the people."

"Do it or they'll be a riot," I say.

"But it's not true," he says.

"Huey," I whisper, "I'll take care of it."

I hold up his hand, trying to get the crowd's attention. Huey stretches forward his arms, shouting hellos to the people; he looks like a prophet, pointing the way, smiling joyfully, elated with freedom, telling the people to disband and go to De Fremery.

"I don't want to mislead them," he tells me.

"Well, Huey," I say, "just do it and I'll tell them later."

He makes the announcement, pleads for them to give the car some room. He drives off in the Volkswagen and I rush toward the crowd. They're already in the streets chanting, marching. I inform them we can't have a rally today, but will at the end of the week. Huey's back, I tell them; there's no rush: he's going to be with us for a long time.

First Huey sees his parents; both sickly and old, neither has dared the courthouse throng.

"My father was concerned Huey finish school," remembers Melvin. "He'd ask the question, 'Do you think he's ever gonna finish?' Because Huey was a forever student. When he saw Huey, my father started crying. He told Huey he had thought he'd never see him outside the prison again. It was the first time I had ever seen my father show emotion about it."

Then he goes to Alex and Elsa's. For the next days—weeks, actually—Huey meets Party members, journalists, black and white radicals.

Huey's jubilant in this element. He gives wonderful interviews, answering questions with explosions of theory, anecdotes, and humor, sipping Vas, his favorite. He loves everyone. A movement journalist comes in with a friend from Gay Liberation. Huey's never even seen the person before, but he grabs him, giving him a hug. I thrill to see him. He's at his best, generous, caring, greeting people, making them feel at home. We light up joints and in a while I'm expounding on Timothy Leary, calling him a dope fiend and saying he's a malign influence on the movement and that it was idiotic for Weathermen to bust him out of prison.

"Come here," Huey says from the kitchen.

I wander in, joint in hand. I feel grand; Huey's back.

"What's up?"

"You don't know how funny it is to hear you putting down Tim Leary while you've got this joint in your hand."

"Is that right?" I'm so stoned I don't even realize I'm holding the joint. "My God, Huey, you're right!"

I laugh and take a Ritalin; I live on them now, Ritalins and massive doses of vitamin B. But maybe now with Huey out some of the pressure will subside and my stomach will calm down.

"Give me some," Huey says after he asks me about the pill.

He throws the capsules in his mouth, starts chewing them like candy.

"God! What are you doing? You're just supposed to swallow them."

He crunches away. "Boy! I really like these things! These are great!"

The only sour note is Huey's attitude toward G. He's never seen him, keeps inquiring who he is.

"That's G.," I tell him. "Geronimo."

I bring Geronimo over and tell Huey our latest plan. We've come up with a solution for putting members on ice when they get in trouble with the law. We'll have them hole up down south like gangsters in movies about the thirties. No white person would ever know about a couple of new brothers living in Rockville. They'd be completely anonymous, forgotten about. G. and I talk about the plan with the Central Committee. We don't intend to turn the place into a revolutionary center—there aren't many significant military targets near Jackson—but a retreat where members can hone their military skills undercover. Agreeing the idea sounds good, the Central Committee has postponed starting the plan until Huey's release.

"I don't agree with that," Huey says.

"What do you mean, you don't agree with it?" I ask. "This is what we've been working on. Geronimo's the Minister of Defense—"

"*I'm* the Minister of Defense," Huey says.

Geronimo laughs to calm the tension. "That's right," he tells Huey.

Huey has hundreds of questions about the organization. In the mornings I go over; we sit on the bed like in the old days and I tell him what's going on in the Party.

"How do you work this stuff with women?" he asks.

"Everybody can choose to be in relationships or not," I say.

"Yeah, but David," he says, "how does that work for you?"

I explain the ways people cope. Huey is disbelieving. Never cowed by official lines or Party doctrine, Huey always says what he thinks is the truth. And he doesn't believe my version of things at all. When he presses me, I tell him about me, Pat, and Brenda; I explain my conflict—my sense of duty to Pat, my pleasure in Brenda's company—describe the scene with Pat and the gun and my complicated schedule, staying with one, then the other, splitting my time between the two.

"And now you're gonna have two families," he says. "No wonder you have an ulcer, David."

"I got the ulcer from pressure," I say.

"No," he says. "You can't resolve this conflict between the two sisters. You think you're controlling them. They're controlling you."

When I protest, Huey drives the point home.

"Pat most of all," he says. "She controls you in a negative way. She gets you angry. Makes you react. She keeps on you and you're always angry and upset."

Of course he's right; I don't commit myself to Brenda because I'm still tied to Pat.

"She's controlling you," he says. "You've got to be indifferent to her. And you've got to pick. Because you're never going to get a balance this way. Besides, how do you feel about Pat having relationships?"

"I'm all right with that," I say. I tell him that I've informed Pat she can relate to other men.

He studies me a moment, not like Eldridge, distancing himself, but trying to read me, as though I pose an interesting puzzle for him.

"No," he says finally, "I don't believe that."

"I'm certain of that," I say.

Now he's laughing. "No. I don't believe that at all. You may believe it, but it's not true." He's completely absorbed in the conversation. Now, he says, when a man sees his woman making love to someone else, he commonly feels two emotions: anger and desire. Which would I act on? he asks.

"I'd probably beat her up," I say.

"That's very interesting," Huey continues, "because you can see by that reaction how violence and property are linked together. Whereas if I related to my sexual response—my desire—I would make love to her, rather than brutalize her.

"Has Pat been with another man?" he asks.

"No," I say.

"Then all you're talking is still theory," he says. "You haven't resolved to test yourself yet in practice."

Then our conversations about the Party are cut short. There's a shoot-out in Marin County. Busting into a courtroom, Jonathan Jackson, the younger brother of George Jackson, seizes a judge and frees three inmates standing trial. Jonathan demands George's freedom in exchange for the judge. The police open fire, killing Jonathan, two of the three other inmates, and the judge.

The event produces powerful repercussions. Huey and I are angry and distressed by Jonathan's sacrifice. I've worked with Jonathan. Since Huey's first communication about George, we've assisted Angela Davis and the Jackson family, giving them money and assigning members to help promote their case. Only a few weeks before, Jonathan stayed at my house along with his mother and Angela. But I've had absolutely no idea that he planned anything like this; the loss of his life appalls me.

But Eldridge lauds the act. "The focus of our contact with the system was the court situation," he writes later on. "Mass mobilization campaign is a symbol of one form of dealing with that. . . . Another alternative way of dealing with it is the case of Jonathan Jackson. . . . The type of action that Jonathan Jackson took has everything to do with the way the Black Panther Party was moving, helping to create the right climate, helping to discredit the judiciary and turn people against it so that the gun would be picked up."

Huey disagrees totally. He considers Jonathan's sacrifice noble, supremely courageous. He also believes Eldridge is pursuing his own politics of spontaneity, rather than building a party, based in the community, of which the military wing is a part. "Any action which does not mobilize the community toward the goal is not a revolutionary action," he writes. "The action might be a marvelous statement of courage, but if it does not mobilize the people toward the goal of a higher manifestation of freedom it is not making a political statement and could even be counterrevolutionary."

Jonathan's act also starts a larger drama. Later on rumors say Geronimo knew about the plan in advance and, at the last moment, refused to let Panther cadre join Jonathan. I don't know whether or not Huey was aware of this. In any event, a year later George is killed in a shoot-out with prison guards only a few days after he wills all his possessions to the Party—and this is followed by a series of seeming revenge deaths, including that of Huey's bodyguard Jimmy Carr, that will remain shrouded in mystery.

All this is yet to happen. Our immediate political reaction to the tragedy is a heightened sense that we must get on track about the Party, clarify our understanding of the past and future. We arrange to go to Santa Cruz for the weekend, just Huey and I and Melvin and his wife; there we can review all this without interruptions.

Before we leave, Huey delivers his first speech, at Merritt College, making good on the rally we've promised people the day of his release.

Now Huey has never liked public speaking. Bobby's public style has been one of his primary contributions to the Party. Huey's great in small sessions, enthusiastic, intense, funny. But before large groups he freezes; his voice gets high—the soprano that used to be a cause of fights back in school—and his style stiffens; he sounds academic, goes on incessantly, and becomes increasingly abstract, spinning out one dialectical contradiction after another.

He argues he shouldn't speak. But he's the leader. People wait for his vision; the rapid-fire brilliance of his newsreel prison interviews has inspired a whole generation of radicals.

So he speaks.

"It couldn't have been more terrible," remembers Alex. "He went on absolutely endlessly, philosophizing for at least an hour and a half. He lost his audience. It was didactic and way over everybody's head. These kids had heard Eldridge and Bobby, and Huey's speech made perfectly clear to them that he was indeed not the poster on the wall."

We go to Santa Cruz, staying in a cabin near redwood forests. Huey's keyed up, disturbed by the contradictions between himself and Eldridge.

"How are we gonna have a constitutional convention?" he asks, referring to a plan of Eldridge's that we've implemented: a gathering of radical groups in Philadelphia the next month for the purpose of rewriting the American constitution, the first step in building a national united front. "This is nonsense. What does it mean? A constitutional convention assumes we have a government somewhere."

He thinks the idea leads us away from our primary task, organizing locally. To him the convention comes from Eldridge's grandiosity — Eldridge will build a great national organization instead of concentrating on powerful local bases.

But most of all Huey hates Eldridge's internal effects on the Party.

One afternoon we are listening to Tchaikovsky's "Pathétique" Symphony.

"Huey, I didn't know you liked classical music," I say.

"Yeah," he answers. "Don't you remember Melvin used to teach me piano."

"What's it called?"

"The Pathétique."

"Path-a-tique," I repeat. *Stille Nacht.* All these unknown languages. I'm in a good mood, pleased at renewing my friendship with Huey and spending this valuable time with him.

"You know, David, I don't know you anymore," Huey says suddenly.

"What are you talking about?" I ask. This is Huey; you never can predict where he's going.

"I don't know you," he says, staring straight at me, challenging me.

"I'm David," I answer. We're in a large room with a picture window framing the woods outside.

"Are you?" he asks. "Because you don't act like David. You act like Eldridge. When I sit here and listen to you, I might as well just turn on Eldridge. Everything you do is like Eldridge. I don't know who you are. You're an impersonator. You're not authentic. You're not David anymore."

His attack stuns me. Choosing between Huey and Eldridge is unimaginable; the two are my idols. Huey has frequently expressed his disapproval of Eldridge, but what he's saying now is more than a criticism of a style: it's an accusation of betrayal. But how can I betray Huey by identifying with someone who has done so much to get him free?

"Why are you attacking me?" I say. "Everybody in the Party acts like Eldridge."

"That's exactly right!" he answers. "Everybody acts like Eldridge. The profanity. Eldridge's style. Eldridge has taken you guys down his direction. This isn't the way of the Party. It's not the vision of the Party."

"But Bobby —" I start to say.

"I didn't leave the Party with Bobby," he answers. "I left it with you. Bobby's never opposed Eldridge in anything. I don't even blame Bobby for April 6. I blame you. Because I left the Party with you!"

*   *   *

Huey's reproach hurts. It's his greatness: he cuts to the bone.

Bobby fantasizes, Eldridge excoriates.

Huey's power is greater than either of theirs. He speaks the truth. I hate and love him for it.

All night I try to answer him in my mind.

Of course I followed Eldridge, I say. What else should I have done? The man was the embodiment of Malcolm.

Plus, you lauded Eldridge, praised his book.

So of course I went along.

And now you accuse me of betraying you for doing what I thought I was supposed to do. What kind of logic is that, Huey?

Except my defense leaves me feeling vulnerable. I'm using Huey to explain my own actions. Not taking responsibility. I'm empty inside, guilty of Huey's accusations: there is no me, only someone who tries to find himself in other people, other people's ways of being, Devil Dogs and Gene Kelly and Huey Newton. There's nothing I'm whole about. I'm in and out of the Party, a revolutionary and working man, father and lover. Who's David, the real David? All this time I've thought I was doing good work, keeping the Party together, strengthening us. Now Huey says I've simply been following someone, showing me to myself—just as he pointed out my dependence on Pat.

I call June.

"Well, what do you think about what he said?" he asks.

"You know Huey," I say. "He's a master of logic. The man is indubitably correct. I can't fault him on that."

The next morning I tell Huey my decision.

"Listen," I say, "I think you're right. I need time. I want to get out. I'm tired. I did this out of friendship, and now you're out so I can get out too."

But Huey has also thought about things.

"David," he tells me, "you've demonstrated a greater friendship than I've ever known. I don't know that I would have given you the leadership of the Party as you've done me."

I'm not sure how to respond. He's praising me; but he's also saying I'm weak.

"Well, it's yours," I say. "I did this out of friendship, not for anything else."

"Because you could easily isolate me now," he says. "These people are loyal to you, not me. Like Geronimo."

"You're wrong about Geronimo," I say. "He's sound. Besides, you're the leader. No one else could create the Party. The Party wouldn't exist without you."

We talk outside, walking together. The air smells fresh and wet. My stomach kills me; I'm always tired, and when I go to sleep I'm wired, too nervous to fall out.

"I think the Party should give you something as a gesture of my gratitude. I think we should buy you a house."

"No, Huey," I say. "I really want out. I need to be with my family. What you said yesterday is true. Undeniably true. I don't know who I am."

But now Huey pleads, says he needs me. He doesn't know all the workings of the Party. I've got to introduce him to members, take him around.

"Then you can rest," he says. "That's all you need. You need to rest."

A month later Brenda gives birth. We name my second daughter Dassine, honoring the Palestinian rebellion. I commute between Brenda and Pat. A tense comradeship exists between the two.

"When I started showing, Pat would ask me questions: 'How do you feel?' and stuff like that," remembers Brenda.

Then after the baby came, Pat—later Dassine called her "Pat Pat" — told me things like "wash the baby's tongue because it cakes up with milk." She enjoyed Dassine. She was like an aunt, both to Dassine and myself.

But it was real funny. I got Dassine's ears pierced when she was about six weeks, and my mother would send me all these gorgeous little teeny stones from Alaska to use as earrings—gold nuggets, diamonds, rubies, little pearls. Little teeny things. But Dassine was always losing them. It would just freak me out no end. Every week she'd lose one of her earrings. I'd call my mom: "You need to send me another pair of whatever." This went on for the longest time. Later you told me that Pat would throw the earrings away. That was her way of getting back at me. I had to laugh when you told me that. But I spent a fortune on the earrings!

Chapter

25

HUEY and I start our tour. On the plane to New York—our first stop—we continue discussing Geronimo.

Huey says the Party's too militaristic. The Party runs survival programs, but the Party itself is not surviving. We must forget Eldridge's fixation about armed struggle. The state wants to destroy us—that's the lesson of the Marin courthouse shoot-out. The police were so scared they killed the judge rather than let Jonathan and the others set a revolutionary example.

"The first step is getting rid of Geronimo Pratt," he says.

"That's crazy," I say. "Geronimo is very loyal and we need him."

I tell him how Geronimo's military and political organizing helped keep the Los Angeles chapter together after Bunchy's death. Plus, I trust G. because he's one of the most loyal Party members, like June or John Seale. Pat puts it perfectly. "I never knew no bad side to Geronimo," she says. "He was very intelligent, very disciplined, very mannerable. Southern." When we stay in Marty's house in New York we sleep together in the back room, like I used to bed down with my brothers on the pallets in Mobile. Geronimo's beyond suspicion.

But Huey's adamant.

"Geronimo is working against us," he says.

"I don't know where you're getting this stuff from," I answer.

Huey doesn't answer. I look out the window and feel like there's no plane beneath me, as though I'm floating, lost. Geronimo's my faithful comrade in arms. If Huey says Geronimo is disloyal that means Huey's skeptical about me. But is that what he's saying? Huey doesn't mince words. If he doesn't trust me, why wouldn't he tell me?

But Huey keeps his own counsel. Without telling me, he has already received bogus FBI letters warning him against me.

On August 13th, 1970, the Philadelphia Field Office had an informant distribute a fictitious BPP directive to Philadelphia Panthers, questioning Newton's leadership ability. The Philadelphia office informed FBI headquarters that the directive "stresses the leadership and strength of David Hilliard and Eldridge Cleaver while intimating Huey Newton is useful only as a drawing card. It is recommended this directive...be mailed personally to Huey Newton with a short anonymous note. The note would indicate the writer, a community worker in Philadelphia for the BPP, was incensed over the suggestion Huey was only being used by the Party after founding it, and wanted no part of this Chapter if it was slandering its leaders in private." Headquarters approved this plan....

The deep flow of play, Huey and I say, a Zen phrase for disregarding the surface things and focusing on inner, hidden reality. Huey must have been thinking he was doing that, not telling me the truth, following his own way.

New York is sticky, hot; between the humidity and the buildings you can hardly breathe. Marty drives us to meetings with lawyers; besides the substantial contributions the Party has received, Huey and the Party are besieged with offers for books and movies, and Huey wants to consolidate all moneys into a company called Stronghold.

The issue creates political tension with the New York Twenty-one lawyers and the defendants themselves.

"The first slight tension came after the police raid on the LA headquarters," Marty remembers.

You asked me for some money to bail some Panthers out. It seemed like the most natural thing in the world. I sent it.

That began the drumbeat of the New York lawyers: "How could you do this?"

Relations only got worse. They kept up this canard that really pissed me off: that the Party wasn't supporting the Twenty-one.

I remember a meeting in a coffee shop. I argued my point very strongly. "This is one party. I know how the money was raised. I know the motivation for the people giving it. It's one struggle. If guys in Winston-Salem need financial support, it's ludicrous for us not to give it. We've paid every lawyer here everything you've asked."

Then something happened that put them through the roof. The New York Panthers were under one hundred thousand dollars bail apiece. We couldn't raise all that money. For a complicated reason and because of another matter, I went to another lawyer, Victor Rabinowitz. Victor had a brilliant idea. Under New York State law at that time, you could put up a bond for bail. Well bonds don't always sell at face value. If interest rates go up, the price of existing bonds go down. And there were New York State bonds selling for twenty-five cents on a dollar. So Victor said, "Let's buy some New York State Dormitory bonds for twenty-five thousand and we'll give you a one-hundred-thousand-dollar bond." New York State later changed the law on that, but that was Victor Rabinowitz's idea and there's no doubt in my mind that no one else could have produced it.

Then a French fashion photographer/filmmaker made a movie about Eldridge Cleaver, which a major distributor wanted to handle. I suggested a theatrical lawyer do the contracts. The fact that I gave the business to someone else really bothered the Twenty-one lawyers. I said to them, "Guys, you want more money, ask for it. You're entitled to be paid for your work. You just shouldn't be paid with other kinds of work. You should be paid for the work you're doing."

After the business meetings, Huey holds a press conference at the chapter's Harlem office. He speaks of internationalism, the Party programs. Then he drops his bomb: he calls the Party a shambles.

"What do you mean, a shambles, Huey?" I confront him afterward. "We're on a roll! Breakfast programs! We got one hundred thousand newspapers going out every week! What do you mean shambles?"

Huey restates his opinion of Eldridge's influence. We have no security, he says; jackanapes are everywhere. (Plus informers; the government later claims sixty-seven paid Party informers.) Eldridge's plan to create a national popular front with this crazy Constitutional Convention completely counters Huey's original vision. Instead we must build strong local organizations. Of course the survival programs are good. But we must forget the whole military aspect or we won't survive at all. And he's back to Geronimo.

But I'm beyond Geronimo now. Huey has insulted, repudiated, rejected me.

"Well, you founded the Party," I say. I fume inside, but try to stay cool with him. "It's your idea. Now whichever way you want it to go is all right with me. I want out of here anyway."

But where am I going to go? By myself I am nothing but obligations I can't possibly meet. Plus, leaving the Party will endanger me: I face years in prison and can't afford my own lawyer. Besides, my legal battles come from working with the Party. To fight on my own would be suicide. I've never wanted to leave the Party more; but there's no place to go. The Party *is* home, where I am accepted; anyplace else is exile.

In Chicago Huey awes and fascinates Rush.

"I remember his eyes were deeply set back in his head," remembers Rush,

and he had this strange look—that might have come from the prison thing. He ate cold chicken from the refrigerator. Which was something I had never done before. But I began to like cold chicken too. He talked about Fred—he had seen the movie *The Murder of Fred Hampton*—how much respect he had for Fred. He had a tremendous impact on me personally at the time. Huey showed a person who *exemplified* the mind and the body—he had a developed body and a developed mind. He was a man of thought and a man of action.

But the cadre are dubious. They interrupt his PE class, looking to me for approval.

"These guys didn't even *know* Huey," remembers John Seale, with whom Huey talked when he came back.

They were wanting to take orders from you. Because you would go in and give an order, and these guys would follow the order to the T.

They never had made *contact* with Huey.

"David, well, what do you think?"

Asking you that.

It made Huey paranoid. He mentioned that when he came back. He said, "I didn't know what to expect down there. They're looking towards David, and I'm supposed to be in charge of the Party."

Huey thought, I guess, everybody should look to him too.

One of Huey's doctors, Tolbert Small, who sets up free medical clinics with the Party, also speaks to Huey about the problem.

"I got the feeling that he didn't like to have any strong male leadership around," he remembers. "I recall meeting with him once and saying, "You've got to have criticism and self-criticism, you can't just have a 'yes' organization." He agreed with me. He told me when he first got out of prison everybody on the Central Committee would listen to you and they wouldn't pay any attention to him. But now they were listening to him."

Even the Oakland cadre are disappointed with him.

"The day Huey came out, everybody was very excited," remembers Brenda.

The expectation was, "Just mess with us now! Our leader is back! We're gonna be a force to be reckoned with for real!" Although people felt more of a commitment to, say, Bobby, you, and June. But it was like, the Leader!—that's what Huey represented to a lot of folks. People really wanted to spend time with him, wanted to have him instruct the PE classes. Then the couple of times he did the PE sessions, he was talking about the dialectics, and a lot of people didn't understand what he was saying. I remember one example he gave. "How can two objects occupy the same space at the same time?" That was the question we were supposed to think about. The answer was, "Well, they can't, unless each takes on the characteristics of the other." But people were like, "Well, what is he talking about?" The looks on their faces. They couldn't grasp where he was coming from, or they had expected something different.

At the next Central Committee meeting Huey disregards Geronimo every time he speaks and criticizes the plan for a southern underground as stupid, counterproductive. When Geronimo defends the idea, Huey ignores him, then trashes his comments.

Afterward G. comes up to me. "What's wrong with the guy?"

"I don't know," I say. I can't repeat Huey's outlandish and insulting accusations to G. "He has this attitude."

Hoping Huey will change, I argue with him about G. whenever the chance arises.

"He's an agent," Huey tells me. "I've got information he's not working in the best interests of the Party."

Frustrated, divided in my loyalties between the comrades who worked to free Huey and Huey himself, I challenge him. Besides, I believe that Huey's really saying that he suspects me, questions my judgment.

"Okay, Huey, okay," I say. "I'll tell you what. I don't believe any of what you say and I will prove to you he's not."

I ask a psychiatrist who supports the Party to administer a sodium pentothal test. Then I go to Geronimo.

"A guy who I expelled from the Party got next to Huey's brother Walter, who was drinking wine down in Los Angeles," Geronimo recalls, and told Walter Newton — Sonny Man — that I never really expelled him, that he's still plugged into my underground, and I just gave word for him to kill Huey, so I could take over the Party. Plus, Huey had been told from various sources — which later turned out to be police — that I was very egotistical and wanted things centered on me, and organized all these infrastructures under the auspices of the Ministry of Defense, and that when he gets out of prison he should make sure that I turn over everything to him, otherwise I'm gonna pull a coup d'état, kill him, overthrow the Party, and call the shots. Especially because Eldridge Cleaver and I were so close and I was so well liked in the New York chapter, the Philadelphia chapter, and I had opened up most of the South. He was told I was training guerrillas in the mountains, in Santa Cruz — I've never been to Santa Cruz in my life! They said I was training guerrillas to break George Jackson out of prison, that I pulled the guys back from joining up with Jonathan in the breakout — which is a lie because I don't know nothing about that; Huey said he was advised not to involve himself and that he stopped it and, as a result, little Jonathan ended up going by himself to the Marin County thing — which Huey said surprised him — and that caused a whole sector of the movement to want to kill Huey! But then the rumor was put out that I had all this laid out. All this was a lie.

But I don't know any of this. So to allay their suspicions I volunteered to go through any kind of tests they would do.

I think the idea's foolproof. If Geronimo fails, Huey's right. But if G. passes and I know Geronimo's no agent; it pains me even to ask him to take the test — I can put an end to Huey's madness, his dismantling of everything we've created.

Myself, Emory, and June escort G. to the psychiatrist's house. G. sits there as we give him the shot, perfectly erect, round moon face, sparkling eyes. He answers all our questions about incidents and people without hesitation, talking in his Southern accent. Afterward the doctor pronounces the verdict: nothing G. has said would suggest he's an agent.

The proof frees me. Now I've got some tangible evidence to quiet Huey. And I'm sure Huey will listen to the results because I've always known Huey to act rationally in the end.

"The guy's a professional," he says.

We're talking in the penthouse; the place is only two bedrooms overlooking downtown Oakland but sounds grand, and we make it sound grander by calling it the Throne. Huey's hated the poster of him as a king; now it seems we all conspire to turn him into what he wishes most not to be.

"What do you mean?" I demand.

"He knows what he's doing. He was in the Army. They trained him about this stuff."

I'm stymied.Huey's acting like a district attorney; he's not going to let anything contradict his presuppositions.

But I can't abandon G. I play my last card. Let G. go south, set up the cadre; maybe when he's away I can work on Huey, get him to see the light.

"Okay," Huey relents. "But whatever happens, you're in charge of him. I don't want to have anything to do with this. It's on you. Whatever happens, you bear the responsibility."

Yet even at his worst, there remains something irresistible about Huey — a charm and sweetness even more magnetic than his logic.

"You two together made an interesting pair," remembers Brenda.

Huey would go on and on and on and on sometimes. All night, talking. You would go, "Okay, I'm going, Huey."

"No, man!! Wait a minute, wait a minute."

He wouldn't let you go. We'd be up standing at the door for hours.

I remember Huey coming over to the house. He'd be talking about something. He was very fast, always.

"You know, man —" and such.

And you'd be in bed.

Huey would take off his clothes and pull back the covers and lay down and you'd run everything right there from the bed. It was very funny. If somebody came in, they'd say, "Well, where's the Chief?"

"Oh, he's in the room."

"Okay." They'd come in. "Oh, hi."

And that's the way it would be for that day — business conducted in the bed.

I always thought Huey just didn't like to be alone.

The Constitutional Convention sharpens Huey's conviction that something's wrong in the Party.

The weekend before the convention, the Philadelphia police command a raid on the chapter offices; after a half hour of resistance — and wounding three cops — the members surrender. The police chief forces the male cadre to strip, parading them naked, gloating to the press he's caught the "big bad Black Panthers with their pants down."

The attack infuriates the fifteen thousand people who come to the conference and also scares the cadre into taking extra security precautions and conducting body frisks that delay the whole assembly and annoy the white left. Huey has prepared a major address. Michael Tabor, a New York Twenty-one member, precedes him. He and Richard Moore, "Dharuba," both out on bail, are the best-known defendants in the case. Huey's all right about some of the New York cadre—he likes Zayd Shakur, a small, tireless member who has dedicated himself to freeing his brother, Lumumba, and the others—but has problems with Tabor and Moore. Dharuba postures constantly, a "murdermouth." Tabor is too eager to please: when he visits us in Oakland he brings a gram of coke, New York's special drug, even though he's famous for a speech about his past drug addiction. (We publish the talk as a pamphlet, *Capitalism Plus Dope Equals Genocide,* advertising it on our back page with our full catalog of posters, buttons, books, and records.) Tabor styles himself as an Eldridge-type orator; his speeches are profane, wandering, provocative. "Power to the brothers and sisters who have taken to the rooftops," he says. Then he raises his hand, making the fist. "No more fists!" he thunders. "Now it's like this!" And he unfolds his fingers, turns them into a gun.

Huey follows. The crowd wants to love him—he's the star. But they don't understand anything of his treatise on American history: "The people of today stand waiting for a foundation of their own life, liberty, and pursuit of happiness. The civil rights movement has not produced this foundation, and it cannot produce this foundation because of the nature of the United States society and economy. . . . They have produced programs of welfare and unemployment compensation, programs with sufficient form to deceive the people but with insufficient substance to change the fundamental distribution of power and resources in this country." Huey's frustration with public speaking builds up. He's annoyed when he comes offstage and, increasing the tension, there's a security breach: his bodyguards have vanished.

"These people have no analytic sense," he tells me, referring to the crowd. "They're hung up on Eldridge's slogans and revolutionary talk. They're not used to analytic lecturing."

We walk around, waiting for security. I'm worried. The cops would like an incident with Huey Newton. Meanwhile strangers come up, asking Huey questions, starting conversations. We move away, but security still hasn't shown.

"By the time security arrives we'll have walked all the way to California," I say.

The joke isn't funny. We've got to do something.

A car drives up, the guy behind the wheel honking. "Where you going? Come with me!"

"Come on," I say to Huey. "Let's go with the people."

Huey regards the proposition dubiously, but joins me. The ecstatic driver turns out to be a Party member who takes us to his house, where he invites neighborhood friends and family. We eat and drink, talk to the people, laugh at how the bodyguards must be freaking out at our absence, forget about the bogus Constitutional Convention.

Two months later we hold the second meeting of the convention in DC. The weekend is a disaster. After promising Kathleen will come, Eldridge keeps her in Algeria; meanwhile Howard University backs out and refuses to give us space, and the only people who show up are already converted white movement types. In six months the massive popular appeal of the antiwar and radical movement has vanished. Kent State has scared away the thousands who last spring seemed ready to become revolutionaries.

Now the people who attend only want to promote their own programs. We're preaching armed struggle, while they're breaking off to form their own factions. In the past, conferences would attract new people. This is a scruffy-looking, mangy crew. They don't inspire confidence. I wouldn't want to join them.

Shortly afterward—the details of this nightmare run together and my time sense is vague—we go to New York. Tabor comes up to our hotel room with a beautiful young woman member of another Third World revolutionary organization.

Tabor behaves erratically, is uptight; then he departs, leaving the woman behind. Huey doesn't say a thing. But I know what he's thinking: the woman is to lure him off his guard so he can be killed. He starts enjoying the situation. Power is the ability to define a phenomenon and make it act in a desired manner, he says. Can he control this threat?

"There's something going on here," he tells me when we're momentarily alone. He's hyped, the danger revving his energy.

"I don't know, Huey," I say.

The woman comes back in the room. Huey gets in the bed with her, fooling around.

I'm tired as hell. "Huey, run that woman out. I want to get some sleep, man."

"No, just come on, get in the bed."

"I don't want to get in the bed. I want to go to sleep."

But Huey's made up his mind.

I trudge back inside, grab a blanket and some pillows.

"I'm going to sleep," I say and settle myself in the bathtub, locking the door, stuffing the pillow right under the faucets.

Besides, I can't handle any more sexual complications in my life. Huey's skepticism about my agreement with Pat has haunted me. One night I'm tested. Pat stays at the Throne—she's still working as the Party's Financial Secretary—later than usual.

"What are you worrying about Pat for?" Brenda asks.

"She should be back," I say.

Brenda and I discuss that I'm not truly ready to share Pat, and I call.

Pat remembers it differently.

"Brenda was over at *my* house, and I was over at Huey's," she recalls.

Him and you got on the phone and said that Brenda was over there. You set this up—I found that out afterwards—to see if I would stay there with Huey.

Huey said, "You know, you shouldn't go over there with David because you're gonna get to fighting and acting a fool."

I said, "No. I won't."

We talked and talked and talked. And drank.

He said, "Where are you going?"

I said, "I'm going to call David and tell him I'm not coming home."

He said, "Well, just don't call him."

I said, "No, I got to call him and *report*."

He said, "What'd David say?"

I said, "I'll stay over."

So I stayed over there with him.

I came home the next morning, and you and I had one of them *long* talks. I don't even know what it was about. But it was kind of hurting to me, because it's always like I have to share you. Because you're the baby of the family.

Even after all my intellectual and emotional preparation, when Pat tells me her choice, I feel empty inside, robbed. The image of her being with someone else—even Huey—torments me. The feeling's intensity amazes me. I love Brenda. Yet she's not part of me like Pat. In my loss and hurt I want to cling to her, hurt her.

But I can't simply do what's best for me. My behavior will set an example for the Party. As leadership I must seize this opportunity and show the cadre that the Party's seriously committed to sexual equality and both men and women can have more than one lover if they want. I remember Huey's admonition. Violence or love? Love can keep this together. And that's what ultimately matters above everything else—keeping ourselves together as a unit, alive, bonded. Pat and I make love.

Chapter

26

HUEY'S suspicions prove to be right. The tension grows between him and Eldridge.

The FBI sees the conflict as an opportunity. After the Constitutional Convention fiasco in Washington, the Los Angeles bureau writes to FBI national headquarters suggesting they send a fake letter to Eldridge intending to "provoke Cleaver to openly question Newton's leadership. . . . It is felt that distance and lack of personal contact between Newton and Cleaver do offer a counterintelligence opportunity that should be probed." The LA bureau also suggests "that each division which had individuals attend the [Revolutionary People's Constitutional Convention] write numerous letters to Cleaver criticizing Newton for his lack of leadership. It is felt that if Cleaver received a sufficient number of complaints regarding Newton it might . . . create dissension that later could be more fully exploited."

Through the winter the FBI men continue their subtle warfare. Playing on our every weakness, their manipulation, in conjunction with the legal and military attacks we have sustained, succeeds in magnifying Huey's insecurity, Eldridge's impetuous egoism, the Party's own confusion. Their massive campaign—we are targets of 233 of the 295 FBI counterintelligence program authorized "black nationalist" actions, and that does not include infiltrators and provocateurs working for local police or Red squads—destroys the foundation of our strength: our mutual trust and respect.

*   *   *

317

In Alabama, G.'s underground unit self-destructs. The guys call, complaining they need money, they're bored, they're in trouble. They have stupid shoot-outs, lack any self-discipline, and Geronimo can't control them. We create a telephone tree to avoid speaking to them on the bugged Central HQ lines. They use the wrong numbers anyway, saying adventuristic, incriminating things. Even when we chastise them, they continue in their unrestrained ways. In early December the police capture Geronimo in Dallas and transport him to Los Angeles for a murder trial.

Huey's limitations as a leader—his shyness, his passion for abstract ideas—become more apparent. He suspects the Party members don't respect him. He's adamant in his support of Bobby and Ericka and the other New Haven defendants, and critical of the Constitutional Convention for distracting people's attention from the upcoming trial. He's also unhappy that members seem confused about the roles of Party leadership. "They think the Chairman is more important than I am," he says.

Rush and I try to deal with the problem. From my reading of Kim Il Sung, I propose we call Huey the Supreme Commander. Then we think the title too militarist; we rename him the Supreme Servant.

Rush buys Huey a swagger stick.

"I remember going to the military store and buying him that swagger stick," he says. "I bought it as symbolic of the fact that he was the 'Supreme Servant,' or the 'Supreme Commander.' I bought it out of respect. Totally out of respect. I had a lot of love and respect for those guys."

We contribute to his glorification in the paper. One centerfold contains a picture of Huey sitting in a chair like a king, shafts of light radiating around his head. "Let Us Hold High the Banner of Revolutionary Intercommunalism and the Invincible Thoughts of Huey P. Newton, Minister of Defense of the Black Panther Party and Supreme Servant of the People," ends an article.

But the outside movement—white and black—remains largely unsympathetic to him, interpreting everything about him from the most critical point of view. The FBI leaks the penthouse's address and monthly rent to a *San Francisco Examiner* reporter, and we must waste time explaining to the movement the rationale for the expense and Huey's new title.

He also lacks any rapport with crowds. Huey bores them. They come to be awed and end up angry.

"You have a mistaken idea about intellectuals," Huey explains to me in his frustration. "They do not know how to think. They know facts, but they don't know how to think. They don't understand concepts. But I'm relaxed with concepts. That's why I talk so long. Because it's hard to reduce very complex concepts to simplifications."

People are also impatient and dismissive of Huey's new theory. In prison, Huey has developed an analysis of the present political moment. Nation-states, he argues, are things of the past. Nationalist struggles, even revolutionary ones, are beside the point. Capital dominates the world; ignoring borders, international finance has transformed the world into communities rather than nations. Some of these communities are under siege—like Vietnam—and others conduct the siege, like the United States Government. The people of the world are united in their desire to run their own communities: the black people in Oakland and the Vietnamese. We need to band together as communities, create a revolutionary intercommunalism that will resist capital's reactionary intercommunalism. The idea certainly describes political reality better than anything else. (And nothing that's happened since changes my judgment. Oakland is an intercommunal city—you can't figure out the ethnic origins of its young people—and capitalism has now pervaded every part of the world. My brother-in-law Paul, in Mobile, lives in a farmhouse that reminds him of his family home; but he buys Korean-made cellular phones and considers himself a gourmet of the Cajun cooking which Paul Prudhomme has marketed into a new international taste treat.)

The new idea further confuses Party members.

"When we were putting the articles and the editorials in the paper, people would say, 'Well, what does this mean?' and, 'Why are we doing this?'" remembers Brenda. "Then there would be discussion of it at the PE classes. After, people were going, 'Oh, okay.' Because just off the top, they didn't relate. A lot of people were very nationalistic in coming to the Party; some of them were black *only.* They didn't *see* it as being a part of a big picture."

The left also reacts defensively to the new idea.

"You guys aren't very consistent," they say. "First you're nationalists. Then you're internationalists. Now you're intercommunalists."

"So what?" we say. "That means we embrace change. We examine ourselves and correct our mode of thought."

"Well this isn't what Marx says," they answer.

"Well we're not Marxists," we answer. "We are dialectical materialists, and if that means that we come up with different answers than Marx, we're all right with that, because Marx wasn't a Marxist either—he was a dialectical materialist too."

Something else fuels the left's criticism of Huey. They like us picking up guns and shooting it out with the pigs. But they don't want us as theoretical leaders. Certainly their response is as uncomradely as possible. Seeing a movement fragmented into gay groups, women's groups, Third World groups, et cetera, Huey proposes a general theory to define this phenomenon and channel its energy. The movement replies by telling him he's boring and irrelevant.

Simultaneously the FBI goes into high gear. They forge letters from Connie Matthews, Huey's personal secretary: "We must either get rid of the Supreme Commander," one ends, "or get rid of the disloyal members." Another, purportedly written by a member of the Young Lords, the radical Hispanic group, attacks Eldridge's weak point: "Your talk is nice, but your ideas and action is nothing. You are gone, those you left behind . . . are afraid to even come out among the people. The oppressed of Amerikkka cannot wait. We must move without you." Alerted to the plan's success by informants, the FBI national headquarters encourages the local offices to press harder: "The present chaotic situation within the BPP must be exploited. . . . You should each give this matter priority attention and immediately furnish Bureau recommendations . . . designed to further aggravate the dissention with BPP leadership and to fan the apparent distrust by Newton of anyone who questions his wishes."

It's after the New Year, 1971. In a stupid letter, the New York Twenty-one criticize Huey, naming Weathermen the vanguard. The Central Committee thereupon expels the Twenty-one and Geronimo from the Party. I don't care about the Twenty-one—I'm relieved to see them gone—but I'm loyal to Geronimo.

"I won't do that," I tell Huey when he requests I write the expulsion letter. "I'll go along with the decision but I won't write the letter."

Elaine Brown—now a member of the Central Committee—does.

Soon after, Huey, Rush, and I go to New Haven, where Don Freed has arranged a week-long seminar between Huey and Erik Erikson, the famous psychologist and philosopher. The trip starts badly when Huey speaks in Boston about intercommunalism. "We see very little difference in what happens to a community here in North America and what happens to a community in Vietnam," Huey says.

We see very little difference in what happens to a Black community in Harlem and a Black community in South Africa. . . . What has happened is that the non-state has already been accomplished, but it is reactionary. . . . I mentioned earlier the "negation of the negation." I mentioned earlier the necessity for the redistribution of wealth. We think it is very important to know that as things are in the world today socialism in the United Sates will never exist. Why? It will not exist because it cannot exist. It cannot at this time exist anyplace in the world. Socialism would require a socialist state, and if a state does not exist how could socialism exist? So how do we define certain progressive countries such as the People's Republic of China? We say: they represent the people's liberated territory. But that community is . . . only the groundwork and preparation for the liberation of the world — seizing the wealth from the ruling clique, equal distribution and proportional representation in an intercommunal framework . . . [because] in order for a revolution to occur in the United States you would have to have a redistribution of wealth not on a national or an international but an intercommunal basis.

"He said some really good things in that speech," Marty Kenner remembers. "One thing he said is you have to share first assumptions with someone to even argue with them. But he also was so academic — Huey had a desperate need to show he was more complex than the poster image. I remember Stew Albert's comment: 'Right on, and on, and on, and on.'"

Frances Carter has a similar memory. "I wanted to find out what intercommunalism meant," she says.

Huey did this big dissertation on it at one of the colleges. It was too much for the average community member, and the average Party member couldn't internalize it, so how could we explain it to the community? When we started talking they wanted to hear about the Oakland shoot-out and that kind of stuff, and were kind of disappointed when they didn't. Intercommunalism was fine for Erik Erikson or the Yale students, but not for the grass-roots community. You couldn't present it to them that way at that particular time.

Huey leaves completely frustrated; he has spent a lot of time organizing this speech.

"I don't want to make public speeches," he says. "I can't do this. It's not what I do. Bobby's going to have to. I can't."

He decides we must set up an Ideological Institute, where he can articulate and expound on his vision of the Party, a place where Panthers can be steeped in understanding not what to think, but how to think.

"You were saying something a while ago about the problem of simplifying your ideology for the masses," a student asks him at the start of his week-long seminar with Erikson. "Could you say a little more about it?"

"Yes," Huey answers. We sit in a book-lined room, Huey and Erikson on opposite sides of a wide library table, Huey matching this world-renowned

German intellectual moment-for-moment in their discussion. "That's our burden. So far I haven't been able to do it well enough to keep from being booed off the stage, but we're learning."

The scene at Yale is very tense.

"Everything was paranoid, stressful," remembers Marty, "people running around, lots of whispered conversations. Huey was surrounded by bodyguards who wanted to kill him, in front of an audience which wasn't necessarily friendly. A nightmare: he's speaking about intercommunalism and psychology with Erikson in the seminar room while outside there are all these subplots swirling around him."

The last night of the seminar Connie Matthews disappears with Tabor and Dharuba. Matthews takes some of Huey's personal documents; the disappearance of the two members of the New York Twenty-one puts at risk the other defendants in the trial—no one can get bail now. We brand the three "Enemies of the People," denouncing them on the cover of the newspaper. Zayd Shakur tries to make peace, but another round of FBI activity sabotages any possibility of reconciliation. "This dissension coupled with financial difficulties offers an exceptional opportunity to further disrupt, aggravate and possibly neutralize this organization through counterintelligence," FBI headquarters writes to twenty-nine field offices at the start of February. "In light of above developments this program has been intensified . . . and selected offices should . . . increase measurably the pressure on the BPP and its followers."

Eldridge receives a forged letter from the New York Twenty-one criticizing Huey.

Melvin gets a letter warning that Eldridge and members of the New York group plan to kill him; he tells Huey the letter must be from someone "inside" because the note contains so much specific information.

At the same time D.C.—staying with Eldridge in Algeria—has a letter sent to him warning Eldridge not to let Kathleen come and work with us in America because we might hurt her.

"I can't risk a call," reads a letter to Eldridge sent under the signature of Big Man, "as it would mean certain expulsion. You should think a great deal before sending Kathleen. If I could talk to you I could tell you why I don't think you should."

By the end of February, the San Francisco FBI office reports, "fortunes of the BPP are at a low ebb. . . . Newton is positive there is an informant in Headquarters. Cleaver feels isolated in Algeria and out of contact with Newton. . . ."

Meanwhile we're organizing for an Intercommunal Day of Solidarity to be held in Oakland for Bobby and Ericka and the political prisoners charged with the Jonathan Jackson shoot-out. The voir dire in Bobby and Ericka's trial—the longest one ever—is almost over. Sams has turned state's evidence. What Garry must prove is that Sams, not the Party, is responsible for the killing. We have arranged with Eldridge that the Oakland rally will start a nationwide speaking tour for Kathleen. But a few days before the rally, Eldridge tells Huey Kathleen won't come. Huey argues with him. Kathleen's the focus of the political defense campaign for the New Haven trial, he tells him: it's sabotage if she stays away.

Eldridge stonewalls, like April 6, never answering me. He's got his plan. He does promise to join us live on a local television show, "AM San Francisco," talking to us from Algeria as we appear in the studio.

He uses the opportunity to start his war. Live, over the air, Eldridge says I and June should be expelled because we've taken the Party down the wrong road.

Huey refuses to conduct the Party's business in public. But as soon as we're off the air, he goes to a phone.

"You dropped a bombshell this morning," Huey says.

"I hope so," Eldridge answers.

"Well, it was very embarrassing for me," says Huey.

Eldridge thinks he has the upper hand. "Well, it had to be dealt with."

"Well, I have to deal with it too because I think it was unfair because when you say things like that it should be to the Central Committee and discussed openly and not outside, you know?"

Still cool, Eldridge starts to answer why he chose another way. He's misread Huey entirely; no one who grew up with Huey would ever commit Eldridge's miscalculation.

"Hello," Huey interrupts. "You listening? The Intercommunal Section is expelled."

"Right on," says Eldridge.

But Eldridge is clearly stunned by the decision. "If that's what you want to do, brother. But look here, I don't think you should take such actions like that."

But this is a fight; Huey loves fights. "As far as I'm concerned you can go to hell, brother."

"Say, Huey—"

"I'm going to write the Koreans, the Chinese, and the Algerians and tell them to kick you out of our embassy."

"Say, Huey—"

"And to put you in jail. You're a maniac, brother."

"Say, Huey —"

"Like Timothy Leary. I think you're full of acid this morning."

"I think you should slow down, brother, because that's not going to work."

"Well, I think it will. . . . You know I'd like a battle, brother. We'll battle it out."

"Say, Huey, that's not the best way to deal with it."

"We'll battle like two bulls; we'll lock horns . . . but I think I've got the guns."

"I got some guns too, brother."

"All right. You put yours to work and I'll put mine. But I'm not a coward like you, brother, because you ran off and got Li'l Bobby Hutton killed and I stayed here to face the gas. But you're a coward because you didn't attack me this morning, you attacked the Chief. You attacked him but you wanted to say my name. So you're a coward, you're a punk, you understand?"

"Say, Huey —"

"You're a punk!"

"I think you've lost your ability to reason," Eldridge goes. He's desperate now.

"Hey, brother," shouts Huey. He wants the fight to begin immediately. "You heard what I called you and that's what I feel about you now. You're a punk!"

"I wouldn't call you that," Eldridge starts.

But Huey hangs up.

Immediately after, Huey and I are scheduled to go to Boston to meet with Bernadette Devlin, a leader of the Northern Ireland independence struggle; she wants to demonstrate solidarity with us.

"My cousin Betty and I were dispatched to pick up Devlin," Marty remembers.

Inexplicably the car doesn't start. I pick up the hood and there's a foreign device inside. I took it out and got the car started. Later someone said it was a timing device for a bomb. I always felt it was put there to scare us — the trouble with me in those days was that my adrenaline talked louder than my fear.

There were lots of bizarre scenes during that period. Escaping from Yale after the New York people had split and denounced you and Huey, keeping out of sight for a few days at the suburban home of Warren Bishop, an eccentric stockbroker who had bankrolled part of the New

York left with his picks in horse races. I remember the contrast between you and Huey. You were quiet and withdrawn. Huey had never seemed more relaxed—he was freed from a Party he didn't feel comfortable with and eager for a battle with Eldridge.

For the next month I spent a lot of time driving around with you and Huey. Huey was thinking out loud. The Party had taken a wrong turn, he was saying. The original idea of the guns was to embed the Party in the community and protect the community. But the result was to emphasize the gun and isolate the Party from the community, concentrating all Party resources into getting comrades out of jail and legal defense work. He kept saying how some of the Party's best comrades had been gunned down by the police—Bunchy, Fred Hampton. And the guns had also just brought fear into the community—people were scared that a Party branch would bring a gunfight with the police. Plus, the guns drew a certain kind of person to the Party, reemphasizing the military aspect among the cadre. And finally we weren't winning the gunfights. For every shootout like Los Angeles where the Panthers resisted pigs, we had ten instances where the offices were destroyed—they were even destroyed in Los Angeles.

So from a political and military point of view Huey thought the Party had to change. You never said much then. But in retrospect I can imagine your feelings: the Party you had worked so hard to build was falling apart and turning in on itself.

The New York and New Jersey chapters declare allegiance to Eldridge. At the office we get calls—"You'd better not come outside. We've got a bullet for you." We're not worried about the East Coast; neither chapter represents significant numbers. Then we get the information that a member of Eldridge's faction—Robert Webb, who came to the Party through D.C.—has been shot and killed in New York. A few days later members of Eldridge's clique capture, torture, and murder Sam Napier.

Marty—who has become close to Sam—comes out to Oakland for the funeral.

"Nothing ever shook me up in my political life as much as the murder of Sam Napier," Marty says.

I thought it was so unjust. Sam had never been involved in the military aspect of the Party. He only worked on distribution. He was defenseless and his murder was unspeakably brutal: he was caught unarmed and unprotected in the newspaper distribution office in Queens, tied to a bed, tortured, shot to death, then burned. The murder was fratricide. The assassins grabbed the two-year-old child Sam was taking care of in the office and literally threw him out the door, giving him lasting injuries, and two young neighborhood kids who happened to be in the office at the time were locked in a closet and left in the fire. Not long after, two members of the Twenty-one, Dharuba and Jamal Josephs, a teenager himself, were arrested and convicted for being part of the gang who killed Sam.

I rode with Huey in his car to the church for Sam's funeral. Huey was shook up in a way that I had never seen him. You were always surrounded by Party members — whenever you visited a city, you stayed up all night talking to them in their homes. Huey felt remote from many rank-and-file members. But not Sam. He felt loyalty and a closeness. He was really torn up — maudlin, depressed, distraught.

The FBI sends Eldridge a copy of the paper announcing his expulsion with an anonymous note: "This is what we think of punks and cowards." Then they forge a letter under my name that goes out to all the foreign solidarity committees. "You are advised," the fake letter reads, "that Eldridge Leroy Cleaver is a murderer and a punk without genitals. D.C. Cox is no better." Referring to Webb's shooting, they write, "Leroy's running dogs in New York have been righteously dealt with. Anyone giving any aid or comfort to Cleaver and his jackanapes will be similarly dealt with no matter where they may be located."

Shortly after, the FBI declares its program a success. "Since the differences between Newton and Cleaver now appear to be irreconcilable, no further counterintelligence activity in this regard will be undertaken at this time and now new targets must be established. David Hilliard and Elbert 'Big Man' Howard of National Headquarters and Bob Rush of Chicago BPP Chapter are likely future targets. Hilliard's key position at National Headquarters makes him an outstanding target. Howard and Rush are also key Panther functionaries.... San Francisco and Chicago furnish the Bureau their comments and recommendations concerning counterintelligence activity designed to cause Newton to expel Hilliard, Howard and Rush."

Huey proceeds with his plans: we will centralize the Party in Oakland and train everyone at the Ideological Institute.

"Most people in Chicago didn't want to go there, because they were pretty practical folks," says Rush.

I didn't force anybody to go out there, and most people began to look at other options. They were beginning to get kind of tired of what was going on. We had created something in this city. Now they began to resent things: I remember when I sent our bus and the printing press we had acquired out to Oakland. Plus, we weren't getting the kinds of community support we had been used to. The local congressman was taking the issue of police brutality and getting all kinds of responses from that. People just wanted to move on, wanted to do something. So they said, "Rather than go out to Oakland, we're just gonna disband. We're just gonna leave." One by one they began to peter out. We could have rebuilt the chapter here. But I didn't. A lot of Huey's actions . . . you know, were becoming more and more disheartening.

At first I share this feeling. I resist Huey. But he wins me over with his argument. He has a vision of change. We must take charge of the institutions of the community, he says. We'll use Oakland as a base. He sees the Party becoming a political machine, like Daley's in Chicago, a force to be reckoned with so that anybody who wants to have power will have to come to us. He's not interested in actually holding office, but in representing the needs of the people. Plus, he's doing what I've always wanted and never gotten from Eldridge: giving us the means to think. Party members are proud. We're listening to Huey, who is a peerless intellectual force; even Masai can't challenge him in debate. He's not simply handing us conclusions, but providing us with an ideology, concepts for long-term protracted struggle, an analysis of revolution:

> We recognize that the political machine in America has consistently required Black people to support it through paying taxes and fighting in wars, but that same machine consistently refuses to serve the interests of the Black community. One of the problems is that the community does not have a structure, organization or vehicle which serves its needs and represents the people's interest. You can no more have effective politics without a structured organization than you can have a man without his shadow. Oppressed Black people—*the lumpen proletariat*—did not have a structured organization to represent their true interests until the Black Panther Party. . . . A truly revolutionary vehicle . . . is made up of a number of characteristics: . . . a small, but dedicated cadre of workers . . . a distinct organized structure through which the cadre can function . . . revolutionary concepts which define and interpret phenomena, and establish the goals toward which the political

vehicle will work. . . . The political vehicle of the people must be guided by a consistent ideology which represents nothing more than a systematic and organized set of principles for analyzing and interpreting objective phenomena. An ideology can only be accepted as valid if it delivers a true understanding of the phenomena which affect the lives of the people. . . . The Black Panther Party was born in a period of stress. . . . We dared to believe that we could offer the community a permanent political vehicle which would serve their needs and advocate their interests. We have met many foes; we have seen many enemies. We have been slandered, kidnapped, gagged, jailed and murdered. We know now, more than ever before, that the will of the people is greater than the technology and repression of those who are against the interests of the people. Therefore we know that we can and will continue to serve and educate the people.

Listening to Huey, we don't mind that we're smaller; we believe we're stronger, that we have shown the left you can survive turmoil and contradiction and once again demonstrated our resiliency and leadership—a leadership that's together for the first time ever because in May Bobby and Ericka are finally found innocent.

"We were dancing in the streets," remembers Frances. "Even the jurors. Everybody was out!"

Then the charges from April 6 return. Because the case has already been dismissed once, I don't take the retrial seriously. The prosecutor is known as the "Panther District Attorney," building a reputation with his conservative politics and aggressive courtroom tactics. Still there's no new evidence; he has managed to get convictions for three other defendants from the shootout, but I figure we'll be able to turn the trial around, use the courtroom to unmask him as a legal vigilante.

Even if I do some time, Huey tells me not to worry, a short prison stint will be good. The police confrontations are behind us. I'm due a rest. I'll build myself up, return to my family; things will be fine.

"You should stay home," he says, "I'll take over from here."

"What are you talking about," I answer. "I work! I need to work. To go to the office and do stuff!"

"You need to rest," he assures me.

"I don't," I answer. "I need to work and be at the helm administering the Party. Don't tell me to take a rest."

But a gap has opened between us. I've always been impatient with cadre who complain Huey doesn't spend enough time talking to them. Contrary to, say, myself, or June, Huey has no gift relating to people; he's a brilliant theoretician and leader and should exert his energies in those fields.

But now I begin to feel some distance from him.

Huey continues to protest against people idolizing him—making him the object of our own cult of personality—yet does everything possible to centralize power in his hands, corralling the Party into Oakland.

Plus, his relationship with James Carr also makes me wonder. Jackal Dog is outside the Party, not subject to discipline. He and Huey have their own thing going. One day Jimmy asks me for some money for ammunition and a reloader—we manufacture our own bullets in the Peralta Street basement that we have converted into an arsenal, including a shooting gallery.

I don't even think about giving Jimmy the money; he's with Huey, so of course I give it to him.

Later Huey reprimands me. "Why'd you give him the money?"

I'm taken aback. We don't hold out on one another in the Party and I certainly haven't been told to treat Jimmy differently. "He's in the Party—"

"Don't do that!" he says. "I need to know everything. I deal with Jackal Dog."

I become suspicious: Why does Huey want his own security?

Besides Jackal Dog acts vaguely threatening. "We're building a squad, man," he tells me as we drive around. "No one will match us." During the defection, I get calls at my house. "Hilliard, I'm gonna mash you like a potato." I recognize Jackal Dog's voice, expressions.

"Well come on, then," I say. "I'll be standing outside in ten minutes. You and me. Come on." He never does.

Huey insists I've got things wrong.

"Just stay out of it. It's not your business."

The trial begins. I've thought that Garry will represent me, but a couple of weeks before the trial, Garry says Bobby needs him to finish off charges from Chicago and that Vincent Hallinan will be my lawyer.

Hallinan is a revered name in left-wing circles; he ran for president on the Progressive Party ticket in 1952. But the choice leaves me apprehensive. Hallinan's old and used to a politics different from ours; his wife is very bourgeois, minks and jewelry, hair done every week—when I see her, I think that if she were holding a cup and you walked by, she would automatically give it to you to take to the kitchen. Elsa Knight Thompson, the woman who shares an apartment with Alex Hoffmann, also dresses finely and comes from Mrs. Hallinan's generation. But I never feel Elsa considers herself su-

perior; she's a comrade, devoted to the working class, and a journalist: she
wants to find out what's happening, what the story is. The Hallinans don't
have any curiosity, but seem arrogant and snobbish. When Pat and I take
them out, trying to acquaint them with the Party in the short time we have
available, educate them so that they'll understand us and the Party, they
don't click with us. I sense that they believe us to be simple and don't feel
good about the situation at all: I want someone else to represent me, but
Charlie assures me Hallinan is able, will give me ample representation.

I agree reluctantly.

The trial is a disaster.

The district attorney, as a peremptory challenge, is able to secure an all-
white jury. Then Hallinan can barely make a case. He issues no objections to
the prosecutor's theatrics. Hoping to terrify the jurors, the DA drags in a bin
of guns, lifts up an assault rifle called a Trooper, and claims its mine. I look
at Hallinan to object; he's quiet. Over and over again I wait for Hallinan to
fight, and he never does.

Then he calls me as a witness. I don't want to be on the stand. What can I
testify to? I have no idea what the DA knows. Holding up a map of the
streets around the shoot-out, Hallinan asks me questions. I don't want to answer; any statements I might make can only lead to the DA asking more
questions. I'm frustrated and furious, try to dodge his questions, act confused. Plus, I haven't told Hallinan the truth about April 6 anyway because I
don't trust him sufficiently; he's not Charles. My evasive answers make me
look stupid and deceptive to the jury. Hallinan gets mad and insistent, pressing me further. The more I try to elude his questions, the more persistent he
becomes. His strategy is absolutely indefensible, but he ends up blaming me
for my testimony. In a later statement he says:

> While my acquaintance with David Hilliard has been of short dura-
> tion, I believe I have learned enough of him to give a reasonable esti-
> mate of his character. In the first place, he is a much more limited man
> than I had gathered from the few talks I had with him. This should not
> be surprising in view of his birth and childhood in the repressive at-
> mosphere of a southern state, his early marriage . . . and the generally
> neurotic pattern which seems endemic in poor black males. . . . This
> last quality had a disastrous consequence on the trial of the case, since,
> confronted by a jury while on the witness stand, he "blew up," was un-
> able to understand a simple street map [and] . . . this neurotic disposi-
> tion is further attested to by the fact that he was suffering from gastric
> ulcers. In my opinion he is a man easily influenced by those whom he

admires. Apparently this led him into a philosophy of violence . . . when the Black Panther Party seemed committed to a violent solution of the enormously crushing problems of Black Americans. . . . Apparently in the absence of Huey Newton and Bobby Seale, the local branch fell under the domination of Eldridge Cleaver, whose conduct and statements can be described as little less than psychotic.

Plus, Party support is negligible. The Party launches a David Hilliard Free Shoes program to publicize the case, but there are no posters, banners, demonstrations. Huey doesn't attend the legal proceedings.

"When you were going to trial, Huey would never go to court," June remembers.

> Everybody in the Party was asking why Huey wasn't going to court, why he wasn't supporting you when you and the rest of the Party membership had supported Huey when he was in jail. But when you asked Huey these questions he would say that he couldn't go because he wasn't allowed to and that it wasn't in your best interests for him to be there. That kind of a thing. By him being the leader of the Party, I at first accepted his analysis.
>
> Then I saw less and less Party members being allowed to go support you. They were being sent out into the community on a daily basis to raise funds and to sell newspapers, instead of packing the courtroom. I started thinking and noticing the difference between the way you were being treated when your trial was going on and the way Huey and Bobby were treated when their trials were going on. In the back of my mind I started wondering, "Something's happening here that I'm not aware of."

Marty is also shocked.

"I came out to Oakland during your trial," he says.

> At the time my role in the Party was changing. Defense had gone the way of confrontations with the police—one of the reasons why your trial was a kind of anachronism. My new task was going to be finding new sources of revenue—Huey wanted the Party to turn to business to finance its survival programs, and I was going to work on book deals, speaking engagements, and other commercial ventures that would earn money for buying or renting space for health clinics, schools, and other programs.
>
> While in Oakland, I went to the trial. I had never taken your case that seriously. I had never really thought of you having a real problem. Then I went to the trial. I saw you had this lawyer who was not up to the fight. I

couldn't believe what was going on. I got very angry. And the other thing that impressed me was how depressed you were.

I said, "David you've got to fight back!"

I went to Huey. He was funny about the whole thing. He had a lack of concern. He was off on his trip, involved in a different world, talking to a new coterie of intellectuals and some Hollywood types. The scene up there seemed so removed from Party life and reality. Things were disintegrating. It was a sad and disorienting time.

I don't complain. I won't change Huey's mind. And maybe jail is a good way to disengage myself from the Party. Plus, I feel in the pull of something large and incomprehensible. Huey's behavior mystifies me. His rejection is so difficult to accept that I overlook it, imagine reasons and explanations, waiting for things to change. The possibility of spending real time in jail, long time, never sinks in. Anyway, I have no more fight in me. I'm used up. Life seems dreamlike, foreordained. Several days before the verdict, Brenda stays overnight at Huey's; later she tells me he seemed so alone. The sentence is indeterminate, six months to ten years. While I'm still in the county jail the kids from the Party school come to visit. Patrice is first. She sits on the other side of the glass screen. You speak and put your ear to the window to hear. She has Pat's long, beguiling face, but her eyes seem resigned, angry, bewildered. Of all our kids, she's been the least happy at the school. She's wanted to live a quieter, more stable life; now I'm off to jail.

"I don't want to leave you here," she says. "I want you to come with me."

I tell her I'll be home soon.

"I love you, Daddy," she says to the glass.

I nod, tell her everything will be all right.

The rest of the Party kids must say hello and time's up: they're ready to take me to prison.

Part

THREE

Chapter

27

NOW I've got only two priorities:

How do I survive?

How do I get out?

I can't fool myself. I'm in a new world here, run by its own rules and rulers. Unless I get some power over the situation—define the phenomenon and make it act in a desired fashion—I'm at risk: prison has a way of pulling you in. Every time you enter jail you run the chance of never getting out. Huey's release is the exception—one reason his case is historic. I'm more keenly mindful of George Jackson's experience, an indeterminate sentence that now threatens to end in execution by the state.

The guards are my primary worry. These guys live under much more pressure than they're used to, never knowing if a rebellion will break out, scared for their own lives. I'm a black communist who threatened to murder Richard Nixon. I'm sure any number of these Hitler's helpers—as George calls them—would like to kill me.

And murder is only one form of death. A death by a thousand cuts is the administration's more probable plan for me, guards provoking me about petty stuff, getting me to react so they can write me up with a One Fifteen, entrapping me in a maze of reprimands, lockups, and disciplinary procedures that degrade and punish you and eventually add to your time. "Strip 'em," they order capriciously as you come back from the iron pile in the yard, and you've got to undress and spread your ass. Or you're returning from a visit feeling good, having momentarily escaped the oppressive prison world, only to find your cell completely torn up, letters from your wife strewn about, pictures on the floor, everything trashed—and not for any reason other than to remind you that your life is in their hands. Or the most dehumanizing thing of all, turning you into a number, not a name, not David Hilliard, but B35378.

Then there are the inmates. I feel solidarity with these guys, of course. They are aggressive, desperate people, quick to anger and slow to trust; many have spent years in solitary. I can't take anything for granted with them. Plus, I must keep away from "prison politics," from focusing on trivial privileges—fights in the television room between the Aryan Brotherhood and young blacks over whether to watch "Grand Ole Opry" or "Good Times," negotiations over packs of cigarettes—permitted by the authorities; pursuit of these symbols of power and status can turn casual exchanges into tests of loyalty and end with your life lost over a pack of Kools.

Finally there's a self-imposed pressure from my political commitment. As a Panther leader I must maintain a rigorous standard of conduct. Because of Huey, Eldridge, Bunchy, and George, inmates strongly identify the Party with revolutionary practice inside the prisons. We're one of the chief organizations to have addressed inmates, ideologically mobilizing them, endowing them with a sense of purpose, challenging the violence they use on one another and their acceptance of the brutal view of life—individualistic, competitive, racist—that underpins prison life. A Party chapter has even opened in San Quentin. As a leader I must set an example, even at the risk of putting myself in jeopardy.

So I must be strong. I must remember the authorities base their power on fear—fear of isolation, fear of losing your privileges—and that independence is my only equalizer to their domination. I must remind myself that privileges are a trap, isolation a good thing, not a bad one—you can use isolation to build yourself both physically and spiritually—and promise myself to avoid the corruption that comes from having nothing. I recall Huey's article, "Prison, Where Is Thy Victory?"

> The prison cannot gain a victory over the political prisoner because he has nothing to be rehabilitated from or to. He refuses to accept the legitimacy of the system and refuses to participate. To participate is to admit that the society is legitimate because of its exploitation of the oppressed. This is the idea which the political prisoner does not accept, this is the idea for which he has been imprisoned, and this is the reason he cannot cooperate with the system.

And my resolution must be even stronger because times have changed since Huey's incarceration. Then we were building a movement that centered around Huey's freedom. Now the Party's energy concentrates on survival programs and creating a political machine; freeing political prisoners has disappeared as a priority.

Emulating Huey's prison life is hard. Isolation probably suits Huey in a way—not that he enjoys solitary, but people put him uptight: he functions best when he can control his stimulation, concentrate on his thoughts, channel his energies.

"When Huey got out he was always on the go and moving with no time sense of day and night," remembers Alex Hoffmann. "I couldn't put that together with the way he was in prison. While he was in jail, especially in the Alameda County Jail, where I saw him regularly, he would go into some self-induced yogi state and come out calm and focused and you could talk to him for hours; he was warm, friendly, totally in control of what he was saying and doing."

But I miss outside stimulation, my friends, music, the Party's noise, life, and pressure. At night when I sleep—they give you sedatives; prisons are pill pushers—I feel doomed. The despair-ridden life of prison seems inescapable; loneliness—the impossibility of reaching out to Pat or Brenda, speaking to Marty or Huey, having a drink or killing an hour in a movie—overwhelms me. I'm in the Reception Guidance Center at Vacaville, a ninety-day psychological evaluation period, your introduction to the California prison system. Longing for companionship—I'm used to wrapping my arms around a woman's warm softness when I sleep—I wait for the drug to work. When I doze off, I'm on my back. In my sleep, I drift upward; around me the air thins. I float into a netherworld, without direction, substance, or texture. I try speaking, but make only inaudible sounds, try breathing, but gasp for oxygen. I know this place from other, past nightmares, but I always escape, woken by the person next to me. Who will wake me now? My isolation haunts my sleep, a new part of my bad dream, telling me I really will die, waft away, disappear. I force myself out of sleep, willfully breaking the tyranny of the unconscious.

Where am I?

Alone.

In the cell.

Me, David.

Am I sure?

Absolutely. I know from my stomach, my constant companion, that stabs me with pain. (The prison doctor—rumor says he has worked in South Africa—tells me to treat the ulcer with baking soda.)

I turn on my side; I know I can fall asleep in this position. A new thought scares me: I won't die, but Mother will and I'll never see her before getting out of here. The possibility terrifies me. You've got to overcome this, I tell myself. You must. I lie on my side; I sleep.

Outside, Huey proceeds with his plans for the Party to create a partly liberated community, an area to serve as an example for other black neighborhoods, in the same way the Oakland chapter provided a model for the other branches earlier on. While the Party has continued to serve the people, operating the school and institute, giving away bags of groceries, and using the paper—David Du Bois, the stepson of the great thinker and writer W. E. B. Du Bois, is now editing it—to educate the community, Huey has rechanneled the Party's direction, calling for an alliance between the Party and the church and black businesses.

"Black businesses which have the interests of the community at heart will be able to contribute to the people through the community programs of the Black Panther Party," he writes in August 1971.

> These free programs will help the community to survive and thus deter the genocide which is always a threat to our existence. . . . In return for these contributions the Black Panther Party will carry advertisements of these businesses in our paper and urge the community to support them. . . . In this way we will achieve a greater unity of the community of victims—the people who are victimized by the society in general, and the Black capitalists who are victimized by the corporate capitalist monopolies. . . . Through this new approach the Black capitalist will contribute to his own negation by helping to build a strong political vehicle which is guided by revolutionary concepts and serves as a vanguard for the people. . . . We will heighten the contradiction between the Black community and corporate capitalism, while at the same time reducing the contradiction between the Black capitalist and the Black community.

He even changes the Ten Point Program. "The words written in 1966 do ' not fully reflect the needs and desires of our people in 1971," announces a statement in the June 26 issue of the paper. "Therefore the platform and program has been temporarily removed from our paper, until such time when

Masai Hewitt

David at Vacaville prison

On leave from Vacaville, David and Pat with sons Darryl (*right*) and Dorion at Bud Hilliard's grave site

Tony Gibson at Vacaville

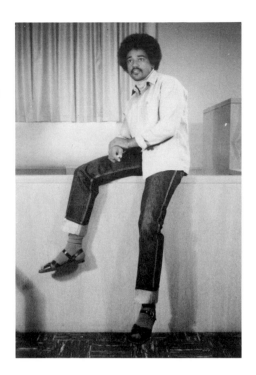

Tom Hayden, David, and comrade Josiah H. Chinamano at a Campaign for Economic Democracy benefit, 1975

David Hilliard, 1992

words can be arranged and organized into a program and platform which more accurately reflects and defines the present needs and desires of our people." (A year later the revised version appears, stressing our internationalism and broadening the demands.)

Huey hatches other visions.

"I had printouts of the elections in Emeryville," remembers Mickey Phillips, referring to a tiny consolidated village wedged between Oakland and Berkeley.

> I showed him where he could win the mayor's election with 600 to 800 votes and the city council with 200 to 300. I said, "Look, what we need to do is get all the troops and move 'em into Emeryville. I'll find apartments or whatever. We'll put fifty to a house, and we got the election."
>
> He said, "That's great! I'll put a tollbooth across the freeway, charge fifty cents for people to cross. Bobby'll be the mayor, David'll be the chief of police. We'll have our own community."
>
> Shortly thereafter a dump was filled over and a condo complex was built, pricing us right out of the market.

He also opens the Lamp Post, a nightclub he buys from his cousin with the eleven thousand dollars he requested from defense committee funds. He plans to establish the Party's own Bos'un Locker, a welcoming, neighborhood place. I listen to the stories, imagining the scene; the club's a dream come true for me, and not being able to join the future parties is one of my true disappointments.

The Lamp Post comes to symbolize a new influence guiding Huey: *The Godfather.* Before, we've used Cuba, Algeria, and China as examples of revolutionary struggle. Now Mario Puzo's novel provides the organizational map, a patriarchal family, divided into military and political wings.

Dr. Tolbert Small notices the new spirit. A community physician, he has provided crucial aid in our campaign against sickle-cell anemia, a genetic disease specific to blacks that has attracted little notice and almost no money: in 1967, volunteer organizations raised only one hundred thousand for research and treatment. After publicizing the disease in the paper, we have, with Small's help, established nine free testing clinics, publicizing the problem so successfully that Nixon himself mentions sickle-cell in that year's health message to Congress. "The thing I always remember about the

Party was, when I started the health clinic I'd come in and there would be some cadre reading the Red Book," Dr. Small says. "By the time I left the Party, I'd come in and the same cadre would be reading *The Godfather.*"

Huey's also using drugs, not only alcohol, but cocaine—and not in our previous, limited fashion.

"We acquired the Lamp Post," remembers June, who's working closely with Huey during this time.

> After, we started getting in contact with these guys that run the after-hours joints, trying to get them to contribute to the community programs. Every time we'd make the rounds they'd have big stacks of cocaine, and they knew who he was and everybody treated him with respect, so they'd just throw the stuff out to him. Huey started using the coke on a daily basis. Then he started coming down to the Lamp Post and had this upstairs office and started using it as a base for his getting high.

Meanwhile I'm analyzed by the prison authorities. Group therapy, individual counseling, Rorschach and IQ tests, a full battery. I go into the cubicles, say hello to the shrinks; self-analysis interests me, though I refuse the intelligence tests and Rorschach: the IQs are geared to white, middle-class people, and I don't want them using my interpretations of the pictures as an excuse for medicating me.

"How are you feeling?" one guy says. He acts in an aloof, reserved manner; the prison psychologists, like cops, each have their own style.

"Somewhat depressed," I say. I'm in jail; what does he expect? I feel like it's time to go home.

But he's not really interested in me, what I've done, the history that the Party has made. All he really wants is to prove I'm an outlaw. Any true regard for me is absolutely contrary to his function and sensibility. His job is simply to see me as a criminal and offer me a rehabilitation program that will repudiate everything I've done before coming to prison.

"How do you deal with that?" he asks.

"I'll read," I say. "Study. I can endure this."

"You strike me as a lonely person," he says.

"I am," I answer.

But these people don't respect honesty. Instead of trying to understand my thoughts and feelings, they interpret everything I say or do as manipulative.

"Hilliard has attended . . . regularly and been very verbal," states an evaluation of my group therapy. "Other inmates have been greatly impressed and it has been difficult to arouse any discussion or any difference of opinion. Those few inmates who do express or even question Hilliard are easily silenced by his fluency. If permitted to do so he will certainly dominate the group." The psychologist who administers the IQ writes, "[Hilliard's] refusal . . . is based upon philosophical reasons. It is felt, however, that the real reason for his failure to cooperate is his fear of failure." He dismisses my comments about my loneliness out of hand.

> Hilliard attributed his loneliness and restlessness to the situation in the world today . . . [explaining] that he could find little opportunity for rest or solace until people were no longer hungry and until men's minds were freed. . . . This . . . would make it appear that he entertains some rather masochistic, yet grandiose ideas about his own destiny. I get the impression that if he were not really suffering he would act in such a way as to invite it. He seems to have a need to make a martyr of himself, as though he wishes to become somebody famous but does not know how to go about becoming famous in any other way.

He responds to my candor with calculation:

> . . . perhaps [Hilliard] was rather lonely either on the basis that other Blacks would not want to associate with him and adversely affect their own reputations or on the basis that he simply is not as well known here and tends to blend in as just another inmate in contrast to his status in the community. . . . Possibly he then would have to rely more upon "establishment" members for emotional support . . . this would be something akin to the process which occurs in types of psychotherapy in which the individual is subjected to emotional or sensory deprivation initially and then receives emotional support from selected sources in order to modify attitudes and behavior.

The report's conclusion demonstrates the system's hypocrisy. Although the doctors find nothing pathological, nothing antisocial about me, they suggest I be put in D Quad, the section of the prison reserved for psychopaths and mass murderers. "Hilliard is simply not viewed as a menace to society," the doctor writes. "Nevertheless, he is recommended initially as a special designation case because of the interest of law enforcement agencies and the resulting publicity." Another doctor is even more to the point: "Subject does not appear as a serious management problem as long as he is not given an opportunity to organize and/or persuade impressionable Blacks to his anti-establishment philosophy." Any prospect for release is remote. "Inmate plans to return to work for the Black Panthers," the report states. "This seems unwise in view of his offense."

D Quad holds maybe a hundred of us. One Chinese man has murdered eight or nine family members. Another inmate thinks he's Michelangelo.

"I'm Michelangelo," he says every day.

Well, I'm from the South and used to dealing with mental cases and strange people; this man's no weirder than Waterhead or Crazy Mary. "Hey, Michelangelo," I answer, "how you doing?"

One day Smitty confronts me in the yard. He's a psyche commitment, a known murderer who's treated with Prolixin, a powerful sedative.

"The guards tell me you guys are racists," he says, "and that I can't join because I'm a Native American."

"That's absolutely untrue," I answer. "We're internationalists."

Other inmates stand around, watching. In prison your life's public, everyone watching how you handle yourself—me especially because of my high Party position.

"I'll prove to you we're not racists," I say. "This is my daughter. We identify with Native Americans."

I show him a snapshot of Dassine with her grandmother in Alaska; bundled up in a parka and furs, Dassine looks like a papoose.

Smitty stares at the photo. "You're not lying," Smitty says joyfully. "I want to be in the Panthers."

"Well," I say, "we can do that. I'll have Huey write a letter himself saying you can become a member of the Black Panther Party."

For the next week Smitty tells everyone he's joining the Party; the guards harass him, saying he's crazy, the Party's all black.

Meanwhile I press June to get Huey's letter; I don't want to disappoint Smitty and be bludgeoned to death at dinner.

Finally the proof appears signed with a flourish, "Servant of the People and Defense Minister of the Black Panther Party, So Let It Be Done." I hand Smitty his membership, go off to lift weights. A couple of minutes later I hear a ruckus break out.

"What's going on?"

"You'd better come, David. Smitty has a bat! He's chasing the guards around the quad, saying they lied and the Panthers aren't racists, and he's your bodyguard!"

Then my stay is cut short: George Jackson is killed. The San Quentin guards claim he tried to escape; lawyers and inmates say the guards assassinated him.

Three guards and two other inmates are dead. Two weeks later, on September 9, 1971, partly in response to George's murder, the prisoners in New York State's Attica rebel, holding forty guards hostage in exchange for their demands, including amnesty. After seven days of negotiation—at their request, Bobby appears at the prison—the national guard and state police seize the prison, killing thirty-nine people, including ten hostages.

Shortly after, the authorities transfer me. "It has come to my attention that this man has been enlisting both blacks and whites in the service of the Black Panthers, or so a number of grossly psychotic inmates have alleged," writes the prison psychiatrist. "He is in the process of rapidly creating chaos, increasing my hospital admissions, aggravating psychoses, upsetting unstable people. Insofar as I can ascertain he is not psychotic himself and has no place in D Quad. Please find him another home now."

That night, around nine, the guard comes up.

"Hilliard, roll 'em up."

I gather my clothes and belongings, march outside to a small bus with narrow seats, chicken-wire pressed into the windows so you can't see. We take off, five or six prisoners, two guards, one with a gun, driving through the California night.

"I'm going home!" one inmate repeats. He's ecstatic. "They said I was going home!"

"I don't know where we're going," another inmate answers. Then he indicates his worry: "They're not supposed to transfer prisoners at night."

We squeeze our knees into the small space in front, try to read road signs.

Our first stop is a jail for the criminally insane; once you're committed, you never get out.

The guard calls the guy who's going home.

"You told me you were taking me home," the guy protests. He starts crying as they push him out of the bus.

"I don't want to go here!" he screams. "No! I want to go home! I've been in prison thirteen years! I want to go home!"

Now we know we're being relocated, but no one knows where. The bus keeps driving.

Soledad—O Wing, where George and the other brothers were charged with the guard's death. We clank off the bus—we're all chained—and spend the night.

"Hilliard, roll 'em up."

Inside the bus my stomach tightens, twists on itself, burns and aches.

San Quentin—sheriffs and guards line up to view me as I clank down off the bus.

"Hilliard, roll 'em up."

Day dissolves into grayness, a foggy darkness, then black. The bus dips down, descending off the road into some tunnel, then up, out into a fake, strong white light.

"Come on, let's go."

We march out to a greeting party.

"Jesus, he's a little guy," one sheriff says. He holds an ax handle— their choice of weapon, stronger than a nightstick. "You look like a big guy in the paper."

I'm quiet. I'm not going to show any attitude. I've never seen it from outside, but I've arrived in my new home: Folsom.

The warehouse.

Drink water and walk slow, Eldridge and Bunchy used to say about the place:

Drink water because you never get enough food.

Walk slow because you have all the time in the world.

Chapter
28

NEXT day they start processing me. I quote from the psychologist's report:

It is to be noted in the psychological testing he refused to do most of it but the opinion of the Psychologist was that he was of low normal mentality. I would agree with this, although this man has very good use of language and he is rather glibe in his speech. However, upon analysis one sees that, like so many visionaries he deals in generalities. There is also a certain amount of grandiosity about this man and he throws psychological terms around rather freely. He is evidently one of the high members of the Black Panther Party and he describes of a seminar with Erickson at Harvard and Hucy Ncuton was also there and they spent an evening at Erickson's house. He describes the Black Panther Movement as a "process." It is quite evident that this man is very sincere in his devotion to helping the Black people, but it is not quite so clear how this goal is to be achieved. . . . He has somewhat of a lack of general information, for example, I pointed out to him certain things about the French revolution and he was not familiar with it at all. On mental examination, this man refused to subtract seven from one hundred and I do not know if he was able but at least he said mathematics was not to his liking. His memory is intact and he was able to name the last four Presidents in reverse order and his interpretation of the proverb, "People who live in glass houses should not throw stones" was rather concrete, in that he said the other people would throw the stones back and break the glass. Personality disorder, obsessive compulsive personality.

They put me in the Adjustment Center—a prison within a prison of five-by-seven, concrete-walled cells each supplied with a one-inch cotton mattress pad and toilet. Paper, pencils, and books are prohibited; *Christian Science Monitor*s and prison-approved books are the only reading material allowed. The food is shoved under the door. Visitors are almost impossible to clear. The side-by-side cells only allow you to talk out into emptiness, answering responses that come back from disembodied voices. You take your once-a-week shower in front of four guards armed with ax handles.

"Folsom Prison is made with piles of rocks," says Sandy Turner, a Quaker whom Huey recruits to serve as my spiritual adviser while I'm in prison, "and really looks like a dungeon in the middle of the English Channel or something out of *Les Misérables*. I never went there when it wasn't raining or foggy. It was a miserable, terrible place."

The only time out of your cell is one hour a day in the yard. My first week I'm eager to see who's in the general population; one guy here has actually written a poem about me called "The Chief."

It's only October, but the air here is already raw. Like the rest of the prison, the yard is concrete. The guards patrol from a catwalk, holding thirty-ought sixes.

Soon as I enter the recreation area, a skirmish erupts, guys tumbling on one another. The guards shout and shoulder their rifles; I can hear the triggers cock.

"Get back, Chief," a comrade yells.

"It's a setup!" someone else shouts.

A buddy grabs me, pulls me to the wall; someone steps in front of me. Everyone acts quickly and coolly; no one wants to give the guards an excuse to shoot.

"Break it up!" guys yell. "Break it up!"

"They want an excuse to fire," one guy tells me.

"I hope they don't fire off," my comrade says. "Once that bullet starts dancing off the concrete it never stops."

We stay hunkered down until everything returns to normal. When the hour's up, I walk back inside.

"Hey, Hilliard," a guard calls. "Next time we're gonna do you like we did George Jackson."

"Is that right?" I answer. "Well thank you very much. I appreciate that warning."

Next day, I stay locked up. I've learned my lesson: no halfway here, people play for life stakes.

"Just leave me alone and let me be," I tell the guard when he says I can go outside. "And by the way, my stomach is in serious trouble and I would appreciate it—"

The doctor will take care of it, they say.

The first few weeks are fine. I read what's permitted, do push-ups and sit-ups, sleep, get to know my two neighbors.

James Holliday is a longtime inmate, nicknamed "Doc," a member of the Businessmen, a Central Los Angeles gang Bunchy dealt with. Doc Holliday schools me in prison life, always telling me to keep my toilet clean.

"Why?" Cleaning the floor and toilet is one of the few ways I can maintain my pride of place, anyway—they allow you so few personal items in the cell—and I spend two hours daily swabbing down with the cleanser and rags they give me. But Doc's warning is directed toward something other than hygiene.

"I'll tell you when the time comes, Cool," he says. Cool's his nickname for me; I seem to be gaining respect from other inmates with my disciplined approach to doing time. "Just keep it clean."

On my other side bunks Raymond Scott. Raymond doesn't call me anything; Raymond doesn't speak: he communicates through messages.

The trustee walks by and puts a note through the bars. "From Raymond."

I open the folded paper and read the flowing, ornate letters: "Are you feeling okay today, comrade? This is from Raymond."

"I'm fine, Raymond," I say, speaking out to the open passage before me. Actually I'm extra fine because of his concern. "How are you? You okay?"

But Raymond doesn't answer. Doc tells me Raymond studies Yoga and practices a severe spiritual discipline. Not only doesn't he speak, Raymond hardly makes a sound. I listen, waiting to hear him flush the toilet, turn on his bed, anything. Nothing. Raymond can speak—Doc assures me Raymond has vocal capability—but refuses to; the guy is utterly self-contained.

"Hey, Raymond, you okay?" I call out.

Silence.

The trustee passes. "From Raymond." Through the bars he passes an orange, round and firm, big as a softball. My stomach is killing me—they still aren't providing any serious medical attention—but I strip the skin. The sweet smell permeates the cell. You're lucky to be in California. There's gold in them thar hills. Singin' in the rain. I picture my arrival in Oakland, glorious Bud driving up on his motorcycle with his cap and handsome salt-

and-pepper mustache, and myself approaching the Chinese fruit stand, staring at the nectarines, coveting the plums, the new kid in town.

"Thank you, Raymond," I say.

Silence.

After a while Raymond's quiet becomes its antithesis, an answer more comforting than words.

Then one night our tray count is short. Every time they feed you, they slip the tray under the door and you slide it back when finished. Twelve trays in, twelve trays out: they must get the same number back because a tray could be a lethal weapon.

"We're short a tray," the guard announces.

"Who's got the tray," everyone is saying.

"You got the tray?"

"Not me."

Down the line, until Raymond.

Silence.

"Oh, oh," says Doc. "Hey, Cool. Raymond got the tray. Tell Raymond to give the tray up. He respects you. He might give it up."

I don't know what's at stake. "I'm not gonna tell the man —"

Doc knows better. "Cool, you'd better tell Raymond to give up that tray, man."

Everybody in the tier is listening.

"I'm telling you, David, they're gonna shoot tear gas in here. It's gonna be a mess if they don't get that tray. Now tell Raymond to give it up."

I don't need any more convincing. "Raymond," I say, addressing the air, "you say you respect the Party and Huey and everything. Now give up the tray so we don't get gassed."

Silence.

"Raymond," I say, "come on, man. Give up the tray. Nothing's gonna come of keeping it except we get gassed."

Silence.

I try once more.

"Doc, he's not gonna give up the tray."

"All right, Cool," says Doc.

Guards mass at the doors, masks covering their faces. Water starts rushing, gallons gushing over and over again, a wave suddenly in the concrete tank.

"Now remember I always told you, keep your toilet clean," says Doc.

"That's right," I say. I'm not sure what to expect, but I hang on his words, really furious at the bars before me — the fact that I'm penned in and something's about to happen, something I'm powerless over.

"Well, this is why."

The wave builds, tumbling over itself, the noise reverberating in the cell-block.

"They're gonna shoot tear gas in here and what you're gonna do is get down on your hands—"

The guards come in and I'm already kneeling, my face plunged into the bowl, the cleanser's caustic scent stinging my nostrils, the water pouring down the sides over my hair.

"— and put your face in that commode and keep flushing."

I hold down the flusher, my eyes stinging from the water, the noise of the gas now louder than the surge down the sides, the acrid smell and liquid dust of the tear gas filling the block, my knees clamped on the concrete, as the guards enter Raymond's cell and whack him, over and over, cursing and shouting, until he's taken out unconscious.

Raymond never makes a sound.

The next day I have my first visit with Sandy Turner, my spiritual adviser—the authorities have denied passes to nearly everyone. I'm marched through the vast kitchen where the general population eats—rows of tables patrolled by guards with rifles stalking the catwalks overhead—to the visiting room, a cubicle screened in by a wire mesh woven so fine you can't stick even your little finger through, and can only feel flesh by pressing flat up against the grid.

"What do you want from this relationship?" Sandy says. She's a short, curly haired woman, no-nonsense; she looks straight in my eyes when she talks and her energy seems purposeful, not distracting.

"I want someone to talk to," I say. "I want to keep thinking and feeling. I want to remain human."

Sandy is Huey's idea, my own Alex Hoffmann. Securing Sandy, with her energy and determination, almost single-handedly compensates for his previous neglect of my legal situation.

Recently settled in the Bay Area, a close friend of Arlene Slaughter, Sandy has been working with Fred Bennett—head of the East Oakland chapter—on the local Breakfast for Children program. One night Fred—who's a member of the Soledad Brothers Defense Committee—appears at her house, speaking ominously about his possible disappearance. The next day he vanishes. Out of love, Sandy begins a campaign to track him down, calling hospitals, checking John Does, and dealing with the Party.

"I got nothing but rude replies," she remembers.

"Lady, it's none of your goddamned business. Why don't you just hang up and forget it. We don't want to deal with you anymore, and if you're gonna get pushy, lady, we don't need you." Because the Panthers assumed that Fred had defected. At least that's what I understand.

Then one day in April I got a telephone call from Huey Newton. He apologized for the Party acting kind of rough with me and said he understood I was very concerned about Fred Bennett and might have some ideas and would I like to come and talk to him.

I met Huey. I liked him enormously. He was just out of prison. He was drug-free; he was a beautiful human being, a very caring person.

We worked out a strategy for trying to tease out some information about Fred. We published an edition of the Panther paper saying, "What happened to him?" Where was he? The next day the sheriff in Santa Cruz County admitted he had a bag of bone chips that were what was left of Fred Bennett, that he'd been sitting on since December. I was appalled that such a nice person should have such a god-awful end—because they shot him in the back of the head, and then they set his body on fire, and then they broke up the remains. I mean it was *awful.*

But what that did was, I met Huey, I liked Huey, and later on I was called on to be of service, in a different capacity, when Huey decided you were going to jail, and he wanted me to figure out a way to be the person who could visit you.

Huey plans for Sandy to be his voice to me in prison.

"What Huey saw in me was persistence," says Sandy.

I don't think he expected me to think for myself. I don't think he looked at me as a person; he saw me as a tool.

He was concerned about you. He told me that you'd grown up together and that you had run the Party while he was in prison and Bobby was in prison, and that you had been the person responsible for many of the programs. You were old friends who loved each other, and he wanted you to make it. Huey knew the guards would play every opportunity to make your life miserable and to finally kill you if they could.

He said to me, "People like us when we're on the street, we drink, we take drugs, we work all the time, we're under terrible pressure, we're under threat, we never get enough to eat, we never get sleep, we never have time to think. And when you go to prison, that's an opportunity to build yourself, to *make* yourself a stronger person."

And that's what he wanted you to do. He didn't want you to be soft. He wanted you to be like Malcolm X. He wanted you to *study;* he wanted you to nurture your body; he wanted you to be such a giant no system could overwhelm you. He didn't think you would have the same steel discipline he had, but it turned out you were very strong. You were just strong in a different way.

I don't feel strong; I feel I'm hanging on. Solitary doesn't grind me down; I sleep fine now. But I no longer have to dream my netherworld; I'm in it, cut off from everyone, speaking into the empty air. I try to hold on to something solid; not memories of Brenda or Pat — because remembrances of women are sirens that will lure you, destroy your resolve — but puzzles to make me concentrate. I recall books I read in San Luis Obispo, recalling and analyzing incidents and sentences from *Siddhartha* when Sandy visits. Frustration drives me crazy — maybe frustration's the animal inside my stomach eating at my will and patience. I send out messages to Huey, the Party, my lawyer, and no one answers! Now I see Sandy once a week. We spend all day talking and arguing; she's the target for my every emotion. I find I can say anything to her because she always responds, never abandons me.

But even Sandy can't get me what I need: a lawyer, money for my commissary, the basic things you must have to survive in prison. Every week it's the same — I ask Sandy and she returns empty-handed, blaming the Party.

"You were very needy in prison," Sandy says.

For instance, a prisoner is dependent on having money on his books in order to buy canteen. But the Party didn't send you any money on the books. Another thing you wanted was a lawyer who would respond to you in prison. That was also not forthcoming. So you would be asking for things, and they would be saying, "No," and I would be the messenger, the person who went back and forth.

Part of the problem was that I don't think people in prison were the highest priority for the Black Panther Party. What they were doing in Oakland, or what they were doing in the rest of the world, was a priority. Once the guys went off to prison, whether it was David Hilliard, or Charles Bursey, they were gone. They may or may not have had a visitor arranged for them, but that was about it. And you wanted a lot. You wanted to stay in contact with the outside, you wanted a lot of visitors, you wanted to keep your connection as close as possible, and that was just building for conflict and strife.

There was also Huey, the disciplinarian. I kept getting a message from Huey, and a little bit from June, about, "David should be strong. David shouldn't be asking for things." Though Huey himself had lots of books and visitors in prison. But it wasn't, "Do as I do." It was, "Do as I say."

Then there were fights over policy. The Panthers wanted you to toe the line, and they wanted me to do what they wanted, and it became very clear, very early, that I didn't work for them. I was working with you. I came back with your desires and I wanted it in a regularized way. The Party wanted to call me up at six o'clock in the morning and say, "You can't go today. We're sending so-and-so. You go next week." That wasn't the way I was gonna function. If I was gonna do this, if I was gonna change my life to accommodate this activity, then I needed to be in charge of when I went—not at the convenience of the Party, but at your convenience. It was very clear you wanted me to come on a regular basis, because the couple of times when I didn't go, I got an outraged message from you, saying, "Where were you?!"

After a while we had enough disagreements that I had to stop trying to communicate with them.

And what's going on with the Party, anyway? On the surface everything seems to be going as planned. Bobby is about to run for mayor and Elaine for city council—the Party's entrance into electoral politics—and the captions have changed from things like "Blood to the horse's brow" to "Hey, Mister, what you doing to the poor man, Lord knows, you oughta quit it."

But I'm beginning to hear strange stories, and not only from antagonists, but Pat, John, and June, too.

"I first noticed the change in him after George Jackson was killed," Pat says.

Busy—that's what I called Huey, Busy, because he was always moving around—was going to the racetrack. Usually the crowd from the racetrack would come in about five. But Huey came in about three that afternoon, hollering and screaming, "And they killed George! They killed George! And they killed George!"

After that he went in the back and didn't eat anything. Then he was drinking some cognac. He drank for two or three days. Walked around holding his stomach. Let his beard grow.

I felt he was hurt. I think George's death brought home to him that he wasn't invincible. But after that he just became very suspicious. Yeah, suspicious of everybody. His cousins, his relatives, his brother.

"Huey started believing everybody around him was against him," says John Seale.

Even on the streets. I remember an incident where a guy walked up to Huey and recognized him. An African guy.

"Hey, mon, I know you! I know you!" You know—eyes bright, smiling.

And Huey: "Who the hell is this guy? Is this the police?" He started talking "police"—police all the time.

And Huey was snorting a lot of cocaine at the time. Cocaine started coming around more and more and more. A movie producer we knew had a big play in that. We went to LA and stayed with him—two or three times I went down with them—and there was cocaine there—matter of fact there was a lot of cocaine there. I'd snort once or twice. But Huey keeps snorting it. Just keeps going.

I said, "Man, you ought to give that stuff up. You're fooling with this stuff too much."

He quit fooling with it for a few weeks. Right back on it again. To see this man abuse his body that way—it blew my mind!

I talked to June. "The man's killing himself! What can we do?"

He said, "I've tried, John."

But what could you do? If we weren't around, somebody else would bring it to him. If he said, "Bring this up," the guys are gonna bring it!

My abandonment means I must deal with my medical problems by myself.

Over time, the symptoms in my stomach have changed. At first, I sometimes felt a burning at day's end. Next the discomfort became a constant demanding ache. Now the pain intensifies every day, some weird growth inside me, taking over my whole life, making me do what it says—bend over to ease the agony, spend hours on the toilet, not eat. I tell myself the hurt's psychosomatic, that I can overcome it. But the monster defies me, growing stronger as I weaken, feeding on me.

And no one listens. The prison doctors ignore me. When I insist on going to the infirmary, they accuse me of malingering, refuse my requests for stronger medications. I can't eat the jailhouse food and the authorities won't permit a special diet. One day Mickey Phillips visits. (Simply seeing me is a major victory. They make Mickey wait forever, telling him I'm in the yard while I'm still in the cell, then fluoroscope him for any concealed weapons; and Mickey, who's no stranger to guns, is scared by the forbidding catwalks and armed guards that ring the place.) When he sees me, we touch hands, the flesh of our palms pressing against the meshed wire.

"I can't eat," I tell him.

He gets some chicken soup from a vending machine, sliding a straw he pinches together through the tight wire. I close my lips around the plastic and taste the warm liquid.

A guard taps Mickey on the shoulder with his nightstick. "That's forbidden."

I suck furiously to finish before the guard confiscates the treat.

"You don't have to use your stick," Mickey protests, trying to start a dialogue.

"Let's go," the guard says, holding the nightstick in position to slap Mickey again. "Your visit's terminated."

At night I get sick, unable to hold down food. When I throw up, blood specks my vomit. My black stools signify internal bleeding; when I see them floating in the toilet, I feel I am looking at the sign of death. I can't think about anything. One day June tells me the news: our sister B.B. has been killed in a drug-related incident—her husband has always been a heroin dealer and addict. The details pass by me; I can't register the loss.

"The Party's gotta do something," I say. "Exact a consequence. You tell Huey."

"All right," says June.

"Tell him," I demand. "The guys that did her can't go unpunished. Tell him."

One day I faint from the pain and my weakness.

My cellblock mates bang their cups against the bars, shouting the prison refrain: "Man down! Man down!"

The prison doctor gives me more baking soda.

"We gotta do something, Cool," Doc Holliday says. "They're playing with you. They want to start something."

I figure the Party will protest. But some days pass and I get no visitors. Inside the cell I know I'm dying, my strength and will vanishing. Then the guards tell me someone's here. I get myself together—the cell has no mirror so I always guess how I look, asking Sandy—and take the walk through the kitchen, feeling dizzy and weightless, my body ready to topple at any moment. I concentrate on getting to the cage, where I can sit down. They open the door and I fall into the seat. Gwen, Huey's girlfriend and assistant, sits opposite, a beautiful woman with the deepest set, blackest eyes I've ever seen: Gwen is half black and half Greek.

"David?" she says. Her eyes show her panic and shock.

"I'm sick, Gwen," I tell her. "I think I'm bleeding inside. I need help. You've got to help me. They're gonna let me die."

That night Gwen calls Sandy, telling her she thinks I'm dying. Sandy goes into high gear, contacting state representatives and Ron Dellums, who comes and visits me. When I wake, I'm holding his hand. We're crying; I'm alive. They transfer me to the hospital unit and Sandy visits me.

"You needed a blood transfusion," Sandy remembers, "but they said that you had such unusual blood they couldn't get it. I went to see you and said, 'What are we gonna do? You need a blood transfusion.' You said, 'It's okay. I'll make it. Don't worry about it.' We got you moved, and once we got you to Vacaville, no matter how hard they tried to get you back, we never let them move you away."

Chapter

29

VACAVILLE is the medical facility. Prolixin-medicated HVP—high violence potential—inmates shuffle down the halls, the drug leaving them palsied, their hands and legs constantly shaking. In some way the hold of the authorities over you here is more insidious than the brute force displayed in Folsom: the fear of return to San Quentin or Folsom keeps you in line.

Still, the place is a lot less dangerous and easier to cope with than Folsom— there is sunny weather, conjugal visits, reading privileges, freedom to wear whatever clothes you want. The gays like the place especially because they can walk around in bikinis, some of them so skilled in transforming themselves that they certainly look like women from behind. One day I enter my cell and La-La appears from under my bed. He's a boxer; he knocks guys out so he can perform fellatio on them.

"We can have a good time," he tells me.

"Well, La-La," I say, "I'm very flattered you're attracted to me. And I want to be friends. But that's not what I do. So I'm saying no."

La-La doesn't press the issue. Part of the Party's influence is to protect members in prison, other inmates knowing we'll exact consequences on people outside if any harm befalls our comrades.

The threat keeps peace in lots of dangerous situations. One day, after therapy—we've got group sessions every morning—Charles Bursey comes and says Leroy, a lifer, is after him for some money. Charles is a dear and lovable comrade, but he constantly gets caught up in prison politics.

I move quickly to defuse the situation. Stuff happens fast in prison and I don't want the situation to explode: if Bursey gets killed for seven dollars I'll have to exact a consequence.

I meet Leroy in the company of another inmate friend, Long Beach.

"Leroy," I say, "what's happening?"

We're in the wing—the hall looks like a hospital corridor—outside our separate rooms. Guards stand by, but I can't rely on their presence to inhibit Leroy; Leroy's got a knife up his sleeve and won't hesitate to use it: he's already in for life.

"Your man is mine."

"Listen, Leroy. I'll give you the money," I say.

Inmates walk by, sensing something's happening, not stopping to find out what.

"Bursey is a Panther," I say. "He's not gonna get into a prison squabble over some cigarettes. That's not our style. We don't let ourselves get distracted with this petty stuff. So let me give you the money and it's over."

"I don't want to take the money."

"Well, I think you'd better take the money."

Leroy gets angry. "What you got to do with it anyway?"

"Well, Bursey is a Panther. I'm a leader of the Party. So this is also my responsibility. And I don't think you want to press this situation. I'm telling you, the reasonable thing would be to take the money."

"I'm not taking any money," he answers. We both keep our voices down, out of earshot from the guards. "Matter of fact, you're talking for the man and you want to pay for the man, you can take the killing for the man."

Long Beach steps between me and Leroy. Beach is one of my prison comrades. He's served over fifteen years for murder; but he has developed himself, becoming an accomplished artist—Ron Dellums is proud to accept a portrait Beach has done of him—and through Sandy I've gotten the Party and Arlene to work on a parole for him.

"Anybody's gonna go down, it'll be you, Leroy," Long Beach threatens. "All this stuff with a knife don't make a difference to me. I been here as long as you. You're out of line. The man's trying to make a deal. You're pushing this stuff beyond reason."

Leroy listens to Long Beach. "Beach, you know, man, what are you in this for?"

"This man is reasonable," Long Beach answers, meaning me. "You don't know what you're getting into. Now it's between you and me."

But I want to control the situation; I don't need Long Beach jeopardizing himself and raising the stakes. I quickly act on Bunchy's old advice.

I sit down.

"No, no, Beach," I say. "That's all right. I can handle this."

I address Leroy. "Sit down, Leroy," I say.

"I'm not gonna —"

"You want to fight, we can fight later," I say, settling on the bench. "Let's talk for a minute."

I don't say anything else. Leroy can walk away, start a fight, or seat himself.

"What's up?" he says, sitting at the far side of the bench.

"Look, Leroy," I say, "I know I might not win this situation. But I can guarantee you something. Your family will not survive it. Anybody can tell you that. We can carry out these threats. So if you want your family to suffer because of seven dollars, then make your move. But you won't have a family to go home to. That's all I got to say."

Leroy measures my words. Then: "What about the money?"

"Money's yours, Leroy. I'll take it off my books."

He stands up. "All right."

Soon after, I'm walking to the gym and see a tall familiar guy coming toward me in his whites. The uniform signifies he's just entered the system, but Temptation Tony can bring style to even standard issue. Tony Gibson is a comrade of George's, known for his martial arts prowess and faultless personal style. The first time I've met him was in a holding cell a while ago. I noticed a powerful-looking man, immaculate and confident, talking about George and the Soledad Brothers while dressed in a burgundy velvet suit with leather boots tucked up under three-quarter-length pants that ballooned out on the bottom like a Scottish golfer's. Tony was thrilled when I introduced myself: he knew me from George's praising references to my Soledad Defense Committee work.

Now we embrace each other like old friends.

"They're trying to send me to San Quentin," he says. "I'm a diabetic."

"That's no good," I say. "We gotta keep you here. In the hospital wing."

I speak to Sandy, telling her Tony's a marked man at San Quentin because the guards know he's a comrade of George's and that he's sick besides.

"And don't forget my silk shirt," I remind her.

"How can you ask me to help out this guy and get you a silk shirt at the same time!"

We've been arguing for weeks, Sandy insisting clothes are a sign of bourgeois self-indulgence and no one should go around dressed fancily.

"Sandy," I say finally, "you got it all wrong. The idea of revolution is not that nobody wears silk shirts. It's that everybody wears them."

Sandy tells me she'll do her best—which is always phenomenal.

"I was always burdened, after a visit with you, with a long list of things to do," she remembers,

and the guards didn't let me write things down, so I had to remember everything till I got to my car. I was supposed to call somebody's mother-in-law in Vallejo and find out why they hadn't visited, and I was supposed to call the Party and tell them there was this nice guy three cells away who hadn't had a visitor in fourteen years.

There was one guy who used to come down to the visiting room who was an epileptic who had not had good medical care. We got medical care for him and got the authorities to recognize he wasn't bad, but mad: I talk about the "mad-bad" continuum in prison, the bad guys you beat up, the mad guys you feel sorry for.

There was also a paraplegic who you found one day in infirmary. You heard the guy crying in his room. This guy had been in a shoot-out with the cops and had been hit in the spine and was paralyzed. He wasn't going anywhere. Every night at six o'clock they locked him up, because he was maximum security, because he was a *danger*—a paraplegic who can't get out of bed, who can't help himself. If he drops something, it's gone. If he chokes, he's choked. He's locked in a hospital cell overnight. This is because of the nature of his *crime,* not because of what kind of prisoner he was. You carried him out to the yard—it was the first time the guy had been out in the *sun* for I don't know how long—brought some attention to his custody so he could at least watch television in the evening instead of being put to bed at six o'clock at night, got a program for him at a nearby hospital where he could get some training in bladder control.

I found visitors for *hundreds* of prisoners, in the time I was there, that you asked me to do that. Some of them were Quaker visitors, some of them were Panther visitors. There were guys who wanted to write letters to a woman! They hadn't seen a woman in ten years. *That's* the kind of stuff that I was doing.

We even did something for Sonny Barger's wife, the leader of the Hell's Angels. She wasn't allowed to visit him. I went through all kinds of convolutions through my legislative connections to grant her permission. Finally we win and she gets up there to see Sonny and gets arrested for having handcuff keys on her key chain!

Sandy's work pays off; Tony's transferred permanently to Vacaville and we convince the guard to let us share adjacent cells.

"I owe you one," he says.

We befriend each other, Tony working me out on the iron pile, while I tell him about the Party's practice and dialectical materialism. One day he says Kumasi—another member of George's cadre—will soon join us. I'm excited. Huey's imprisonment began the connection between the Party and George; I'm broadening and deepening the alliance.

But Kumasi's cool to me. When he arrives he walks up as I stand near my cell. He's served three years in the Folsom Adjustment Center, a guy with incontestable prestige as a front-line solider in the prison war with the Aryan Brotherhood and against the administration, someone known for his incorrigible ferocity as a fighter: he's actually taught Tony karate, and is never beaten, which is how you stay on top in prison, like gunfighters in the old West. But he looks nothing like his reputation. He's handsome as a movie star, speaks in a smooth, superbly controlled voice, and is never at a loss for words or curses.

"I'm glad you're here," I say. "I hope we can be comrades."

"Well, I don't know," he says. "We'll have to talk. I don't expect you to betray your party, but there's a lot of disagreement with things that have happened."

"The Party's the Party," I say. "Our deeds are public record. We exist to serve the people. If we've done stuff that's retrograde or wrong we are not only bound to discuss it—we welcome that discussion because we believe we'll become stronger."

Kumasi and I start meeting regularly, walking around the yard. I tell him about my Party role and the organization's history. He tells me fantastic stories about people getting jumped on in bars, stuck up, brutalized by Party members, and that Huey's called Boss of the Bosses, that he's coked out and fired up.

"I don't know what you're talking about," I say. "The Party isn't into that individualistic gangsterism."

But Kumasi isn't the only one. Guys frequently confront me now, telling me I'm fooling myself, Huey's gone bad, putting me in the vulnerable position of defending things I don't know about.

One day I visit with Pat and the kids in the cafeteria. Patrice mopes around Pat; she hates the visits. Meanwhile Doe and Darryl play at the vending machines. Darryl does his mischief—Darryl's always doing mischief—while Doe's affectionate eagerness ingratiates him with other visitors; he's become particularly friendly with a guy named Big Bob Wells, who's told Doe he's been inside for forty years. Pat sends Trice off for a moment, then asks me whether I still love Brenda. I say yes: I dream of Brenda, fantasize about living with her when I get out.

A woman walks up holding a child.

"Look at me!" she shouts. "You made my baby an orphan!"

I don't even recognize her at first. Then I realize: it's James Carr's wife.

"What are you talking about?"

"Jimmy's dead. Huey's a murderer. I'm gonna get him. You'd better—"

"I don't know what you're saying—"

"My baby's an orphan!"

Later I hear that James Carr has been ambushed and killed outside his house. Soon after, I hear rumors there's a contract for me.

"That's the kind of stuff I was talking about," Kumasi tells me.

We're in our usual place, sitting near the iron pile.

"Well, I don't know anything about that." I tell him about the strained relations between me and Carr.

"There are people who hold you responsible for James Carr's death," he says.

"My role was to run the programs and Party," I explain. "I don't know about this stuff."

But I sense Kumasi's reserve; he's still waiting for me to prove I deserve his respect, his granting me equality with himself as a warrior.

I repeat the stories to June.

June looks away. "Don't bother about that," he says. "Think about getting out."

"What do you mean, 'Don't worry about that?' What are you guys doing? Everybody up here hating the Party? What's happening? What's Huey doing?"

"We're taking care of things," June says.

"No you're not," I say.

He knows what I mean. I keep asking him whether the Party's avenged B.B.'s death. All this *Godfather* stuff we're into, at least let our muscle work to protect our own.

"Well, Huey says he can't do that. We can't be about disciplining every dope dealer and user in America."

"Well, from what I hear he's disciplining the ones he wants to."

"That's what Huey says," answers June.

"I don't care," I say. "That is not sufficient. You guys are destroying the Party and he can't even do what I want. That's not sufficient. That's definitely not sufficient. I need to talk to Huey. Huey's got to come here."

But Huey doesn't come, write, or call.

Plus, he seems uptight about my comradeship with Tony and Kumasi. The connection excites me. I'm organizing, bringing people into the Party. Tony's important, providing us access and respect in the jails and gangs, the kind of warrior Eldridge never could deliver.

But Huey acts standoffish about Tony. I never get the little favors I request—a note or signed book—to reciprocate Tony's devotion.

"I'd like Huey to get in contact with Tony," I tell June.

"Huey wants to know why you're talking so much to Tony," June answers.

"What do you mean? Tony loves the Party. He would never sabotage us. He's completely loyal. What's Huey's problem anyway?"

Huey never answers.

We talk past each other.

What's David saying? he asks June.

What's Huey doing? I ask June.

Sometimes I imagine the scene—June and Huey alone in the Throne, late at night, the telescope staring out the window.

"Well, what did David say?"

June looks around. For all his strength, June has a gentle face, especially when perplexed. And now he's perplexed because he's answered Huey, but evidently not correctly.

"I told you, Huey. David wanted to know—"

Huey rises, walks around the room, stares through the telescope. June waits; it's anybody's guess what Huey will do next. Enough time has passed for him to have forgotten the question.

Huey comes back to his chair, sits down. "What did David ask?" As though June hadn't answered the question.

"Huey, I told you, man—"

"You trying to read me?"

"I've answered your question."

"You're trying to read me. You can't."

Huey gets up, looks through the telescope, comes back to the chair.

"What did David say?"

The senseless stories keep getting worse. I tell Pat and Brenda—I'm seeing both of them—to stay away from Huey; I know this man and the trouble he can cause. But Pat depends on him since I've been in prison, and Brenda always thinks she knows best anyway. June seems lost. Huey sounds like he's gone off. Meanwhile June tells me that Huey claims Pat is relating to other men, trying to work me up. Brenda says some of the Party women are now being used as prostitutes. The Party continues some excellent community work but sounds increasingly like a split organization, a reflection of the split in Huey's own personality, two halves operating in completely separate spheres.

"What are you guys doing?" I demand of June.

The original idea of the Lamp Post has become perverted. The club wasn't supposed to be associated with the Party; now Huey comes in all the time, making the ownership clear. The Squad—his group of strong-arm men—rips off drugs from dealers, then sells them back through the contacts at the club. Huey attacks people without warning, terrorizing customers and Party members. No one calls him on his behavior, but everybody talks about it behind his back. As the mayoral campaign proceeds—Bobby eventually wins an impressive forty-two thousand votes, forcing a runoff—the Party changes focus.

"In July of '72, I went to California," says Marty.

I met Huey in LA, where he was staying with his Hollywood friends— they had become a fixture in his life. Over the last year my role had changed a lot. I had lost contact with you and nearly all the Party members I had worked with regularly when you were the Chief. Now I was primarily a business agent, dealing with Huey, and we had done well, helping finance the Party's transition by selling several books, including a posthumous volume by George Jackson. (Some people tried to claim a split between George and the Party. Actually, the week before his murder at San Quentin George had sent me legal documents turning over all rights to his writings to the Party.)

Anyway, this was the first time I really had a chance to hear Huey's vision of the new Party—the Party since he had come out of jail and you had gone in.

Besides the beating the Party had taken from the police, Huey sensed the sixties were over. He would never express it that way. But he clearly felt that history was changing and the Party needed to transform itself— and this was an insight he had had long before anybody else—as early as before the defection.

His plans for the Party were radical. He saw the need for a strategic retreat. He said that people had been consumed by the Party full-time and that this had distanced them from the community. Now they were to work regular jobs and integrate their lives into the community. The future was going to be leaders like Elaine Brown — people who were at ease in every kind of social setting, from the streets to Hollywood, and who could move in establishment political circles, raising money from the state government and exerting leverage in the Democratic Party. Plus he had very ambitious plans to create a school that would function as both an educational model and center for political work in Oakland — and through his Hollywood connections had found new sources of financial and intellectual support. In fact, he was attracting leading progressive educators at the time.

I was impressed with the thoroughness of his vision. But there was also a troubling side to the change. Another aspect of his agenda was to purge the Party of representatives of the older Party, the Party that existed when he was in jail, and were loyal to you — the veteran leaders who had survived the police raids, held fast during Eldridge's defection, and stayed loyal through the move back to Oakland, even though for many of them that meant abandoning strong bases in their own communities. It wasn't a matter of the political decision. There was a dismissive attitude towards old comrades that was really offensive to me, a harshness. Most inexplicable to many of the Party's best cadre was Huey's hostility towards Masai Hewitt — both an intellectual and warrior, Masai seemed an embodiment of both the old and new Party.

The kookiest manifestation of all this were the asides to me by the new crowd that you were part of a plot to kill Huey. One of Huey's Hollywood companions kept saying to Huey that he should tell me about what you were doing — "Tell Martin about David!" he kept repeating, implying there was something sinister. But Huey simply refused to take the bait. I felt he didn't believe a word of what he was telling his new friends about you but was using these stories as an excuse for his dismissal of these old comrades. I was also struck by how incredibly focused his new friends were on Huey. Their fawning and flattery seemed more appropriate for a movie star than a political leader.

Finally there was Huey's choice of Elaine as a leader. In recalling the local leadership to Oakland Huey had provided himself with an incredible array of talent, including Audrea Jones, the Boston chapter leader; Bobby Rush and Lynn French, the leaders of the Chicago branch; and Omar Barbour and Jamil Young from Sam Napier's distribution center. But he chose Elaine as his top lieutenant. The choice amused him. Elaine was fast-witted, real smart, and highly articulate. But she also continually caused problems for Huey because there was always a lot of friction between her and the other comrades. She used her fast tongue against other Party members; many gave her a wide berth because she was so quick to detect slights against Huey and then use the supposedly offending comment to score a point against the comrade who had made it. (She also made no secret of her contempt for Huey's companion and assistant, Gwen, whom she clearly believed was unworthy of the leader and occupying a place that should have been hers.) Her loyalty was very valuable to Huey. Her weakness was her strength: she had no place to go, could organize no independent base. Huey would chuckle that she might be a son of a bitch, but she was his son of a bitch.

June feels the impact of the changes.

"He was deteriorating—going downhill with that coke and alcohol— staying up all night snorting that stuff," June says.

Bobby and all of them become aware of it. The rank and file was constantly wondering what was going on. Why was the Servant doing those things? Didn't he know that was going to be something *used* against the Party membership as a whole? They're trying to explain the actions to the community. Well, there's *no* way you can explain that. So they were telling community people that they don't know, they don't think it's true. Or, "We'll find out," try to have an explanation for them next time, but that's the only thing they could say.

Huey's bodyguard would constantly tell me how much out of control Huey was becoming, because he'd go to those after-hours joints and get in fights, take advantage of those guys. Take those guys' drugs and money and pull guns on them, shooting up the place. His bodyguard was becoming more and more fearful; in fear of his own *life*.

Every once in a while Huey'd call me to the apartment. I'd go up there and talk to him all night. He wanted me to go with him to the islands, Barbados or Trinidad.

I told him, "No, I don't think I should go. I should stay here. Somebody needs to be here to see that the Party functions on a daily basis."

He said, "No, you want to stay here and take care of your little brother—look out for your little brother."

When I refused to go, he got highly upset. From that day, I had a feeling that either something was going to happen to me or you. That's what I convinced myself. Nothing concrete that I can actually say, just a feeling.

To this day I believe if I had gone, you would probably have been dead when I came back.

Pat complains about Huey constantly. She tells me that he orders her to visit him on the days she visits me, that she can't take the Party car to drive to me, that she's disciplined for six months.

"Busy's going crazy," Pat tells me in one of the trailers the prison provides for conjugal visits. "Something's happening."

A couple of days later, I'm reading and the loudspeaker blares, "Hilliard, report to the attorney's room."

By now I've gotten rid of Hallinan and Garry is overseeing the case because he feels so guilty about what has happened. Walking into the room, I'm eager and excited: Hallinan has handled the case so badly there's not much grounds on which to appeal, but maybe there's some good news. Besides, I'm to appear for a parole hearing in a few days, and Sandy thinks my model behavior might give me a chance.

I open the door and my FBI agent sits there with two other guys.

"Hello, David," he says. "We'd like to talk to you."

I want to use whatever information they have, so I sit down.

"Look, David," he says, "things are really a shambles out there. Newton's constantly getting into fights. He rides around in a new Marquis. We don't know where you guys are getting your money from."

"I don't know," I say, "I'm inside here."

"That's just the point," he says, always the salesman. "We want to make you an offer. We need some stuff on Newton. When you get out why don't you tell us about him?"

"No," I say, "I don't think I want to work for you guys."

He remonstrates with me. Don't I know what's in my best interest? Newton's no revolutionary, just a thug. The Party's a cult.

"I still don't want to work for you."

He gets up. "I'm sorry, David," he says. "We'll see you next year."

"What do you mean, 'next year'?"

But they're already gone.

"Tell Huey to call me," I insist to June next time I see him.

"Man, you don't understand," June says. He's hunched over, speaking low, like he's still hauling that wagon of wood.

"I don't care about understanding. Get him to call me."

"He's going away," he says. "Going to the islands for his birthday. He'll call you when he gets back."

I leave him and go through the doors to the main prison. A line of guards stand there on one side of the hall; opposite them the brothers mass, angry, ready for trouble.

"Bursey got hit," they tell me.

"Hilliard," the captain says, "we want to talk to you."

I see Tony and Kumasi watching. "Well, wait a minute."

The brothers want some action. "A white guy just hit Bursey. We can't let this stuff go."

Tony and Kumasi wait to see what I do.

"Where's Bursey?"

"In the hospital."

"Where's the white guy?"

"They took him away."

The guards are ready to attack. I gather myself and turn to address the brothers.

"Well, I tell you what I'm doing," I announce. "I'm not giving any order for any white guy to get stabbed. That's exactly what these guards want me and you to do. We can't even get the white guy that hit Bursey, and I don't even know how bad Bursey's hit. So I'm not talking to you and I'm not talking to the guards. I'm going to see Charles."

"Bursey—" I say when I get upstairs.

"It's all right, David." He lifts his gown; a dressing covers a small puncture wound.

When I come back down, Kumasi walks over, sticking out his hand. "You're a true professional," he says.

"Hurricane," adds Tony. "That's what I'm calling you. You're the calm in the eye of the storm."

Huey returns and the stories about the trip are bizarre. At some point Huey presumably meets a witch doctor—Huey's always believed in Hoodoo—and stages an all-night challenge match, pitting his command of dialectical materialism against the shaman's supernatural powers. Huey comes out shaken. Another story claims he's afraid the priests will use a piece of hair he left in a cab to gain power over his soul. Another says that somehow a day was lost, that the other people on the trip can't account for one twenty-four-hour period.

Whatever has occurred, he acts more suspicious and meaner than ever. (Later the story comes out that he received a letter saying the Hilliards planned to kill him, another FBI plant. Certainly the police abet his self-destruction; their constant surveillance of him fails to intercept any of the cocaine moving into his house.) He keeps cutting me off, not writing, sending tapes, or answering calls; my requests go untended. I'm frantic, angry, scared; the dissolution of our relationship and decline of the Party is unimaginable and unthinkable, and I remain unshakable in my belief that if I can only get to Huey, speak to him directly, all the confusion will end and conflicts disappear.

"Tell Huey to call me," I say to June. "I've got to speak to him. Tell him."

Chapter
30

BY January people start to leave.

Marty's the first to go. "Huey's plans for me became increasingly bizarre," he remembers.

"Why don't you run the bar?" he said to me one time.

I said, "Huey, I didn't join the Black Panther Party to be a Jewish businessman in the black ghetto."

He said, "But Martin, you've got four thousand years of experience."

After that I stayed away until January. During my stay, I visited Huey's apartment one night—one of those horrible nights when he wanted to talk philosophy and drink brandy, walking around without his shirt while the fog rolls in and I'm freezing and exhausted.

Then, out of the blue, he says, "There's some people moved in next door who want to kill me. Come with me."

Gwen was sleeping, his bodyguard not around.

Huey goes out in the hall and kicks in the door. I'm with him—like an asshole. I see he has a .357 Magnum in his hand.

Inside are two guys and a woman.

He says, "Okay, up against the wall. I want to talk to you."

Then he says, "Martin, go get a pillow."

In my naïveté, I thought he wanted a pillow to sit on. The pillow's to put around the gun as a silencer.

That's when I broke out in hives. I said, "Oh my God."

I run into the apartment next door, saying, "Gwen, this guy's crazy."

Ultimately Huey's bodyguard came and got him. Meanwhile I had broken out in hives, and I'm saying, "What am I doing here? Either I get killed for no good reason, or he kills somebody and what am I supposed to do? Go to jail for not testifying against him? Or testify against him? Who wants to do that? Or to see an innocent person killed?" I decided there was no way this thing could come to a good end and that I was through.

At the time *Ramparts* editor David Horowitz was doing an outstanding job on building academic and financial support for the Party's community school in Oakland. The new crew provided me with a ticket out. I was thankful to Horowitz for creating the opportunity for me to distance myself from the scene in Oakland and to do this in good conscience and not only out of fear.

Mickey's next. One afternoon in the Lamp Post Huey asks him about a house Arlene has arranged for me and Pat to buy. Mickey knows nothing about the deal and says so. Huey answers by ordering his bodyguard to hit him.

"I got a split lip," Mickey remembers. "Then two Party members took me out to the car. One said, 'What happened?' I told him. 'I don't *know* what the hell happened with that house. If I did, I would have *told* him. There's nobody *stealing* nothing here.' They said they were gonna bring it up to the Central Committee. 'We can't have this.' I said, 'You guys are gonna get yourself in trouble.'"

Then Gene. "Huey didn't want me to go to jail to see you," Gene recalls.

Saying it wouldn't be beneficial. He made some little, terrible threats about "not helping David's family" and stuff. Also some people gave him some more lies—like you're gonna get me to do something to harm Huey.

I said, "Huey, where are you coming from? We're here to help you! How do you think we could ever, ever think about doing any kind of harm to you? Or even go against any of our principles? David has meant well. You can't mess with the man's family. He's in jail, man. You can't do that. Hey, I want to see him. Don't worry about it. Let's talk about something else."

But somebody put some stuff into his head, and then he got to think it. I had never seen Huey like that.

Later it was mentioned that Huey was saying, "Gene is getting too popular."

He came down at the Lamp Post and said, "I don't want you around here anymore."

I was asking him, "What is happening, man?"

It hurt! It just hurt!

I said, "I don't want your woman. I got my hands full! Huey, come and tell me something else. Don't tell me about some women. They've got women out here, a dime a dozen! Who cares about all these women? They're not no major thing between me and you. If we're gonna have a problem, it ain't gonna be about no woman."

I said, "What do you think I'm gonna do to you? You're the Minister, you're supreme! Can't nobody take your place. You're you! There ain't but one Huey, and won't ever be nothing but one Huey—like there ain't but one Bobby or David. Everybody has got their little self person. All right, man. You go your way and I'll go mine."

He just had this ego about being a man—that macho stuff! He always wanted to do that. That was one of his little hidden things. He was insecure about that. He had to prove something, be something more. I mean he's dynamite already. He ain't got to prove nothing to nobody about no woman. He's Huey. I think that was one of his little problems. It seemed like he always had that little thing on him. I don't know why.

Rush follows. "I didn't see anything wrong with Huey living in the apartment," Rush says.

I knew the rationale behind it: he should have been protected.

But the gangsterism I couldn't relate to. If I wanted to do that, I could have joined the Stones, or the Disciples, or some other kind of thing. Gangsterism was everyday activity in Chicago. It wasn't something that I was impressed with.

Then there was personal things. One time I went up to the Throne and Huey was in the bed. We were talking. I was being questioned about activities in Chicago. I saw he had this Browning automatic real close by. I felt threatened, personally threatened. I hadn't felt that before. Then I began to focus more on other things I had heard, because I hadn't been treated like that before.

A little later they asked me to come to Elaine's apartment. There were a lot of other people there. Everybody was sitting around in a semicircle, and then there was a chair sitting away from everybody else. I went and sat in that chair. After a few moments they asked me to step in the next room. Then they told me to come back and this guy who I had brought in and trained and was the head of the East St. Louis chapter told me I had to get out of Oakland, I had been expelled. And that's when I left.

Brenda's next.

I told Huey I didn't want to sleep with him anymore. I said I didn't need that aspect of a relationship, I wanted us to be friends, and maybe I could help fill in the void you left. "We can talk. You bounce things off of me, and I can give you my input," I said. "I'd like to do that."

We were talking on the phone. He didn't go off or anything, but he didn't like it. I felt a tension after that. He didn't like me seeing anyone else. Whenever I would deviate from my schedule, it was, "Where is she?"

Other things were happening that I wasn't really that happy with. I would hear "mud-holing." Before discipline had been on that joking kind of level. But these incidents sounded serious.

Then I went out with this guy.

Shortly after, I ended up at Huey's house. He told me he was gonna beat me. They were gonna get me for breaching the Party rules, beat me because I was out of line.

I told him he couldn't beat me. I was very afraid.

I went to the Lamp Post and called my mom and told her to come over with the truck because I needed to get away. She said okay. Her and my cousins came over very, very early that morning. I just moved my stuff and left.

June called me that night. "You're gone."

"Yes."

Then Bobby called me. He didn't sound very happy, didn't sound like the Chairman. He told me they were gonna have a Central Committee meeting and I needed to come. I said okay.

June called back and said, "Don't come. They're gonna do something to you."

I said, "Okay. No problem."

I think they were gonna mud-hole me or something. I don't know.

June called me back the next day. He told me I had been expelled and I wasn't to see you anymore and could not have anything to do with any

Party members. I had to take Dassine out of the school. I told them I wasn't gonna stop seeing you. When I went that following weekend, you asked me what had happened.

Brenda's story makes no sense. Huey has accused her of sleeping with a youngster. Brenda's infidelity angers me, but Huey has no cause to complain about her sexual indulgence: her actions concern us; she's certainly never betrayed the Party. I refuse to give her up.

"I don't understand," I tell her.

We sit in the visiting room, surrounded by the usual intimate chaos, families fighting and loving; sometimes guys get their wives to masturbate them in the corner, the guards pretending not to see.

Brenda says Huey wants to make a deal: if I stop her visits, I can see Pat.

"The Party doesn't make that decision for me," I say. "You're the mother of my child. I'm visiting with you and visiting with Pat. He can't dictate my personal life. He knows where my loyalties lie. He's going too far. I don't do this. If I've got to choose between principle and passion, then I pick passion. I've got to speak to Huey."

That Sunday June comes: Pat's been expelled.

"I was very hurt," Pat remembers, "really hurt by Huey because he wouldn't give me any answers."

I said, "Who's been telling you? What's making you act the way that you're acting?"

Then he'd say, "Well, you know me too well."

That was one of the things he said that made me know he was really very paranoid. "You know too much about me," he says. "You know too much about me."

I looked at him and I said, "Well, I think it's okay that I know this about you. I mean what is it about you that I know too much about?"

The next two days are nonvisiting. When I phone June that night—everyone gets five minutes; you line up and someone in charge calls your name and clocks your time so no one abuses the privilege—he's not home.

"Huey called me up and said we had to talk," June remembers.

He said he didn't want to fight with David. He found that David had aligned himself with some brothers in the prison, and taken a position against him.

I said, "What are you talking about?"

He said, "Well, you come back here, you keep going up there and seeing David. You're in the middle of it!"

I went home that night and he called and told me that David *and* I was expelled from the Party. That shocked the hell out of me.

I asked him, "Why are you expelling David? David's locked up, he's up there. Expel *me*, but why are you expelling David?"

"No, no! *Both* of you are expelled, *both* of you are expelled!"

I told him, "I'm gonna need a little money." I had access to donations of maybe ten to fifteen thousand, but I said all I need is twenty-five hundred. Later on I found out that he'd told everybody we stole the money and that I was a *counter*revolutionary, and it was all part of a plot to overthrow him and take his Party away from him. All this stuff being said and done from a person I never thought would resort to that type of lying and deceit, back-stabbing tactic. But I guess it was a combination of drugs and that constant pressure he was under, dealing with the people in the street, while the police were hounding him.

Frances goes with him: "June told me he's *expelled,* and so was David. I said, 'What's going on here?' He said, 'Well, look. I'm gone.' He told me he was going to Alabama. I could imagine how he felt—because leaving you was just like when I had to leave Peggy in Niantic. 'Wait a minute,' I said. 'Don't go without me. I don't want to be here.' He says, 'Well, you can come if you want.' From that point on, we're together."

The next day is Tuesday, last day of the nonvisiting period.

"Hilliard," the guard says, "down to custody. You got a telephone call."

My heart beats fast, stomach tightens. I'm not anticipating news from Huey or the Party; I'm sure my mother has died.

Guards stand around in the captain's office, waiting for me.

"It's your wife," one says and hands me the phone.

"David," Pat says. She sounds hysterical. "You've been expelled."

I can't say anything. Pat knows nothing; the phone is bugged, all calls in and out of the prison recorded, and I'm onstage for the guards.

"Okay, Pat," I say. "Give me a minute. I need to call Huey."

I hang up, look around. The guards watch mutely; they're enjoying this humiliation. I can't ask them to leave. One of them gestures to the phone: go ahead, get jammed, be my guest.

Gwen answers at Huey's number.

I'm peremptory, the way I act when I'm into serious business.

"Yeah, Gwen, this is David."

"David!"

She tries to control her voice. This is bad: she doesn't want to be on the phone.

I stare at the floor, closing myself off from the guards.

"What's this about my expulsion?"

Gwen pauses, then: "Huey, this is David. He wants to talk to you."

I hear his voice, high, insistent, furious.

"I don't have to talk to David," he shouts. "I'll send someone to talk to him."

"Gwen—"

"I'm sorry, David." Her voice breaks; she can't say what she wants; there are no words left between us. In the background I hear Huey's voice, edgy, driven.

"I'm sorry, David. I'm sorry."

She hangs up.

The captain stares at me. "Everything okay?" he says. "Need to call anyone else?"

All I want is to be in my room, alone. When I get there, I have nothing to do. I sit and breathe, smell the air, feel I'm alive. Then I remember my circumstance: *I don't have to talk to him!* I curse Huey out in my mind, my anger boiling. Motherfucker! You goddamn right you got to—police right there, and you saying you don't have to *talk* to me—when I gave you back the Party! And, *plus,* I've got no protection now, no organization to cover me!

Tony comes by.

"David, come on. We're going to the iron pile."

I don't say anything. I don't ever want to move.

Tony waits a moment, then: "You've got to come, man."

We've been reading Aleister Crowley and have adopted a phrase from one of his books, "Thelema, Do As Thou Will," our new motto.

"Man, you got to get to that iron pile and take it out on those weights. Thelema, brother. Don't show those niggers you can be broken. You got to come out of here stronger than ever."

Tony's the most aggressive guy I've ever known. Kumasi says he's so aggressive that he'll even turn on himself. But right now he's speaking truth.

"All right," I say.

I lift the weights while composing a letter in my mind, assembling the phrases, sorting out what I want to say; it's my last attempt to contact Huey, and I speak with my heart as well as my mind, hoping my words can reach through whatever has come between us.

"Huey, I have tried always to give what you expected of me, striven to become what you are by following your example. You said in a conversation we had that I had proven my loyalty to you. Here I will quote you, 'I went to Prison and you had control of the Party, you could have made it anything you wanted it to be. I am back home now and you have given it back to me, you are truly my friend.' There are various and sundry reasons regarding my expulsion. I will not attempt to explain them simply because I do not understand what's happening. I wish to reaffirm my loyalty, Love, and friendship—it is steadfast, undiscouraged by the recent developments. Am I correctly informed that my expulsion was because of my refusal to stop seeing Brenda Presley? Those charges are true. I love her in spite of her amoral, sensual, libertine nature: that's all I have to say by way of explanation regarding that situation. You have taught me well: suffering is no stranger to me. 'I will ride the Whirlwinds of Change While You direct the Storm.' You have full control of your organization and I bear no ill will against you. I am not your enemy and you know it. I want to be your friend, Huey, not because I fear you, but because I love you."

Toward morning I wake up realizing something: Huey never wanted to avenge B.B.'s death because I was already in bad standing. My anger at his betrayal builds inside me. Why didn't I see all this coming beforehand? I have no release for my remorse and fury, so I throw myself on the floor and do push-ups, thinking of Huey all the time. When I stop B.B. comes to my mind, at the train station, in her polka-dot dress, waving good-bye. *David, take care of—*

My anger ebbs into grief.

Father.

Bunchy.

Fred.

Mark.

Li'l Bobby.

B.B.—gold tooth gleaming, laughing as I run around the room singing, Caldonia, what make your big head so hard!

Black Gal! Black Gal!

Chapter
31

DURING the next days the visiting room fills with people, Pat, Brenda, Alex, Gene McKinney, personal friends. No one understands what's happening. When the Central Committee voted on my expulsion, Masai and some others evidently defied Huey. (Soon after, Masai is beaten up and thrown out.) Alex tells me he and Elsa Knight Thompson have been talking to Huey. Huey's accusations are incomprehensible, and he refuses to listen to reason: at the same time he never expresses anger to them when they defend me, a reaction consistently reported by everyone, including Donald Freed and Marty.

"Huey offered me a totally nutty story about Brenda Presley and some teenager who needed to lose his virginity," Alex remembers.

> And Huey was shocked, shocked, shocked. Now *please.* I was not impressed by the reasoning and made it clear I was not impressed. I kept suggesting that one of the problems was the method of communication. There was totally screwed-up communication going on. Huey was going off on these flights by then, and I don't know that *anybody* could have conveyed what Huey was rambling on about, but certainly June couldn't, so everything got screwed up.

The only person absent is June. No word from him. That night I get a letter:

David,
    I was with Huey after he come back from his trip to the Islands of the

26 of Feb. He started off by telling me how he enjoyed his trip and how he was almost hoodooded. We were up all night and many things were said and discussed. . . . He started telling me about all of my previous insults to him. I get led into a lot of things because of my slowness in grasping things I guess. . . . Then he started talking in parables and lost me. He did ask me if you were sitting across the table from me and pulled a gun on me what would I do. I said that I would probably try to shoot you first. He disagreed, which he is right on that. . . . Somewhere along he said he resigned from the Party and I couldn't resign and no one could change his mind. . . . David there are lot of things that was said that I don't recall right now but there were similar charges against me. . . . He asked me to call after I got settled. I said that I would. . . . I will be back to see you as soon as I can get some things squared away here.

June

Soon after, I hear the last piece of news: Bobby's been thrown out. Now all the leadership that guided the Party from its inception are gone—dead, exiled, jailed, expelled.

Sandy pursues my release while Charlie Garry files retrial motions. One day he tells me guards have intercepted a letter from an inmate: there's a contract on me for twelve packs of cigarettes.

"You're in danger," Charlie says.

"I'm not even in the Party anymore," I answer.

"You know how these things work," he answers. "Contracts are forever. Your life's in jeopardy. Take yourself out of the general population. Put yourself in the custody of the guards."

I look away, not answering; the small consultation room adds to my sense of feeling trapped.

"David," Charles says, "you've got your family—"

"I don't hide in prison," I say. "I can't do that."

"You're not hiding."

"I'm here and I'm gonna be here. I can't hide. Besides, police don't protect Panthers."

"You're not a Panther," Charles argues, not meaning to wound me but to force me to see things clearly. "Things are different now. You're a prisoner."

His words sink in. "That's right," I say, "I'm a prisoner. I take my risks with other prisoners."

When I tell Tony the information, he reassures me, saying I shouldn't worry and that he already knows the name of my killer, Baby Ray.

"Twelve packs of cigarettes," I say. "They could at least be twelve cartons."
"It's all right," Tony says. "Be cool."

The next morning I meet Kumasi in the yard.
"What's going on?" I say. "I don't understand."
Kumasi pauses. Then: "Man, it's a vendetta."
"What?"
"They're out to kill people."
I'm still lost.
"Explain it."
Kumasi starts at the beginning. In the early sixties black inmates divided themselves into two gangs, the southern Californian Black Mafia, and the Bay Area mob. Both were strong-arm pressure groups. But George Jackson managed to unite them under an umbrella group.

"George was just an amazing man," Kumasi says. "He was a mix—quiet and thoughtful, pragmatic and incorrigible. All of us would be arguing. He'd take his own counsel, then say, Check this out, comrade. This is what we're gonna do. And you listened. Because he was right. Just a very quiet, very studious-looking guy—you know, with his horn-rimmed glasses, he presented almost a square look—with tremendous physical self-confidence. His control inspired people. He just drew your attention. You could have a yard of two or three thousand convicts, and he comes out with guards and suddenly there's just a feeling, an emotion that just stood you still. It was hard to contest him intellectually or physically. I would browbeat people, call them names. He'd tell me to shut up because his manner was to ask you a question and, if he didn't like the answer, draw you to come to the right conclusion. He would simply develop a formula and go with it. Methodical. Don't mess with your foe, he would say. Instead he would instruct us to kill our man in two point five seconds. Two point five seconds, comrades, go straight to the heart. Without any braggadocio. Just a very calm, very confident, very capable individual.

"So George took all the most desperate and aggressive guys—the long-term Adjustment Center guys, the front-line soldiers in struggles with the administrations—and gave them a single purpose, melding them into this umbrella group called the Black Militant Front. He politicized them and trained them into a cadre whose primary purpose was to educate themselves and get out of prison and develop cells on the street and train others—develop a revolutionary movement based on Che Guevara's foco theory, the outside arm of the movement inside the prison.

"Eventually he organized the Black Guerrilla Family out of the Black Militant Front. Our stance was that the war was on. You kill one of ours, we get three of yours. George said, we gotta stop going for the puppet and go for the puppeteer.

"At the same time the Party was developing. Well, George identified with the Party program and the Party's stance. He was very impressed by the Party's internationalism. So we became supporters of the Party.

"When the split with Eldridge happened we kept a neutral stance. Our position was that the Party had to be kept alive at all costs—even if you had to get rid of some people to do it. Our theory was that the Party should disarm; we would take over the military wing and the Party would be purely a propaganda and political unit.

"August seventh happens. Huey was blamed for Jonathan's death because Huey was supposed to have given assistance so no one would get killed. But he pulled it back.

"Afterwards I understand George held Huey responsible. Meanwhile James Carr—who had been transferred to San Luis Obispo and whom we delegated as Huey's personal bodyguard—got out. We gave him authority to act as George's proxy; his job was to establish the connection between those of us inside and outside.

"But then things don't work out right. Every time a Black Guerrilla Family functionary got out and was supposed to do things, he would wind up dead. Plus, George gets murdered, which makes Huey worried because there are lots of people now angry at him and wanting to kill him and there's a scramble for leadership in the organization. Then James Carr is murdered—which we understand is ordered by Huey.

"So now the plan evolves to take over the Party, completely eliminate the Central Committee one by one, slowly, over time, so we'll keep the organization. We believe we can organize outside because we have already organized the most extreme characters and brought together the most antagonistic foes in prison. So we figure we can certainly do it on the streets—which turns out to be completely wrong, since prison is a controlled environment and it is in fact much harder to mobilize people politically on the streets. Anyway, the whole plan never gets full sanction—but a contract is put out on the whole Central Committee. When I got here I had to be cool with you because there were lots of people who felt you had ordered assassinations of people. I told everybody I would get close to you, that they should stand back, I would expose myself—in case you were out to get us. But then I got to trust and like you. Later, when Baby Ray told me there was a contract for you and some others, I said he had to come through me before he could get to you, and exerted leadership with Tony. That's what stopped him. But I think from Huey's perspective he saw you hanging with Tony and me and he got worried. He wanted you to declare yourself. He was scared you'd flip on him. So when you wouldn't, he flipped on you."

The California sun bakes us with its hard midmorning light; there's no wind in the hot, cloudless air.

"We saw ourselves as dead men," Kumasi continues. "The retributionists. We weren't getting out alive so we were willing to sacrifice ourselves, strike the blows that other people couldn't afford. The Nat Turners. Now I don't know what will happen. Whole new group of guys coming out inside. I'll tell you something. The world changes, David; with or without you it's gonna change and not necessarily the way you want it to. You done your time, man. Get out. Go live your life."

I spend another year in Vacaville, trying to comprehend what has happened.

Some days I'm consumed with hate. I focus my rage on the guys coming in. I can't understand them. "Jess B. Simple niggers," Tony calls them. They're different from our generation, apolitical drug gangsters whose violent crimes are usually directed against blacks. They should be the Bunchy Carters of the future, but unlike him they are entirely and solely interested in what they can get. I coin a phrase to describe their mentality: not the politics of spontaneity—that would be a step up in consciousness for them—but the politics of *in*stanteity.

But I also enjoy periods of great calm. Toward the end of my stay, my brother Bud dies, his heart giving out. Drawing on my recent experience, I write a memorial for him:

When he died I was in despair, as any man well might be. But soon, pondering on what had happened, I told myself that in death no strange new fate befalls us. In the beginning we lack not life, but form. Not form only, but spirit. We blend in the one great featureless, indistinguishable mass. Then a time came when the mass evolved spirit, spirit evolved form, form evolved life. And now life in its turn has evolved death. For not nature only but man's being has its seasons, its sequence of spring and autumn, summer and winter. If someone is tired and has gone to lie down, we do not pursue him with shouting and bawling. He whom I have lost has lain down to sleep for a while in the great inner room. To break in upon his rest with the noise of lamentation would but show that I knew nothing of nature's sovereign law. So let Theodore sleep—may he rest in peace!

Everyone says I should let the Party rest too and get on with my life.

I follow their suggestions, concentrating my energies on securing my release. Every night I call Arlene and ask her how I'm doing, meaning whether her political influence and Sandy's indefatigable pursuit of my case is making a difference.

"You're supposed to tell me, David," she jokes.

"What's happening with the Party?" I ask her.

"Don't worry about that," she says. "Just come home. Things will work out."

I keep sifting through what's taken place. Something's gone wrong, I figure. Because it seems to me impossible that the man I have known since childhood could be involved in the incomprehensible behavior of the last couple of months. "Listen, David," Huey used to say to me, "you can do anything, murder, anything, as long as you have a definition for the situation." But this situation has no definition. None at least that I've heard from any of the people I speak to. And yet I'm sure Huey himself could give me one: one of his greatest gifts is his ability to clarify the most complicated realities. When I get out of prison, I think, we'll meet together, just Huey and I, and make sense of everything.

Then I hear the latest news. Huey's disappeared, he and Gwen gone to Cuba in order to escape charges of murdering a prostitute. The Party's under Elaine's leadership.

One day I get the usual call. Down to the office.

My FBI agent greets me as an old friend now.

"David, you look good," he says.

"I feel good." Sandy has set up an employment situation for me, eliminating another reason for denial of my parole.

"Look, David," my agent says. "The Party's gone. So we're gonna let you go home. You'd like that wouldn't you?"

"Yeah, I'd like that. I think it's time I go home. But I'm not working for you guys."

"We can offer you twenty thousand dollars," the guy says.

I tell him no, I'm only eager to go out and resume my work with survival programs. I feel strong, having withstood all his suasion; I've lasted and triumphed without him.

"Well, all right," he says. "We won't argue. You go out. We won't bother you. There's no reason to. There's nothing left there anymore."

Chapter
32

ADJUSTING to outside is hard. I've spent the last year preparing to come out, hearing the news from Oakland and setting up my life: the promise of a job (through Sandy), a house (through Mickey and Arlene), and money (through an old-time Party supporter) until I'm on my feet. "I have been asked whether I have changed since my period of imprisonment," I write to Sandy shortly before leaving Vacaville. "My answer is yes and no. Physically I have changed. I am timeworn, older than I was when I arrived here! Have my ideas changed? No, but my knowledge of applying them has developed—through much concentration and study."

But all my mental and emotional readiness proves insufficient for the altered reality I meet.

For one thing the Party is completely different. The paper still appears, and the school—the Oakland Community Learning Center, led by Ericka—is now highly regarded, but other survival programs have disappeared. While I've been inside, the government has attacked us again, the IRS and other agencies harassing the members of the East Bay business community who give the programs financial support. The free testing for sickle-cell anemia has been crippled because the FBI has urged Oakland police to arrest Party members for making unlawful solicitations and planted news stories trying to discredit the program. They have also served Arlene Slaughter with a patently false indictment, hoping to scare her and her many political contacts away, and conducted three separate investigations of racketeering against the Party, none of which develops evidence to support the charges.

Yet under Elaine's leadership and even without the survival programs, the Party has become a political power in Oakland. Taking off its berets and leather jackets and putting on three-piece suits, the Party has realized Huey's vision of a "people's political machine," an organization that exercises influence at both local and state levels, forcing bureaucracies and institutions to address the needs of the black community, attracting accomplished intellectuals to aid in Party work, winning appointments and grants.

But the community's changed also. I'm in culture shock when I walk around. There's absolutely no politics on the street anymore. Before I went to jail, politics was a constant part of the environment. I couldn't go a block without meeting someone selling a newspaper or passing posters announcing a rally or demonstration; plus, of course, Telegraph Avenue and the area around Berkeley always boiled with student rebellions and street fights between cops and protesters. Now the main action on the street is drugs and prostitution. The openness of this activity stuns even me. It used to be the nighttime was the right time for making love, as Ray Charles sings — that's why prostitutes were called ladies of the night. Now the women work the streets at high noon, presenting a beauty parade of young bodies in bathing suits and hot pants. The kinds of kids — Asians, whites, blacks, Hispanics — who four or five years ago were chanting, Free Huey! and Power to the People! are now flaunting their bodies or dealing on the corner. Oakland's no longer the city of the Panthers, but a wide-open good-time town, a place where guys come from around the state to score with women or drugs. The economic foundation of the city has altered. The Oakland of my youth was a working-class town, people holding down nine-to-fives. Now the community seems increasingly devastated. Attempts at enterprise don't last. There's no support money for small businesses. It's 1974; under Jerry Ford people are living on the margin — a friend opens a beauty salon or bar one week and the next week it's gone. It's impossible to believe that a short while ago this community was politicized; now politics is a foreign word.

When I speak to people about this change, express my shock, start to piece together what's happened, they give me double-talk. Most simply act as though I'm harping on something bad in a self-destructive way. Those that do talk give Party-line opinions, blaming Huey for embracing capitalism and abandoning what they consider to be the Party's previous revolutionary stance.

"You know, I think I gotta contact Huey in Cuba," I say one night to my old buddies. We're at Regent Street, the three-bedroom house Arlene secured for us while I was in prison.

One agrees. "That's right, David. You guys grew up together. You can work it out. You need to talk."

But everyone else says no. "You don't want to do that, David," one of them tells me.

I pour myself some more Armangac—I've bought a quart, my drink of choice—and fill their glasses.

"Well, I do," I answer.

"Don't get hung up on him. We got a party for you." Their name for coke. We spread, chop, and sniff the powder. Coke was still an elite, rarely used drug when I went in; now everybody seems to have it.

I try out my thinking on them; convincing them will bolster my confidence in my own understanding of the situation. "Huey's complex," I say. "He's hard to read. Worst thing in the world you can do is to try and second-guess that guy." Mickey himself—even after being hit—has suggested Huey might be pursuing some subtle strategy, figuring my expulsion will ensure my safety in prison, persuading other inmates that Huey and I are antagonists, rather than friends.

My friends interrupt me before I finish.

"I'm telling you, David, things have changed. You don't want to talk to him."

I take another toot, get amped. I look around the house: no posters, leaflets, action. Real quiet compared to the usual frantic pace inside the Panther office. The difference depresses me. I take another toot.

"Yeah," I agree, "but if we talk—"

"You should stay away. These guys are dangerous. You should leave them alone."

I drain my glass, pour some more.

"Man, you don't understand. Huey's crazy."

They spell things out, telling more reports of rip-offs, beatings, a prostitute being shot.

I nod, acting like I'm taking in what they're saying, but following my own thoughts: *they* don't understand; *they* have things figured wrong; *they* don't know Huey as well as I do, haven't worked with him as closely. Their stories describe a person completely alien to the one I know. Huey can be extreme—taking things to the limit is part of his genius—but he's never been vicious or petty. I feel sure there's something left out or wrong in these accounts, like I'm hearing a translation that's missing words. My friends are street hustlers anyway; beating somebody's their way of life. Maybe Huey did what they claim. But I'm also sure they're not mentioning something about the incidents, something they did, something they provoked. Other-

wise their versions of Huey's behavior are simply too out-of-bounds because, except for my expulsion—and I'm sure by now that Huey threw me
out because he was given wrong information—I've never known Huey to
be cruel without some compelling reason.

"Is that right?" I say. I drink and toot, act amazed at the tales, already
wanting this conversation to stop.

"I'm telling you, David," one says. "Things aren't the same as when you
left. Don't talk to people about the Party. People don't like the Party now."

Later, I leave, go to Brenda's. I've decided before leaving jail that we'll live
together. I won't break altogether with Pat; but I love Brenda and hope we'll
be able to build a life together. I've lived and loved with Pat before the Party,
know the world of being a father and husband with her. Brenda and I have
only been together inside the Party, but our relationship has always entailed
a more complete coming together than that of Pat and me, and I figure the
intellectual and emotional compatibility we have enjoyed will continue. She's
working as a secretary; I'll get my job soon. We'll live together as I slowly
disengage from Pat and keep seeing the kids. Things will work out.

Driving over I formulate my plans. Tonight makes it clear I must proceed
the only way I know, the way I've been taught: make a concrete analysis of
concrete situations. Oakland's my town, my home. No one knows these
streets as well as I do. I'll drive around, visit my old spots, talk to people,
find out for myself what's going on.

Next day I start, apprehensive, hopeful.

The liquor store:

Hey, David. Hugs, handshakes. The usual questions about jail, congratu-
lations on getting out.

What do you hear about Huey?

Guys shake their head, look grim.

That nigger was going around terrorizing everybody, David. Best stay
away from him.

In De Fremery, under the trees near the Victorian mansion community
center:

It ain't like when you left, David. You guys had the respect of the community then. It's different now.

Old friends, ex-Muslims, small-business owners, street people.

They say Huey was—I start, relating some rumor I've heard.

David, that's nothing, they interrupt, and tell a much worse story.

"You guys got to be wrong," I say finally. I've been drinking for some
time in an after-hours joint. I feel compelled to defend Huey; after all, these

accusations refute my past judgment. "You niggers are just bad-mouthing Huey behind his back. You wouldn't be telling Huey that to his face. I don't want to hear that stuff."

A guy answers me angrily. "You know what?" he says. "You're absolutely out of your mind. This man *mis-used* you, *mis-used* everybody. Look what he did to you. You're in danger and you don't even know it."

Everything's upside down. Huey's in Cuba, but word on the street says the Squad's still active and even has a contract out to hit me. I've helped train guys like the ones presumably out to do me in; the threat makes me feel like Malcolm when he broke with Elijah Muhammad and faced members of the Fruit of Islam who had once been his lieutenants and were now under orders to destroy him. Plus, with all the changes that have happened, I'm no longer confident in my reading of the current of the streets—the comings and goings, gestures, greetings, and attitudes that signify what's really happening.

I don't even know the faces of my enemies—faceless faces, George Jackson used to call them. One night J.J. and I are drinking at a bar and some young guys walk in.

"See those guys?" J.J. says over his cognac. "They're Panthers."

I look around for someone I recognize. "Where?"

He gestures to the kids. "Those dudes over there."

I feel like I'm back in prison: people I don't even know are out to harm me. I'm like a space traveler who's landed on an unknown planet, finding out everything for the first time—except that the planet was once my own home, the place on earth where I could relax.

I'm not even sure now about my old friends. Driving on the freeway, Pat sees Emory in a car ahead of us. We race alongside.

"Emory!" I shout.

Emory stares straight ahead.

I figure he can't hear me and roll down the window, stick my head out. "Emory! Emory!"

Emory keeps looking straight ahead, ignoring me.

"Pat, honk the horn! Emory's trying to act like he don't know me!"

Pat honks and I shout, but Emory—Emory! we worked together ever since the day after the shoot-out, the first morning on the bus, riding around saying, Free Huey!—never breaks, finally driving off, leaving me.

I call up old members, June in Alabama, Masai, Big Man, trying to piece things together, find out what's happened, what devastation has wiped out my life.

They all say the same. Masai relates the story of his beating. Guys hit him around the head and back, trying to kill him, then took him in a car and dropped him off at Dr. Small's house, saying he had fallen off a truck. They answer questions with unrepentant hostility; they curse Huey, curse the Party, curse their time in the organization as though the Party were the worst thing that ever happened to them.

"They don't understand," I tell Brenda. We talk at night after she comes home from work and before I go out to meet people in the clubs.

"I'm gonna speak to Melvin. Melvin understands Huey. He loves Huey. All these other guys have always had their own agendas."

I meet Melvin at his home; he's teaching at Merritt College, a respected member of the academic community.

We wrap arms around each other.

"Hey, Melvin," I start, "let me tell you something. I need to get in contact with Huey." I still believe that one conversation with Huey will solve all the problems; I'll be able to lead the life I imagined waited for me when I went to prison: days doing Party work, nights at the Lamp Post.

Melvin scowls, shakes his head. "Wait until he approaches you."

"Well, I'm eager to talk to him," I persist.

"It's best to leave that stuff alone." He has already adopted the attitude everyone assumes when I bring up the subject, hearing me reluctantly, nodding without agreeing, acting as though I'm making a fool of myself and that he's too good a friend to embarrass me by calling attention to my willful delusion.

But I press on. This is Melvin: we've been through a lot together. "It's the Party," I say, "I can't forget it."

No equivocation or evasion now. He looks straight at me. "I'm telling you, David," he says. "Leave Huey alone. For your sake. You don't know what you're getting into. He's even accused me of trying to kill him."

"I want to find out what happened," I say.

"You're not gonna find out. Leave it alone. All that stuff will work itself out in time."

Later that night I call June.

"There's something I don't understand," I say.

"Just get out of there," he tells me.

Which is what he's done. But I can't do that yet. I have a sense of pride. Oakland is my home. You don't make me leave until I'm ready to go.

Personal matters aren't working out either.

The kids aren't happy. Patrice wants us to lead a Brady Bunch family life completely antithetical to our reality. Meanwhile the boys are lured by the streets.

"When you got out of jail," says Darryl,

I was trying to catch up on all this stuff I missed—hanging out all night going to parties, having a girlfriend. That's when I started running the streets. Everything out there was fun to me. It was a *game,* going out, stealing a car, driving around, or running and snatching a purse. Going to jack somebody—you catch them coming out of a bar, coming down the street, pace them for a minute, then run up, just grab them and one punch to the head and snatch their wallet or jewelry and go on about your business. Never used a weapon. It was a challenge. Some days you'd get two hundred, some days you'd get a penny. We had about eleven boys. "The Berkeley Boys." I was "D." That's all they'd call me. I was known through town—a known character. If you wanted clothes, jewelry, pistols, cameras, and that kind of stuff, you looked for Darryl or one of the gang—"them youngsters." You knew I was taking folks off because I used to get busted and call you. A couple of times you said, "Well, I told you. Stay in jail. I'm not coming to get you. You *need* to be in jail. You'll learn your lesson if you stay there."

The promised jobs disappear. Past Party supporters who are now local politicians give me little more than lip service. Plus, the available jobs represent a serious step down from my Party experience. When I finally secure employment—as a field rep for the Service Employees International Union—I'm temperamentally unprepared to start at the bottom; I've helped create a world-renowned organization, and I'm used to making decisions.

Plus, we never seem to have enough money. One change that has occurred since I went to jail is that the world is aswirl with things; you feel a constant pressure to buy the hottest fashion, eat in the newest restaurant, purchase the latest piece of electronic equipment. When I went in people constantly discussed politics; now all they talk about is real estate. In the years of the Party we always preached the collective spirit, tried to practice socialism within our organization. Now everyone's out to amass as much for themselves as possible—a Yahoo mentality has taken hold.

Resenting our never having enough, I make plans. With Brenda I start writing a book about my experiences. And I experiment in dealing coke—everybody is trying to subsidize their income by dealing. Using parts of my money, Brenda's paycheck, and Pat's welfare stipend, I buy a quantity. But I never sell it. Instead I get caught up using the drug. Well, I tell myself, I'll only use a gram, then sell the rest. Before I know it the drug has disappeared. Now I've not made any money and lost the five hundred I used to buy the stuff—which, as often as not, was supposed to go for rent or something. The new debt compels me to think about selling some more coke. I buy even more to double or triple my money and end up further in debt. And I never guilt-trip, because I promise myself that the next time I won't use any. Feeling more confident, I imagine a new plan that will pull me out of the morass; I get more money and repeat this process, becoming my own best customer.

Regent Street becomes unaffordable, and Pat and I move to a cheaper single-family rental complete with a genie that makes the garage door go up and down—Patrice's suburban dream come true—and an orange tree in the backyard. Pat plans for me to buy the new house, but I've agreed only to provide the greater share of the rent: I still spend half or more of my week with Brenda, still hope to end up living with her.

But breaking with Pat seems almost impossible. I'm assailed by guilt at the thought of abandoning her. Yet moments between us are never satisfying or peaceful; however we start, we always end up drinking or tooting and going after each another.

Plus, Pat doesn't seem to have the self-respect that would compel her to break off our relationship for her own sake. No matter what I do, no matter how my actions might humiliate her, she continues to accept me. Part of her denial is to refuse to recognize that I'm in a relationship with Brenda. When I'm at Brenda's, Pat calls in the middle of the night or on weekends, drives over when she feels like it, issues peremptory demands on my time and money, never respecting the fact that I'm actually trying to create a new life with this person.

"Why don't you make a decision," Brenda demands. "You're not living with Pat, and the way she acts is very disrespectful. Either tell her to stop calling or go back. You've got to draw some clear lines here."

But clear lines means committing myself to Brenda, and I'm not ready for that. Lots of contradictions arise between us. I'm used to giving orders and having them carried out and am not prepared to extend the sexual equality we shared in the Party into everyday life. But to Brenda, we're simply lovers—I'm not the Chief of Staff anymore—and my word doesn't carry any special weight. Plus, after her experience in the Party she's used to making her own decisions; she refuses to return to a traditional relationship now.

I read her independence as rejection. When she suggests that maybe I shouldn't stay with her as often or at all, I burn with abandonment and betrayal.

"I gave the Party up for you," I say.

"What do you want me to do?" she answers. It's after work and she's putting away stuff she's bought for the house. "I'm not responsible for what the Party did. Huey says that. But it wasn't me. You'll find out. I'm not responsible."

I accuse her of loving Huey, betraying me by sleeping with other men while I was in prison.

"I didn't want to do that," she defends herself. "I was doing it for the Servant."

I tell her she's lying to herself. I believe I've given up everything to be with this woman—my wife, kids, the security of the Party. I feel she owes me something.

"If I loved Huey," she answers, "why did I leave the Party? He wanted me to stay. He wanted me to abandon you for him, and I didn't do it. That's why he was mad."

"I put my life on the line for you," I say.

Brenda turns her back on me, small and sure of herself, hanging things in the closet.

"You're absolutely selfish," I tell her.

"What do you want me to do?" she explodes. "Why are you doing this to me?"

Then a situation occurs that brings everything to a head. Brenda befriends a girl who lives next door. I warn her against the relationship: one Party rule is to limit socializing to members. But now Brenda thinks she has to branch out. The girl has friends of her own, street people, and though I warn Brenda not to let these guys up, she goes ahead and the place is robbed.

"I told you," I say. "I told you not to bother with those unprincipled people, and you didn't listen."

Brenda confronts the girl, saying she knows the girl stole the stuff, threatening her. A couple of days later we see the girl with members of the Squad and she's boasting that she now belongs to the Panther Party. I understand what's happening: she's gone to the Squad to protect herself against me and Brenda. I'm scared and edgy anyway—I'm drinking constantly and using coke—and this situation is completely unacceptable. I can't have these guys next door; for all I know they could be waiting to kill me. I go to confront them, knock on the door and walk in. The girl's with two guys from the Squad. I remember one from when he first entered the Party, a fourteen-year-old who idolized Bunchy.

"Hey," I say, "how you guys doing?"

I wait, standing there exposed, looking at them.

"What's up?"

No answer but their stares. I laugh, turn around, and leave: I've made my point.

"David," Brenda warns me when I get back, "you've got to be careful. You taunted them. You can't mess with those guys."

I tell Tony Gibson about what's happened—he's recently been released and has come from Los Angeles to put together a dope deal.

Tony says he wants to put a hit on Huey when Huey returns from Cuba. "Guys in LA will do what you tell them to," he says. "All you have to do is give me the order."

Tony's talked like this before, when we were in prison, after my expulsion. "Yeah, I'd like to go one-on-one with Huey," he'd say, "discipline him." But now that the possibility of taking action is real, I must make clear that his idea is completely unacceptable.

"I won't do that," I say. "Huey could have killed me many times. Whatever he's done, he's never hurt me."

Then I fall out with Tony because he gives Brenda a diamond ring: he knows my problems with her, and I suspect he's trying to get her away from me. I tell him to take back the ring.

"What's wrong with you?" he says. "You know what? I'm gone."

That night I speak to June.

"I knew you were drinking," he says.

I talked to you and Pat and family members. They told me you were just about out of control and they were concerned about you. I had been on a drinking binge myself after that whole situation. Drinking every day, depressed about what had happened to the Party and that we had to leave Oakland, and not liking the way I left, humiliated by that. Frances finally threatened to leave me. She just couldn't deal with it anymore. I said, "Well, we've come through all this turmoil and hard times, a drink of alcohol isn't gonna cause separation. I never liked drinking anyway. Alcohol hurts me and makes me sick."

"I don't know what's going on," I say.

"Come down here," he says. "You got to get away from there."

I meet Alex Hoffmann and tell him I feel empty.

"David, the problem's not outside," Alex says. "Nothing is going to be right until you get right with yourself."

I agree. Right with myself. I certainly can't do that here. I'm back and forth between Brenda and Pat, and Brenda is in misery, losing weight, crying a lot. One day I walk into the apartment and find new furniture.

"Where'd you get this furniture?" I demand.

"I got a severance check," she says.

"Why didn't you tell me," I start. "I give you all my money and you hold back on me. After everything I did—"

I scream about her hiding money and her selfish nature. When everything calms down, Brenda says she can't deal with this, maybe we should break.

I know she's right: as angry as I am, I can see the relationship is destroying her. I go to Pat, ask if she wants to try living in Alabama.

"It happened quick," Dorion remembers.

It was just like, "Come on! We're going to Alabama." We were packed in the car and gone. Me and my brother was excited about it—driving all the way across country. When I got to Alabama, I had a frightening dream. In Oakland I had just learned to whistle with my fingers. In my dream I was being kidnapped. I saw my dad or someone a block away. But the guys were grabbing me by my hands, trying to shove me in the car. I was fighting them, trying to stay out of the car. I could feel myself trying to call the person that I saw down the street, but the person couldn't hear me. I woke up sweating, scared and everything.

The next day I saw a friend who knew how to whistle with no fingers. Man, I told him, you got to teach me—because inside I was scared. And I learned that very day.

Chapter
33

THIS is David, the guys in Mobile say, he comes from California—the future. I haven't been back since my father's death, and the attorneys, politicians, government workers who are my new acquaintances represent the new, post–civil rights Mobile: black-populated Prichard and Spring Hill, Martin Luther King Boulevard—not Davis Avenue—and an integrated city administration. Among them I'm a legend and VIP, a prime mover in the Black Panther Party, an historical figure with stories to tell and experience to relate. I can scale the heights, Bunchy used to say when he felt particularly confident, and the same spirit moves me now. When some local whites harass Darryl on the way to school, I go to the principal and mayor, telling them I'm David Hilliard, former Black Panther Party Chief of Staff, and that I'll mobilize the black community if they don't put an immediate end to these racists' terrorizing my kids with guns. The mayor promptly assures me he'll station a patrol car in the area. Soon I'm named head of a four-person staff on a CETA ex-offenders program, securing work for just-released inmates and setting up job programs. Plus, I rent a palatial three-bedroom house complete with a lush backyard, creek, and brick barbecue pit. The rent seems almost nothing to me, coming from Oakland, but the grandeur of the home impresses the local people, adding to my prestige.

I celebrate my success in my usual way: I drink, have a party. But the liquor only succeeds in calling up my loneliness and anger. Despondent, bitter, I think about Huey, Brenda, mull over events. Then I buy some coke, using the drug to bolster my confidence. I never imagine my drinking and tooting to be in any way self-destructive. To my mind the drugs don't affect my behavior: I can drink all night without ever throwing up or staggering, and I certainly never associate my anger or insane behavior with the drugs — my rages at my family or other loved ones, my drug schemes, all seem normal ways of getting over.

Patrice hates the change.

"I didn't want to go to Alabama," she says.

This was the fifth, sixth move since the Black Panther Party, within a year's time, from home to home, house to house. As soon as you're comfortable with one place, then all of a sudden you come home, it's time to move again. When is this gonna stop? I'm tired of moving. Let's stay in a shelter or anything as long as we have a place to consider home. The moving meant we didn't have any friends — our friends were only for a few minutes.

She complains the entire ride to Alabama. Why are we going? Everything was fine back in Oakland. She liked our new house. At every stop she calls her boyfriend, coming back to the car steamed and furious. She acts as though I have purposefully made her life miserable. I don't know what to tell her. One night she says she often lies in bed and cries, that she's frustrated and tired.

"I think about committing suicide," she says.

We sit on my sister Sweetie's porch; she and her husband, Paul, live in a rambling farmhouse on forty acres outside of Mobile; other relatives often drop by without warning, and there's always food to eat.

"Well, you can't give up, Patrice," I say. "You want to become a model. You can go to school in Atlanta. It's a big city. There are lots of black colleges there and lots of opportunity."

"I was searching for love," she remembers.

When I tried to tell you what was wrong, you told me it wasn't true. Neither you nor Mom were *listening* to me. I needed to talk to you, to share with you about my experiences in the Black Panther Party, what it had done to me, how I *felt*. I wanted some reassurance, whether we would be a family or not, or whether we would continue moving from here to there, and would our life continue being chaotic, and if there was someplace I could go, or something that I could do to try to understand what I was feeling and what was going on. I tried to tell you what I had been feeling from when I was a little girl and I first heard you beat up Mother and how I had felt since you'd been out of the Black Panther Party—how you didn't spend time with us, and how when my brothers were involved in a golf tournament and baseball, that you were never there. I *wanted* to share those feelings with you.

What can I tell her? Apologize for the Party, the best thing in my life? Tell her that her father is going to transform himself completely? Even as I speak to her my mind is partly elsewhere, remembering Brenda, hating June for leaving me, obsessing over some aspect of my expulsion or what happened with Huey.

"It doesn't make sense," I say to June when he repeats—at my insistence—how Huey expelled Brenda. We're in BK's "hit house," one of the illegal bars where people get around Alabama's blue laws by selling repackaged liquor for a dollar a shot, precursors of the crack houses about to spread throughout the country.

"It's not gonna make sense," June answers, "whatever I tell you."

I pour myself another shot of gin from the mayonnaise jar in which they serve the alcohol—they don't use regular liquor bottles in case the police make a raid. I persist like Huey would, refusing to accept what June says. "And that was the reason?" I say.

"That was the reason," June says. He's looking down, wanting to end the conversation.

"There's got to be more," I say.

"The reason is there was no reason. What do you want out of the man? The man was crazy. If it hadn't been that reason it would have been something else."

I take this in and put some more ice in the drink. I want to return to another insult.

"Well, June," I say, "why didn't I ever get a message from you."

"I sent you a tape and a letter," he replies.

Not good enough, I think. "What'd you jump up and leave for?"

"I did what I had to do," he says.

One night, I get an idea. I'm planning to buy some coke off a guy. I'll rip him off, I think. Strong-arm the guy, take the drugs. Act the way the Party did when I was in jail. Why not? Get June to come along. That's what he was doing when I was in jail. Why won't he do it now?

I drive to June's, tell him the plan outside his house.

"You're drunk and out of your mind, David," he says. "Forget this stuff. What are you talking about? 'I'm gonna take this man's drugs.'"

Another rejection. I don't argue. I've got a gun—a .380 Beretta—in the car; I'll do the job myself.

Liquor fueling my anger, I drive to the guy's place. I feel absolutely justified in taking this dealer's dope and his life. I picture myself going up, knocking on the guy's screen door. Hey, David how are you? then—

The guy lives on a street of shotgun shacks, two-bedroom houses with small porches. He's not home. I circle the cottage, cursing and furious.

"You looking for somebody?" a passerby asks.

"I'm taking a walk and it's none of your business," I say. I storm back to the car, thwarted and furious. I need to get my anger out, but no one's around. I drive to June's, the unused gun in my pocket; if I hadn't spent that time talking to June the guy might have been there.

Outside June's the loud static of the insects' buzz rises and falls. The air is suffocating, a combination of the funk of the Prichard paper mill and the low tide.

I knock on the door. "June! I gotta speak to you."

June comes out, wondering what I want.

"I'm angry with you," I say. "You left me. It was very cowardly what you did. You're a punk. You lost your nerve. You were scared."

"Be a damn fool if I wasn't," June answers. "Anybody would have been scared under that situation. You're dealing with a madman."

His answer only makes me angrier. "You ran off and left me."

"My life was in danger, David," June answers. He speaks in his softest voice, trying to explain. "I didn't have time to contact you. I had to get out of there. If I hadn't I probably wouldn't be standing here talking to you now. And you probably wouldn't be talking to me."

I want to get away from the unbearable night, leave the smell, the noise, the reasonableness of June's answer.

I pull the gun out of my pocket.

"You're not angry with me," June says. "You've got a point to prove."

I extend my hand, pointing the gun at him. I plan to shoot him, not kill him: I don't want to make Mother mourn. I'll shoot him in the leg, exact a political consequence.

"Yeah, I've got a point to prove," I say. "I'm gonna shoot your ass."

June sees the gun. He pauses, then speaks: "Go on. You feel like you got to shoot me, go ahead and shoot me."

I cock the gun. "You don't want me to shoot you, June. You're scared."

"You're damn right I'm scared," he says. "I was scared then, I'm scared now. But go ahead and shoot if it's gonna make you feel better."

He waits for me.

I aim at his leg.

"I never thought you were gonna shoot me," he says now.

You were searching, trying to find out what had happened, what it was that you had done to bring about the expulsion. You wouldn't allow yourself to believe that you didn't do anything—because Huey had said you had done something, and what Huey thought had more power over you than your own self. You were searching for a cause, a reason, and it was beating hell out of you. But I never thought you were gonna shoot me. Maybe I was a little naive. But if you had wanted to do something, you had plenty of chances. Instead it seemed to me you were acting out of frustration and anger.

I lift the gun, holding it waist high. Blow his leg off. I've drunk a lot, but I'm not drunk. Matter of fact, after I shoot June I'll go to the bar and get another drink.

"I'm gonna shoot your fucking ass."

June doesn't move.

June: still and solid as a rock.

I pull the trigger.

The gun bucks up as the bullet buries itself in the ground, exploding a mound of earth.

June doesn't move.

Pat and Frances run out, screaming.

I can't even shoot the man. I get back in the car, drive off.

Later that night I call Brenda from the bar.

"I'm on my way to California," I tell her. "We got something to talk about." Tonight I'm going to deal with all the wreckage of my past.

I lie to Pat and drink the entire flight to Oakland. An ex–Party member meets me at the airport and we drive to Brenda's house.

I walk into Brenda's place and see the new furniture. Immediately I'm back arguing with her, wanting to hurt her, furious at the sacrifices I've made for her. Everything about her strikes me as selfish and calculating. I scream about the furniture. Crying and scared, Dassine runs and calls Brenda's mother. When I become physical Brenda dashes to a closet. I see her take a gun—

"Bitch!"

I jump on her, drag her down. She's got a gun we used to keep for security against the pigs. "You gonna kill me!"

"I was keeping it from you!"

Her mother comes in and reaches in her purse. The Party member takes my gun and points it at her: "You pull that, I'm shooting." Only a moment away from mayhem, I get my sense back, tell him to stop.

"I never want to see you again," I say to Brenda, knowing she only wants one thing: for me to get out of her life. "If I see you again, I'll kill you."

I go back to Alabama. Soon after, Patrice runs away, taking a bus to Oakland, where she spends a week with her boyfriend. When she returns, I find out she's run up more than five hundred dollars' worth of long-distance calls on Frances and June's number. June says he can't pay the charges—they've already paid one outlandish bill—and asks why I can't control my daughter. I'm enraged at Patrice. We've gone through this all before, and I've told her if she wants to speak to this guy every night she must call him collect—otherwise he's just pimping me, as well as her.

Now I look for her, finding her on my brother Allen's porch.

"Patrice," I say, "I understand that words don't mean much. I'm a Panther Party member and I don't trust words anyway. I asked you not to call—"

"Well I didn't want to come here anyway," she answers.

"Well you don't have to be here. Go anywhere you want. But you're not fucking me over, and since you don't understand words, you understand this—"

"I'd seen you hit and be very mean to my mother," Patrice says.

But you'd never hit me in my life, and I was fifteen years old.

That was it.

I said, "This is the end. I am not gonna take this, I am not gonna deal with this."

I got bus fare and moved back to Oakland. I got pregnant with my son. I did it on purpose because I was searching for love. I felt like that was the *only* way that I could love someone, or someone would love me back.

I went to a nursing school; it happened to be very racist. There was only three black students and it was very challenging. My mother didn't support me, you didn't support me—anyway I wouldn't have called to ask your advice if you had paid me to. I was on my own. I didn't have anyone I could go back to. I saved my little money that I earned from working as a dietician's aide and paid my way. I took a six-month course. It cost six hundred dollars. It was a very hard course. One of the other black girls — who came from somewhat of a very bougie family — assisted me. Her mother and I would go to the library and do research. My teacher was an older white lady, and she did *not* like black kids at all. In the beginning of the class she told me that she didn't think I would make a good nurse, and that I would probably need assistance, and I was too young, and that I should go ahead and be focusing on going to college and not wasting my time working at no hospital. Just real discouraging things. At the end of the course she came and told me she was very proud, that she didn't think I was going to be able to make that course and pass the state exam. But I made it — I made it! And I had no one to come to my graduation.

No one tells me I'm out of control. My life proceeds as though I'm living a normal existence. Weeks I spend working. Every day I visit the hit houses with my brother Allen. Set them all up, I say, acting like the big shot. Why not? I got cash in my pocket. We need to get a good time going. Some of the places are forlorn: a guy or two sits in the living room, as likely as not unconscious from alcohol, in front of a television soap opera; a young kid waits to deliver a bottle or two to a good customer, the woman who runs the place works in the kitchen under a forever turning fan. Others got jukeboxes and women and you're happy to stay all day and night. I go in, start drinking and become sentimental, remembering Brenda. I play records we used to listen to, trying to bring back my California life, even while I swear never to return to Oakland because the city is death. Unable to escape the past, I find the present unbearable. When my boss tries to implicate me in some trouble, I blow up. We're at a meeting and he attempts to hold me responsible for some misappropriation of funds that's his fault. No, I tell my co-workers. You obviously don't know who you're dealing with. I don't need your job. I can go back to California, work longshore, and you'd better give me my check right now because if I have to wait for it I'll probably get violent. Next day we pack our bags and drive away from Alabama.

"I'm starting to figure out, 'What's with my parents, always moving?'" remembers Dorion.

That started to bother me because I saw so much inconsistency and that the inconsistency in your lives in turn was gonna bring inconsistency to mine. I saw you taking me away from an opportunity. I had friends and everything; I didn't want to leave. I even tried to get you to talk to my football coach. But your mind was made up that you weren't gonna stay and for some reason you didn't want me to stay either. You were just ready to go.

Okay, I tell myself, Alabama's not the answer. We'll find a new home. I'll overcome difficulties. Nobody bests me. I'll survive.

Chapter
34

"DOING geographics," the program calls it—trying to find a new life by changing where you live.

Los Angeles is first.

Through personal contacts, I get a job at Tom Hayden's new political organization, CED, the Campaign for Economic Democracy. At first I earn a stipend provided by a movie executive who's an old Party friend. Hoping to get elected representing all-white Santa Monica, Tom has little interest in the South Central LA black vote. Then money for a solar energy experiment becomes available and I serve as a conduit between local organizations and a funding organization. Plus, I arrange movie screenings throughout the black community at which Jane Fonda comes and speaks about rent control.

The job makes my life schizophrenic. Nights I sleep at my sister's, one of the featureless stucco-and-slat houses that line the flat Los Angeles ghetto streets. Days I drive into Beverly Hills and Santa Monica, hobnobbing with executives and movie stars who support Tom and Jane. Every morning I pass from the glaring, shadeless streets of Compton to the palm-lined boulevards of Beverly Hills. The journey from the hidden-away destitution to the ostentatious opulence feels like a million miles. I often spend the time remembering my trips here as a Panther, first spending time with Bunchy, then later meeting stars, and the stark difference of purpose between my present and past life rebukes and scorns me.

The flaunted wealth of the Hollywood community—riding the freeway every other car I pass is a Rolls or Mercedes—embitters me. I despise their egoism while envying their fortune. One night Tom holds a party at Helen Reddy's house. Tents dot the rock star's tennis courts and Jags and stretch limos fill the parking lot. Small people—midgets, I guess—dressed as leprechauns serve food, their size and green garb celebrating Tom's Irish heritage. I spend the evening talking about left-wing politics and economic democracy.

"Where's the democracy?" I say to Pat when I come home. It takes a good forty-five minutes to drive from their manicured lawns to Compton's cookie-cutter single-family houses. "They should share their money. Then they can talk about democracy. Make me a movie star. Put me in one of your films and pay me three or four million dollars for standing in front of a camera and acting out a role."

One weekend we visit Tom and Jane's ranch in Santa Barbara. I fill the two days strategizing while burning with resentment. Toward the end a movie producer who's an old friend of Huey's greets me warmly.

"Huey hopes you get in touch with him," he says.

Defying the advice of his closest friends, Huey has returned from Cuba in the past year.

"Huey came back to fight the charges against him and to take charge of the Party," Melvin says.

It was not a move that I encouraged. I didn't want him to come back. He had to face the same kind of threats from government agencies and individuals. I told him so, by telephone, when he was in Cuba. I encouraged him not to come back, to make himself useful there—go back to school, pursue his continuing education, become a useful member of that community. We even talked about going to medical school. The Cubans were open to almost anything Huey wanted to do. They appreciated his being there, and they were good hosts.

Charles Garry tried to get him to stay too.

But Huey didn't want to remain in exile, and the next thing I heard was that he was coming back.

He arrived in good shape. I confronted him about reports I had heard that he had even feared I might harm him. He said he had a mental breakdown. I accepted what he said, and what that did, of course, was end that conversation, so I couldn't get on his case.

"You gonna call him?" Pat asks.

"Of course," I say. "I love Huey. Besides, I got some questions to ask him."

We meet at a restaurant in Jack London Square. Two guys from the Squad sit at the bar, checking out whether Pat and I are alone. After a few minutes they leave. I don't mention the precaution, though their presence amazes me: Does Huey still think I might hurt him?

But Huey himself couldn't be more gracious. He looks strong, handsome, buffed from lifting, exudes good spirits, and acts as a perfect host, kindly, considerate, gentlemanly, witty — when he wants, Huey can display a trenchant wit, describing people and events precisely, employing his acute intelligence for comic effect. He asks me about my job and I describe my increasing discomfort — the solar energy money is running out, and Tom seems increasingly uninterested in black support. I draw a weekly check, but feel irrelevant and guilty: I don't want to take money for killing time. I tell him about the SMG, the Sunday Morning Group, regular meetings held with Masai and other ex-Panthers; I've tried to get them to put together a proposal so we can get some solar energy money, but Masai and the others seem obsessed with the Party, constantly retreading the Party's mistakes and failures much the same as I do when I'm drunk. Huey and I recall some old times, and finally he apologizes for my trial, taking personal responsibility for Hallinan and explaining that FBI letters and false rumors fed his suspicions of me. I listen, charmed but still skeptical: he hasn't mentioned the bodyguards. Then, as we're leaving, he rises to the occasion as usual:

"I have to tell you, David," he says, "that I brought bodyguards and you only brought Pat. I'm really ashamed of myself."

It's a new world. There's no comradeship anymore, no movement, no leadership. People spout left-wing pieties to feel good about themselves; everything is a circus of individualism. Why should you hold to the old tenets? No one does. I live in a world of crass material values now, not community; everybody seizes their own privileges; I want my share.

The changes affect the black community. Everything is much more extreme. The kinds of fights Huey and I used to have in high school, for instance, are now deadly affairs.

"It was right before Christmas," Dorion remembers.

You had just given me fifty dollars and I was also working at Burger King so I had seventy-five dollars in my pocket and I was gonna go get me like a little ten-dollar bag and have some weed to smoke with my friends.

I got in my friend's car — Darryl, who we called Horsehead because he had a big, huge head, looked like the Elephant Man. Darryl's gonna drive me to get the pot. And my brother and some other guys go off for a moment.

Darryl knows the gang members. And there was this one guy in a wheelchair who was a gang member, a Blood member—that's how he ended up in the wheelchair.

The guy in the wheelchair ensued to question Darryl Horsehead about talking some mess about his family and punking him.

So the guy puts his wheelchair between the car and the door so it can't close and pulls out a handgun and grabbed Darryl by the shirt collar and started pistol-whipping him while I'm sitting over in the passenger seat. He's popping him in the head with the butt of the gun and I'm saying to myself, "I hope this fool don't decide he wants to *rob* me." Because he was out there when I asked Darryl, "Do they have change for a fifty?"

Blood's running all down Darryl's face and the guy pulls Darryl down and puts his head in his lap and reaches over and points the gun at me and says, "Give me your money."

"Man, what are you talking about, man? I ain't got no money. What are you talking about?"

He's like, "Don't give me that shit, punk, or I'll *shoot* you. I don't play no games."

"Man, what do I got to do with this? You know, I don't even *know* you. Why are you gonna take *my* money?"

"I don't want to hear it. Just give me your money."

Trying to be slick, I pull the fifty out of my pocket.

"You got more money than that, man! What do you think I am? A *fool* or something? Pull it all out before I shoot you right now!"

"Man, it ain't that serious. Here, you can *have* the money!"

He rolled off and I hopped out of the car and ran in the house real fast. "Daddy! Darryl! The guy in the wheelchair robbed me, robbed me!"

You were like, "Where is he?"

"I don't know, I don't know! He went down the alley."

You gave us the gun to go find the guy and get my money back.

We couldn't find him. But two weeks later my brother saw the guy. I guess the guy had a bad reputation, because he went grocery shopping late at night. Darryl ran home and said, "Doe, Doe, I seen the guy! Come on, come on!"

We took the gun again, got in the car, and caught the guy right at the corner. I knew the guy didn't remember who I was; he was just robbing somebody—that's why I was so pissed off about it, because he didn't give me any respect.

We rode up, caught the guy right at the corner, flicked the lights of the car, and when he looked up just shot a couple of times. I don't know what ever happened to him, but at least he *knows* that *somebody's* out to get him. He can't be just fucking over people. So I felt somewhat relieved. But I never got my money back anyway.

The other new thing is the drugs. One day a friend tells me I should try the latest variation of cocaine. You take a vial of coke, mix the powder with the right amount of baking soda and water, and stir. When the stuff begins to harden along the side, you slowly immerse the vial into a pot of boiling water—always being sure not to close the vial too tightly because otherwise the cocaine will explode. Once the mixture liquefies you remove the vial, placing it immediately under cold water; the rock that comes out is called crack.

Pat and I experiment at our house, Darryl looking on.

"Pat," I say before we begin, "listen to me. You gotta do this right. Don't hold the smoke. This stuff will give you a heart attack. Plus, you won't even get high swallowing. You get high when you exhale through your nose."

But Pat doesn't listen. She sucks on the pipe, doesn't exhale, like she's smoking a joint, and falls straight over on her face.

"Daddy!" Darryl screams. "Mommy's dead!"

"No, she's not," I say, "get some ice. She'll be all right."

The drugs make me crazy. Liquor starts my self-destruction; cocaine guarantees it. Always needing money for the drugs, I constantly convince myself I can concoct a scheme to score and get out of debt. My sense of values and truth disintegrate. Later, when I start smoking crack all the time, my obsession becomes truly limitless, and all I care about is hearing the boiling of the pots and seeing the rock forming in the bottom.

When the CED job runs its course, I figure out a plan. A woman with millions loans me fifteen thousand to buy a house. The small place needs remodeling into a two-bedroom, but I figure I'll use the money to secure the property, pay for the work and mortgage while I also start repaying her because soon I'll get another job. But I don't find a job. Instead I drink and use. As the money shrinks, I cast about for a way to get even financially, get my feet on dry land. As usual I snort the drugs I mean to sell and go into arrears on the mortgage and the monthly loan payments. Convincing myself I can get out of the jam with one more buy, I end up deeper in debt. Finally the house is foreclosed. I've got five thousand left. I write the woman a note, telling her the situation, and leave.

We go to Oakland, leaving Dorion behind — he thinks he has a career as a college athlete and doesn't want to change schools again.

Oakland's full of the past. One night Alex Hoffmann invites me to a party for Ron Dellums.

"I went to pick you up with my roommate — not lover — who was a black, gay, younger guy. He reminded me a lot of you in some ways," remembers Alex, "And I wanted the two of you to meet. We went by your house and banged on the door. You were hiding out. You didn't want to come out or go, and I sort of physically dragged you out of bed and schlepped you to this party where everybody was overjoyed to see you, including Ron. But you had a real hard time."

I don't want the pressure of their love. Their approval shames me. I can't fulfill their vision or expectations of me, and their presence simply serves, unintentionally, to humiliate me.

Other friends from the past appear. J.J. tells me he's got some monster crack. I tell him I prefer to snort, basing does nothing for me. J.J. says I must be doing something wrong, wasting the drug by not preparing it correctly.

He cooks the powder, returning with a perfect rock, not the flaky residue I manufacture. We light up and I inhale, letting the smoke out my nose.

J.J.'s right. This is it. No more tooting for me.

"J.J.," I say, "I tell you what we're gonna do. I got five thousand in my pocket. I want to buy an ounce. You're gonna teach me how to cook it, and we're gonna make some money."

My desire's insatiable. Nothing can compare to this sensation, not any other drug, not sex.

"Tell you what," says J.J. as we smoke. "I got a house. You got no place to live. But you got all this money. Now I'm your partner so I'm not trying to run any game on you. But you pay this debt I got with this dealer — only seven hundred dollars — and you and Pat can just move into my apartment tonight. I'll move the bitch who's living there out. Don't worry about me. The girl can find someplace else to stay. And I can live with my old lady."

Now we're set. I still have my longshore card. I'm glad to be home and to reacquaint myself with old friends.

On my birthday Huey calls and invites me out. When I get to the restaurant he's organized a surprise party.

"Huey," I say, "you got to try this new drug."

"Absolutely not," he says. "I don't understand that stuff. It doesn't do anything to anybody. I think you guys are wasting your money."

"You're wrong," I say. "You don't know how to smoke it." Then I joke, "And it's a good thing you don't. The way you be putting it up your nose, you don't need to smoke it. Once you start smoking, the world's in trouble."

Huey thinks I'm joking, but the next week I take him to my friend's crack house and leave him there to experience the drug on his own. Several days later my friend calls:

"David," he says, "how could you bring Huey over here? I can't get him out."

Huey gets on the phone. "David, you were right. I wasn't smoking it right. But I'm doing it right now. Come on over."

I drive to see him. Huey's eyes shine like headlights. He talks nonstop, elaborating a plan to dominate the drug trade. Plus, he's figured out the drug. He rambles on, explaining his theory that the drug brings out your extremities. For instance, J.J. and I are givers, generous, so when I take the drug I look for somebody to share it with. But with others the drug will accentuate their violent side.

"Well, I always thought I had pretty much of an influence over you when you got out of hand," I say.

Huey changes his manner, becoming cold, severe. "That's very arrogant," he says. "I don't even know myself from one day to the next. The man I sleep with is not the man I wake up with. How are you gonna control me?"

I feel myself thrown back into the past, when I could never be sure of what was going to happen and was always jumpy, worried about what Huey would do next, all my attention focused on his moods and thoughts, rather than my own. And I know that if I stay in Oakland and keep smoking I won't be able to resist the pull of the man. So I make up my mind. I tell him no, I'm out of the plan, I've been here before. In the program they talk about moments of clarity, when all the self-deluding tricks that guide you through your addiction vanish and you see yourself clearly. But the realization, like the addiction, is a process and this moment is the start: over the next years I'm in a constant combat, trying to convince myself I can control things.

I tell Pat and Darryl to pack their things, we're returning to Los Angeles. I don't want anything to do with this man, he's a terrible and terrifying influence on me, and we're leaving immediately.

"I made a decision to stay here in Oakland with the girl I got pregnant," Darryl says.

I told you I didn't feel like going through the same that we just came from. All this traveling was too much pressure. Arguing, moving from place to place. My life was like a merry-go-round. Soon after, I got busted for possession of dope. I did something like three months for that in Santa Rita. Then I made a decision: I don't want to live like my father. I don't want to be going to the penitentiary for four years. So I decided to slow down. I turned towards my kids—I had a little girl and a boy was on the way. Started spending all my time with my little girl and selling drugs on the side. I got jobs, landscaping, painting, anything to survive. For three years I worked as an automobile mechanic's helper, but then I found a quicker way to make money, delivering dope.

Back to Los Angeles.

We live in Hawthorne, with Dorion, pooling our paychecks. I bounce around—job, scheme, job. I work as a courier until I can't get security clearance. I collect unemployment, buy a cheap auto insurance policy and smash up my car, hammering and breaking the lights and fenders right in the streets. Money is meaningless. I go through a thousand or fifteen hundred a night on drugs. I call up old friends and make up stories, telling them my car's broke down or Pat's sick—will they wire money? Western Union becomes my lifeline to alcohol and crack. Needing steady pay, I hire on as a gas-station attendant. The salary's not enough. I call up the husband of the woman who loaned me money.

"I don't want to hear from you ever again," he says. "What you did was absolutely unforgivable."

I live with my sister, then she throws me out. I find a Party friend who invites me to stay with him and get a job packing meat while Pat lives with Dorion. My new housemate doesn't realize I'm drinking, drugging. He wants to believe the best of me—everyone does. He offers me his van, refuses to accept that all my money and energy turn into smoke. One night I come home broken-spirited because I don't have the money to get high.

"I'm so depressed," I cry. "My life ain't coming together. Let me have fifty dollars."

The man doesn't want to believe my state of demoralization. "It's two in the morning, bro. What are you gonna do with fifty dollars?"

I start making up a story—

"You high, David? You using drugs?"

I'm indignant. "Fuck you mean, man, using drugs?"

Immediately he knows the answer. "You gotta leave my house, man. You don't do nothing. You just lay around."

I'm into my act. "Fuck you. Want me to be your slave. I don't slave for nobody. Fuck you."

And back to my relatives.

Because I don't care anymore.

My only predilection is to keep my high going.

Which is what happens when you smoke crack. You always want to increase the high. You never feel you have enough. The drug brings out the dog in you, the most animalistic, selfish side of your nature. You never want to share it, suffer compunctions about how you get the money to buy the drug, what you must do to take that first hit. You don't have time or energy to concentrate on thoughts about anything but obtaining the drug itself. I smoke and think that I could withstand anything—even the death of my mother—with an ounce of coke. Not simply because the drug anesthetizes you—that answer's too simple—but because the drug involves you. Your life becomes a matter of finding the drug, preparing the drug, using it, going on the mission of finding more. The drug wipes out any possibility of seeing yourself or the world in perspective because the drug becomes the world. If there's a hundred people in a room smoking crack, all their attention will focus on the center of the table where the dope lies on the plate and whoever's hand happens to be holding the pipe.

One morning I drink a half-pint of Christian Brothers after I smoke. The room closes in on me, the walls squeezing together. I've never even suffered a blackout when I drink so I believe what I'm seeing is actually happening. I break into a sweat and run next door, pounding on the door, telling them to call the fire department, desperate for help. I have another moment of clarity, promise myself I'll stop this madness, go back to Oakland, get straight. Pat and I pack and go up the coast once again, living with Trice in a project. I work longshore—driving Hondas from the huge ship containers, side by side with guys half my age and with twice my seniority—and make two promises: I won't see Huey, won't use drugs.

I blow my first paycheck on crack and tell myself no more lies. My mind speaks to me: Never, I say, never never never never am I ever going to spend a day without smoking. Smoking is how I want to spend my life until the day I die.

Chapter

35

COMING from Connecticut, where he's relocated with Frances, June rescues me. Mother fares poorly. The staff in her nursing home steal her stuff, a new television, gown, and slippers we buy her disappearing immediately. When my sister Sweetie offers to take care of her June suggests I escort Mother to Alabama, then come north and stay with him. The proposition's a chance to leave Oakland, free myself from the past.

I agree immediately. Of course logistics and environment will solve my problem. I guide Mother's wheelchair onto the plane, proud to be taking her home, finishing the trip we began thirty years before. Connecticut will definitely be a new start, without drugs, without madness. Also without Pat. Because clearly Pat and I don't help each other but feed off one another's weaknesses, always fighting, harming ourselves and others, locked into an endless, futile battle.

In Connecticut, I again use old Party contacts to set myself up, securing a job as an organizer for the New England Health Care Employees Union and borrowing some money to rent a nice house. I feel myself again, revved up, confident. Pat joins me and when I speak to Dorion and he sounds lost, afraid that he'll drift into selling crack, I encourage him to come too, maybe go to school out here, make a break from California. I'm not smoking, just tooting and drinking—I meet with union members while indulging in three-martini lunches—and my work, mapping successful strategies against union-busting agencies, goes well.

Then Pat and I start fighting.

"I used to hate you and Mom getting into arguments," says Dorion.

I remember in Connecticut you and Mom got into it, arguing in the car. I was eighteen at this time.

I went off: "Why don't you stop arguing now? You guys are acting like kids! All you do is argue all the *fucking* time! You make me mad, you make me *mad!!*"

Still, things weren't so bad because you got up and went to work every day. I still saw you as my dad, the organizer, effective in what you were trying to do.

But then you started tripping again, dating one of your co-workers.

The woman's a union rep, a friend of both Pat's and mine. We party together at our house, drinking, dancing. Pat accepts my flirtation with the woman, knows when we start sleeping together. In my mind, my want and affection for this woman is as intense and true as the need and love I've felt for Pat or Brenda. She represents another beginning. I pursue her.

The alcohol and drugs make me feel invincible, and I constantly push the boundaries of acceptable behavior.

At the union we plan our next campaign. I resent the guy in charge who explains the union's strategy. Besides, something else annoys me: Dorion thinks that maybe the fact he's my son is negatively influencing his application to the Coast Guard, and I've been on the phone with a congressman arguing for my son.

"Teach that to someone who needs it," I say to the union head. "I'm winning campaign after campaign. I don't need your method."

Of course I'm wrong; it's my drunkenness that takes offense.

"I'm supposed to teach you," the guy starts.

"I don't need teaching," I answer. "Don't bother me with that mechanical approach. I have a style. I have an ideology. I use what I learned in the Panther Party. I make a concrete analysis of concrete situations and apply what I know, and that works—"

The guy argues. "In the union we—"

I pick up a chair. "Don't tell me nothing," I say. "Matter of fact, I don't need no teaching, and I resent you implying that I do."

People defuse the situation and everyone talks away the conflict: I drank a little too much, the guy acted in an insulting fashion, there was a misunderstanding—people find as many excuses for drunk behavior as a drunk does. I should see my outbursts as a warning—it's taking less and less to set me off—but my alcoholism shields me from any criticism. The tension between my work and my drinking increases until I lose control. At a regional convention I enjoy four or five martinis and walk into the meeting hall when the president is calling a vote.

"Are there any nays?" the president asks from the podium.

"You want a nay?" I say. "Nay." I have absolutely no idea what he's talking about. I'm clowning, acting like Richard Pryor.

"Hilliard," the guy says, "you just voted against wage increases for the staff."

I pretend I was joking, but the next day the local president tells me I need help. They'll admit me in a program, set me up with disability and continue my paychecks, and after thirty days I can return to work. I agree, arrange for disability, and go to the recovery program. Soon as the counselor starts talking, I tell him I don't have a problem; my only problem is not having enough money to drink all I want. I pursue the argument with the same energy, vehemence, and logic I once used to argue the rightness of the Ten Point Program. I can work when I'm on alcohol, matter of fact work better than most other people. So there's definitely no problem, and even if there were I belong to an organization and practice a way of thinking that has turned this entire world around and can challenge any concept in his program, which I don't need.

And Pat and I go back to Oakland, living with Patrice, hooking up with J.J.

"Man, I like that," J.J. says when he sees my soft wool overcoat.

I don't need the coat; I'm out of the snow back east, in Califa.

"For a sixteenth you can have it."

I cook the powder, start smoking, speak to Huey. Life resumes. Pat and I move into an apartment in the Acorn, a downtown-Oakland housing project, low buildings separated by breezeways, sparse trees and battered playgrounds. I get odd jobs. The personnel woman at Del Monte looks at my application and tells me I've been blackballed from the company for all the trouble I used to cause. I work on an assembly line, stacking boxes, confused and jamming the lines because I still can't figure out the patterns.

On Christmas the family gathers at Trice's. I cook two honey-glazed ducks; Trice works all day and I've been helping out, picking up John and DeMario, her kids, and making dinner. Tonight I want to do something particularly nice for the family. But something always goes wrong between Pat and me, Pat smoking all the drugs or cashing a check without me.

This time when I start yelling—she's drinking too, which she's not supposed to do because she has diabetes—Trice blames me for the fight.

I defend myself. "It's not me, it's Pat, who smoked up all my goddamned drugs, and now she's drinking up the alcohol. It's her. Put her out. She's causing the problem."

But Trice takes Pat's side. "Daddy, get out of here. You're aggravating her."

The kids are crying and John—Trice's oldest—is getting into this now. I hate their instant allegiance to Pat. I've been trying to do something good.

"Aggravating her!" I say. "Smoked up all the damned drugs, and now she drank up all my brandy."

I pick up the tray with the ducks. "The hell with it then. I'll leave your house."

I figure I'll go to Darryl's—I've got three kids; if one won't take me, another will—and the police catch up to me.

"Where are you going?"

I stand outside Trice's holding the tray, the ducks browned, crisp, sweet looking.

"I'm trying to get to my son's house with my ducks, if you'd just get the fuck out of the way."

We tussle in the street, the ducks flying out of the pan, and I spend Christmas in jail. When I get out, I call the woman back in Connecticut.

"I miss you," I say.

"I'll send you a ticket."

I pack my bags, leave Pat a note, drive the car to the airport, and fly off, high above San Francisco, thinking this time I'm gone for sure. I arrive, file for my unemployment, get into the life, going down to Bridgeport, where I buy crack. The woman and I plan to stay together—I'll be with her forever, I think—and rent an apartment. Then we fight when she finds out I've used her credit card to get a cash advance for the smoke, and I'm gone, back to Oakland, thinking, What the hell am I doing here? I'm better off back home.

But Oakland's the same as Connecticut; the drug demolishes all differences between places and people, reduces all of life to its demands. My days are delusion and madness. When the woman in Connecticut becomes pregnant, I say I'll stay with her, participate in a Lamaze birth. After the delivery I stay with her, taking care of the child. My schedule is simple: the woman leaves for work, I bundle up the baby, go down to the dope house, collect my pipe—the dealer keeps it for me—go home and smoke and drink. I run up bills at the liquor store, make trouble with the neighbors. The woman and I fight. I've got hells on both coasts and think I don't need her anger, I've already got one wife, take the baby one morning to its grandmother, kiss the child, pack my bags, and leave.

Everything in Oakland is alien to me.

In my worst rage, confusion, and despair, there have always remained two poles in my life: my family and the Party. Together they gave my life sense. Without the Party, my family life was a hopeless future, a meaningless knocking about from one job to the next, a desperate search for survival; I never even understood what I wanted for myself, could never articulate my longings and anger until I read Malcolm and worked with the Party because it was only then that I found a language to express what I thought and saw, words that reflected my experience of the world and my wishes and ideas about changing it. And once I had the Party, my family provided me with a sense of loyalty, comradeship, and solidarity that inspired my hopes and love for the organization.

Now my addiction wrecks these two pillars. Huey is absolutely right. The drug obliterates any sanction in your personality; everything that's evil in me emerges and tries to destroy all my relationships.

I exploit all my Party contacts.

"You would call me from time to time," says Mickey. "There were always reasons for money. Anything but *dope,* but I knew it was dope money, and it got old. I think the last go-around was you needed food or something. I said to Pat, 'I'll get you some groceries, but I'm not playing into this, Pat.'"

The groceries go for drugs too. After we buy and unpack them—proving to Mickey or whoever has paid the bill that the money is for food—I rebag everything, take the packages back to the store, tell the man I've got to leave town because my mother's terribly ill and I need the money for airfare.

Even the police become aware of our humiliation and despair. Pat and I move around, living anywhere—later on we stay in any kind of shelter, including a car, and sometimes sleep on Trice's back porch. An old Party member from Chicago—he was sleeping in Fred's house the night of the police raid and still carries a bullet from the ambush—lives with us until he fights with Pat.

"You got to go," I tell him. "You're disrespecting my wife and my house. You've got to cool down."

He leaves. I go back to the pipe and hear a crash—he's kicked the door off the hinge.

"What are you doing?"

He slams the door with his foot, insane from drinking wine.

"Do it," I say. "It's not my door. You're a good comrade. I don't care. Just get out of here. You've absolutely lost it."

He grabs a hatchet, marches down the street, trying to chop down telephone poles.

"Man, you better put that ax down before the police come and shoot your ass," I say.

"I'll defend myself," he answers. He attacks a telephone pole. "I'm still a Panther. That's what's wrong with you guys. You guys are not Panthers anymore."

"They'll shoot you," I say, grabbing his arm.

"They used to call me Roscoe," he replies, "but now they call me Bosco."

I have no idea what he's talking about. "What?" People are calling the police; the man's completely mad, chopping one pole after another.

"Because I used to carry a roscoe."

Then I realize: a roscoe is a name for a .22.

He assaults his new target, knocking out a chunk of wood.

"They used to call me Roscoe. Now they call me Bosco."

I get him away, but people have seen me with him, and the next day when Pat and I go at each other, the cops come immediately. I've been smoking dope and there's a bit left in the pipe; plus, matches litter the floor. Some people have joined us — guys like me to relate Panther stories, trading a little drug for memories of the Free Huey movement and the Party's early days. The cops — a rookie and a sergeant who's one of the old Oakland cowboys gone to seed in his own way — go into the bedroom.

"Look at this," he tells the rookie, pointing to some photos from the old days. "This is Newton. This is Seale. You know who these guys are?"

I walk into the bedroom, tell him he doesn't have a warrant, following the Pocket Lawyer to the end.

"Aw, sit down, Hilliard," he says. "We're gonna take your ass to jail anyway."

He's more interested in the photos, flipping through the pictures of us in our black leather, showing them to the rookie. "These guys were Panthers," he says. "Really a sad lot. Newton's high off crack these days, Hilliard—"

He goes on, ignoring and degrading me. Except of course I've degraded myself.

At one point, he turns. "Hilliard, how'd you ever manage to get hung up into this shit?"

Before I even start to respond he turns his back to me, giving his attention to the rookie. Listening to him, I despise myself. His contemptuous words and attitude humiliate me worse than any jail strip search. Finally he starts to leave.

"Why aren't we arresting him?" the rookie asks.

"Don't worry about it," the sergeant says. "All he's gonna do is go buy some more crack."

They leave and the place quiets. I fill the pipe. With the intake of smoke, my heart races, feeling like it will jump out of my chest. I clutch the pipe more tightly, never wanting to let it go, wanting to get over the initial rush. I know that if my heart slows, I'll be better, able to take another hit. And it has always quieted itself. I go to the window, breathe, the oxygen calming me. There. The pipe's in my hand, ready to be lit again. I don't even remember the incident of a half hour ago.

The kids experience the horror.

"When you and Mom got back to Oakland, you started calling, maybe once or twice a month, saying you needed money because of the rent, or the car broke down," says Dorion. He's doing well in the Coast Guard and is living near Los Angeles.

So I'm going in my savings account — I had maybe sixty-five hundred saved up because I was following your plan: "Get into the service, save your money, and get all you can out of it." Patrice would call, telling me you and Mom were doing drugs, but I didn't believe it because I had faith in you and knew you wouldn't let the drugs *do* that to you. And *not* experiencing the drugs, I didn't know how powerful they were.

Finally I made a trip up to Oakland to play in the basketball tournament for the Coast Guard.

That Saturday, before our game, I picked Darryl up and he wanted to show me where you and Mom were staying. He took me to Sixteenth or Seventeenth Street.

I had never seen you and Mom in this condition.

There was no furniture, just a hardwood floor, and then in the bedroom a mattress, and a little TV. You were sleeping on the mattress with a sheet. I didn't really see any clothes, dishes, no *anything*.

When I got in the house, I'm like, "Daddy! What you guys doing sleeping in the house and no lock on the door!" Because he had kicked the door in or something on one of his binges or something. That's when I *really* knew something was wrong, because I'm like, "My dad is living in an apartment where there's not even a *lock* on the door." Never in a day!

I stayed there for about fifteen, twenty minutes. Pissed off. I couldn't believe it. I was totally disappointed and hurt. I gave you and Mom twenty bucks, told you I'd see you later, and told my brother, "Let's go."

I think from that point on, I stopped being supportive of you and Mom. I just felt so let down—especially by you because I don't so much want to *be* like you, but I did and do believe in the things you stand and stood for, and based on those principles, I would like to follow in your footsteps, because there's so much that needs to be done, not only for blacks, but for minorities *period*—which people don't understand about the Black Panther Party, that it was for poor and oppressed people everywhere.

I cried about it. I would drive in my car because I felt so lonely. It touches me right now. You were always such a positive image that to see you go down like that was so *hard!* But I never gave up on you, and I also knew I couldn't let you bring *me* down but that I had to do what was best for me, and that was turn my back on you.

"Go away," I tell Pat.

She stumbles after me on the street, crying and cursing. But I'm adamant. I'm going to a dope house with a guy who robs cars.

"You're my wife. Go away."

I give her two dollars to take a bus and follow the guy. All night I play look-out as he boosts baby seats, clothes, and stereos from parked cars. We carry the stuff to Cypress Village, another project, and enter the shooting gallery. A guy props himself against the wall, a spike sticking out from his neck. It's maybe four o'clock in the morning and my partner has been promising me someplace to bed down.

I look around. "Where we gonna sleep?"

"Here," he says.

He stretches out on the concrete. Other people lie on the floor, everyone sealed off in their own drugged-out world. I lower myself onto the hardness, curl into a ball, trying to shelter myself. People are shadows in the sparse, early-morning light. The place smells putrid, the stench of human desolation. Death is all around: I'm in the hold of a slave ship during the middle passage.

I struggle to my feet and begin to walk.

I'm tired, more exhausted than I've ever felt before. All I want to do is rest. But I have nowhere to go. Neither Trice nor Darryl will let me in be-cause I always cause problems—whenever I enter Trice's house, her youngest son, my grandson DeMario, starts crying, miserable to see me.

Your life's over, I tell myself.

I must get help, I think.

With a quarter I find in my pocket I call 911, tell them I'm having a heart attack. When the emergency people finally arrive, they laugh at me. I'm a crazy crackhead.

"I need help," I tell them. "I want out of my life."

They drive off, leaving me alone. Huey's in prison somewhere, serving time for one of the endless cases that have become his life — the government has charged him with fraud and income-tax evasion as well as local drug crimes. And even if he were around I wouldn't see Huey because in my insane state he'd only make me even crazier. But I get an idea, a brilliant idea! There's no one else; I've used up all my friends, comrades, lovers, family — I'll go to Eldrige's!

I pound on his door.

Eldridge opens up, peering at me. We haven't seen each other since the night before he left for Cuba.

"Eldridge," I say, "I need some help. I'm fucked up off drugs."

Eldridge stares at me, starts asking questions.

What does crack do to me?

How does it affect me?

On and on. Of course he's no help.

I get up, continue my wandering, absolutely alone. Over the next few days, I manage to earn some money and spend it immediately on dope. I plead with Patrice to take me to the emergency room, but she refuses — my credit is used up with her — and I get another idea. I throw away the blood-pressure pills in my pocket and stagger into Emergency by myself, telling them that I've just swallowed fifty pills. The stunt wins me a few days in the psyche ward. Then the psychiatrist tells me they have to let me out.

I'm desperate. I know I'll die on the streets. Do these people want me to die? I walk over to the administrator of the hospital's drug program, saying I must be admitted. When the woman behind the desk tells me I need insurance, I start screaming, "I'm not going anywhere. You *have* to give me a room, and I know that you have a space here for people that don't have insurance. You *have* to! One room! 'Cause I can't go back out there!" A tantrum — because my life is in the balance.

Taking pity, the woman calls the longshore union.

"David!" the longshore benefits guy asks me, "do you want to come to a program and straighten yourself out?"

"I'm gonna die if I don't," I say.

He tells me I've got a couple of hours to take a bus to San Rafael and claim a bed allocated for the indigent at a particular program. The bus costs six dollars and I'm penniless. I borrow the money and go to the bus and think:

One more bottle of Wild Irish Rose.

Because I'm going into treatment and I'll be okay.

I check for the bus — it's far down the block.

I go into the liquor store. There's a line.

The bus is coming —

The line moves slowly —

My mind tells me there'll be another bus.

The bus doors open with a whoosh.

I get on.

Chapter
36

FROM the first I do the program my way.

The second day my counselor asks me to write about myself. I fulfill the assignment. I say my problem with drugs and alochol is unique because of my background and experience and that no one drinks as much as I do or spends as much money on drugs. I also say that my particular philosophy lets me see the world with a clarity most other people don't enjoy.

My counselor reads the statement.

"You think your problem's unique—nobody's like you, nobody's ever drunk as much as you, nobody ever spent as much money on drugs as you. Plus, you're a Black Panther Party leader. You know how to change societies and your leaders are Huey Newton and Eldridge Cleaver and your friends know how to do everything. But your friends don't know one thing. They don't know how to stay sober. What do you think about that?"

"They don't want to," I answer.

"I don't think so," he says, then presses the point. "Listen, you're gonna have to give up your understanding—"

I cut him off. He's proposing a much bigger challenge than anything I've imagined. I'm prepared to stop using drugs and liquor. But I'm certainly not ready to forsake the way I've learned to think over the last twenty years.

"David," he says, "you're going to learn how to stay sober. Your problem has three levels—physical, psychological, spiritual. In order to stay sober you're gonna have to give up everything you know, because the problem lies deep within your belief system. Deep within your belief system, in your innermost self, you think drugs and alcohol are good and will bring you quick relief from emotional and situational discomfort, leaving no negative results. That's your fix—it's fixed you all your life. Now you've got to learn to transfer that dependency on alcohol and drugs to a power greater than yourself—which means following the program and going to the meetings."

I know what he's saying: I've got to fire my understanding and hire a new one. The AA one. The program presents me with a new and complete way of thinking, like the Party did; now I'm confronted with the Twelve Steps instead of the Ten Point Program and the Big Book instead of the Red Book. Plus the program has its own slogans—"You're only as sick as your secrets," "Keep it simple," "Save your ass, not your face," read posters on the wall. I'm simply not sure I'm ready to sign on.

I go to my first AA meeting. I don't think I share anything with the members. I see the people sitting in the fold-out seats as drunks, wrecks. I'm different—Chief of Staff of the Black Panther Party.

Then I'm supposed to share—I'm David, I'm supposed to say, and I'm an alcoholic/addict, and then tell them my experiences and secrets and listen to their responses. But the idea that these losers can tell me how best to conduct my life is ridiculous. What are these people able to offer that Huey couldn't?

You're powerless over drugs and alcohol, they say, and your life has become unmanageable.

Don't tell me I'm powerless, I think. My life struggle has been to gain power, to claim some space in which I exert my understanding, speak my piece and am heard—and, together with the others, we accomplished that!

You're powerless, they repeat. Otherwise you wouldn't be here.

Of course I don't believe them.

When I leave recovery—and I'm physically sober—I continue to pursue my own program, placing greater faith in my judgment than AA's. They tell me half measures will avail you nothing. You must go to any lengths to stay sober: stay away from any "slippery" places—bars, dope houses, old friends who sit around and drink all day, attend ninety meetings in ninety days, get yourself a sponsor.

Instead I contact my old friends, visit meetings irregularly, and depend on my own willpower to overcome temptations. In my mind I'm recovered: I'm off alcohol and drugs. What I don't understand is that I've only arrested my addiction; my disease is chronic, irreversible, and progressive. So I disregard the warnings, constant flare-ups of drunk-like shouting or cursing, going off, my alcoholic mind setting me up for a fall, recurring dreams in which I'm smoking crack and from which I wake up feeling hung over and terrified that I'll smoke again, overwhelmed by a sense of impending doom, one drink or hit away from relapse.

I also live with Pat. When my counselor warns me the program won't work if I stay with someone who's drinking, I tell Pat to go to the program, fighting about this until she agrees, saying she'll do it for me, not for herself, to keep the relationship alive. Soon after, though, I smell alcohol on her breath when we sleep together at night.

There are other problems. On the longshore, where I work, I'm still on the B list—the roster of those with the least seniority. The fact that I've so little to show for my efforts over the last twenty years is a constant indignity.

I also feel humiliated by the kids, the dealers and would-be dealers who now proliferate throughout Oakland, driving Beamers, dressing like million-aire athletes in three- and four-hundred-dollar sports outfits, wearing gold, arrogant and violent. Their presence rebukes me: I should be able to talk to them, deal with them—they're the sons and daughters of the people the Party organized. Instead they exhibit a cool and complete disrespect for me. Move your car, they order one morning when I park in a space they use to deal. Who do you think you're talking to? I want to answer. But you can't reason with these fools. They pull out a gun and I move.

One day the family holds a picnic, scores of us gathering in a city park for a barbecue. A nephew gets into a fight with some teenagers. We don't worry about the scuffle until I spot some youths checking us out. My niece starts arguing with the boys, telling them we're grown-ups and to leave us alone, but I stop her: the kids carry coats draped over their arms and it's eighty degrees.

"Come on," I whisper to her, "let's get out of here. They've got guns."

We pack up, everybody hurrying to put away grills, blankets, and food. A girl comes running, saying the kids are making phone calls: we've got to get out before their friends arrive.

Suddenly bullets spray the place. We're in a crossfire. I hug the earth, feeling like I've returned to April 6.

"Get down," I yell, scurrying around on the ground. "Stay down!"

The bullets dance for an hour it seems, the Uzies popping like firecrackers, the dirt jumping in the open field, before the guys run out of ammunition.

When the silence happens, everyone's terror-stricken, afraid of getting up.

"My baby's been shot!" my niece cries. Her eight-year-old daughter lies on the ground in shock.

"Don't wait for the police," I say. "Get her to a hospital."

We're lucky, the doctors tell us when we arrive: the bullets passed through cleanly and she'll survive.

But the incident doesn't end. The cops arrest one of the attackers, and now we're afraid that his buddies will retaliate. I'm terrified every morning when I go to work, fearful the guys will drive by and kill me or shoot up our house. The feeling is so powerful that I bring the family into therapy to help all of us get over the shock of the incident.

Plus, I become consumed with a general hatred toward all male black youths. I despise them—with their jogging suits, caps, and hundred-dollar Nikes.

What happened here? I think. Twenty years ago these guys would have been Panthers. Now they're violent, undisciplined, apolitical, fratricidal maniacs. I have never felt such hatred toward another black person as I do toward these youths. I've been able to withstand every attack and failure of the Party, but not this—the existence of these kids seems the complete nihilistic repudiation of everything the Party stood for. I want to kill them.

It's Alabama where I relapse.

My brother Arthur is dying of esophagus cancer while living with Sweetie. He has deteriorated rapidly over the last months; I visit every time he declines. Each return is more tense, painful, torturous. The last time I go Arthur has shrunk to ninety pounds; he lives in constant excruciating pain. But he refuses to be taken care of by the hospice workers.

"You got to go to the hospital," I tell him. "There's nobody to take care of you. You need around-the-clock treatment. You won't even allow these hospice workers to help you. You're in bad enough pain as it is."

"If I wanted the hospice workers here, I would have called them myself," he answers.

His refusal infuriates me: he even worries about getting addicted to the morphine they give him for pain. My frustration at his stubbornness becomes unbearable. I walk into the living room. June drinks a beer.

"Fuck it," I say. "I've been sober a year. I can handle a beer."

"Sure," June agrees, not knowing anything about the disease of alcoholism. "Much liquor as you've drunk, one beer won't hurt you."

Of course, I can't handle the beer. I'm an alcoholic. It's the first, not the last drink that gets you drunk. In my mind I hear the AA people saying, One drink is too many and a thousand's not enough. I'm ashamed of myself—but my alcoholic mind is already programming me, telling me I only had a beer, I'm not stumbling or anything, I shouldn't be so hard on myself. Besides, I can go to a meeting when I get back to Oakland, talk about it there. Later that night I figure that nothing happened from the first, so I take a second.

The next morning I'm scheduled to leave. While I'm packing the news announces a plane crash in Dallas, where I have a stopover. There are terrible thunderstorms and tornados throughout the Southwest. I know that flying is the worst thing I can do, but I need to get back to work and any postponement means additional costs. As soon as we're in the air the turbulence hits, the plane bouncing through air pockets while passengers shriek with fear and grip their seats. The flight attendant comes by with the drinks, I order a vodka—

By the time we land I've had three miniatures. I'm met by Gene and the family.

"Let me have a drink," I say as soon as Gene pulls out the pint of gin he always carries.

"You drinking again?" Trice asks.

I start to explain about the turbulence and Alabama, the bottle already touching my lip.

It takes only six months this time for me to reach a "pitiful state of incomprehensible demoralization," as the Big Book says. Working only to collect enough money for drugs, I find refuge with Pat in a relative's empty house. Our days are spent in a desperate mission for drugs.

"Well, I know you said we wasn't gonna smoke no more, but I'm just gonna buy one twenty-dollar rock."

We're in the Western Union. Some still-faithful friends have wired us money. We promise each other we'll pay some bills, and Pat purchases money orders. But we leave the orders blank. We go back to the house, smoke the rock. Soon as we exhale, we start fighting, Pat repeating all this ancient history, accusing me about women and other abuses, bringing up Brenda and old high school girlfriends.

Her obsession with the past reminds me of Huey.

"David, let's compare war stories," Huey says when we smoke. "How you feel asking people for twenty dollars? We used to be stars. Now we're fallen stars."

"David, you never loved me," Pat says. "Why did you need all those other women."

I don't want to hear any of this madness.

Party history.

Personal history.

Let me smoke. I don't want memories. I want oblivion.

"Patricia," I say, fuming, "how can you talk to me about somebody I was with in *high school?*"

The question only charges her up; we fight and smoke and the money orders disappear. Now we have no cash, no dope, and no paid bills.

"You smoked up all my dope! Gimme the money."

"I don't have no money."

"Gimme the money orders."

"We used up the money orders. If we had made them out we wouldn't have cashed them."

I give up my job altogether, renting rooms in a house to prostitutes for twenty dollars. When June visits I invite him to stay, telling him I got girls.

"No, man," June answers, "I'll go elsewhere."

"Well, the idea is, June," I explain, "that I'll rent out these rooms. Turn the place into a brothel. Sell food and liquor. Make money."

I'm lying on the mattress; the room's empty except for a television set, matchbooks, a crack pipe, and wine bottles.

He says, "You got to get yourself together. You really got to see yourself. You're really in bad shape."

"What's the matter with you?" I say, taking offense. "This is a pretty nice life. I've got all the women I want, got all the free drugs, and got this house with five rooms in it. I'm satisfied."

When we meet up later I try convincing him to visit Huey.

"I don't want to see Huey," June says. "I got nothing to say to the man."

I argue with him. Huey's just been released from prison. Inside he's met G. — G.'s served eighteen years already on a charge most legal experts consider very dubious — and they've discussed what happened in the Party. We can talk to him —

"Fuck Huey," June says. "What the hell's wrong with you? I don't care if I ever see that man again. Leave that stuff alone."

"You got the man wrong," I say. "You misunderstand."

"David," he answers, "Huey's crazy, and you're getting crazy just like him."

I fight with everyone in the family. Darryl and I battle three or four times a week. One night I grab a gun and chase him, threatening to shoot him; another time he threatens me with a knife. Dorion stays away. Patrice sides with Pat and calls the police.

"Call the police!" I dare her.

I slap Trice and bang around some pots in the kitchen. She pushes me. I don't care. I'm sick of her favoritism. Pat's the problem, always the problem.

Give her twenty dollars for drugs and now she's smoked up the dope and there's no money.

I stomp outside. Don't even want to be in Trice's house. I try to act nice and she shrinks away from me as soon as I enter like I have the plague. Her son John disappears. Patrice is shouting, telling me to leave. The house is too small anyway, and there's always noise, no place to rest, no place to think, no one listening to my side, Pat telling me I should get the drugs, I'm the smart one who can figure out the latest scheme, even now a provider, and the kids only and ever sticking up for her.

A police car rushes onto the corner, lights flaring. The cops run out. I stand on the lawn and see drawn guns.

"You motherfuckers," I shout. "You're gonna try to kill me like you did Bobby Hutton!"

The cops draw closer.

I strip off my clothes in the driveway.

"Now shoot me, motherfuckers! Now you won't get away with this shit!"

One day the Vietnamese buyer of the house where I'm living offers me two thousand dollars to move. I agree immediately and make my plans: buy my grandkids some clothes and put a down payment on an apartment for Pat and myself. Get things right again.

Only a few weeks pass before Pat, myself, and another woman are smoking up seven hundred dollars. When Pat goes to take the woman home I find a check stub in the garbage for a hundred bucks.

"What's this?" I ask her, soon as she returns.

"I got paid."

"Where's the money?"

She tells me she and the woman smoked the money up.

I'm outraged. "You go with this bitch and smoke up my goddamn seven hundred and spend your money and don't give me none of the dope?"

I pick up a broom and smack her with the straw.

"Fuck it," I yell. "Get out of here, before I kill you. You do that dirty shit to me! It's been prison, it's been guys, anything you can imagine heaped on us in this relationship—and you start lying to me and spending money and crossing me for some other person and it's gonna be these fucking drugs that break us up."

I go to bed. I don't want to see Pat, think of Pat. I turn and she stands there, armed with a knife.

"Take this, motherfucker," she says, and springs, gashing my leg with the knife. "I'm tired of you jumping on me."

Pat runs from the room. But I'm not going after her. I lie there amazed, looking at my bleeding leg, stupefied by the attack. In all our fights, we've always limited the harm we'd do to one another. Now we've entered on a death trip; one of us will kill the other. In my daze, I get up, wrap a tourniquet around my leg, and drive to the dope house.

The guys in the dope house stare at the wound. The blood has saturated the cloth bandage. "What's wrong with your leg? I'd go to the hospital."

I buy some more dope and go back to my house. I know exactly what I'm going to do.

"David," a friend says, "let me take you to the hospital."

I sit by the window, the pipe never leaving my hand, smoking, smoking.

"No," I tell him. "I don't need to go to a hospital. I need to be reminded of what's going on here, because when I finish this one, I'm gonna go and clean my act up."

On Monday morning I call my union and ask them to send a car: I want to go into a drug program.

This time I take no chances, do everything by the book. Ninety meetings in ninety days, regular sessions with the therapist, dependence on a sponsor. I abandon my previous ideas — Panther philosophy, Marxism, Hinduism and Buddhism, all the stuff I've ever talked to Huey about. Instead I make a leap of faith, telling myself this program has the answer and that if I follow the program I'll strengthen myself enough to do without the drugs and liquor. I accept the new teachings unequivocally now. My life had become unmanageable because of my addiction. I am powerless over people, places, and things. There's a power greater than myself that can bring me to sanity. I cannot trust my mind because my mind is programmed to self-destruct, to con me into addiction by telling me I'll find relief from my anguish in drink or drugs.

Every day a new struggle presents itself. Anytime I face pressure or frustration I'm prepared to go off and get drunk. Anytime I get angry, my mind tells me I should find a drink. *That sure smells good,* a voice inside says when a friend pours a cognac. *You can have a beer today,* another voice tells me soon as I awake. The program says everybody has a committee in his or her mind of different voices. I have a whole government — ten thousand voices including my family, Huey, the Party, records, signs, and smells, all letting me know in different ways that it's okay to have a drink.

The hardest thing is transferring my dependence on drugs and alcohol to the fellowship. My impulse when I'm angry — the emotion that most commonly leads me to use — is *not* to call my sponsor, *not* to drive down to the church or school and go into the basement, sit down, listen to the others, raise my hand and speak. In fact, every fiber in my body and soul says the opposite: that if things are bad, a drink will make them better. But then I remember the hopelessness of my last days, that the program has worked so far, that I can keep coming back and staying away from that madness step by step, minute by minute. I force myself to make the call, get into the car, and the effort works. I study the Big Book like I once read the Red Book, finding new insights every time I open it, using it as a guide and support.

One thing I refuse. I continue living with Pat. In every area of my life I surrender to the judgment of the program, but I keep my relationship with her apart, convinced that sooner or later she will come around, still believing in my heart of hearts that I have some control over her, can change her.

Slowly, I begin to bring back the people whom I've wounded. Make a fearless moral inventory of yourself, the program says, and I begin with my family.

"I didn't visit you in recovery the second time," says Patrice.

I had nothing to do with you. Then you came here to apologize to my husband and kids, let me know what triggered your relapse and also let us know that you wanted to try and live a normal life, and to encourage me to start going to Alanon, and to start reading more about alcoholism and whatnot.

You wanted to take the kids to the movies — *Ghostbusters*. At first DeMario was a little skeptical. But then they got excited. Now every Saturday they look forward to Grandpa coming over to go to the movies. A couple of times you took them up to the marina, fishing. You made an *effort* every other weekend to try to become friends with them, especially DeMario, to show him your good side. You bought them birds. DeMario was very interested in dinosaurs, so you got him a nice collection of dinosaurs, books on dinosaurs. You sat down with him and read the books, bought him a nice globe for Christmas. You did things that they wanted their grandfather to do in the beginning.

Now they love their grandfather to death. I think if you *ever* went back to drinking again, those two guys would be *crushed,* because they've seen that part of it and they don't like to talk about it. Don't *mention* to them that their grandfather used to drink. They get very defensive. They don't want to hear that: "That's not my grandfather. He used to be like that, but he's not like that now."

I also begin to reconstitute my relations with my friends. I write notes, apologizing for my behavior, facing my own shame.

"I was going to lunch at a Vietnamese restaurant in downtown Oakland, and the restaurant was closed," says Brenda.

If the restaurant had been open, I would have never seen you. I walked back to the car and was sitting down when I saw these legs coming by. They came up to the window, and they had on some jeans and some snakeskin cowboy boots.

You said, "Brenda, you're not gonna speak to me?"

I went, "David!"

It had been nine years since I had seen you. We talked for a long time, I gave you my phone number. We went to dinner and you started seeing Dassine again. Which was good for her. Because she always refers to you, even when she's talking to Patrice, as "my daddy." Patrice says, "I think he's my daddy too, don't you think?" Dassine says, "No! He's just my dad."

I even manage to visit Alabama. Sometime after I get out of my second recovery, my brother Arthur dies. We must go down to the funeral. I want to stay away — deaths are occasions for drinking, plus Mobile is forever associated in my mind with alcohol — but family obligations and feelings won't permit an absence. I prepare myself, talking to my sponsor, going to meetings, and feel okay about the trip, when a new challenge unsettles me: Arthur will be buried in Rockville, near my father's grave, and in accordance with custom, we, his brothers, are to dig the grave the day before the ceremony.

Throughout the night and the drive north, I'm anxious. I'm not a gravedigger, don't want to be climbing around in the earth. We pass through the small streets of Jackson, drive up into the hills and meet our guide: a local man from my father's generation must take us to the right spot in the rural cemetery and oversee the preparation of the grave.

"Gotta be six feet exactly," the old man tells us.

We measure off the plot then start. One by one my brothers shovel the red dirt as the old man looks on. I calm. The earth smells fresh in the morning air. My fear dissipates. I climb down and dig.

"Make those sides nice and smooth," the old man says in the country accent common in Rockville when I was growing up. He seems from another century, stuck in the old country ways; yet his kids use FiloFaxes and fly in from DC to visit him over the weekends. "Dig that deep. Hard rain comes, you don't want water getting underneath and the casket floating out now.''

I concentrate on the work, remembering Arthur and his temper and stubbornness.

"Stop your conflummicks," my father warns as Arthur sneaks up behind him while my father plays checkers.

But Arthur won't stop; this is the guy who takes B.B. at her word and tries chopping off her toe and later on jacks off his .22 to let us know he's coming home on Friday nights. Of course he touches my father.

And the checkers go flying across the room.

"You kissified bastard!" shouts my father.

I pat down the earth. The darkness and closeness of death dissipates as I participate in his burial. We're part of the same community in death as in life—part of a circle not bound by flesh, but spirit.

"That's right, David," the old man coaches me. "Nice and smooth."

Nice and smooth. This is your home, Arthur, I think. Rest in peace.

With Mickey and some other people I begin to organize help for mothers of crack babies, addressing on an individual level the madness and communal self-destruction I myself have been part of—and which the Reagan years have been only too eager to allow.

The question of political activism is the one part of the program with which I seriously disagree. The program talks about alcoholism solely as an individual disease. Now it's true that I could never have cured myself of alcoholism by changing the society: I had to change myself. But the program also says that the one thing we can't afford is anger. Turn it over, they say, let go, let God. Well I believe in anger—righteous indignation. I come out of a meeting and a cop harasses me simply because I'm black, of course I'll get furious. And there's no reason in the world for me to accept it. To accept inhuman behavior is to deny your own humanity—you'll think you're worthless, and being worthless you'll start drinking. The program is powerful because it tells me I do have a choice. But I can't choose not to forgo political and social activism: my spiritual well-being means there must be something added to the Twelve Steps, attacking the dehumanizing conditions in which I was forced to live and which for millions have become not better over the last twenty years, but much worse.

The one person I don't see is Huey. My one contact is running into him at Melvin's. I hear he's doing better, off drugs, then the opposite. I feel I must keep myself steadfastly away, concentrated on my own sobriety, never letting anything interfere with it, because the daily struggle to remain sober is so demanding, my own balance so delicate, and also because I know that this time if I fail there's no reprieve: there's always another high, but there might not be another recovery.

The one time I break my vow about Huey is in early August. A journalist writes a column commending the Party and saying Oakland should build the Party a memorial. All right, I think, I'll call Huey. He says he thinks we should leave memorials to the people, see what they think about it.

Soon after, my mother gets sick. Pat goes down to help her. I'm working longshore, coming home at three in the morning. I'm wired usually; I'm used to rising early in the morning from my days on drugs, and I walk around the house, nervous, going from room to room, a one-house version of geographics. Just as I get to sleep the phone rings. I figure it's Pat. She usually calls in the morning.

"David," Melvin says, "wake up. Huey's dead."

Epilogue

SO of course I'll tell the truth.

Huey would want his eulogy to be honest.

Huey wasn't all right. By his own admission. The man didn't deceive himself. "No," he said to me the last time we saw each other, "I'm not doing well at all." He knew his worth and the waste of his talents. He knew we were — I mean the society — in a very catastrophic situation in which an entire generation of black youth and a legacy of struggle were being systematically trashed. In his last statements he was always furious at his own irrelevance and the apolitical nonsense of the times.

I don't want to deny him that anger and frustration.

I don't want to deny my own anger and frustration. Bad enough that I suffered through this tribulation. At least let me show something for my pains.

So I'm not interested in speaking about Huey the myth, but Huey the man. As Huey himself, the most fearless truth-speaker I've ever known, would want me to.

During the days before the funeral, as I decide what to say, pressure mounts. By the day of the funeral I feel I have been tested by Huey once again. Not since going into recovery have I had to face as much tension.

First there's the question of what I'm going to say. Melvin has indicated that he approves my decision to speak about Huey's drug problem, but I still

433

don't know Huey's family won't be upset, and I don't want to cause these people more pain.

Then I must face the constant presence of liquor. For the last nine months I've lived in a cocoon, assiduously avoiding any situations where alcohol or drugs might be present. But I can't do that here—people are doing what they do at funerals. And every moment is a test for me—because you never know when you might take that drink, but I am certain that if I do the drink will not be the last one.

Plus, I'm under the tension of once again being in the media, arranging things and speaking publicly, an attention I haven't been subject to in fifteen years.

So I'm constantly on the phone with my sponsor, attending meetings with Mickey, checking my spiritual pulse, seeing if I feel strong.

Hi, I say, standing up, my name is David and I'm a drunk.

Hello, David, they say. The ritual of fellowship.

Well, it's a very hard time for me, I begin, because my friend Huey Newton has just been murdered. He was my buddy from childhood and I was with him in the Black Panther Party.

Many of the faces in the fellowship know this—they've been around for a while—but they nod, encouraging me to go on.

Now I'm very shaky, very close to having a drink. But I'm here because I need to hear stuff and be fortified. Because now there are cameras everywhere and people are asking me what I think, and that sort of celebrity stuff has a tendency to make you think you're somebody you're not, and I must be very, very clear that I'm not the Chief of Staff of the Black Panther Party but a drug addict and an alcoholic who can become a truly very pitiful and demoralized character, and I don't want to be.

Well, David, they say, you don't have to be. You've got a choice. You don't have to drink. Remember this: if you don't take the first drink or hit of cocaine, you don't get high. Keep coming back.

The image of sharing solves my biggest problem.

Throughout the last couple of days I've been trying to picture myself giving Huey's eulogy. Because my image is giving a speech, as we used to for our other martyrs—Fred, Bunchy, George. But now I don't want to give a speech or political analysis. I simply want to tell my story—to share as I would at an AA meeting.

So, I realize, that's exactly what I must do.

I keep in mind certain things:

I want to be simple—keep it simple is one of the tenets of the program, a reminder that confirms Fred's frequent advice: I speak really well when I talk with emotion, say what I believe, and stay away from abstract concepts.

I also want to be humble. To express my thanks at still being here, to rekindle in others gratitude that they also have survived.

But most of all, I want what I say to be relevant to Huey—the Huey I knew. I don't want to verbalize, make some philosophical statement about history or the state. I want to vindicate Huey as he lies in that casket. I want to let people know Huey was no different than the rest of us and to bring some honesty into the situation. I want to acknowledge the truth, tell Huey's story and my own. Everybody is so afraid to accept the truth of Huey. But what is there to be afraid of? Huey represented the best of all of us. It's simply shame that doesn't let us accept the truth of what he became.

But I am not ashamed.

I remember something my sponsor once said. "This is a spiritual program of recovery, David, not a religious program. You don't have to believe in religion. We're talking about God. God—G-O-D. That could be a Group of Drunks."

A group of drunks.

Well, a group of drunks is certainly whom I have always placed my faith in: my friends, whom I love whatever their shortcomings, and the beautiful comrades with whom I fought in the Party, my blessed family, and now the million-plus souls who daily attend meetings and struggle to pursue their lives without alcohol and drugs, we're all a group of drunks. A group of drunks might sound insulting to sober-minded, straight-laced citizens; to me the phrase spells God, a fellowship of healing. I certainly have faith in their capacity to change and create change because I have seen this my whole life. So I'm all right with that—I can certainly assent to faith in that great host.

I write the speech:

Huey's spirit certainly lives.

As Huey would say, Nobody gets out of life alive. But death does vary in its significance.

And Huey's spirit lives because Huey's life was so significant and he's done so many important things:

Huey was a philosopher.

Huey practiced his philosophy.

Huey was a gentleman warrior.

He had a complete and resolute acceptance of death. He never feared death. Huey knew who the Buddha at the head of the Garden was. He often told me that he would embrace death, but that he would also always struggle for the principles he lived for.

So, to me, Huey represents the very best that humanity has to offer.

I feel right now that we need to talk about some very serious things.

Huey has been attacked in the media about his drug addiction.

I want to say that Huey's problem with chemical dependency represents all our weaknesses here in America. To focus on his chemical dependency really doesn't allow us to see him in the proper context. We get blinded to the programs and ideals that he was about.

So our correct focus is to deal with the solution—not only to Huey's problem, but to America's problem: drugs and alcohol. Because Huey's problem was not a problem unique to Huey. It's a societal ill. And to point the finger at Huey as though he's some sort of social deviant is wrong: he's a product of this society. His problem is larger than it has been presented— that he was a doped-out, crazy psychopath.

We should attack the disease, not Huey.

I personally am no different from Huey. The only thing that separated me from Huey was the fact that I was in an AA fellowship.

What needs to be done is to use Huey's death as a national clarion call and a springboard to come together.

We should move to try to do intervention in our own loved one's lives so we don't continue to lose our loved ones and even our race by this new oppression of drugs and alcohol.

And I want to say that in a sense we're all Huey's co-dependents when we try to turn our heads and act like we don't understand what's happening. We've got to do some personal housecleaning. Because my son and your son and other younger mothers and fathers out there—they are substance abusers.

I want to serve notice to them: if they haven't touched bottom yet, they will.

And to the other suffering alcoholics out there—and I know what you look like; you look like the people in this audience—I tell you that there will come a time when your willpower alone won't carry you through your problems.

So we've got to work and save our race.

These are frightening and insane times.

But Huey's always said that when we have moments like this we should seize them.

So I'm going to do that now:

I CHALLENGE YOU TO TAKE SOME ACTION, TO MOVE FOR-
WARD, TO DEAL WITH THE PROBLEMS I WAS A VICTIM OF MY-
SELF.

The next morning I'm ready, squirrelly, but ready.

I drive down with Dorion. The church sits on a wide, open street in East
Oakland, near the school that was the Party's last institute. People already
pack the avenue.

I go through the crowd, greeting long-lost faces. Some are missing:

Masai and Charles Bursey are both dead. Masai died of a heart attack; a
brain tumor has killed Bursey.

Peggy Carter, Frances's sister, has passed away some time ago, a victim
of complications brought on by the arthritis she suffered from serving time
in jail.

An alderman in Chicago—everyone there of course knows his past, and
he goes around saying that he wants to be the first Panther in the House of
Representatives—Bobby Rush still feels too bitterly about his expulsion to
come.

G. remains in jail.

Gene McKinney doesn't show either. "I started to go to the memorial service—I meant to," he says.

But I had other things to do. Life goes on. But you know I'll always be
with Huey. No matter what. He was a brother who tried to get things
going right. That thing was going *so* good—people could see things
coming together, see those children eating. That's where our minds were
coming from: let's do something about something, make a step, make an
effort. That's what the path of the Party was about: it was about life!

But many others do come. Marty is with me: I haven't seen or spoken to
him since my madness in Connecticut. I called him up one night, saying that
the woman's brothers were coming after me with guns. David, he answered,
I can't take this anymore, this is the eighties!

There's a celebratory air to the solemnity: we have survived. The press
and police always presented as us vicious, brutal. But the fact was always that
the Party grew strongest when it spread from families—the Newtons, Seales,
and Hilliards in Oakland, Bunchy's gangs in Los Angeles, the Shakurs in
New York, Bobby Rush's political cadre in Chicago. We trusted one another.

"It's a thing I will never forget," says Alex Hoffmann. "It was in the early days and Huey was telling me some story—I don't remember the content—which was incriminating, though not about his case.

"I said to him, 'Huey, why do you trust me?'

"He said, 'Oh, I don't know. Beverly said you were okay.'"

We arrange loudspeakers for outside, get ourselves together on the podium.

The ceremony begins. I'm sweating the whole time.

The speeches go on.

A preacher.

City official.

H. Rap Brown—now a Muslim minister named Jamil Abdullah Al-Amin.

Bobby coming onstage with his beret.

The lights blink and the mike sputters. The generator's failed—there's always something wrong. Someone saves the day with a bullhorn.

The wait seems endless—longer than my wait at Golden Gate Park.

For one last time I question myself. What am I going to say? Then Bunchy urges me on: You're a Panther, you've got words, good words, I demand you talk more.

My mind clears, focuses. My purpose is plain. I will extenuate nothing, apologize for nothing, eulogize my dear comrade as he dwelled *this* side of glory, the near side of Heaven, the side that falls short of immortality's perfection, the side by which we mean life.

Ericka finishes.

My turn.

I step close to the bullhorn so my words can be heard.

"This is a hard one," I say and give the time-honored salute: "Power to the people."

I face the crowd.

This moment is my witness.

I speak.

Postscript

WILLIAM O'NEAL, the police agent partly responsible for the deaths of Fred Hampton and Mark Clark, murdered himself, throwing himself off a bridge into oncoming traffic.

Bobby Rush was elected to the House of Representatives.

Geronimo remains in jail.

Eldridge Cleaver was recently arrested for possession of crack cocaine.

Pat Hilliard has entered a rehabilitation program.

On August 28, 1992, my son Darryl Hilliard died in the hospital of medical complications. At the time he was living in Los Angeles, off drugs and alcohol, working full-time, raising his two children.

This book is dedicated to his living memory.

Index